RELIGIOUS ENCOUNTERS WITH DEATH

RELIGIOUS ENCOUNTERS WITH DEATH

Insights from the History and Anthropology of Religions

Edited by FRANK E. REYNOLDS
and EARLE H. WAUGH

THE PENNSYLVANIA STATE
UNIVERSITY PRESS
University Park and London

Library of Congress Cataloging in Publication Data
Main entry under title:

Religious encounters with death.

Based on papers prepared for the annual convention of the American Academy of Religion held in Chicago, 1973.
Includes index.
1. Death—Addresses, essays, lectures. I. Reynolds, Frank, 1930– II. Waugh, Earle H. III. American Academy of Religion.
BL504.R44 1976 291.2'3 76–14981
ISBN 0–271–01229–3

Designed by Marilyn E. Shobaken

Printed in the United States of America

Contents

Contributors

Donald Capps, Associate Professor in the Psychology of Religion at the School of Theology, Phillips University, holds a Ph.D. from Chicago. He is co-editor with Walter H. Capps of *The Religious Personality* and with Frank E. Reynolds of *The Biographical Process*. He has published articles in *Social Research*, *Journal of Church History*, *Journal for the Scientific Study of Religion*, *Journal of the History of Behavioral Sciences*, and *Journal of Religion*. He is working on a book tentatively titled *The Personality Factor: Essays in the Psychology of Religion*.

Glen W. Davidson, Chairman, Department of Medical Humanities and Chief, Department of Psychiatry, Southern Illinois University School of Medicine, holds a Ph.D. from Claremont. Previously he taught at Colgate and the University of Chicago. He is the author of *Religion, Culture and Medicine: An Annotated Bibliography, The Gypsy's Journey: A Study in North American Culture, King Mohammed V of Morocco*, Sermons in *Sermons Preached in the Colgate Memorial Chapel*, and *The Pound Fishers: a photographic essay*. He is General Editor of the Augsburg series on "Religion and Medicine" and author of *Living with Dying*.

Mircea Eliade, Sewell Avery Distinguished Service Professor at the University of Chicago, has also taught at the University of Bucharest and at the École des Hautes Études in Paris. His works include *The Myth of the Eternal Return (Cosmos and History)*, *The Sacred and the Profane*, *Patterns in Comparative Religion*, *Birth and Rebirth*, and *Yoga—Immortality and Freedom*.

Wolfram Herrmann was granted the degree *Doctor theologiae* for the thesis *The Significance of the Prophets in the Historical Design of the Deuteronomist* (*Die Bedeutung der Propheten im Geschichtsaufriss des Deuteronomisten*). He teaches Old Testament theology at the Theologischen Seminar Leipzig, a church institute connected with the theology faculty of the University of Leipzig.

Winston L. King, Special Professor, Department of Philosophy, Colorado State University, holds a Ph.D. from Harvard. Among his publications are *Buddhism and Christianity*, *A Thousand Lives Away: Buddhism in Contemporary Burma*, and *Introduction to Religion: A Phenomenological Approach*. He is currently working on a book on meditation in three Buddhist contexts: Theravada, Zen, Jodo.

David R. Kinsley, who teaches religion at McMaster University, holds a Ph.D. in History of Religions from Chicago. His works include "The Taming of the Shrew: On the History of the Goddess Kālī" in *Studies in Religion/Sciences Religieuses*,

"Without Kṛṣṇa There is No Song" and "Through the Looking Glass: Divine Madness in the Hindu Religious Tradition" in *History of Religions*. His most recent publication is *The Sword and the Flute—Kālī and Kṛṣṇa: Dark Visions of the Terrible and the Sublime in Hindu Mythology*.

David M. Knipe is in the Department of South Asian Studies at the University of Wisconsin, Madison, and Chairman of the Graduate Program in the Religions of South Asia. He holds degrees from Cornell, Union Theological Seminary, and Chicago (M.A., Ph.D.). He is the author of *In the Image of Fire: Vedic Experiences of Heat* and articles on Hinduism, Vedic studies, and Indo-European studies in *History of Religions* and *Journal of Asian Studies*. In 1971–72 he was in India as a Senior Research Fellow of the American Institute of Indian Studies and in 1974 he made films in India for his series, *Exploring the Religions of South Asia*.

J. Bruce Long teaches Asian religions, Asian Studies Department, and is coordinator of the Religious Studies Program at Cornell University. He holds a Ph.D. in History of Religions (with a specialization in Indology) from Chicago. He has done field work in India and is a Fellow of the American Institute of Indian Studies. He is completing a study of the early history of Śaivism and an annotated bibliography on the Mahābhārata.

Franke J. Neumann, a member of the Department of Philosophy and Religion, Virginia Polytechnic Institute and State University, holds a Ph.D. from Chicago. He is a member of International Congress of Americanists, member of *Société des Americanistes*, and Fellow *Instituto Interamericano*. He is author of "The Dragon and the Dog: Two Symbols of Time in Nahuatl Religion" appearing in *Numen: International Review for the History of Religions*, "Eagle and Serpent: The Concept of Duality in Pre-Hispanic Mesoamerica" in *Perspectives in Religious Studies*, and "Sacred Material in Aztec Ritual" in *History of Religions*.

Cyrus R. Pangborn is Professor of Religion and Chairman of the Department at Douglass College, Rutgers. A graduate of Kansas Wesleyan and Yale Divinity School, he received his Ph.D. in Religion from Columbia and taught at the University of Iowa until moving to Rutgers. His interests in contemporary Hinduism and Zoroastrianism have been shaped by studies in India as a Fulbright Research Scholar (1962–63) and as a Fellow of the K.R. Cama Oriental Institute in 1971. He has contributed to the *Journal of Bible and Religion* (now *Journal of the AAR*), *Christian Century*, *Prabuddha Bharata*, *Swami Vivekananda Centenary Volume* (1963), and *Contributions to Asian Studies* (edited by K. Ishwaran, 1973).

Benjamin Ray, who teaches history of religions at Princeton University, holds a Ph.D. from Chicago. In 1972 he was a Visiting Professor at Makerere University,

Uganda, where he did field work on the royal shrines of Buganda. He is author of *African Religions: Symbol, Ritual, and Community*, and articles in *History of Religions, Uganda Journal Religion*, and *African Studies*.

Pesach Schindler, born in Germany, received his B.A. from Brooklyn College, M.S. from Yeshiva University, and Ph.D. from New York University. His doctoral dissertation dealt with *Responses of Hassidic Leaders and Hassidim During the Holocaust in Europe, 1939–1945, and a Correlation between Such Responses and Selected Concepts in Hassidic Thought*. He has contributed to various journals including the recent "Faith after Auschwitz in Light of the Paradox of Tikkun in Hassidic Documents" in *Sidic*. He is writing the major article on Hassidism and the Holocaust in the *Encyclopedia of Hassidism*. Dr. Schindler is Director of the Israel office of the United Synagogue of America.

Victor Turner, Professor of Anthropology and Social Thought, University of Chicago, has done field work in Africa, Mexico, Europe, and Celtic countries. He is author of *The Ritual Process: Structure and Anti-Structure, Dramas, Fields, and Metaphors, Revelation and Divination in Ndembu Ritual*, and *The Pilgrimage Process*. He is also General Editor of the *Symbol, Myth, and Ritual* series.

Frank E. Reynolds holds a Ph.D. in History of Religions from Chicago. He has done field work in Thailand, has served as a visiting professor at Stanford and Notre Dame, and is now Chairman of the History of Religions field and Associate Professor of Buddhist Studies at Chicago. He is the author of *A Guide to the Buddhist Religion*, co-author of *The Two Wheels of Dhamma*, and co-editor of *The Biographical Process*.

Earle H. Waugh, Chairman, Department of Religious Studies, University of Alberta, holds a Master's in Philosophy from McMaster University and a Ph.D. in the History of Religions from Chicago. He is the author of "Jealous Angels: Aspects of Muslim Religious Language" (*Ohio Journal of Religious Studies*) and "Muhammad as Model in the Sufi Tradition" in *The Biographical Process*. He is researching a book on the biographical image of the Prophet and serving as project director and consultant for a film series on religious diversity in Alberta.

Alford T. Welch, a member of the faculty in Religious Studies at Michigan State University, holds the Ph.D. degree from the University of Edinburgh. He has translated and edited the English edition of Helmut Gatje's *Koran und Koran-exegese, The Qur'ān and Its Exegesis: Selected Texts with Classical and Modern Interpretations*. He is organizing an anthology of articles on Qur'ānic studies.

Preface

Despite the universal existence of myths, ceremonies, and conceptions associated with death, scholars have not given these human expressions the extent and depth of consideration that, by almost any standards, they deserve. This collection of essays reflects the relatively new awareness among historians of religion and anthropologists of the wealth of original historical and ethnographic materials concerning death, as well as the possibilities of exploring the religious perspectives they express. Eleven of the fifteen essays in the collection are based on papers originally prepared for the Annual Convention of the American Academy of Religion held in Chicago, 8–11 November 1973, where scholars from many academic disciplines shared insights from their areas of specialization and suggested general categories for handling such data. Of the four remaining essays two (those by Ray and Davidson) represent original contributions solicited by the editors; the remaining two (those by Herrmann and Schindler) were originally published in other contexts. All of these essays have been especially adapted to preserve the concreteness and complexity of the original manuscripts, while at the same time presenting the materials and interpretations in an idiom accessible to readers who are not specialists in the particular disciplines of the authors, or in the particular cultural areas on which their studies are focused.

None of the authors whose work is represented in this collection presumes to say the last word about the phenomena associated with death, even in his own particular area of expertise. However, in the papers contributed, each scholar has come to grips with a specific body of important material and has presented it in a way designed to highlight man's perennial encounter with his own mortality. Moreover, by placing these essays concerned with a common theme together, we hope that the special nuances revealed in each of these bodies of material will be highlighted, and that the grain of a more total picture may begin to appear.

The original conception of the topic and the solicitation of papers was the work of Frank Reynolds, who was at the time serving as the Chairman of the Asian Religions/History of Religions section of the American Academy of Religion. When he was awarded a Fulbright/Hayes Faculty Research Fellowship, which took him to Thailand for six months, the basic work of drafting the introduction and editing the individual papers was carried on by Earle Waugh. The final writing of the introduction and the final preparation of the collection were carried out cooperatively by us, and we jointly share the responsibility for the enterprise as a whole.

Although many persons have contributed to this book in the various stages of its development, we wish to express special thanks to Harry Partin of Duke University and to Stanley Lusby of the University of Tennessee, both of whom served with

Frank Reynolds on the Steering Committee that organized the program of the Asian Religions/History of Religions section of the A.A.R. and acted as consultants in the selection of the papers presented at the A.A.R. meeting. We also wish to specially mention the assistance given by Victor Turner of the University of Chicago, who, in addition to making his paper available to us, took a great interest in the project and made invaluable suggestions as we engaged in the editing process. William F. May of Indiana University and Luther H. Harshbarger of Penn State made valuable suggestions regarding coverage and organization. We are, in addition, most grateful to Gösta Ahlström and Chaim Lipskar of the University of Chicago, who made suggestions that led to the inclusion of the articles by Wolfram Herrmann and Pesach Schindler. We are also appreciative of the work of John McCarthy, who prepared the index. Finally, all of the contributors were most responsive to our requests that they rewrite and adapt their own manuscripts, and they deserve full credit for the collection as it has finally emerged. As editors we believe they have produced a book that will provide the reader—whether professional scholar or interested layman—with new insights into some ways in which man, through the ages, has encountered death, come to terms with it, and, in some cases at least, transcended it.

Frank E. Reynolds

Earle H. Waugh

RELIGIOUS ENCOUNTERS WITH DEATH

Introduction

Our first acquaintance with death is probably hidden in some moment of childhood: the lifeless form of a beloved pet who no longer responds, a parent whose normal gait becomes Emily Dickinson's "wooden way" after something happened called "Grampa dying," pictures in the media of someone very still and said to be "dead." The lines that communicate death's total meaning to us must be long and complex, for, as we shall see, death imagery, responses, and comprehensions are carried in many languages of experience.

Most of us regard death as some kind of end. In fact, death has meanings that go far beyond any conventional sense of finality. Wittgenstein once noted that death was not an event in life, thereby implying that none of the common categories of knowledge can legitimately decipher its reality—from that standpoint even the most erudite scholar remains a dilettante. The essays in this collection attempt to let death appear in whatever form religious experience has allowed it to take, without imposing on it the conclusion drawn from the everyday understanding of "end"; the color and variety encountered here indicate that the texture of death's meaning is rich indeed, far outstripping any single-minded perspective.

Like the other great crises of life, death is the catalyst for wide-ranging responses: vibrant emotions, obsessive fears, intensive self-questioning, giant swings from ornate ritual to quiet meditation. Where, on the one hand, accepted and conventionalized activities offer the support of society's forms in the face of death, on the other their very regularity and inflexibility may contribute to a collapse under the absurdity of death's presence. The immediate result of this explosive new element in life is the birth, in effect, of a new "language." Though not necessarily verbal, it is a genuine attempt to cope with and give expression to a violent new challenge. True, language has some basic structures, but at its cutting edge little is reverenced; it is always roaming around on the periphery of established norms, developing nuances and subtleties that may give totally different insights in time. No living language depends for communication on a one-to-one relationship between an object and its description; such conceptions may accord with technical usage, and, in fact, some limited meaning is required if translation is to be possible. Nevertheless, it is the freedom and vitality at the horizons of language that give it style and texture. Confronting death creates this new language: the way is opened for articulating emerging experiences in consort with other moods and attitudes, and individuals wander down many paths trying to make sense of the conjunction of themselves and that peculiar occurrence at that particular time.

It follows, then, that it is impossible to detect the many currents this experience has provoked in human consciousness. Even the most careful scholar can bring preconceived models when researching the subject and this too must be regarded as part of man's creative interaction with the termination of earthly existence. The essays in this book may be read in a similar vain, with the cadence and flavor of each an aid in perceiving the reality of death as mankind has encountered it.

Nevertheless, most of us admit there are some assertions about death that cannot be changed; statements like "all men are mortal" seem to say something definitive about mankind. But on closer scrutiny it is only one of a whole set of propositions that could be maintained with equal conviction from a specific point of view: "all men are eternal," "all unreal aspects of men are mortal," "some men are immortal." Clearly these cannot all operate within the same meaning system, but they all have legitimacy within their own contexts. Ultimately, then, constancy and structure do operate in the ways we look at death, but their claims must always be judged in the light of their perspective. It is the conflict and tension arising from these points of view that bring us back to religion, for, as we shall see in the selections, religion composes a "language" about death that becomes a normative model for interpreting that reality.

Another issue that will soon be evident in the material is the commonness of patterns: an identical motif may appear in separate cultural situations, or a strikingly similar ritual activity may be found in radically different social climates. These have posed and continue to pose problems for the contemporary researcher. How can social and cultural forms produce such a dazzling array of differences and yet speak with the undeniable voice of unity?

Some hints at explaining this phenomenon are found in the following essays. For example, Mircea Eliade explores the mythic formulas that populate our religious and imaginative worlds; he sees at the core of our being the constant creating and re-creating of meaningful conglomerates from those forms. He suspects that the locus for this vitality is in the unconscious, but he does not probe this possibility; rather he is content to point out the conscious dimensions of these mythic formulas and their links with past cultural expressions. Winston L. King explores the Samurai Suzuki Shōsan's contention that all formations of life and death must be existentially experienced and then transcended. What it means to exist after death for Suzuki Shōsan cannot be translated into any of the available metaphors with which the uninitiated adorn their afterlife; indeed, any casting of the continuum as *life* and *death* is to have missed the entire point of Zen teaching. There is, in fact, no "life" that death can be either before or after, if it *is* at all. Thus this view presupposes that even the most sacred human designations must be destroyed if real meaning is to be found.

But there are other patterns evident in the material: for example, the universal abhorrence of death and the inherent conservatism of death rituals. Are they not recurring motifs that derive from basic attitudes and moods exemplified in the interaction of man with death? In an effort to probe these problems, we have centered discussion on five models: disjunction, continuity, transition, integration, and transformation.

Disjunction

The anguish of the ruthless separation is captured by Johannes von Saaz's thirteenth-century *Death and the Plowman*:

> Until now every hour was for me one full of happiness and cheer; the days and nights were short and never anything unpleasant; every year was for me a year of grace. Now suddenly I'm told: forget. I'm told to spend my days now crying and ceaselessly lamenting, full of misery and sadness, drinking muddy wine, clinging to a brittle, withered bough! So now you see me blown by every wind, straining in a wild, angry flood, ever at the mercy of the waves, vainly weighing anchor. Therefore will I shriek without end: Death, be you accursed![1]

Despite the miracles of medicine, death plays the game according to its own rules—the main event is outside our control. For the Plowman, such capriciousness was an outrage. The established fabric of life was slashed without warning, second chance, or acceptable alternative.

Response to this disruptive aspect of death has taken several forms: Cyrus R. Pangborn highlights the ritual activity that, in the Parsi community in Bombay, marks off the living from the dead: no one is allowed to touch the body of the deceased except professional body-bearers; death is a pollution, and the attendants must cleanse themselves by ritual baths, and they must wear white apparel during the performance of their duties; the distinctiveness of the death-state is insured by the rite of the "sight of the dog," and the entire moment is sacralized by the continuous recitation of prayers, beginning with the confession prayer of the dying individual.

David M. Knipe discloses another aspect of this element of disjunction: from the moment when the dying Hindu individual whispers, "Now is my breath the immortal wind, this body is ashes," until he is firmly established among the fathers in the other world, the ritual is fraught with concerns for impurity. This has even led to the shortening of the daily ritual activity from one year to a symbolic twelve days, thus lessening the amount of ritual pollution to which the family could be exposed and insuring that the re-creation of the individual's body in the other world be completed. Such concerns point not only to the potential for evil to the members of the family still alive, but also to the relationship with the other world that would be imbalanced if all were not carried out according to prescription.

The images stressing the absolute separation of this life from the next underscore this disjunction: In his discussion of the gatekeeper motif, Franke J. Neumann elucidates the important complex associated with death in Mesoamerica. There is a guardian of the doors to the beyond, and the ambiguity before it is preserved in the figure of hʔik'al, which is "neither man nor animal, neither social nor antisocial. He welcomes company, but with murderous intent. He is to be found principally in those transitional zones of an in-between," and the disjunction points to the religious objections of seeking the other world before it comes to the individual.

Interaction between the moral domain and disjunctional models is also indicated here. "Natural" death in Qur'ānic passages is only one dimension of early Muslim ideas concerning death, notes Alford T. Welch. Some passages elevate the notions of "second death," that is, death associated with the eternal death of the damned. Acceptance or rejection of the salvation offered in the Muslim community is not based on conceptions of a sinful human nature, as it is in Christianity. Rather the individual is free to make a choice, untrammeled by structures built into his decision-making mechanism that would turn him away from the truth. Personal destiny is the total responsibility of each individual. The condemnation of injustice and moral failure hinges on acceptance of the prerogatives offered by God and presented to mankind by the Prophet; all activities, including dying, follow logically from that great moral choice.

Then, too, there is the tension that results from death, bringing disjunctional models into operation at both psychological and sociological levels. The anger and antagonism generated in Bugandan society by the random killing of faithful attendants is probed by Benjamin Ray. From whose perspective do we speak when we think that death can be as important for the servant who dies as for the king who dies? What of the tensions that arise in our own situation, such as those between Dr. Christiaan Barnard and his associate Dr. Terry O'Donovan when they were waiting for the death of the heart donor in their first historic operation:

> "I'll not lift an instrument until the EKG line is flat," said Terry O'Donovan.
>
> I nodded, knowing how he felt.
>
> All the years of our training, all the structures of our belief rested on one concept —to protect life, not to take it. Yet what life were we protecting in waiting for this heart to die—and perhaps injure itself? Certainly not Washkansky's. Nor could we take away the life of Denise Darvall, for it had already been removed from her. So this was not another temptation to commit the Great Transgression—to cross the line and play God, to decide when a life should be terminated. Here there was no decision to be made by us. It had already been made. Denise Darvall was beyond the possibility of living. Clinically, she was dead. Her heart lived on, yes—but it had been supported by us, to reach this moment when we could take it to a man waiting in another room.
>
> "What do you say, Chris?"
>
> Marius spoke as though he knew my thoughts—and believed we should take the heart now.
>
> "No, we must wait until it stops."[2]

Finally, it should be noted that disjunction implies an uncoupling, but not a severing; religion views the span from birth to death as the steppingstone to another life. The key is the word life. The religious person operates with the conviction that the span of years on earth is but a moment in a continuum. Death is a disjunction, but not a termination. The results of this affirmation can be seen in many death phenomena: death has a meaning, a purpose; life has transcending realities; man has a soul, and so on. From this perspective our contemporaries have become more religious. Astrology, tarot cards, occult ministrations, seances, and scientific research into psychical phenomena are indicators of a complex fascination for life beyond. The role this plays in our lives may well be outside our ability to comprehend, for, if we follow Heidegger, even our own being is itself defined by its stance toward the nothingness of its death. But this model, which is designated in this chapter by the term continuity, deserves closer study.

Continuity

> To everything there is a season
> and a time to every purpose under the heavens:
> a time to be born;
> a time to die. . . .

Religious man has insisted that death be viewed differently from other crucial events in life since it is tied to a larger ordering of reality. The conception that seems to be present in Ecclesiastes, as well as in many other religious writings, is that life and death reside in the same purposive dimension as all other significant elements of experience, and therefore the meaning of existence is related to this undergirding order in the universe. At one level these interpretations see death as part of natural law; at another they regard death as a prelude to a future life.

A fine discussion of such complex orderings of reality is Wolfram Herrmann's study. For Herrmann, the ancient Israelites accommodated the ideas of human mortality, borrowed from their Canaanite neighbors, to their conviction that a fundamental disruption between man and God had brought death about. But the Israelite insisted that the universal dictum that all would die could be broken by some—as reflected in Enoch and Elijah. This belief, however, did not overcome all the difficulties for it raised new questions about why just those individuals should be given such special preference. This, in turn, posed new ethical and religious problems. In any case, the *raison d'être* of death is in a transcendent order beyond personal control, and life and death are only two events in the ongoing expression of the transcendent authority resident in Yahweh.

Ancient Hindu mythology involves a strong recognition of a dimension of transcendence, and the continuity of life is assured through this dimension. According to J. Bruce Long's interpretation, the message of the dominant myths and reflections concerning death that appear in the *Brāhmaṇas*, the *Mahābhārata*, and the *Purāṇas* is that whereas the truly wise man knows death is radically disjunctive, he is also equally cognizant of the transcendent reality through which continuity is guaranteed; in fact, as Long deciphers these myths and accounts, the quintessence of the wisdom they reveal is that these two seemingly incompatible truths must be held together as complementary perspectives that balance and penetrate one another if individuals are to free themselves from the power of death and attain true Immortality.

Finally, Victor Turner approaches this element of continuity between life and death from a completely different perspective. In his words:

> When I came to investigate Catholic Christian pilgrimage processes, sensitized as I was to the role of the dead in African initiation and other "passage" ritual, I soon became aware that these, too, were pervaded by ideas about how precisely the living and the dead were interconnected, but that these interconnections were consistent with voluntaristic religion, and indeed, the total culture in which they were embedded.

Turner goes on to elucidate the manner and diversity of this continuity between earth-life and death-life in the Catholic pilgrimage beliefs in the west of Ireland and focuses on the pilgrimage to Knock in County Mayo. He finds evidence that there is not only a continuity in the belief-systems between the states of life and death, but that those on pilgrimage are themselves metaphorically placed in an in-between state, neither in death nor in life, and are capable of communion with those who have gone on ahead, especially saints, prophets, or heroes.

Transition

In this section we draw your attention to another closely related phenomenon represented in these papers: transitional states. We have already caught glimpses of this theme in Turner's discussion of pilgrims who put themselves "in the in-between state of life-in-death." The complexities of the state identified by Turner as "liminal," or betwixt-and-betweenness, and explored in some detail in his article, are much better left to that eminent essay. What we wish to do here is draw attention to the role this state plays in the material outlined in David R. Kinsley's "The Death that Conquers Death." For example, in Nāmadeva's hymn, it is said that

> we should always think of death . . . in whatever pursuit we might be engaged. As when a thief is being carried to the hanging place, death is approaching him at every step; as when a man is plying his axe at the root of the tree, its life is diminishing every moment, similarly, whatever we may be doing, we must suppose that death is always approaching us.

Death becomes a living presence, dominating the expression and direction of life. It is as if some talented artist had shifted the relation between the images of our world and the space around us so that the brooding presence of death fills the entire horizon of our lives. As a consequence, the inner dynamic motivating the individual's life is the negation of ordinary life structures, such as relatives, friends, social situations, until all the normal meanings of an individual's life are regarded as of no ultimate worth. The many rites described by Kinsley involve a ritual exteriorizing of the total complex of personal worth and the subsequent relegation of that conglomerate to transience and death, as prefigured in the third *Sannyāsa-Upaniṣad*, where the renunciant is told to deal with his body "as if it were dead." Having placed everything behind the veil of death, the "presence" in the painting melts into the image of the deity. The devotee has literally moved through a series of interior and exterior acts that have killed him as a normal individual, overcome his ideas of personal death, and transformed the reality of death into a deity of great glory.

Integration

Claude Lévi-Strauss noted that the function of myths of death is to maintain a proper distance between life and death; in one sense, this is also the function of religion. It is, after all, only those elements outside our ken, cut off from our awareness, that can provoke terror and issue fearful challenges to us. Death is not a monster from chaos. It is part of the furniture of life.

The techniques involved in this integration vary from culture to culture, and perhaps from person to person. The validity of this view is reinforced in a remarkable series of articles appearing in *The Pennsylvania Gazette*, written by Professor Archie Hanlan, who was dying of cancer (and who did die before the series was completed). His progressive disintegration and how people responded to him and he to himself demonstrate that death is integrated into life at proper distances and maintained there at all costs. Dying, he says, is "the real pornography of our time—the dirty business that is to be shunted out of the way, the dying patient who is to be shoved off in a ward where he won't offend or bother other people."[4] But, from our standpoint, his most fascinating insight came from the pious Christian people around him, who continually bombarded him with Bible verses in an attempt to have him adopt their views toward death:

> To those people my unwillingness to meet death on their terms, from their religious point of view, is itself very threatening to them—that I either have to believe as they do, or their own belief-system will really have been shaken. And maybe that's true, not only in terms of religious points of view, but other points of view of dying. Maybe that's what's so difficult for all of us to face: that in looking at our own mortality we may find some assumption we have made about living very much shaken up.[5]

Moreover, it is not just the fact that Dr. Hanlan and his Bible-quoting acquaintances differed on the point of view of death; it is rather that for both, death has a proper place in life, and death beliefs are significant in the way people establish meaning for themselves. The various methods involved in this enterprise would comprise a study in itself, but it is sufficient to indicate, in Earle Waugh's selection, for example, the important role the death of Ḥusain plays in community identity among the Shīʿa. The ceremonies revolving around Muḥarram instill and reenact the mythical history of the community, not only in its celebration cycles, but in its suffering and agony. Through the storytelling, giftgiving, and personal flagellation, the participants revisit the founding events of the religion, and in that superior spiritual moment, they realize the drama of their own death as having meaning only in the sacred history of the Muslim faith. Thus, the meaning of each person's existence is activated by the paradigmatic death of Ḥusain in the dim ages of the past, and his own worth can be seen through his participation in the same plane of reality.

The parameters of the integration theme are expanded by Glen W. Davidson's consideration of seventeenth-century North America. He sees death transform the fathers from ordinary men to ideal types; the way the sons lived, the social organization they developed, and their sense of personal well-being were tied deliberately to the framework of paradigms created by the fathers' deaths. Thus the fathers lived on in ever-renewing rituals that cemented the past and future.

Transformation

Most people are convinced that death is ugly; few have noted the liberation it interjects into experience. The metaphors of death have borne a cloud of theological speculation, so much so that we tend to forget, as Eliade points out, "the fact that death transforms man into a form of spirit, be it soul, ghost, ethereal body or whatever.... Such spiritual transformations are expressed through images and symbols related to birth, rebirth, or resurrection, that is, to a new and sometimes more powerful life." The vigor and delight of this new state of being functions positively in attitudes giving life meaning and is undoubtedly one factor in the surliness and antagonism that focus on the corpse in many cultures.

Consider another positive transformation: André Schwartz-Bart ends his acclaimed novel *The Last of the Just* with this paragraph:

> Yes, at times one's heart could break in sorrow. But often too, preferably in the evening, I can't help thinking that Ernie Levy, dead six million times, is still alive somewhere, I don't know where. . . . Yesterday, as I stood in the street trembling in despair, rooted to the spot, a drop of pity fell from above my face. But there was no breeze in the air, no cloud in the sky. . . . There was only a presence.[6]

Despite the hopelessness and nausea of the Jewish massacres in Hitler's gas chambers, the author's gloom is broken by the insight into the transcending reality of Ernie Levy's humanity. It gave content, direction, and form to the heart awash in despair, brightening that Jewish child with a future. Death, even cruel, heartless death, can transform the horizons of experience into something new and blessed with hope.

No more concrete example of the transformative powers in the presence of death could be found than that treated by Pesach Schindler. Facing death in 1939, a group of Jews were ordered to sing a Hassidic melody.

> When the angry outburst against the Jews continued, an anonymous voice broke through the turmoil with a powerful and piercing cry, "*Mir velen sei iberleben Avinu*

> *Shebashomayim*," We will outlive them, O Father in Heaven! Instantly, the song took hold among the entire people, until it catapulted [the people] into a stormy and feverish dance. The assembled were literally swept up by the entrancing melody full of *dveikut*, which had now been infused with new content of faith and trust.

In a very different context, Benjamin Ray discusses royal funerary rituals in Buganda, vividly describing the way these rituals have been utilized by Uganda's General Amin in order to transfer an aura of sacrality and legitimacy from the ancient lineage of kings to his own person and rule. Ray's study makes it clear that this modern African leader has understood the possibilities for transformation inherent in these traditional rites of community death and renewal, and that he has effectively adapted them in a contemporary setting.

In another vein, consider this transformation: Lincoln lived and died as all men, but the drama of his death transformed his ordinariness into a transcendent image. Donald Capps pursues the mechanics of this transformation in "The Death of Father Abraham: The Assassination of Lincoln and Its Effects on Frontier Mythology." Biographers succeeded in presenting Lincoln either as a frontier hero or as a "representative man"; they had less success in making him a single individual, given the incompatibility of these patterns. The event of Lincoln's death resolved the conflict by raising the folk hero to the level of a Great Father. This model then fit into the martyred Christ-image. His tragic death transformed him from a complex human being into a universal figure with religious connotations. Indeed, his death signaled that God had transformed the naive confidence of a nation into the chastened attitude of a child before his father.

Finally, consider the transformative abilities of the dead, which, as Victor Turner points out, are able to mediate between "domains that are normally classified as distinct." The result of this metamorphic activity is that a "communitas" realm is established outside the definitions of normal social control, from which spiritual benefits may flow. The fantastic sacred power of the dead is hardly better portrayed than in David M. Knipe's "Sapiṇḍīkaraṇa"; the triple world of the immigrant dead is virtually created by ritual activities of the living, and the ancestors are maintained by the myriad attentions of those attending the rites. The interchange between two worlds is such that the living relatives are absolutely responsible for the eternal well-being of the family-group to which he, himself, belongs. Death rites not only transfer the dead to their proper levels in the world beyond but transform the living into creators of the order in which everyone may find his place. The ritual participants operate at a level of cosmic significance far beyond their role in the ordinary scheme of things.

We hope this brief prelude will provide an introduction to the wealth of the following contributions. However, because death has an intensely personal consequence, whether the interpretations given here are suggestive is secondary. Engagement with the subject itself has religious overtones, and the ultimate success of this venture lies in its capacity to stimulate each individual to develop a personal "language" of death.

Notes

1. Johannes von Saaz, *Death and the Plowman* or *The Bohemian Plowman*, trans. Ernest N. Kirrmann (Chapel Hill: The University of North Carolina Press, 1958), adapted by Jacob Needleman in *Death and Bereavement*, ed. Austin H. Kutscher (Springfield, Ill.: Charles C. Thomas, 1969), p. 102.

2. Christiaan Barnard and Curtis Bill Pepper, *Christiaan Barnard, One Life* (New York: Macmillan, 1969), pp. 359–60.

3. P.V. Kane, *History of Dharmaśāstra*, vol. 2 (Poona: Bhandarkar Oriental Research Institute, 1941), pt. 2, p. 942.

4. *The Pennsylvania Gazette*, February 1973, quoted in *The Chronicle of Higher Education*, 3 December 1973, p. 18.

5. Ibid.

6. André Schwartz-Bart, *The Last of the Just* (New York: Atheneum, 1960), p. 422.

Comparative Studies

Without Other there is no Self, without Self no choice between alternatives.

Chuang-Tzu
[A.C. Graham]

Mythologies of Death: An Introduction

MIRCEA ELIADE

Evoking the life-crisis of an Australian aboriginal male, W. Lloyd Warner writes, "The personality before birth is purely spiritual; it becomes completely profane or unspiritual in the earlier period of its life, when it is classed socially with the females, gradually becomes more and more ritualized and sacred as the individual grows older and approaches death, and at death once more becomes completely spiritual and sacred."[1]

Whatever they may think of death, a great number of our contemporaries will certainly *not* agree that death is a "completely spiritual and sacred" mode of being. For the common nonreligious person, death was emptied of any religious significance even before life lost its meaning. For some, the discovery of the ineptitude of death anticipated the discovery of the absurdity and the meaninglessness of life. As an anonymous British psychoanalyst is reported to have said, "We are born mad; then we acquire morality and become stupid and unhappy; then we die."

This last sentence—"Then we die"—admirably expresses the Western man's understanding of his destiny, but it is a somewhat different understanding from that found in many other cultures. There, too, people strive to pierce the mystery of death and to grasp its meaning. I do not know of a single culture where such a sentence—"Then we die"—would not be taken for granted. But this flat assertion of human mortality is only a pretentious platitude when it is isolated from its mythological context. A coherent and meaningful concluding sentence would be, " . . . and *therefore* we die." Indeed, in most traditional cultures, the advent of death is presented as an unfortunate accident that took place in the beginning. Death was unknown to the mythic Ancestors and is the consequence of something that happened in primordial times.[2] To learn how death first appeared in the world is to understand the cause of one's own mortality as well; death occurs because such and such a thing took place in the beginnings. Whatever the details of this myth of the first death may be, the myth itself offers an explanation of personal mortality.

As is well known, only a few myths explain the advent of death as a consequence of man's transgressing a divine commandment. Somewhat more common are the myths relating mortality to a cruel and arbitrary act of some demonic Being. Such mythic themes are found, for instance, among Australian tribes,[3] and in the Central Asiatic, Siberian, and North American mythologies,[4] where mortality is introduced to the world by an adversary of the Creator. In contrast to this, among archaic societies, most of the myths explain Death as an absurd accident and/or as the consequence of a stupid choice made by the first ancestors. I am sure you will recall the innumerable stories like "Two Messengers" or "The Message That Failed," which are especially common in Africa.[5] According to these stories, God sent the chameleon to the ancestors with the message that they would be immortal, and sent the lizard with the message that they would die. But the chameleon paused along the way, and the lizard arrived first. After she delivered her message, Death entered the world.

Seldom do we encounter a more appropriate illustration of the absurdity of Death. One has the impression that he is reading a page of a French existentialist author. Indeed, the passage from Being to Non-Being is so hopelessly incomprehensible that a ridiculous explanation is more convincing because it is ridiculously absurd. Of course, such myths presuppose a carefully elaborated theology of the Word: God could not change the verdict for the simple reason that, once uttered, the words *created* reality.

Equally dramatic are the myths that relate the appearance of death to a stupid action of the Ancestors. For example, a Melanesian myth tells that, as they advanced in life, the first men cast their skins like snakes, and came out with their youth renewed. But once an old woman, coming home rejuvenated, was not recognized by her child. In order to pacify the child, she put her old skin on again, and from that time people became mortal.[6] Last, let me recall the beautiful Indonesian myth of the Stone and the Banana. In the beginning, the sky was very near to the earth, and the Creator used to let down his gifts to men at the end of a rope. One day he thus lowered a stone. But the Ancestors would have none of it, and called out to their Maker, "What have we to do with this stone? Give us something else." God complied; some time later he let down a banana, which they joyfully accepted. Then the ancestors heard a voice from heaven saying, "Because ye have chosen the banana, your life shall be like its life. When the banana-tree has offspring, the parent stem dies; so shall ye die and your children shall step into your place. Had ye chosen the stone, your life would have been like the life of the stone, changeless and immortal."[7]

This Indonesian myth aptly illustrates the mysterious dialectics of Life and Death. The stone symbolizes indestructibility and invulnerability and, consequently, an indefinite continuity of the same. But the stone is also a symbol of opacity, inertia, and immobility, while life in general and the human condition in particular are characterized by creativity and freedom. For man this ultimately means spiritual creativity and spiritual freedom. Thus, death becomes part of the human condition because, as we shall see, it is the experience of death that renders intelligible the notion of spirit and of spiritual beings. In sum, whatever was the cause of the first death, man became himself and could fulfill his specific destiny only as a being fully aware of his own mortality.

The elder Henry James, father of William and Henry, wrote that "the first and highest service which Eve renders Adam is to throw him out of Paradise." This is, of course, a modern Western view of that primordial catastrophe, the loss of Paradise and immortality. In no traditional culture is death regarded as a blessing.

On the contrary, in archaic societies ideas of human perenniality can still be detected, that is, the conviction that human beings, though no longer immortal, could live indefinitely if only a hostile agent did not put an end to their lives. In other words, a natural death is simply inconceivable. As the Ancestors lost their immortality through accident or demonic plot, so a man dies as he falls victim to magic, ghosts, or other supernatural aggressors.

Nevertheless, in many archaic cultures, as the myth of the Stone and the Banana so gracefully suggests, death is considered a necessary complement of life. Essentially, this means that death changes man's ontological status. The separation of the soul from the body brings about a new modality of being. From this point on, man is reduced to a spiritual existence; he becomes a ghost, a "spirit."

In many cultures, there is the belief that the separation of body and soul brought forth through the first death was accompanied by a structural modification of the entire cosmos; the sky was removed and the means of communications between heaven and earth was broken. (The tree, liana, or ladder connecting heaven and earth was severed, or the Cosmic Mountain was flattened.) Henceforth, the gods were no longer easily accessible, as they had been before; they now dwell far removed in the highest heaven, where only shamans or medicine men are able to reach them, doing so in ecstasy, which is to say, in "spirit."[8]

There is also the belief that when man was first made, the Creator bestowed his soul, while the Earth provided his body. Consequently, at the moment of death these two elements return to their sources, the body to earth, and the soul to its celestial author.[9]

Such analogies between cosmogony, anthropogony, and death indicate, so to speak, the "creative" virtualities of the act of dying. It is well known among traditional societies that death is not considered real until the funerary ceremonies are duly completed. In other words, the onset of physiological death is only the signal that a new set of ritual operations must be accomplished in order to create the new identity of the deceased. The body has to be treated in such a way that it will not be magically reanimated and become an instrument of mischievous performances. Even more important, the soul must be guided to her new abode and ritually integrated in the community of its inhabitants.

Unfortunately, little is known of the religious symbolism of funerary ceremonies among archaic and traditional societies. We realize the proportion of our ignorance when, by a piece of luck, a contemporary anthropologist has the opportunity to witness an adequate funerary ritual and to have it explained to him. Such was the case with the Colombian anthropologist Gerardo Reichel-Dolmatoff, who in 1966 attended the burial of a young girl of the Kogi tribe of Sierra Nevada de Santa Maria. The description published by him is still insufficiently known; it certainly merits being summarized here.

After having chosen the place for the grave, the shaman (*máma*) executes a series of ritual gestures and declares, "Here is the village of Death; Here is the ceremonial house of Death; Here is the womb. I Will open the House. The house is closed, and I am going to open it!" Following this, he announces, "The house is open," and shows the men the place where they should dig the grave. At the bottom of the tomb they put small green stones, shellfish, and a snail's shell. Then the shaman vainly tries to raise the body, giving the impression that it is very heavy; it is only on the ninth try that he succeeds. The body is placed with the head toward the east, and he "closes the house," which is to say, fills in the grave. There follow other ritual movements around the tomb, and finally all return. The ceremony lasts about two hours.

As Reichel-Dolmatoff remarked, an archaeologist of the future excavating the tomb would find a skeleton with its head facing east, along with some stones and shells. The rituals and, above all, the religious ideology implied in the rituals would not be recoverable along with the rest. Moreover, for a foreign observer today, the symbolism of the ceremony remains inaccessible if the totality of Kogi religion is ignored. As Reichel-Dolmatoff saw, the "village of Death" and the "ceremonial house of Death" are "verbalizations" of the cemetery, while the "house" and "womb" are verbalizations of the grave. (This explains the fetal position of the body, lying on its right side.) These ceremonies are followed by the verbalization of offerings as "food for the dead" and by the ritual of "opening" and "closing" the "house-womb." A final purification completes the ceremony.

Further, the Kogi identify the world—womb of the Universal Mother—with each village, each cultic house, each dwelling, and each grave. When the shaman lifts the corpse nine times, it signifies the return of the body to its fetal state by passing through the nine months of gestation in reverse. And as the tomb is assimilated to the world, the funerary offerings receive a cosmic significance. Moreover, the offerings, "food for the dead," also have a sexual sense, for in myths and dreams, and in rules of marriage, the act of eating symbolizes the sexual act; consequently the funerary offerings constitute a kind of semen that fertilizes the Universal Mother. The shellfish are charged with a very complex symbolism also, which is not simply sexual in significance. They represent the living members of the family, while the snail's shell symbolizes the spouse of the deceased, for if it is not found in the tomb, a young girl, upon arriving in the other world, "will ask for a husband," which will provoke the death of a young man from the tribe. [10]

This analysis, carried forward so well by Reichel-Dolmatoff, shows how precarious is our understanding of the anthropocosmic symbolism informing any traditional interment, and, consequently, how little we know of the religious dimensions of death and dying in archaic societies. Nevertheless, we are assured of one fact: everywhere in the traditional world death is, or was, considered a second birth, the beginning of a new, spiritual existence. This second birth, however, is not natural as is the first, biological birth; that is to say, it is not given, but must be ritually created. In this sense, death is an initiation, an introduction into a new mode of being. And, as is well known, any initiation consists essentially of a symbolic death followed by rebirth or resurrection.[11] Besides, any passage from one mode of being to another necessarily implies a symbolic act of dying. One has to die to the previous condition in order to be reborn in a new, superior state. In the initiation rites of puberty, the adolescent dies to his "natural," biological condition and comes to life again as a "cultural" being, and from this time forward he has access to the spiritual values of the tribe. During their initiation, novices are considered dead, and they behave like ghosts.[12] In such cases, we witness a fairly veridical anticipation of death, that is, an anticipation of the mode of being of a "spirit." Consequently, in some cultures there is the belief that only those who have been properly initiated will obtain a real postexistence; the others either will be doomed to a larvaelike state or will fall victim to a "second death."

It is not my intention to evoke all the important religious and cultural creations occasioned by the confrontation with death. The cults of the ancestors and heroes, or the beliefs and rituals concerning the collective return of the dead—those periodic masquerades in which some scholars have seen the beginnings of drama—could be discussed in great detail. Whatever one may think of the origin of Greek tragedy, though, it is certain that the ceremonies celebrating the periodic return of the dead gave rise to complex dramatic spectacles, which played a considerable role in many folk cultures.

Particularly creative were the ecstatic experiences of the shamans, that is, their journeys to Heaven or the world of the dead. Representing a momentary separation of the soul from the body, ecstasy was and is still considered to be an anticipation of death. Able to travel in "spiritual worlds" and to see superhuman beings (gods, demons, spirits of the dead), the shaman contributed extensively to the knowledge of death. In all probability, many features of "funerary geography" as well as some themes of the mythology of death are the result of the ecstatic experiences of shamans. The lands that the shaman sees and the personages he meets in his ecstatic journeys to the beyond are minutely described by the shaman himself, either during or after his trance. The unknown and terrifying world of death thus assumes form and is organized in accordance with particular patterns. Finally it displays a structure, and in the course of time becomes familiar and acceptable. In turn, the supernatural inhabitants of the world of death become visible; they show a form, display a personality, even a biography. Little by little the world of the dead becomes knowable. In the last analysis, the accounts of the shamans' ecstatic journeys contribute to "spiritualizing" the world of the dead at the same time that they enrich it with wondrous forms and figures.[13]

There is also a marked likeness between the accounts of shamanic ecstasies and certain epic themes in the oral literatures of Siberia, Central Asia, Polynesia, and of some North American tribes.[14] Here, just as the shaman descends to the underworld in order to bring back the soul of a sick person, so the epic hero goes to the world of the dead, and after many trials succeeds in carrying back the soul of a dead person, as is seen in the familiar story of Orpheus' struggle to bring back the soul of Eurydice.

Further, a great number of dramatic motifs in both myth and folklore involve journeys to fabulous regions beyond the ocean or at the extremities of the world. Obviously, these mythic lands represent the realm of the dead. It is impossible to trace the origin or "history" of such funerary geographies, but directly or indirectly they are all related to different views of the other world, the most familiar being the subterranean, the celestial, and the land beyond the ocean.[15]

I shall have more to say of such mythical geographies later, but for the moment let me recall some other examples of what may be called the creative understanding of Death and the act of dying. In fact, once having been interpreted as a passage to a superior mode of existence, Death became the paradigmatic model of all significant changes in human life. The Platonic assimilation of philosophy to an anticipation of death became, in the course of time, a venerable metaphor. But this was not the case with mystical experiences, from shamanistic ecstasies to the great mystics of the high religions. A Hindu as well as a Christian saint *dies* to the profane condition; he is "dead to the world," as is the case with the great Jewish and Muslim mystics.

All these "creative homologies"—symbols and metaphors brought forth by setting up the act of dying as the paradigmatic model of any significant transition—emphasize the "spiritual" function of Death, the fact that death transforms man into a form of spirit, be it soul, ghost, ethereal body, or whatever. But, on the other hand, such spiritual transformations are expressed through images and symbols related to birth, rebirth, or resurrection, that is, to a new and sometimes more powerful life. This paradox is already implicit in the earliest interpretation of the act of dying as the beginning of a new mode of existence.

As a matter of fact, there is a curious ambivalence, if not a latent contradiction, in many ritual patterns of confronting death. The spiritualizing virtue of death may be enthusiastically exalted, but the love for the body and for incarnate life turns out to be stronger. Although it is true, as Professor W. Lloyd Warner has said, that an Australian man becomes at death "completely spiritual and sacred," this transformation is not greeted with rejoicing. Rather, everywhere in Australia, when someone dies there is a catastrophic crisis. The wailing of women, the gashing of one's head to draw blood, and other manifestations of grief and despair reach a real frenzy. "The collective grief and wrath are controlled only by the certainty and the emphatic reassurance that the dead will be avenged."[16]

Most of these contradictory ideas and behaviors are occasioned by the problem of the soul's localization. There is a widespread belief that the departed ones haunt their familiar surroundings, although they are supposed to be concurrently present in their tombs and in the Netherworld. Of course, such paradoxical multilocation of the soul is diversely explained according to the different religious systems: either it is asserted that a segment of the soul remains near the dwelling or the tomb, while the essential soul goes to the realm of the dead; or it is held that the soul tarries for some time in the proximity of the living, ultimately joining the community of the dead in the Netherworld. Notwithstanding these and similar explanations, there is a tacit consent in most religions that the dead are present concurrently in the tomb and in some spiritual realm. Such a conception, which is widely prevalent in the Mediterranean world, was duly accepted by the Christian church. To be sure, we are dealing here with a popular, pre-Christian tradition, later accepted by the Church. But the same idea was shared even by the most rigorous theologians, such as St. Ambrosius of Milan. When his brother, Satyrus, died in 379, Ambrosius buried him near the body of a martyr. And the great theologian composed the following funerary inscription: "Ambrosius has buried his brother Manius Satyrus at the left hand of a martyr; in return for his good life, may the moisture of this holy blood seep through to him and water his body."[17] Thus, in spite of the fact that Satyrus was supposed to be now in heaven, the martyr's blood could still operate on the Satyrus buried in the tomb. This belief in the bilocation of the dead has nothing to do with the Christian doctrine of the resurrection of the body. As Oscar Cullman rightly points out, "the resurrection of the body is a new act of creation which embraces everything . . . ," and "it is tied to a *divine total process* implying deliverance."[18]

The almost universal conviction that the dead are present both on earth and in a spiritual world reveals the secret hope that, in spite of all evidence to the contrary, the dead are able to partake somehow in the world of the living. As we have seen, the advent of death makes possible the mode of being of the spirit, but, conversely, the spiritualization is realized and expressed through symbols and metaphors of life. One is reminded of the reciprocal translation whereby the most important acts of life are seen in terms of death, and vice versa; for instance, marriage as death, birth as death, and so on. In the last analysis, this paradoxical process discloses a secret hope, and perhaps a nostalgia of attaining a level of meaning where life and death, body and spirit, reveal themselves as aspects or dialectical stages of one ultimate reality. Indirectly, this implies a depreciation of the condition of "pure spirit." Indeed, one could say that, with the exception of Orphism, Platonism, and Gnosticism, the Near Eastern and European anthropologies did not conceive the ideal man as a uniquely spiritual being but as an incarnate spirit. Similar conceptions may be deciphered in some archaic mythologies. Moreover, one can point out in certain primitive millenarian movements the eschatological hope for the resurrection of the body,[19] a hope shared by Zoroastrianism, Judaism, Christianity, and Islam.

The paradox of the reciprocal translation of life symbols and metaphors with the symbols and metaphors of death has attracted the attention of some psychologists, linguists, and philosophers, but as yet (at least to my knowledge) no historian of religions has contributed significantly to the discussion. However, the historian of religions may be able to decipher meanings and intentionalities that have escaped other researchers. The paradox of this reciprocal translation reveals that, whatever one may think, or believe he thinks, of life and death, he is constantly experiencing modes and levels of dying. This means more than just a confirmation of the biological truism that death is always present in life. The important fact is that, consciously or unconsciously, we are perpetually exploring the imaginary worlds of death and untiringly inventing new ones. This also means that we are anticipating death-experiences even when we are, so to say, driven by the most creative epiphanies of life.

To illustrate, let us go back to the mythical funerary geographies discussed a few moments ago. The morphology of such fabulous realms is extremely rich and complex. No scholar can vouch knowledge of all the Paradises, Hells, Underworlds, and counterworlds (or antiworlds) of the dead. Neither can he assert that he knows all the roads to these wonderlands, though he may be certain that there will be a river and a bridge, a sea and a boat; a tree, a cove, or a precipice; a dog, a demonic or angelic psychopomp or doorkeeper, to mention only the most frequent features of the road to the land of no return.[20]

What interests us is not the infinitude of these fantastic lands, but, as I said, the fact that they still nourish and stimulate our imagination. Moreover, new lands of no return and new roads to reach them safely are continuously discovered in our dreams and fantasies, or by children, poets, novelists, painters, and film makers. It matters little that the real meaning of such lands and landscapes, persons, figures, and actions is not always clear to those who consider or imagine them. European and American children still play the hotch-potch, ignorant of the fact that they reenact an initiatory game whose goal is to penetrate into and successfully return from a labyrinth; for in playing the hotch-potch game, they symbolically descend into the netherworld and come back to earth.[21]

Thus, important and revealing is the fact that mythologies of death and funerary geographies became part of modern man's everyday life. The French proverb *partir c'est mourir un peu* is often quoted, but it is not an illuminating example. Death is not anticipated or symbolically experienced only by going away, departing from a town or a country, or similar actions. Neither everyday language with so many picturesque evocations of Hells, Paradises, and Purgatories nor the many proverbs referring to them give full justice to the creative role played by the imaginary universes in modern man's life. Since the early 1920s, literary critics have been successful in deciphering the mythologies and geographies of death in works of fiction, drama, and poetry, and historians of religions can go further and show that many gestures and actions of everyday life are symbolically related to modes and levels of dying. Any immersion in darkness, as well as any irruption of light, represents an encounter with death. The same thing can be said of any experience of mountaineering, flying, swimming under water, or any long journey, discovery of an unknown country, or even a meaningful encounter with strangers. Every one of these experiences recalls and reactualizes a landscape, a figure, or an event from one of those imaginary universes known from mythologies or folklore or one's own dreams and fantasies; of course we are seldom aware of the symbolic meaning of such experiences. But what matters is that, though unconscious, these symbolic meanings play a decisive role in our life. This is confirmed by the fact that we simply cannot detach ourselves from such imaginary universes: not when we work or think, not when we relax and amuse ourselves, not when we sleep and dream, not even when we vainly try to fall asleep.

We have repeatedly noticed the ambivalence of the images and metaphors of death and life. In the imaginary universes, as in so many mythologies and religions, death and life are dialectically related. To be sure, there are also nightmares provoked by terrifying funerary figures. But in such cases we have to deal with initiatory experiences, though we are rarely aware of this fact. In sum, even modern Western man, in spite of his religious ignorance and his indifference to the problem of death, is still involved, consciously or unconsciously, with the mysterious dialectics that obsessed our archaic ancestors. Death is inconceivable if it is not related to a new form of being in some way or other, no matter how this form may be imagined: a postexistence, rebirth, reincarnation, spiritual immortality, or resurrection of the body. In many traditions there is also the hope for a recovery of the original perenniality. Ultimately this amounts to saying, if we may refer to the Indonesian myth again, that the only satisfactory solution would have been for the Ancestors to have chosen both the stone and the banana. Separately, neither one is able to meet man's paradoxical nostalgia of being fully immersed in life, and concurrently partaking of immortality—yearning to exist alike in time and in eternity.

For a historian of religions, such paradoxical drives and nostalgias are familiar. In a great number of religious creations, we recognize the will to transcend oppositions, polarities, and dualisms in order to obtain a sort of *coincidentia oppositorum*, that is, the totality in which all contraries are abolished. To quote only one example, the ideal man is seen as androgynous and as such partakes of both life and perenniality.

The paradoxical conjunction of opposites characterizes, as is well-known, the Indian ontologies and soteriologies. One of the most profound and most audacious reinterpretations of the Mahāyāna tradition, the Mādhyamika doctrine developed mainly by Nāgārjuna, went to the extreme limits of such dialectics. What could be more scandalous, even sacrilegious, than to proclaim, as Nāgārjuna did, that "there is nothing whatever to differentiate *saṃsāra* from *nirvāṇa*, and there is nothing whatever to differentiate *nirvāṇa* from *saṃsāra*"?[22] In order to set the mind free from illusory structures dependent on language, Nāgārjuna elaborated a dialectics leading to the supreme and universal *coincidentia oppositorum*. But his religious and philosophical genius was nourished by the venerable and pan-Indian tradition of paradoxical "coincidences" of being and nonbeing, eternity and temporal flux, beatitude and suffering.

To be sure, such grandiose Indian metaphysical creations cannot be ranked with the paradoxical drives and nostalgias that give birth to the Western man's imaginary universes. Their structural affinities are evident nonetheless, and they break open new and fascinating problems for philosophers and psychologists alike. On the other hand, we must keep in mind the recurrent efforts of the most profound and seminal Western thinkers to recover the existential meaning of death. In effect, though emptied of religious significations as a result of the accelerated secularization of Western society, death has become, since *Sein und Zeit*, the center of philosophical inquiry. The exceptional success—one could almost say, the popular vogue—of Heidegger's investigations illustrates the modern individual's yearning for an "existential understanding of Death."

There is no point in trying to summarize the decisive contributions of Heidegger. But it is important to note that if Heidegger describes human existence as "Being unto Death" (*Sein zum Tode*) and proclaims Death as "the most proper, exclusive and ultimate potentiality of *Dasein*,"[23] he also states that "Death is the hiding-place where Being retreats as into a mountain stronghold [*Gebirg*]."[24] Or, to quote another passage, Death, "as the shrine of Non-Being, hides within itself the presence of Being [*das Wesende des Seins*]."[25]

It is not possible to convey in a clear and simple formula any one of Heidegger's fundamental philosophical conclusions. Nevertheless, it seems that, for him, man takes possession of himself through the correct understanding of Death and consequently opens himself to Being. Indeed, an existence becomes authentic, that is, fully human, when, comprehending the inevitability of Death, man realizes the "Freedom-unto-Death [*Freiheit zum Tode*]." But inasmuch as Death "hides within itself the presence of Being," Heidegger's thought may be interpreted as indicating the possibility of encountering Being in the very act of dying. Whatever a Heideggerian exegete may think of such interpretation, the important fact remains that Heidegger admirably proved the paradoxical coexistence of Death and Life, Being and Non-Being.

A historian of religions would be particularly captivated by Heidegger's acute analysis of the multiform presence of Death in the very core of Life, and of the inextricable camouflage of Being in Non-Being. It is perhaps the historian of religion's privilege, and his highest satisfaction, to discover the continuity of human thought and imagination from prehistory to our own time, from a naive and enigmatic myth like that of the Stone and the Banana to the grandiose but equally enigmatic *Sein und Zeit*.

Notes

1. W. Lloyd Warner, *A Black Civilization: A Study of an Australian Tribe*, rev. ed. (New York: Harper Torchbooks, 1964), pp. 5–6.

2. J.G. Frazer, "On Myths of the Origin of Death," *Folklore in the Old Testament*, vol. 1 (London: MacMillan, 1919), pp. 45–77; Theodor H. Gaster, *Myth, Legend and Custom in the Old Testament* (New York: Harper & Row, 1969), pp. 35–47, 339–40; Mircea Eliade, *From Primitives to Zen: A Thematic Sourcebook of the History of Religions* (New York: Harper & Row, 1967), pp. 139–44.

3. Cf., *inter alia*, T.G.H. Strehlow, *Aranda Traditions* (Melbourne: Melbourne University Press: 1947), pp. 44–45. (Myth reproduced in *From Primitives to Zen*, pp. 140–42.)

4. See some examples in Mircea Eliade, *Zalmoxis, the Vanishing God* (Chicago: University of Chicago Press, 1972), pp. 76ff.

5. See Hans Abrahamsson, *The Origin of Death: Studies in African Mythology* (Uppsala, 1951).

6. R.H. Codrington, *The Melanesians* (Oxford, 1895), p. 265 (= *From Primitives to Zen*, p. 139).

7. J.G. Frazer, *The Belief in Immortality*, vol. 1 (London, 1913), pp. 74–75, quoting A.C. Kruit (= *From Primitives to Zen*, p. 140).

8. Cf. Mircea Eliade, *Myths, Dreams and Mysteries*, trans. Philip Mairet (1960; reprint ed., Harper Torchbooks, 1967), pp. 59ff.

9. See, *inter alia*, Olof Pettersson, *Jabmek and Jabmeaimo: A Comparative Study of the Dead and of the Realm of the Dead in Lappish Religion* (Lund, 1957), pp. 20ff.

10. Gerardo Reichel-Dolmatoff, "Notas Sobre el Simbolismo Religioso de los Indios de la Sierra Nevada de Santa Marta," *Razón y Fabula, Revista de la Universidad de los Andes*, no. 1 (1967): 55–72, esp. pp. 63ff. See also Eliade, *The Quest: History and Meaning in Religion* (Chicago: University of Chicago Press, 1969), pp. 138ff.; "South American High Gods," part 2, *History of Religions* 10 (1971): 234–66, esp. pp. 256ff.

11. Cf. Eliade, *Birth and Rebirth*, trans. Willard R. Trask (New York: Harper & Row, 1958; reprint ed. Harper Torchbooks, *Rites and Symbols of Initiation; The Mysteries of Birth and Rebirth*, 1965).

12. Eliade, *Birth and Rebirth*, pp. 15ff.

13. Cf. Eliade, *Shamanism: Archaic Techniques of Ecstasy*, trans. Willard R. Trask (New York: Pantheon, 1964), pp. 500ff.

14. Cf. *Shamanism*, pp. 213ff., 371ff., 368ff. See also R.A. Stein, *Recherches sur l'épopée et le Barde au Tibet* (Paris: Presses Universitaires de France, 1959), pp. 317ff., 370ff.

15. There is a considerable literature on these themes. The works of Frazer (*The Belief in Immortality*, vols. 1–3) and Olof Pettersson are valuable for the materials collected (cf. the bibliography of Pettersson, pp. 233–41). For a summary presentation, see F. Bar, *Les Routes de l'autre Monde* (Paris: Presses Universitaires de France, 1946).

16. Cf. Eliade, *Australian Religions: An Introduction* (Ithaca: Cornell University Press, 1973), p. 167.

17. Cf. Franz Buecheler, ed., *Carmina latina epigraphica*, no. 1421, quoted by J.P. Jacobsen, *Les Manes*, vol. 1 (Paris: E. Champion, 1924), p. 72.

18. See Oscar Cullmann, "Immortality of the Soul or Resurrection of the Dead?" in Krister Stendahl, ed., *Immortality and Resurrection* (New York: Macmillan, 1965), p. 29.

19. See some examples quoted in Eliade, *Méphistophéles et L'Androgyne* (1962), pp. 171ff. (= *Mephistopheles and the Androgyne*, trans. Jim Cohen [New York: Sheed and Ward, 1965], pp. 137ff.).

20. I discuss these mythical geographies in a book in preparation, *Mythologies de la Mort*.

21. Cf. Jan de Vries, *Untersuchung über das Hüpfspiel: Kinderspiel-Kulttanz*, FF Communications, no. 173 (Helsinki: Suomalainen Tiedeakatemia Academia Scientiarum Fennica, 1957).

22. *Mūlamadhyamakakānikās* 25, 19, trans. Frederick J. Streng, *Emptiness* (Nashville: Abingdon Press, 1967), p. 217.

23. Martin Heidegger, *Sein und Seit*, p. 250, with the commentary of William J. Richardson, Heidegger: *Through Phenomenology to Thought* (The Hague: Martinus Nijhoff, 1963), p. 76.

24. Richardson, p. 574.

25. Heidegger, *Vorträge und Aufsätze* (Pfullingen: G. Neske, 1954), p. 177, with the commentary of Richardson, pp. 573–74.

Death and the Dead in the Pilgrimage Process

VICTOR TURNER

It is appropriate to begin with three quotations, directly connecting the three themes of this study—pilgrimage, death, and salvation. The first is from Leslie Farmer's *We Saw the Holy City*, concerning the Christian pilgimage to Jerusalem: "It was a common custom to bring one's shroud to be cut to the size of the Stone of Unction [in the Church of the Holy Sepulchre]."[1] The second is from Sir Richard Burton's *Personal Narrative of a Pilgrimage to Al Madinah and Meccah*: "Those who die on a pilgrimage become martyrs . . . the ghost departs to instant beatitude."[2] And the last is from Romain Roussel's *Les Pèlerinages à Travers Les Siècles:* "The pilgrim [to Mecca] knows that he will present himself at the Last Judgment covered with his ihram pilgrim's garb [two simple white pieces of cloth]. That is why many of those who fulfill the *haj* wish to be buried in the dress they wore at Mecca."[3]

Only death on the way to or at the shrine makes a pilgrimage a true rite of passage, although pilgrimages are somewhat similar to initiation rites.

Pilgrimages in the salvation religions, like initiation rites in tribal religions, are full of symbols and metaphors for death and are also directly concerned with the dead. The dead may include the founder of a religion, his kin, disciples or companions, saints and martyrs of the faith, and the souls of the ordinary faithful. This is partly because both pilgrims and initiands are undergoing a separation from a relatively fixed state of life and social status and passing into a liminal or threshold phase and condition for which none of the rules and few of the experiences of their previous existence had prepared them. In this sense, they are "dying" from what was and passing into a state which is "dead" to the inhabited world of those living in social systems.

To use terminology favored by A.R. Radcliffe-Brown,[4] initiand and pilgrim cease to be members of a perduring system of social relations (family, neighborhood, state) and become members of a transient class of initiands and pilgrims moving through the fields or lands. The actors in the pilgrimage processes leave a domain where relations are complex for one where they are simple. Their relations with others are, at any rate at first, no longer those of interconnectedness but of similarity: no longer do they occupy social positions in a hierarchical or segmentary structure of localized status roles; now they are assigned to a class of anonymous novices or plainly and uniformly garbed pilgrims, all torn or self-torn from their familiar systemic environment. Again, although a system has characteristic form, and is governed by rules of social and cultural construction, a class of liminal initiands or pilgrims is without form, is a homogenized mass of like components—at least initially. Homesteaders are coordinated by interdependence: pilgrims and initiands are coordinated by similarity, by likeness of lot rather than interdependence of social position. And whereas members of an established social system play roles and occupy statuses that are functionally consistent, there may be no functional relationship among novices or pilgrims. Again, a stabilized social system has a structure, but novices and pilgrims confront one another at first as a mere aggregate, without organic unity.

"System" may be symbolically equated with "life," in ritual, and extrusion from system—as a phase of a ritual or pilgrimage process—with "death," since all that interconnects, integrates, coordinates, all that constitutes the order of daily life for the actors is annulled or abrogated. Metaphorically, the novice or pilgrim experiences "the pains of dissolution." This is one reason why symbols of death, dying, and catabolism proliferate in tribal initiation rites. For example, Monica Wilson writes on what I would call the "liminal" (threshold) phase of the rituals of birth, puberty and marriage, death, abnormal birth and misfortune of a southern Tanzanian people:

> There can be no doubt that the induction [into the ritual situation] and seclusion represent death. Strewing leaves—or laying a litter—which is an essential act in every induction is a sign of misfortune and death; and at the induction of a bride her "mothers" sing: "Go, go and never return," and "We wail a dirge." The mourners, the nubile girl, the mother of a new-born child, and the parents of twins are all [termed] "filthy" and one with the dead; Kasitile [Wilson's best informant] said of mourners: "We have died, we *are* the corpse."[5]

In my book *The Forest of Symbols* I give many further examples, drawn from tribal societies, of symbols and metaphors for death in initiation rites: "The initiand may be buried, forced to lie motionless in the posture and direction of customary burial, may be stained black, or may be forced to live for a while in the company of masked and monstrous mummers representing, *inter alia*, the dead."[6]

Again, among the Ndembu of Zambia, in several types of ritual an officiant known as the "hyena" (*chimbu*), characteristically a snatcher both of carrion and of the young of other species, "snatches" the novices from their mothers to be circumcised in the *Mukanda* circumcision rites, while the blood-soaked site of the operation is called *ifwilu*, "the place of death or dying." Circumcision is partly a metaphor for killing, since it kills the novice's childhood state. Such instances occur frequently in ethnographic literature. Symbols and metaphors (and other tropes) for structural erasure, rendering the initiands faceless, "dark," and "invisible" and anonymous, through disguise, body painting, and use of a generic term of address instead of a personal name ("novice," "neophyte," "initiand") also abound.

But the detachment of an initiand or novice from the system in which he has been embedded may also be positively interpreted as rebirth and growth. From this perspective, the abandoned system may be "death," and the new liminal state the germ of "life" or spiritual development. Thus the shift from complex, interconnected relations to simple relations of likeness may be regarded not so much as a negative dissolution of an ordering, articulating structure, the decay of a complex living organism, but rather as a positive release from the distancing between individuals that their membership of social positions and occupancy of statuses in a system involves.

Structural distance may, then, be an apt symbol for death, the dissolution of distance and rebirth into authentic social life. Individuals may see the move away as an opportunity for a direct, immediate confrontation of others as total human beings, no longer as segments of a structured system. Thus among many West Central Bantu peoples, the circumcised novices become fast friends during a long period of seclusion together, even though before the operation they lived in different villages or even chiefdoms, structured units normally in continuous low-key conflict with one another. Moreover, even the most harmoniously articulated structures in any culture produce some "alienation," for the fullness of an individual's being overflows the totality of his roles and statuses. Structure also provokes competition and conflict, whether of small-scale or large-scale social systems. Social and political systems contain a wide range of offices in addition to chains of command and bureaucratic ladders. There are systems of promotion, rules, and criteria for status elevation and degradation and laws concerning the protection, disposal, transference, and inheritance of property, as well as succession to high office. There are social controls over sexuality and reproductive capacity, rules governing marriage, and prohibitions on incest and adultery. In this many-leveled, ordered, and sanctioned field, individuals find it hard not to envy their neighbor's good fortune, covet his ox, ass, or lands, strive with him for office, compete with him on the promotion ladder, seek to commit adultery with his wife, become greedy or miserly, or fall into despair at their own lack of success. But when they are lifted by initiation ritual or voluntarily elect to go on pilgrimage, they may see the metaphoric death mentioned earlier as a death from the negative, alienating aspects of systems and structure, as an opportunity to take stock of the lives from which they are now temporarily detached, or, alternatively, regain an innocence felt by them to have been lost. They may feel that a death from self, or in traditional Christian terms, from the World, the Flesh, and the Devil, may be simultaneously a birth or rebirth of an identity splintered and crushed by social structure. Ordinary, mundane life may be reinterpreted as the Terrene City; its abandonment is a first glimpse of the Heavenly City. The move into liminality is here, therefore, a death-birth or a birth-death. This is explicitly formulated by Monica Wilson in a continuation of the passage already quoted. Furthermore, this quotation raises the problem of the second term in my title: What is the role of the dead in initiatory liminality? Later I shall examine this role in pilgrimage liminality: now we see it in the tribal initiation of which Wilson writes: "The period of seclusion implies a *sojourn with the shades* [the ancestral spirits], and our hypothesis is that it represents *both* death and gestation. The hut appears as a symbol of the womb in the pregnancy and 'gasping cough' [a Nyakyusa category of illness] rituals, and the doorway which 'belongs to the shades' is a symbol for the vagina."[7] Wilson interprets certain symbolic actions, as when mourners or the girl novice in puberty rites runs in and out of the doorway, to represent rebirth. I have noticed "gateway" symbols not only in African rituals but also as an outstanding feature of the precincts of Catholic pilgrimage shrines, as at Lourdes, Remedios in Mexico City, and Chalma in Mexico State.

Thus there is metaphorical death in tribal rituals, parallel perhaps with "mystical death" in the salvation religions of complex societies and metaphorical rebirth, homologous to "spiritual regeneration." Perhaps ritual liminality may be spoken of as an exteriorized mystical way and the mystic's path as interiorized ritual liminality. During liminality there is also the involvement of the dead—of the ancestral "shades" for the Nyakyusa. The dead also partake of the ambiguous quality of liminality, the state of betwixt-and-betweenness, for they are associated both with positive and negative processes and objects, with life and death: "We have spoken," writes Wilson "of the Nyakyusa disgust for filth (*ubunyali*), which is associated with a corpse, menstruation, childbirth, intercourse, faeces, and all these are identified in some fashion with the shade. Faeces 'go below to the land of the shades.'"[8] There is about all this the image of "dust to dust." But there is an opposite quality attached to the shades. Wilson writes:

> All through the rituals the connection of the shades with potency and fertility is emphasized . . . they are present in intercourse and ejected as semen; they control conception; they control fertility in the fields. "The shade and semen are brothers," said one informant. And another said: "When they shake the millet and pumpkin-seeds (after ritual connection) the seed is semen . . . and it is the shade."[9]

The shades therefore represent both the decay of the body and the spirit of fertility, reminding one of the Biblical seed that must first die before it can yield much fruit, though this metaphor has of course to be seen in the context of a religion of personal salvation, and not, as in the Nyakyusa case, of a religion of community maintenance, where localized community has facets of system, class, and communitas. In the Christian case the death metaphor applies both to the death of the individual from the local structured community and to the death of that organic group for the individual. Nevertheless, both in Nyakyusa pagan and Christian modes of liminality initiands and pilgrims simultaneously undergo the death of social structure and regeneration in communitas, a kind of social antistructure. First they must cease to be members of a system and become members of a class, then they must be reborn in that modality of social interrelatedness I have called existential *communitas*—which might be paraphrased as true fellowship or *agapē*, or spontaneous, altruistic love, if one also concedes that there is a well-defined cognitive or "intellectual" (in Blake's sense) component in the relationship, for it is not a merging of consciousnesses, nor an emotional melding, but rather a mutual recognition of "definite, determinate identities" (to cite Blake again), each with its wiry, unique, indefeasible outline. All are one because each is one.

In this process of death and regeneration—at both social and individual levels—

different religions assign to the human dead a mediating function concerned with keeping the social structure of the system going in its characteristic form, with all its moral and jural rules, by acting as a punitive sanction against any major transgression of the basic legal, ethical, and commonsense principles determining the shape or profile of that system. The dead are also concerned with two extrastructural, perhaps antistructural, modalities: biological (or natural) and spiritual. In the first modality, as in the Nyakyusa case, and quite typical of many parts of Africa and elsewhere, the dead are thought to mediate between the invisible, ideal world of paradigms and archetypes and the sensorily perceptible world of sex and economics, begetting and food production, distribution, and consumption. If the dead are honored, known, and recognized, they will differentially, and in terms of structural differences, bestow blessings. Meyer Fortes's work on *pietas* is pertinent here.[10] But the dead, as we have seen in Wilson's work, are also regarded as powers, as themselves being the "force that through the green fuse thrusts the shoot." In the Ndembu Chihamba ritual, a spirit or arch-ancestor is planted in symbolic form, including the seeds and roots of food plants, in order that people and crops will multiply. And in salvation religions the dead are also regarded as possessing a mediating role in the drama of salvation, the freeing or binding of the immortal human soul, that invisible formative principle, which is believed to survive death, but to undergo punishment or reward for its consciously willed acts during life. The dead have influence over the living and are reciprocally influenced by their thoughts, words, and deeds. The dead can spiritually fructify the living, in Catholic theological thought at least; and it is not only in the folk dimension but also in theological terms that they are regarded as having an influence on the physical fertility, and certainly on the health, of the living. I quote from the *Knock Shrine Annual* for 1968, which records news of all group pilgrimages to the famous Irish shrine and publishes letters expressing gratitude to its mediating saints for favors believed to have been received through their mediation with God. One letter runs: "I wish to acknowledge my thanks to Our Lady of Knock, St. Joseph and St. John for the gift of two little girls and also recovery from heart trouble, and for many other favours and graces over the years. [Signed] A client of Our Lady."[11] This is typical of hundreds of letters published by journals connected with pilgrimage shrines.

I am not competent to discuss the relationship between the living and the dead in such salvation religions (to use Weber's term) as Hinduism, Islam, Buddhism, Judaism, Taoism, and Jainism, to mention only a few of those that profess to offer permanent or temporary surcease or release from the "human condition" of what might be termed structural morality and its behavioral consequences, either of "uptight" virtue or the slavery of sin. But I have in the past few years gone, both as participant observer and observing participant, on a number of pilgrimage journeys to Catholic shrines in Mexico, Ireland, England, Italy, France, and elsewhere. These travels in space led to travels in time, and I have been avidly reading historical records of Christian pilgrimage through the ages.[12]

Personal needs as well as a theoretical and disciplinary interest led to my study of pilgrimages. I have always regarded anthropology as a process of "reculer pour mieux sauter," which may be paraphrased as "going to a far place to understand a familiar place better," which in turn is a partial definition of the pilgrimage process. Pilgrimage is also a rehearsal of the pilgrim's own death. Sooner or later, we anthropologists have to come home having experienced a partial death of our home-born stereotypes and domestic values—a point outlined by Lévi-Strauss in his *Tristes Tropiques*. "Home" for me is the tradition of Western European culture, and, since I have always defined ritual as "quintessential culture," to understand home therefore involves looking at domestic forms of the ritual process.

What I was looking for was, in fact, the characteristic cultural modality of liminality in the salvation religions, specifically that established in the formative period of Christianity. In other words, what was to Christian salvific belief and practice the homologue of the liminality of major initiations in tribal religions? I was looking for a substantial rather than merely formal homology. Superficially, the Christian sacramental system, plus funerary purificatory and some other rituals, might seem to supply liminal phases equivalent to those in tribal and other rites of passage. But in terms of differences in scale and complexity between the societies having these religions, it seemed to me that pilgrimage was to complex salvation religion what the protracted seclusion periods of initiation rites were to tribal and archaic religions.

Christian pilgrimage, as an object of study, may have escaped Western intellectuals because it is too "familiar" to us, too close for comfort, whether we are scientists or theologians. I distinguish pilgrimage from initiation as a locus of liminality by saying that it is, like many features of life in large-scale, complex societies, rooted in optation, in voluntariness, whereas initiation is founded in obligatoriness, in duty. Initiations fit best in societies with ascribed status, pilgrimages in those where status may not only be achieved but also rejected. In tribal societies men and women have to go through rites of passage transferring them from one state and status to another; in posttribal societies of varying complexity and degree of development of the social division of labor, people can choose to go on pilgrimage. This is true even when, as in medieval Islam and Temple Judaism, pilgrimage was held to be of obligation; a variety of mitigating circumstances and get-out clauses made pilgrimage virtually a matter of optation rather than of duty.

Christian pilgrimage, though it became in the waning of the Middle Ages almost a matter of obligation—for those who had committed serious civil crimes as well as religious sins—under the Church's penitential system, remained in principle a matter for the individual conscience. In Catholic theology it was, and remains, an eminently "good work," of counsel, not precept—thus differing from the obligatory "recourse to the sacraments," which may aid the individual's salvation by securing for him many "graces" but cannot, after the manner of an initiation, guarantee it. And this is the crucial difference between the two liminalities. Initiation is an irreversible process, transforming the state and status of the initiand. Pilgrimage is part of a lifelong drama of salvation or damnation, hinging on individual choice, which itself involves acceptance or rejection by an individual of "graces," or freely volunteered gifts, from God. Irrespective of one's intention, one is changed *ex opere operato* by initiation. Moreover, initiation's primary referent is to the total social system. Individuals only have meaning in this frame insofar as it is necessary for the structured group to redefine them cognitively from time to time as members of a class other than that which they belonged to before, and more than this, to alter them substantially to perform the duties and enjoy the rights of that class by means of symbolic action. Initiation rituals are, as Fernandez would put it, "sets of enacted correspondences," metaphorical actions which, by virture of novices' involvement in them, teach them, even nonverbally, how to comfort themselves when they are inducted into their new station in life.[13] They are to be returned, furthermore, to the same structural system, but to a higher level or position in that system.

Life and death are often thought of, in these societies, to be what the poet Rilke called the "great circulation." Rilke, like all poets, was nostalgic for societies where nature and culture were more directly conjoined in metaphor and metonymy than in our literate, industrial society—where, as Eliot maintains, "the shadow" (i.e., scientific objectification, making possible both the use and misuse of nature by culture on a large scale, as well as "original sin") falls between them. Organic processes and the seasonal round provide root-metaphors for cultural processes that are perceived, therefore, as cyclical, and proceed through the life and death of vegetation and the fertility and latency of animals, which mark the annual round. Thus, although initiations are irreversible, in their total sequence they convey the aging individual to the beginning again, to be reborn after the funeral, which is an initiation, as an infant from one of his own totemic clan descendants perhaps. In initiations, too, the fiat of the whole community, expressed through its representative elders, is crucial for inaugurating symbolic action.

Initiations also fairly regularly exhibit the rite of passage form discovered by Van Gennep with its three phases: separation; margin or limen; and reaggregation or reincorporation, conceived of as an irreversible sequence, like the human lives they service and mediate. But pilgrimage, though liminal, or perhaps, better, liminoid, since the liminoid resembles but does not coincide with the liminal, are in principle quite different from initiations. But as salvation religions become routinized, their pilgrimages tend to revert or regress to initiatory devices; they become, in Christian terms, the sacrament of penance writ large, though they never acquire a completely sacramental character. They are not, therefore, necessary for salvation, nor do they become a matter of ecclesiastical precepts. This makes pilgrimage a major expression of the "modern" spirit, the spirit expressed in the primacy, say, of contract over status, in Sir Henry Maine's terms, of ethics over magic, of personal responsibility over corporate affiliation.

Pilgrimage is to a voluntaristic system what initiation is to an obligatory system. That people opt to go on pilgrimage rather than have to be initiated, that they make a vow to a patron saint to be his client by making a pilgrimage to his shrine, to my mind accounts for its paradigmatic charm for such literary figures as Chaucer, Dante, and Bunyan. The plain truth is that pilgrimage does not ensure a major change in religious state—and seldom in secular status—though it may make one a better person, fortified by the graces merited by the hardships and self-sacrifice of the journey. Folk-belief, in Christianity and Islam, does of course insist that if one dies at the holy places, Mecca, Jerusalem, or Compostella, one goes straight to Heaven or Paradise, but this belief lends support to the view that in salvation religions, of the Semitic type at least, stance is all-important for personal salvation. Death sums up and epitomizes the quality of an individual life. But even the best pilgrims may backslide. This is precisely because the will, the *voluntas*, of the individual is the fulcrum of the whole matter. Shift it a bit and past achievement falls to the ground. The role of the social in pilgrimage differs markedly from society's role in initiation. In pilgrimage the pilgrim divests himself by personal choice of his structural incumbencies: in initiation social pressures enforce symbolic, transformative action on the individual. In neither case is communitas ensured; the pilgrim may leave the familiar system and become a member of a class of pilgrims. But he need not necessarily enter a communitas of pilgrims, either in the easygoing Chaucerian fellowship of the road or in the eucharistic communion at the shrine itself, mentioned by pilgrims such as Holy Paula and the Abbot Daniel, whose narratives are included in the volumes of *Palestine Pilgrims Text Society*. In initiation the actor may enter the class of novices without helping to generate a communitas of novices. But the dying from system into class may, in each case, facilitate the communitas experience, the subjective sense of antistructure that has had so many important objective results in the history of religion.

Another difference is that initiation is often localized in a protected place—though its ordeals may be dangerous—while pilgrimage is often hazardous. Pilgrims are exposed to diverse geographical, climatic, and social conditions, sometimes traversing several national frontiers. Although at the end they perform formal rituals, on the way they are vulnerable to historical happenstance. This implication with history is, again, modern. I have recently been studying pilgrimage systems—that is, processes focused on specific shrines—in their historical dimension, both from the perspective of their internal dynamics, their *entelechy*, and from that of the currents of thought, movements of political power, and shifts in popular opinion supporting or assailing them. Pilgrimages, though rooted in atemporal paradigms, experience temporality in ways rather foreign to the protected milieus of initiation rituals. All this is consistent with the emphasis on free will, personal experience, casting one's bread on the waters, the capacity to retract from commitment, and so on, characteristic of salvation religions arising in and helping to shape international fields of social relations, ethnically plural, multilingual, and multicultural. It is worth mentioning that the limen of pilgrimage is, characteristically, motion, the movement of travel, while that of initiation is stasis, the seclusion of novices in a fixed, sacred space. The former liminalizes time, the latter space; time is here connected with voluntariness, space with obligation.

One could ramify differences here, but I will return to the central themes of death and the dead. In the liminality of initiations, the dead often appear as near or remote ancestors, connected by putative ties of consanguinity or affinity with the living, part of a communion of kin beginning with the founding ancestors and, it is hoped, with due performance of ritual, continuing to the end of the world. The dead, as ancestral spirits, punish and sometimes reward the living. Kin are punished for quarreling or for having failed to remember the ancestors in their hearts or with offerings and sacrifices. Usually, specific ancestors punish specific kin or groups of kin. Most misfortune, sickness, and reproductive trouble, in Central African society, for example,. is attributed to the morally punitive action of the "shades." Once recognized, named, and propitiated, however, they become benevolent guardians of their living kin, usually their lineal kin.

The dead are both the jural and moral continuators of the society, formed by their jural descendants, and the procreative biology, the increase and multiplication, which ensures the continuance of the human matter on which that structural form is imprinted. When initiands become their companions in liminal seclusion, they, too, become moral and fertile. When I came to investigate Catholic Christian pilgrimage processes, sensitized as I was to the role of the dead in African initiation and other "passage" ritual, I soon became aware that these, too, were pervaded by ideas about how precisely the living and the dead were interconnected, but that these interconnections were consistent with voluntaristic religion and, indeed, the total culture in which they were embedded.

In a crucial way, the Catholic faith itself hinges on the self-chosen, the voluntary, death of its Founder for the sake both of those who would come after Him, His spiritual posterity, and also of the good pagan dead, neither in Heaven nor Hell, but in Limbo, who had preceded Him, and whom He released by His descent into the nether regions during the three days between His death and resurrection in the body. This *Via crucis*, death, and resurrection paradigm became the inspiration of the early martyrs whose "imitation of Christ" led to their death for the faith and future faithful at the hands of the pagan political authorities. Hence the well-known expression "the blood of the martyrs is the seed of the church," where blood = spiritual semen. Scholars generally hold that after the Holy Places of the Holy Land, the tombs of the martyrs, scattered throughout the Roman Empire, but particularly numerous in Rome itself, became the first pilgrimage centers. They exemplified the supreme act of Christian free will, the choice of death for the salvific faith rather than life under the auspices of state religion. It was also believed by the masses that these places of redemptive self-sacrifice—since their martyrdom was thought to be a projection into history of Christ's redeeming self-sacrifice—were places where heaven and earth came close, even communicated through the media of prayers, miracles, and apparitions. Here there might be "gaps in the curtain."

A miracle, "an effect wrought in nature independently of natural powers and laws," the extreme expression of the rare, unprecedented, and idiosyncratic in experience, is counterposed to order and law, supreme symbols as well as agencies of social structuration, and exemplifies for the faithful the volitional character of faith as against the "necessary cause and effect" character of both natural and state law. Miracles might happen at martyrs' graves, because martyrs gave up their lives for the belief that God alone is above and beyond Nature and is the direct and immediate cause of salvation, defined as the "freeing of the soul from the bonds of sin and its consequences and the attainment of the everlasting vision of God in heaven." Miracles occur fitfully, not systematically or regularly, precisely because they are supreme acts in the drama of free will and grace, creative acts in the moral order.

From these beliefs and other sources, the development of the pilgrimage process became closely linked with the doctrine of the "communion of saints." This postulates that under certain conditions the dead and the living can freely help one another to attain heaven, that is, the beatific vision of God in the company of all the other saints and angels. Roman legalism has worked on the notion of the communion of saints and has come to define it as "the unity under and in Christ of the *faithful on earth* (the *Church Militant*), the souls in Purgatory (the *Church Suffering*), and the blessed in Heaven (the *Church Triumphant*)." In principle, all these people—living and dead—are in the Church in the first place through optation, for even if it was the parents' will that their child should be baptized, it is as the result of the child's own will that that child ultimately attains salvation. God plies the soul with graces, the devil with temptations, the flesh is weak, and the world is full of occasions of sin. The drama goes on until the General Judgment. But the different components of the Church can help one another. In prayer communion or fellowship is most active. The living pray to God and the saints on behalf of the suffering, and to God in honor of the saints. The saints intercede with God for the suffering and the living. The suffering, the souls in Purgatory, pray to God and the saints for others. It is thought to be particularly efficacious if the living seek the intercession of the saints with God on behalf of the souls in Purgatory. Here the system comes closest to tribal animism, for, in practice, people pray most often for and to their own dead kinsfolk.

My own Catholic background and field research among Catholic countryfolk in Europe and Middle America have made me familiar with the doctrine of the *Benditas Animas* (in Mexico) or Holy Souls (in Ireland), that is, the members of the Church Suffering in Purgatory. Purgatory, in Catholic thought, is the place and state in which souls suffer for a while and are purged after death, before they go to Heaven, on account of their sins. Dante's Mount of Purgatory is, of course, the supreme literary expression of the doctrine. Most souls, it is thought, go to Purgatory, if on the whole they have shown themselves to be reasonably moral, decent people, Walt Whitman's "Divine average." These souls are there, either because they have committed unrepented venial sins or, having in the sacrament of penance confessed their grave sins, they have been forgiven but still have to pay a "debt of temporal punishment." They are purged by the pain of intense longing for God, whose beatific vision is delayed, and by some pain of sense, popularly believed to be by material fire. In this liminal period between earth and heaven, institutional faith is the means by which the souls in purgatory can be helped toward heaven or eased of pain by the prayers and sacrifices of the living, especially by the sacrament of the Eucharist; thus, virtually every Mass is, even today, offered on behalf of a named relative of some parishioner. And, although there has been no ecclesiastical decision on the matter, it is widely believed throughout the Catholic Church that one should not only pray for but also to the souls in Purgatory so that they will intercede for the living with God. In popular belief, the Holy Souls do not have immediate access to God—that is part of their purgative suffering—as the saints in heaven do, but their prayers for the living, made while in Purgatory, in a sense, accumulate, and when the Holy Soul finally becomes a saint, and no one knows the hour of this, such prayers are considered to have surplus efficacy for having so long been pent-up. Therefore, so argues the Catholic peasant in many lands, it is a pretty good bet to pray both for and to the Holy Souls, since if you pray for him he will be grateful to you for speeding up his release from Purgatory, and if you pray to him he will carry to Heaven a great heap of your requests for God's immediate attention.

The Holy Souls—and it is fitting to discuss them in November, for the Catholic Church dedicates this month to the beloved dead—resemble the Nyakyusa "shades." They are polluted and polluting, since they are not yet cleansed of adhering sins, but at the same time they are sacred and capable, if remembered and propitiated by sacrifices, of bringing such benefits to the living as fertility of people, animals, and crops, and to fend off or mend afflictions, such as illness, accident, injury, famine, drought, blight, plague, or reproductive disorders. There may well be some delay here, but the outcome is virtually certain. Neither Holy Souls nor Shades are Saints, for these two categories are liminally in-between the *moyen sensuel* of the living and the ideal sphere of the perfectly moral dead. They need as well as bestow help. In practice, too, both Holy Souls and Shades are one's kinsfolk, though in the tribal case kinship, particularly lineal kinship, may often be the very frame of institutionalized social life, while the Catholic prays for and to kin due to residential continuities based on feudal, postfeudal and industrial-rural concrete circumstances rather than on societal axiomatic rule. But in both types of religion a normative communitas is postulated among the living and the dead. The dead need the sacrifices and prayers of the living; the living need the fructifying powers of the dead, either as mediators with Divinity for the living or as a direct emission from the benevolent dead themselves.

Pilgrimage may be regarded as an accelerator of normal liturgical practice. It is popularly felt that the merits acquired by the saint or martyr lent power to masses said on the altar of a church dedicated to him. Also, popes and bishops grant indulgences to those receiving communion there. When the pilgrim reaches his goal, the target-shrine is expected very speedily to perform two rituals of the sacramental liturgical set. These are penance and the eucharist, "confession" and "Mass," as they are usually spoken of. Having made a pilgrimage amplifies these two sacraments in the pilgrim's eyes. These sacraments differ from the others—Baptism, Confirmation, Marriage, Ordination, and Extreme Unction—in not being life-crisis rituals, rites of passage properly speaking, but are rather what anthropologists might call contingent rituals, being concerned with the day-to-day maintenance of concrete individuals and groups in a state of moral, spiritual, and hence (in terms of medical theory which regards body and informing soul as a dynamic continuum) physical health. Thus when a pilgrim asks for a mass to be said for his dead relatives in Purgatory, this mass is thought to be more effective on account of the time, energy, and patience expended on the pilgrim's journey to the shrine and of his other sacrifices—exposure to danger and bad weather, loss of comfort, and his overcoming of temptations on the way. There is a general theory among pilgrims, however vague, that personal sacrifice can be the source of graces and blessings for others. These personal losses may be transmuted, like base metal, through the pilgrim's sacrifice, into the gold of graces and blessings, released from God's treasury, in which are also stored the merits of the faithful in all the ages, for the benefit of those whom the pilgrim specifically names as beneficiaries. In this specificity of benefaction, purgatorial notions most remind us of animistic religions.

It is almost a truism that universal Catholic ideas about the fate of the dead in Purgatory have received most reinforcement from pre-Christian religious beliefs in the western fringes of Europe, in the surviving haunts of the Celtic peoples—Ireland, the Western Highlands of Scotland (Barra, South Uist), Wales, Armorican Brittany, Galicia in Spain. William A. Christian, Jr., recently wrote an excellent account of Spanish folk-Catholicism in the Nansa valley of northern Spain. He writes: "Devotion for and worry about the dead is characteristic of the entire Atlantic fringe from Galicia, through Brittany, Ireland, and England."[14] Similarly Georgiana Goddard King and Walter Starkie have stressed connections in Purgatorial beliefs between Galicia and Ireland, and Starkie has quoted from old traditions how spirits of the dead, temporarily released from Purgatory, have begged mortals, in the twilight, to pray for them that they might complete the pilgrimage to St. James's shrine at Compostella and so have their sufferings remitted.[15] If pilgrims are companions to the dead, it is to the dead of the church suffering; and if pilgrims are equivalent to the dead, it is to the dead in Purgatory.

My own most vivid encounter with the continuity between Celtic animism and Catholic pilgrimage beliefs about the Holy Souls has been in the west of Ireland—though Mexico, too, has its Christian cult of the dead uniting Galician and Asturian beliefs of this type to pre-Columbian Aztec traditions, for example, in the "Day of the Dead" in Morelos, where, on November first, all household members make offerings in the house and cemetery (pantheon) not only for the direct ascendants of the family but for all household residents, including women married into it.

My wife and I spent some months in the summer of 1972 going on and studying pilgrimages in the west of Ireland. The most important contemporary pilgrim shrine in Ireland is that of Knock in County Mayo, where, it is credibly estimated, at least 700,000 people each year visit the shrine during the pilgrimage season, a substantial proportion of the total Catholic population of Ireland, North and South. This pilgrimage is of the type I have called elsewhere "apparitional." The type has become established in the post-Napoleonic, industrial era of Europe and includes such major shrines as La Salette, Lourdes, Pontmain, Pellevoisin, Fatima, Beaurang, and Banneux. The Latin countries of France, Portugal, and Belgium (though here Flemish speakers have also been involved) have been the main sites of apparitions of the Virgin Mary, usually to children, alone or in groups. In most cases a message has been given by the Virgin; at La Salette in France and Fatima in Portugal especially, the message has been minatory and apocalyptic, prophesying disasters for men on earth and Hell for them after death if they do not mend their ways. But Knock, though apparitional, contains no threatening *anima* figure portending disaster for over-technocratic and rationalistic people. The Knock apparition was peaceful and silent. Moreover, it was seen, not by children alone, but by at least fifteen people ranging in age from six to seventy-five. Nor was it the Virgin alone that was seen. A group of people saw a group of supernaturals, or so they believed and testified to with convincing mutual consistency before a commission of three senior priests convoked by the Archbishop of Tuam, under whose aegis the affair came, less than two months after the apparition. On the rainy night of 21 August 1879, during one of Ireland's afflictions by potato famine and in the political context of Michael Davitt's and Parnell's struggles for Land Reform, Margaret, Mary, and Dominick Beirne, Mary McLoughlin, Catherine Murray, and eventually at least a dozen more villagers of the small hamlet of Knock, consisting of about a dozen or more cottages, claimed that they saw "a sight such as was never before seen," near the gable of the village church, itself one of the first fruits of the Catholic Emancipation of 1829. What did they see? Let Michael Walsh take up the tale:

> They saw three figures standing at the gable wall of the church, about eighteen inches or two feet above the ground. The central figure was recognized as that of Our Lady. She was wearing a large white cloak fastened at the neck and on her head was a brilliant crown. . . . She was raised slightly above the other figures. . . . On her right was a figure recognized as that of St. Joseph. On her left was a figure considered by Mary Beirne (the chief informant) to be St. John the Evangelist . . . on the grounds that he resembles a statue of St. John which she had seen in the church at [the coastal Mayo town of] Lecanvy. He was dressed like a bishop . . . held an open book in his left hand . . . and appeared to be preaching. On his left was an altar, full-sized, and on it was a lamb . . . facing the figures. Just behind it was a cross. . . . The figures were full and round as if they had a body and life, but they spoke no words and no words were addressed to them.[16]

One of the informants, Patrick Hill, thirteen years old, testified that he saw "wings fluttering" around the Lamb. Those who relate the Apparition to the Holy Souls often advert to this statement. Some regard the wings as signs of angels, others as indications of the presence of the Holy Souls. The Apparition began about seven o'clock in the evening (8:30 P.M. modern summer time) and lasted several hours before fading away. Despite anticlerical criticisms of varying kinds, for example, that the apparitions had been produced by a concealed Jesuit with one of the primitive magic lanterns of that period, or that they were really a heap of holy statues ordered by the Parish Priest Archdeacon Cavanagh, or that Mary McLoughlin, the priest's housekeeper, a well-known alcoholic, had stirred up the lively fancy of the villagers (none of which hypotheses stood up to the test of evidence), the news of the apparitions spread, crowds soon collected at the gable, miraculous cures were reported, the Archbishop's Commission's report, though not positive, was not negative either, attesting to the honesty of the fifteen witnesses, and a full-blown pilgrimage began, which, with ups and downs over the decades, finally succeeded in obtaining a Papal Coronation for the image of the Virgin of Knock, who is now known as the Queen of Ireland.

I first became aware of the intimate connection of Knock with the doctrine of Purgatory when my wife went on pilgrimage on 20 August 1972, to Knock from Castlebar, Mayo's county seat, twenty miles or so away. This was the Sunday nearest to the day of the Apparition, a day on which many normally at work during the week could attend. She went with Bridgy Lydon, a pious old lady, who spent much of her time traveling, a true palmer, from shrine to shrine. At the Knock Shrine Society Office, Bridgy, an old-age pensioner, gave a "widow's mite" of £5, more than a week's pension, for Masses for the Holy Souls. Later we learned that the people have the theory that the testimony about "wings" or indistinct "flames" seen by witnesses were not angels, that is, beings in Heaven, as some supposed, but were, indeed, souls in Purgatory. As can well be imagined, the theological imagination of several generations of Irish clergy and laity has exercised itself most eloquently on the "meaning" of the Silent Apparition. Most agree that the Apparition itself was a reward to Ireland for keeping the faith through centuries of persecution and it was not a warning that divine retribution would follow loss of faith, as in some of the French and Portuguese apparitions, which manifested themselves in periods of antireligious and anticlerical ascendancy. Many also agree that the Holy Souls believed to be present were those of the countless heroes and martyrs of the Irish struggle, which, since the Reformation, has also been a Catholic struggle against English overlordship. They argue that since for many years Catholic priests were forbidden, under the Penal Laws, to administer the sacraments, including the Last Sacrament, many souls, through no fault of their own, must have died unshriven, so that they would have to spend much more time in Purgatory than they would otherwise have had to endure.

Clerical endorsement of the belief that the Apparition was connected with the souls in Purgatory is not lacking. For example, a Franciscan Capuchin priest, Fr. Hubert, wrote a pamphlet in 1962 for the Knock Shrine Annual, "The Knock Apparition and Purgatory," in which he comments on the fact that the Apparition was seen just after the Parish Priest Fr. Cavanagh had offered his hundredth Mass for the souls in Purgatory. He, therefore, suggests that Our Lady of Knock should "very fitly be styled the helper of the Holy Souls and Mother of the Church Suffering" (p. 3). He then focuses on the composite figure of Lamb, Altar, and Cross seen in the Apparition, illustrates it with a drawing showing wings hovering above the altar, and suggests that this apocalyptic vision was "showing forth of the glorious vision for which the souls in purgatory are continually yearning and to which many of them have already attained through the sacrifice of the Mass which had just been offered the hundredth time for them in the church at Knock" (p. 7). From these and other signs Fr. Hubert concludes that the apparition itself "was due to the intervention of the holy souls" (p. 8). Ordinary pilgrims, the kind that swarm at the shrine every day, have deduced that the Apparition was a response to the prayers of the countless Irish martyred dead, and that it was somehow connected with the Book of Revelation popularly supposed to have been written by St. John the Evangelist, one of the figures by the gable, during the persecution of the then scattered Christian communities by the Roman Emperor Domitian, identified by some of the Irish clergy with the English. Father Michael Walsh has written: "It can reasonably be said that the immediate purpose of the apparition at Knock was to console the afflicted Irish community."[17]

The cover picture of the *Knock Shrine Annual* for 1967 makes the purgatorial component quite clear. It purports to represent the Apparition. But unlike earlier portrayals of this event, it quite frankly places to the left of the altar—now given a central position—and balancing the group of Mary, Joseph, and John to the right (i.e., looking toward the people from the gable), a shadowy crowd of suffering souls in Purgatory, regarded both as the initiators and benefactors (through the prayers of the faithful) of the Apparition. The wings over the altar have now become explicit, full-bodied angels, no longer regarded as suffering souls, now that these have been openly portrayed. In this way iconography follows popular thought.

Irish pilgrims go to Knock to seek help from the supernatural power there with reference to much the same problems and afflictions that send Africans to the ancestral shrines. The *Knock Shrine Annual*, like many Catholic journals associated with pilgrim shrines, publishes letters from pilgrims expressing gratitude for favors received after fulfilling their vows to visit the shrine. They refer mainly to the cure of illness, the gift of children, success in examinations, recovery from operations, the cure of sick farm animals, and similar matters. Often there is reference to the intercession of the Holy Souls. At Knock, the pilgrims feel that the whole church is present in a communitas of prayer. The living pray to Joseph, Mary, Jesus, and John and the angels (the Church Triumphant), for the Holy Souls, the Church Suffering, and to the saints and Holy Souls to intercede with God for them in their own troubles as members of the Church Militant. All this reinforces their faith that death is not extinction, and that the dead of all the ages are still in loving communion.

In the interstitial, interfacial realm of liminality, both in initiation rites and in the pilgrimage process, the dead are conceived of as transformative agencies and as mediating between various domains normally classified as distinct. These include the sensory as against the world of ideas; birth and death, structure and communitas, person and God, culture and nature, visibility and invisibility, past and present, human and animal, and many more fundamental dyads. It is important to note that the symbolic or metaphorical death undergone by initiands or pilgrims puts them in the in-between state of life-in-death, like the seed with rotting husk but thrusting cotyledon in the ground. Illness is one of the signs of this liminal condition and it may be turned to fruitful account if it is made by ritual to lead to an opening up for the initiand of the communitas dimension outside of social structure. In tribal society communitas is associated with physical fertility, in Christian pilgrimage with spiritual fruitfulness. The seclusion camp and the pilgrim's road are also schools in which gnosis (liminal wisdom) is communicated to the individual in passage. Thus when we are outside structure, in initiation or pilgrimage, whether literal or metaphorical, we are, in a sense, in communion with the dead, either the saints, prophets, philosophers, poets, or impeccable heroes of our own most cherished tradition, or the hosts of ordinary people, the "Holy Souls" who sinned, suffered, but loved enough to stay truly human, though now invisible to us.

In that we may fear "destructuration" we may regard our dead as filthy and polluting, for they make themselves known in the liminal space that is betwixt-and-between all "pure" classifications and unambiguous concepts. But if we regard them as part of a space-time communitas of mankind spanning the ages may we not see them, on a wider scale than either the world of the Nyakyusa or of traditional pilgrimage, as a fructifying force, a tradition of grace rather than of blood?

Notes

1. London: Epworth, 1944, p. 79.
2. Vol. 2 (1893; reprint ed., New York: Dover, 1964), p. 183, n.2.
3. Paris: Payot, 1954, pp. 240–41.
4. *A Natural Science of Society* (Glencoe, Ill.: Free Press, 1957), p. 22.
5. *Rituals of Kinship Among the Nyakyusa* (London: Oxford University Press, 1957), p. 205.
6. Ithaca, N.Y.: Cornell University Press, 1967, p. 1067: 96.
7. Wilson, p. 205, my emphasis.
8. Ibid., p. 207.
9. Ibid., p. 205. Quotations are from various informants of the Wilsons.
10. "Pietas in Ancestor Worship," *Journal of the Royal Anthropological Society*, no. 91 (1961): 166–91.
11. Knock Shrine Society, Knock, Ireland.
12. I have visited Guadalupe, Ocotlán, Remedios, Chalma, Izamal, Tizinin, Acambaro, Amecameca, and others in Mexico; Knock, Croagh Patrick, Lough Dearg, Limerick, and Cork in Ireland; Walsingham, Glastonbury, Canterbury, and Aylesford in England; the Catacombs, Santa Maria Maggiore, St. Peter's, Santa Maria Ara Coeli, and other Roman churches of the pilgrimage path within Rome, in Italy; Lourdes in France; and other pilgrimage centers in the Old and New Worlds.
13. James Fernandez, "Analysis of Ritual: Metaphoric Correspondences as the Elementary Forms," *Science* 182, no. 4119 (1973): 1366.
14. *Person and God in a Spanish Valley* (New York and London: Seminar Press, 1972), p. 94.
15. Georgiana Goddard King, *The Way of St. James*, vol. 3 (New York and London: Putnam, 1920), pp. 235–49; Walter Starkie, *The Road to Santiago* (Berkeley and Los Angeles: University of California Press, 1965).
16. *Knock: The Shrine of the Pilgrim People of God* (Tuam: St. Jarlath's College, 1967), pp. 6–7.
17. Walsh, p. 57.

Mesoamerica and Africa

"Be unhappy! Stay alone! If you had not called me, I could have shown you the secret of renewing the skin." The old woman died, and left death behind for all her descendants.

Alur Myth

The Black Man in the Cave in Chapultepec: An Aztec Variant on the Gatekeeper Motif

FRANKE J. NEUMANN

The Problems of Moctezuma

Just before the arrival of the Spanish Conquistadors, the Aztec empire under Moctezuma II was in a perilous state of health.[1] Indeed, Moctezuma's entire reign was not an auspicious one. The extant chronicles speak of many signs foretelling the end of the Aztec empire, clear indications of a serious crisis in a world in process of losing its equilibrium. Following a rebellion of the Mixtecs and a confrontation with Tlaxcala came a severe two-year famine, which was followed by feverish temple-building to appease the gods. Next there was a series of extremely ominous portents. The temple of Xiuhtecuhtli, the god of time, was destroyed, presumably by an act of the gods themselves. Then came the strange appearance of a cone of light in the eastern sky. It is variously described as a luminous bannerlike spirit, or like smoke and flames rising, or as a comet. It lasted, according to the sources, for four years, having an unnerving effect on the people of Anahuac; and it caused Moctezuma to consult his sorcerers and astrologers all the more avidly as they increasingly and insistently foretold of approaching evil and doom. Then came a rash of rebellions, followed by a disaster in connection with the creation of a new sacrificial stone for the temple in Tenochtitlán. There were inextinguishable fires, an appearance of an enchanted crane carrying a magical mirror, the rising and "boiling" of the Lake of Mexico, and the night voice of a weeping woman heard by all the people.[2] In all these auguries, Moctezuma appears to be the one held responsible for impending catastrophe; and accepting his responsibility he underwent lengthy penances and made numerous offerings to the gods, including an enormously increased volume of human sacrifices. It is quite clear that he began to doubt his ability to rule, and as compensation tended to adopt an increasingly authoritarian attitude. Doubtless this internal struggle provoked guilt feelings that drove him to seek a way out of his predicament. We are told that

> Moteczoma [*sic*] then wept bitterly, saying, "O Lord of All Created Things! O mighty gods who give life or death! Why have you decreed that many kings shall have reigned proudly but that my fate is to witness the unhappy destruction of Mexico? Why should I be the one to see the death of my wives and children and the loss of my powerful

> kingdoms and dominions and of all that the Aztecs have conquered with their mighty arms and strength of their chests? What shall I do? Where shall I hide? Where shall I conceal myself? Alas, if only I could turn into stone, wood, or some other earthly matter rather than suffer that which I so dread!"[3]

Finally, distraught, he makes a speech to his chieftains:

> "Truly, O brethren, I now believe that our labors and afflictions will be great and that our lives are about to end. And I am determined to allow death to come just as my brave ancestors did. Let the will of the Lord of All Created Things be done!" He called his stone cutters and ordered that his statue be carved on the rocks of Chapultepec. When the work was finished he went to see his image and wept. "If our bodies," he moaned, "were as durable in this life as this carved effigy is upon this rock, who would be afraid of death? But I know that I must perish and this is the only memorial that will remain of me!"
>
> Moteczoma returned to Mexico and bemoaned his fate again:
>
> "O brethren! I find no consolation! I am surrounded by worries and anguish. Am I greater than Nezahualpilli who was a prophet and would tell of things to come and who died in spite of all his knowledge? Am I greater than my kinsman Tzompantecuhtli of Cuitlahuac who also was a prophet, knowing six hundred and ten sciences, all of which he could explain with the greatest of ease? He also died. What will become of me, then, who am ignorant, knowing no science? How am I to avoid the calamities and ills which await me?"[4]

In despair, Moctezuma then called together a number of his priests, advisers, and magicians,[5] to counsel on how he might evade his troubles and escape to the other world. Although some of the sources appear to attempt either to soften or to evade the issue, it seems quite clear that Moctezuma was contemplating suicide. His counselors advised him that there were several places he might go: *Mictlan*, the place of the dead; *Tonatiuhilhuicac*, "the house of the sun"; or *Tlalocan*, the land of the god Tlaloc—the three traditional destinies of men after death.[6] These three realms, however, are not entirely applicable to Moctezuma's situation.

"The house of the sun," *Tonatiuhilhuicac* (or *Tonatiuhichan*), for instance, was the glorious destiny of those who either fell in battle or died as sacrificial victims, together with women who died in childbirth. They became the *quauhteca*, the "people of the eagle," the loyal companions of the sun. They were the privileged ones, chosen by the sun to live a "life" of pure joy. To them was given the honor of accompanying the sun in a shining and joyful assembly. Brandishing their weapons and shields, singing war chants and simulating combat, the warriors attended the sun during the first half of its journey through the sky. Sahagún tells us that after four years the warriors are changed into hummingbirds and other birds of brightly colored feathers; they return to earth to suck honey from all the flowers. Even enemy warriors were honored in this paradise, because when they died, they too were deemed to have given their lives to nourish that powerful warrior, the sun, who does battle in the sky. For that reason they were said to be the equal of the Aztecs who died in combat. Together with these warriors, women who died in childbirth were also considered companions of the sun. The women comprised his retinue from the zenith to the west, also accompanying the sun with their singing. At the end of the day, the sun and his cortege arrived at the entrance to the subterranean world, located on the horizon. The underworld was then traversed during the night in order that the sun might reappear again in the east in the morning. Thus the west was known as *Cihuatlampa*, "the feminine side," since it was from that region that the "divine women" would come to greet the sun.[7]

The second paradise was one intended for devotees of the god Tlaloc. It was an idealized image of tropical nature: eternal springtime, flowers, warm rain, luxuriant growth, and abundance without need for work. It was a place of unconcern, repose, and peaceful happiness which freed the individual from the problems oppressing him: drought, famine, and war. The famous murals at Teotihuacán show us a garden of abundance where the blessed dead frolic under the benevolence of the god of vegetation.[8] As Alfonso Caso notes,

> The paintings [at Teotihuacán] illustrate what Sahagún relates in his history. A dry bough was placed on the tomb at the burial of the one who had been chosen by the rain god. . . . When the fortunate one reached . . . Tlalocan, the dry bough became green again, indicating that in this place of abundance he acquired a new life. After intoning a long song, no doubt of thanks to the god who makes all things grow, he joined his companions to enjoy a life of eternal happiness spent lolling beneath the trees heavy with fruit on the banks of the rivers of paradise; or he submerged in the waters of the lagoons far beyond death and passed the time singing with his companions, joining in games, and sharing their pleasures. The life of those who had been summoned by Tlaloc was conceived of by the Aztecs, and before them by the Teotihuacáns, as one of abundance, serenity, and blessedness.[9]

Tlalocan was located in the east, first in the warm and humid tropical regions, where the plants grew vigorously in the rain; but later, when the Mexicans of the high plateau subjugated the country, this mythical region was said to lie beyond the horizon to the south, somewhere beneath the waters. This paradise, however, was not for everyone. These fortunate individuals were called by Tlaloc himself, who chose them in a manner that clearly indicated his personal intervention: death by drowning, being struck by lightning, or other means considered related to the god of water.[10] The bodies of these victims, thus honored by Tlaloc, were surrounded with veneration and fear. Only the priests could lead them to their last rest, and they were carried in a litter to the sound of a flute. The individuals thus chosen by the god of rain were not cremated, but were buried.

The great majority of the dead, however, know neither the joys of the "house of the sun" nor the delights of Tlalocan. *Having died a natural death*, these were required to undertake a long, perilous journey under the earth to Mictlan. It was represented as a vast realm of cold and darkness, situated somewhere to the north, over which ruled Mictlantecuhtli and his wife Mictecacihuatl accompanied by their familiar animals: centipedes, bats, spiders, and owls, the latter considered birds of ill omen whose call was held to be fatal to those who heard it.

Mictlan, according to Sahagún, was composed of nine levels below the earth, each presided over by various gods of the dead who always appear in pairs. Persons who died a natural death went there; but on the road, the dead had to overcome a number of obstacles. In order to reach Mictlan, in the successive levels the dead soul had, among other things, to pass between two mountains that clapped together, climb over a mountain of obsidian, be subjected to an icy wind so bitter that it cut like obsidian knives, be pierced by arrows, and pass through a region where there were wild beasts that ate human hearts. Finally he arrived at the edge of the nine rivers, which he must pass on the back of a dog.[11] When he had finally reached the end of his journey, the ninth level of the underworld (*Chiconamictlan*), the dead ceased to be, disappearing into nothingness. In this level Mictlantecuhtli and his consort Mictecacihuatl ruled as supreme. One of the other names used for Mictlan was *Ximoayan*, "the place of the fleshless," where the dead were finally enabled to shed their bodies.

This, then, was the basic structure of the Nahuatl image of the afterlife. Final destiny was determined not on the basis of moral conduct in life but by the nature of one's death. Those who died by drowning, from lightning, or from dropsy or skin diseases went to Tlalocan; those who were sacrificed, those who died in childbirth, and those killed in combat would become the companions of the sun in Tonatiuhichan. Those who ended their days in any other way went to Mictlan, which seemed to be the least desirable of the three traditional realms. In each of these three destinies mentioned, however, there are requirements for entry that militate against Moctezuma's seeking his escape in that direction; namely that he die in battle, as a sacrificial victim, as a chosen one of Tlaloc, or at the very least a "natural" death, that is, not by his own hand. And Moctezuma does not fall in any of these categories.

Huemac and the Cave in Chapultepec

In response to his further entreaties, however, Moctezuma's counselors told him that there was one other alternative, a great secret, the cave called *Cincalco* near Tlacuyoacan, behind Chapultepec.[12] The place was hallowed by tradition, for there, many years before (possibly in 1174), Huemac, the last ruler of the Toltecs, was said to have killed himself following his flight from the disturbed situation in Tula. The sources are somewhat confused on the immediate reason for Huemac's flight, but it appears to have had to do with the right of succession to the throne. Incidents leading up to this problem include various episodes involving either Huemac's daughter and a naked chili vendor,[13] or Huemac's marriage to a commoner, or his dalliance with a prostitute by the name of Xochiquetzal, or his rejection of a Nonoalcan woman for not being wide enough in the buttocks.[14] At any rate we do know that repeated crop failures resulting from droughts had led to internal crises, famine, and war with the Huastecs—a situation that culminated in the flight of Huemac and the Toltecs, energetically pursued by their enemies. Two somewhat parallel stories, of Huemac and of Topiltzin Quetzalcóatl, coincide at this point and become confused in the records; in several instances it is not absolutely certain just whose history is being told. Quetzalcóatl, too, was forced to flee Tollan with his followers, escaping to Veracruz from whence he either embarked by boat for Yucatan where he founded Chichén Itzá, or was apotheosized as the planet Venus. Although the sources disagree concerning the precise manner of Huemac's death,[15] the consensus of the traditions appears to be that he committed suicide by hanging himself, a tradition which, as we shall see, has considerable implication for Moctezuma.

Suicide was apparently a fairly widespread practice in Mesoamerica at the time of the conquest, especially in the Maya area. The reports from the colonial period are all similar. Diego de Landa, and after him Sanchez de Aguilar, indicate how easily the Mayas committed suicide;[16] and Francisco Clavijero says that

> among the crimes charged to the Americans . . . suicide is included. It is true that at the times of the Conquest many hanged themselves, or threw themselves down precipices or put an end to themselves by abstinence; but it is not the least wonderful that men who had become desperate from continual harassment and vexations, who thought their gods had abandoned, and the elements conspired against them, would do that which was frequent with the Romans, the Franks, and ancient Spaniards, and modern English, French, and Japanese, for a slight motive.[17]

But the reports are all notably silent on suicide among the Nahuas. The evidence, or rather the lack of it, would seem to indicate the possibility that suicide was, if not unknown among them, at least subject to disapproval.[18]

Nevertheless, Moctezuma was assured by his counselors that the cave of Cincalco in Chapultepec was "a place of joy and pleasure where men live forever. . . . It was a land of clear, crystalline waters. There grew all kinds of foods; there was the freshness of many flowers."[19]

As Mircea Eliade has pointed out, the cave represents not merely the otherworld, but also the entire universe:

> It is not the immediate, "natural" valorization of the cave as a dark—and hence subterranean—place that enables us to perceive its symbolism and its religious function, but the experience caused by entering a place whose sacredness makes it "total," that is, a place that *constitutes a world-in-itself*. . . . In other words, it is an *imago mundi*, a Universe in miniature. Living in a cave does not necessarily imply going down among the shades; it can as well imply living in a different world—a world that is vaster and more complex because it incorporates various modes of existence (gods, demons, souls of the dead, etc.) and hence is full of "riches" and countless virtualities.[20]

The cave is also the symbol of creation and of life. As Doris Heyden has noted,[21] pictorial representations of caves abound in the Mexican codices, both historical and religious. Indeed, the homeland or source of the Aztecs themselves was called *chicomoztoc*, "in the seven caves," the place of emergence and return, the cave here representing the womb of the earth. Heyden continues:

> Other references in the literature show us the importance of grottos in Mesoamerican mythology and religion. The sun and the moon came out of a cave. Tlaloc, lord of water and earth, lived in caves as well as on mountain tops. Durán describes Tlaloc as "God of Rain, Thunder, and Lightning. . . . The name means Path under the Earth or Long Cave." In the *Primeros Memoriales* we read that in the Etzalcualiztli fiesta the victim representing Tlaloc was sacrificed and then placed in a cave. Tepeyolotl, "Heart of the Hill," was also an earth deity, associated with caves. Finally the God of Fire, Xiuhtecuhtli or Ixcozauhqui, had his abode in the center of the earth, in the "turquoise enclosure," logically reached through caves.[22]

The cave is thus the place of the oracle, a place both to give offerings and receive gifts from the gods, a place of sacrifice and burial, of initiation, a storage chamber for treasure kept by the Powers, a place for prayers to request food or rain. In this connection, Martha Stone reports that a "*puerto*," a word which she interpreted normally as "port," is really, according to her informant, "a place where our ancestors went to make their requests and to perform their ceremonies . . . an enchanted place, a place where there is power."[23]

And so, having determined his course of action, Moctezuma sent his hunchback messengers to make the necessary arrangements for his transition to the other world. And it is at this point in the narrative that a most unusual event occurs.

The Figure of the Black Man

> The hunchbacks went out with the tequitques to seek the mouth of the cave of Cicalco [*sic*], following the instructions of Moteczoma. According to some opinions this cave was situated in a place called Atlixocan between Mexico and Coyoacan, where, say the old men, a ghost used to appear every night, kidnapping the first man it encountered, who was never to be seen again. Therefore, everyone avoided this place at night.
>
> It was to this place, says the Chronicle, that Moteczoma sent the hunchbacks. As soon as they entered the cave they met a black man with a staff in his hand. This man was called Totec, Our Lord. He asked them what they wanted and they answered that they had come to speak to the lord of that cave, Huemac. Totec took them by the hand and led them into the depths of the cave until they were in the presence of Huemac, a god of awesome appearance. After greeting him they offered him the ten human skins and repeated the message that Moteczoma had sent. But Huemac answered, "Ask Moteczoma why he wants to come here. Does he think that he is going to find jewels, gold, precious stones, feathers, and rich mantles like those he now possesses? Tell him that he has been deceived! Let him rejoice in what he had and let him be calm. That which has been fated cannot be avoided."[24]

What is of interest in this account is not only that Huemac is now "lord of the cave" and a "god," but also the rather mysterious figure of the black man who appears only in this one incident and consequently has been completely ignored by the commentators and interpreters. The black man in the cave is a variation of a type of figure known as a threshold guardian of the entrance to a zone of potency or power, the "gatekeeper." He is the "watcher" of the established boundary that marks the passage beyond the veil of the known into the unknown. Such powers that watch at the threshold are dangerous; to deal with them is risky. Yet only by advancing beyond this boundary and provoking the destructive aspect of the powers can the individual pass into a new zone of experience. As Joseph Campbell notes, the passage of the threshold is a form of self-annihilation.[25]

This identification is given considerable support in the light of Sarah C. Blaffer's recent detailed analysis of the figure of the black-man of the Tzotzils, *hʔik'al* (pl., *hʔik'altik*), a winged black demon or "spook" with a reputation for unrestrained sexuality, people-snatching, and cannibalism.[26]

Briefly and bluntly stated, Blaffer's thesis is that the Tzotzils' black-man is, in fact, a bat, although she admits that nowhere in the myths or data from informants is it ever expressly stated that he is in any way even related to a bat. But if she is correct in this identification, it may help to explain that mysterious figure in the Chapultepec cave. In analyzing the connection between hʔik'al and bats, Blaffer notes that both are black, live in caves, are considered scavengers or robbers, and are associated with blood. Indeed, the figure of hʔik'al is anomalous, just as is the bat. Black-man is neither man nor animal, neither social nor antisocial. He welcomes company, but with murderous intent. He is to be found principally in those transitional zones of the in-between: for example, crossroads and corners (places leading in several directions and no direction) and cemeteries where the worlds of the living and the dead come together. He is especially dangerous to persons in areas of tension between two zones: the sick, the insane, those asleep or drunk, those not completely alive or conscious, yet also not dead. And if any creature may be considered anomalous, it is surely the bat! It is a furry animal, yet it flies like a bird. And it is further distinguished by being nocturnal, by living in dark places (principally caves), by sleeping upside down, and in the case of the vampire (*Desmodus rotundus*), by having a blood diet.[27] This creature has been both misunderstood and feared, since it haunts the countryside at night, and disappears with the sunrise. Its domain is the night, a foreign land where man is alien.

With regard to color, Blaffer notes that the name hʔik'al itself is probably derived from the Tzotzil adjective *ʔik'*, "black" or "dirty." That should be neither puzzling nor difficult to interpret, because throughout Mesoamerica black is a color associated with the dead.[28] By extension, it is also to be associated with rottenness and bad smell. To the extent that he is feared as a "spook," black-man is also and at the same time a sort of enforcer of cultural norms, on the lookout for deviant behavior.[29] Interestingly, he is rarely successful against bravery, the issue of cowardice being discussed in tales where hʔik'al accosts travelers asleep on the road.[30]

It is not certain what the original source for this strange figure may have been. The most likely prototype is the ancient Mayan bat-god or bat-demon, which gave rise to a number of features that were absorbed into the symbols contributing to black-man's identity, although there was, to be sure, a lowland Maya god Ikal Ahau, "Black Lord." He was feared by the Tzotzil as a death god, an enjoyer of human flesh, who attacked people at night, and by day lived in a cave.[31]

One parallel Blaffer does not mention is certainly of interest here. In the Kekchi region of Guatemala, the *Queck* (and its Spanish equivalent the *Negro* or *Tronchador*) is a scarecrow having human form. He is black, and he possesses extraordinary strength, sufficient to break the back of anyone so unfortunate as to fall within the Queck's power (hence the name Tronchador). In the Kekchi region, it is held that he is a hybrid of a cow and a man. In the Cakchiquel region, however, he is associated with a Negro slave who possessed some rather diabolical traits.[32]

The question might justifiably be raised at this point as to how one phenomenon in highland Chiapas may be used to interpret another in the central Mexican plateau. I believe, however, that this problem may have been resolved. In a recent article, Robert Chadwick argues that the version of Toltec history recounted in the *Códice Chimalpopoca*, while basically correct, actually recounts the histories of the first and second dynasties of Tilantongo in the Mixteca Alta, rather than of Tollan. He points out the similarities of the careers of Huemac of Tollan and 5-Alligator of Tilantongo, the first king of the second dynasty; and beyond this he argues that the story of Huemac in *Chimalpopoca* is the story of both 5-Alligator and his son 8-Deer and the story of Tecpancaltzin and his son Topiltzin (Quetzalcóatl) in Ixtlilxochitl, Veytia, and Clavijero.[33] And he further advances the thesis of John Paddock that the "Chapoltepec" mentioned in the *Relación of Cuilapa* could well be the present-day barrio of San Juan Chapultepec at the foot of Monte Alban.[34] If this be correct, then the story surrounding Huemac in Chapultepec need not have occurred in the place of the same name near ancient Tenochtitlán and present Mexico City at all, but may in fact have been part of a legendary motif attributed to that site as the stories surrounding Huemac passed into the realm of folk belief. The figure of the black man in that case could very well have accompanied the tale of Huemac on its northward migration.

Summary and Conclusion

This study has dealt with a number of motifs surrounding the theme of death in pre-Hispanic Mesoamerican cultures: the cave, bats, "spooks," the night, and the color black. In the case of Moctezuma, it is evident that his search for a solution to his predicament led him to contemplate suicide, a course of action for which he found precedent in the person of a previous ruler, Huemac, and which then led him to the cave in Chapultepec. There his emmissaries encountered the "gate-keeper," a black man, Totecchicahua, who led the way to a Huemac who is now the "lord of the cave" or a "lord of the dead," and not a spirit in one of the traditional underworlds; his suicide had excluded him from the destinies of other men. The black man who appears in the narratives is an anomaly. His figure is consistent with both h'ik'al and the Queck. He is known to be a "spook" and a "people-snatcher"; yet as a guardian or "gatekeeper" he protects the entrance to this realm lest it be entered unawares. It is not a place, we learn, where one would wish to remain at all. Huemac says:

> Those who bear me company here are also men like him [Moctezuma]. They too enjoyed life at one time; now they suffer, as you see. Behold them and observe how different they look from the way they did when they were alive. We . . . reside here because of the desires of the Supreme One. Therefore, why should he join us here?[35]

Nevertheless, so great is Moctezuma's disappointment, and so oppressive his burdens, that he persists in his desire to commit suicide, and is finally instructed to prepare for entry to the other world.

> Moteczoma . . . put in order the things of the Republic. He also began to prepare for his flight. All of this was done secretly. Having given gifts to his attendants and relatives he ordered his slaves to prepare a place at Tlachtonco for his arrival. They did this, adorning the place with sapota branches and arranging seats made of the leaves of this tree.
>
> When everything was ready Moteczoma entered his canoe and began his watch. On the hill of Chapultepec he saw a cave so brilliantly illuminated that it gave light to all the things of the city, the hills and trees, as if it were midday. Knowing then that Huemac had come for him he ordered his dwarfs to row quickly and soon he reached Tlachtonco. . . . He sat down upon one of the seats surrounded by his attendants and awaited the coming of Huemac. However, it was fated that he was not to escape his destiny.
>
> That night Texiptla, a priest of the temple . . . heard a voice in his sleep saying, "Awake, Texiptla! Behold, your king Moteczoma is in flight and goes to the cave of Huemac." . . . He abandoned the temple and entered a canoe. . . . With great haste he rowed as far as Tlachtonco where he found Moteczoma and his hunchbacks. Approaching Moteczoma he said, "What is this, O mighty prince? What folly is this in a person of such courage as you? Where are you going? What would Tlaxcala say? What would Huexotzinco, Cholula, Tliliuhquitepec, Michoacan and Metztitlan say? Think of the contempt they will have for Mexico, the city that is the heart of the entire world. Truly it will be a great shame for your city and for all those who remain behind you when the news of your flight becomes known. . . . What will we say, what will we answer, to those who ask about our king? We will have to reply that he has abandoned us. Return, O lord, to your throne and forget this folly because you dishonor us." . . .
>
> Greatly ashamed, Moteczoma sighed and on looking back toward the hill of Chapultepec, he saw that the light which had burned there had gone out.[36]

It is not clear just how Moctezuma died in the year 1520, whether at the hands of the Spaniards or of his own countrymen. Doubtless he felt his gods had failed him. After welcoming the Spaniards into Tenochtitlán, he soon found that he was their prisoner. During the course of a battle in which the Spaniards were momentarily forced to retreat to Veracruz, Moctezuma finally met his end, but not by his own hand.

Notes

1. Moctezuma Xocoyotzin ("the younger") ruled as *tlatoani* from 1502 to 1520, and is to be distinguished from his great-grandfather Moctezuma Ilhuicamina who ruled earlier (1440–68). His name is variously spelled by a number of the sources and their commentators as Montezuma, Motecuhzoma, Moteuczoma, Moteczoma, and even Mocthecuzoma. He was succeeded by his brother Cuitlahuac, who ruled only four months. Their nephew Cuauhtemoc (whose fight in defense of Tenochtitlán served to elevate him to the rank of a national hero) was the last of the Mexican kings.

2. Cf., for example, Diego Durán, *The Aztecs: The History of the Indies of New Spain*, trans. Doris Heyden and Fernando Horcasitas (New York: Orion Press, 1964), chaps. 61–68; Bernardino de Sahagún, *The Conquest*, bk. 12 of *Florentine Codex: General History of the Things of New Spain*, Monographs of the School of American Research, no. 14, pt. 13, trans. Arthur J.O. Anderson and Charles E. Dibble, 13 vols. (Santa Fe, N.M.: School of American Research and the University of Utah, 1950–1969); and Diego Muñoz Camargo, *Historia de Tlaxcala*, ed. A. Chavero (Guadalajara, Jalisco: Edmundo Aviña Levy, 1966), pp. 168–70.

3. Durán, *The Aztecs*, p. 248.

4. Ibid., p. 254.

5. *Tequitque* ("conjurers"). Partly merged with the priesthood, the magicians played a considerable role in the structure of supernaturalism in late pre-Hispanic central Mexico. The general class of magicians and sorcerers were known as the *tlahueliloc nanahuiltin*. See Henry B. Nicholson, "Religion in Pre-Hispanic Central Mexico," in *Archaeology of Northern Mesoamerica, Part One*, ed. Gordon F. Ekholm and Ignacio Bernal, vol. 10 of *Handbook of Middle American Indians*, ed. Robert Wauchope, 16 vols. (Austin: University of Texas Press, 1964–75), p. 442. For a discussion of specific classes of magicians, see also Alfredo López Austin, "Cuarenta clases de magos del mundo náhuatl," *Estudios de Cultura Náhuatl* 7 (1967): 87–117.

6. There is one other realm, but it is manifestly inappropriate to the circumstance at hand. This is *Chichihuacuauhco* (literally, "in the place of the wet-nurse tree"), the place of children who died before attaining the age of reason. There they were nourished by drops of milk which fell from the tree. According to Sahagún, *Florentine Codex*, Chichihuacuauhco was located in the house of Tonacatecuhtli ("Lord of our flesh"), where the souls of men are born. On the afterlife in general, see Cecelia F. Klein, "Post-Classic Mexican Death Imagery as a Sign of Cyclic Completion," in *Death and the Afterlife in Pre-Columbian America: A Conference at Dumbarton Oaks, October 27th, 1973*, ed. Elizabeth P. Benson (Washington, D.C.: Dumbarton Oaks Research Library and Collections, 1975); and Jesús Angel Ochoa Zazuzeta, "La idea de la vida después de la muerte," in *Religion en Mesoamerica; XII Mesa Redonda*, ed. Jaime Litvak King y Noemi Castillo Tejero (México: Sociedad Mexicana de Antropología, 1973), pp. 547–51. But cf. the considerable doubt expressed in some of the hymns of the *MSS Cantares Mexicanos*, and discussed by Miguel León-Portilla in his *Aztec Thought and Culture*, trans. Jack Emory Davis, Civilization of the American Indian Series 67 (Norman: University of Oklahoma Press, 1963), pp. 128–33.

7. Sahagún, *Florentine Codex*, bk. 3, pp. 47ff. See also Alfonso Caso, *The Aztecs, People of the Sun*, trans. Lowell Dunham, Civilization of the American Indian Series 50 (Norman: University of Oklahoma Press, 1958), pp. 58–59, and León-Portilla, *The Aztecs*, p. 126. Women who died in childbirth with the child still "captive in the womb" were called *mochihuaquetzque*, "women warriors," or "valiant women." They became *cihuapipiltin* or *cihuateteo*, "deified women." They were not cremated like the warriors but were interred in the womb of the eternal mother earth. Even so, their afterlife was spent in the "house of the sun." See Thelma D. Sullivan, "Pregnancy, Childbirth, and the Deification of the Women Who Died in Childbirth," *Estudios de Cultura Náhuatl* 6 (1966): 87–88. The role of the warriors and women appears to have become confused in the concept of the *tzitzimime*, the planets and stars which, changed into beasts, return to devour mankind at the end of the present "Sun" or age.

8. The reference is to the paradise scene of the lower register of the *Tlalocan* Mural 3 from Portico 2 of Tepantitla. Cf. Arthur G. Miller, *The Mural Painting of Teotihuacán* (Washington, D.C.: Dumbarton Oaks Research Library and Collection, 1973), figs. 160, 163–64, pp. 96–97; and George Kubler, *The Iconography of the Art of Teotihuacán*, Studies in Pre-Columbian Art and Archaeology, no. 4 (Washington, D.C.: Dumbarton Oaks Research Library and Collection, 1967), fig. 3.

9. Caso, *The Aztecs*, p. 60.

10. Ibid. As an example, some victims were said to have been dragged under the water by the *auitzotl*, a fantastic animal who lived beneath the surface in the lagoons.

11. *Mic* is the root of the verb *miqui*, "to die." The journey to the underworld is described by Sahagún, *Florentine Codex*, bk. 3, p. 42. The dog is the incarnation or representative of Xólotl, the "double" of Quetzalcóatl, who descended to the underworld at the creation of the world. On Mictlan as the realm of the dead, and comparisons with other traditions, see Vicente T. Mendoza, "El plano o mundo inferior, Mictlan, Xibalbá, Nith, y Hel," *Estudios de Cultura Náhuatl* 3 (1962): 75–99; and Justino Fernandez, "El Mictlan de Coatlicue," *Estudios de Cultura Náhuatl* 6 (1966): 47–53.

12. Sahagún, *Florentine Codex*, bk. 12, chap. 9, sec. 9. Durán calls the place *Cicalco*, "the place of the Hares."

13. Guy Stresser-Pean, "Ancient Sources on the Huasteca," in *Archaeology of Northern Mesoamerica, Part Two*, ed. Gordon F. Ekholm and Ignacio Bernal, vol. 9 of *Handbook of Middle American Indians*, p. 587. The historical basis of this particular legend is extremely doubtful. It nevertheless illustrates a number of peculiarities attributed to the Huastec: masculine nudism, the practice of magic, and illusionism.

14. On the legends surrounding Ce Coatl Huemac Quetzalcóatl ("One Snake Big Hand Plumed Serpent"), cf. the following sources: *Codice Chimalpopoca; Anales de Cuauhtitlan y leyenda de los Soles*, trans. Primo Feliciano Velázquez, Publicaciones del Instituto de Historia, Primera serie, no. 1 (México: Universidad Nacional Autónoma de México, Instituto de Historia, Imprenta Universitaria, 1945), p. 15; *Historia Tolteca-Chichimeca; Anales de Quauhtinchan*, ed. Heinrich Berlin and Silvia Rendón, vol. 1 of *Fuentes para la historia de México*, ed. Salvador Toscano (México: Antigua Librería Robredo de José Porrúa e Hijos, 1947), pp. 69f.; Hernando Alvarado Tezozomoc, *Crónica mexicana*, Notas de Manuel Orozco y Berra (México: Editorial Leyenda, 1944), pp. 502–7; Konrad T. Preuss and Ernst Mengin, trans. and eds., "Die mexikanische Bilderhandschrift Historia Tolteca-Chichimeca; Die Manuscripte 46–59 bis der National-bibliothek in Paris," pt. 1, Die Bilderschrift nebst Uebersetzung, *Baessler-Archiv; Beiträge zur Völkerkunde*, Beiheft 9 (Berlin: Verlag von Dietrich Reimer, 1937; reprinted, Johnson Reprint Corp., 1968), p. 17.

15. *The Historia Tolteca-Chichimeca*, for example, says that the Nonoalcans killed him ritually by shooting him with arrows (a type of sacrifice known as *tlacacaliliztli*). See Preuss and Mengin, "Historia Tolteca-Chichimeca," p. 17.

16. Diego de Landa, *Landa's Relación de las cosas de Yucatan* [*1570*], trans. and ed. Alfred M. Tozzer (Cambridge: Peabody Museum, 1941); Pedro Sanchez de Aguilar, "Informe contra idolorum cultores del Obíspado de Yucatan [1613]," *Anales del Museo Nacional de México*, 6 (1892): 13–122.

17. Francisco Javier Clavijero, *Historia antigua de México*, trans. J. Joaquin de la Mora, 2 vols. (Mexico: Editorial Porrúa, 1964). Quoted from Francisco Guerra, *The Pre-Columbian Mind* (New York: Seminar Press, 1971), p. 214.

18. There are, however, instances of individuals hanging themselves while under the influence of hallucinations produced by eating mushrooms (*teonanactl*, possibly *Amanita muscaria* or, more probably, a species of one of the three genera *Psilocybe*, *Stropharia*, or *Conocybe*). See Toribio Motolinía, *Historia de los indios de la Nueva España* (Mexico: Editorial Chávez Hayhoe, 1941), trat. 1, cap. 2, p. 25. Cf. Durán, *The Aztecs*, p. 225. Such individuals, however, were held to be inebriated or "witless," and their actions were condemned.

19. Durán, *The Aztecs*, p. 256. The description sounds more like that of Tlalocan. But Moctezuma is quickly undeceived by Huemac, who reveals to him the true nature of the domain over which he rules.

20. Mircea Eliade, *Zalmoxis: The Vanishing God; Comparative Studies in the Religions and Folklore of Dacia and Eastern Europe*, trans. Willard R. Trask (Chicago: University of Chicago Press, 1972), pp. 29–30.

21. Doris Heyden, "An Interpretation of the Cave underneath the Pyramid of the Sun in Teotihuacan, Mexico," *American Antiquity* 40, no. 2 (1975): 134–38.

22. Ibid., pp. 134–35, references omitted.

23. Martha Stone, *At the Sign of Midnight; The Concheros Dance Cult of Mexico* (Tucson: University of Arizona Press, 1975), p. 207. She is speaking in this instance of the *animas* (souls or ancestral spirits) of the *danzantes*.

24. Durán, *The Aztecs*, pp. 256–57. Cf. Tezozomoc, *Crónica Mexicana*, p. 505, where the black man is

called "the old Totecchicahua" ("Our lord, the strong one," or "the strength-gatherer," or possibly "the enforcer"). He appears here also with a staff in his hands. Caves in Chiapas and other places are considered to be holes for communication with the Earth Lord. See Evon Z. Vogt, *Zinacantan: A Maya Community in the Highlands of Chiapas* (Cambridge, Mass.: Belknap Press of Harvard University, 1969), pp. 375–87, 547.

25. On the motif of the "gatekeeper," see Joseph Campbell, *The Hero with a Thousand Faces*, Bollingen Series 17 (New York: Pantheon Books, 1949), pp. 77–89. The entrance to the other world is often found protected by snorting or panting beasts or a snarling dog. See Mircea Eliade, *Shamanism; Archaic Techniques of Ecstasy*, trans. Willard R. Trask, Bollingen Series 76 (New York: Pantheon Books, 1964), p. 295. See also his analysis of the "strait gate" that forbids access to the plane of higher being, and the motif of the "difficult passage," ibid., pp. 482–94.

26. Sarah C. Blaffer, *The Black-man of Zinacantan; A Central American Legend*, The Texas Pan American Series (Austin: University of Texas Press, 1972). One of hʔik'al's more striking features is his sexuality. Blaffer notes that he is possessed of a six-foot-long, death-dealing penis. Women raped by him are "superimpregnated": they swell up and die, or begin to produce children within three days of conception and continue giving birth, one child a night. Blaffer also reports conversations with Zinacantecos about the ritual impersonators of the demon, who wear black capes representing wings (pp. 19–20).

27. Ibid., pp. 7, 37, 68–69, 129. In the light of the emphasis placed on hʔik'al's sexuality, it is interesting to note that the bat commonly stands in an intimate relationship with the goddess of love. See Thomas Barthel, "Mesoamerikanische Fledermausdämonen," *Tribus* 15 (1966): 106f. The Nahuas did not place as much emphasis on the bat as did the Maya. Nevertheless Durán, in his description of *Huey Micailhuitl* ("the great feast of the dead") or *Xocotl Huetzi* ("fall of the fruits"), notes that the leader of the dance wore a costume resembling either a bird or a bat, and that he danced completely out of rhythm with the other dancers, occasionally speaking unintelligibly in a loud voice. See Diego Durán, *Book of the Gods and Rites, and the Ancient Calendar*, trans. and ed. Fernando Horcasitas and Doris Heyden, The Civilization of the American Indian Series, vol. 102 (Norman: University of Oklahoma Press, 1971), p. 207, and pl. 18.

28. Cf. Hermann Beyer, "El color negro en el simbolismo de los antiguos Mexicanos," *Boletín del Centro de Investigaciones de Antropologicos de México* 1 (1956); Samuel Martí, "Simbolismo de los colores, deidades, números y rumbos," *Estudios de Cultura Náhuatl* 2 (1960): 93–128. Blaffer, *Black-man*, pp. 36–37, notes that there are equivalences between black charcoal and dead bodies. The Indians of San Pedro Chenalhó use black candles to represent or communicate with the dead; see Calixta Guiteras-Holmes, *Perils of the Soul* (New York: Free Press, 1961), p. 295. On the use of the color black in funerary rites in Tepoztlan, see Robert Redfield, *Tepoztlan, A Mexican Village; A Study of Folk Life* (Chicago: University of Chicago Press, 1930), p. 143. There are several rather curious instances of black men in the murals at Bonampak, which depict persons of apparent distinction (possibly priests), whose bodies are (painted?) black. Cf. *Ancient Maya Paintings of Bonampak, Mexico*, Supplementary Publication No. 46 (Washington, D.C. Carnegie Institution of Washington, 1955), esp. "The Raid," room 2, structure 1.

29. Blaffer, *Black-man*, p. 125.

30. Ibid., p. 106. In the myths, hʔik'al attacks both sexes, but he is rarely successful against brave males.

31. J.E.S. Thompson, *Maya History and Religion*, Civilization of the Indian Series 49 (Norman: University of Oklahoma Press, 1970), p. 323. But see also the argument of Carmen Aguilera, "Una posible deidad negroide en el panteón azteca," *Estudios de Cultura Náhuatl* 9 (1971): 47–56, who discusses the figure of a black deity, Tzipitl, within the Aztec pantheon. I am inclined to doubt that he is the black man in question here, however. Further with respect to the black man, see Juan Comas, "Hubo negros en América?" *Revista de la Universidad de México* 10, no. 4 (1955).

32. Gustavo Correa, "El espíritu del mal en Guatemala," in *Nativism and Syncretism*, Publication no. 19, Middle American Research Institute, ed. Margaret A.L. Harrison and Robert Wauchope (New Orleans: Tulane University, 1960), pp. 62–66.

33. Robert Chadwick, "Native Pre-Aztec History of Central Mexico," in *Archaeology of Northern Mesoamerica, Part Two*, pp. 474–504.

34. Chadwick, "Native Pre-Aztec History," p. 487, notes: "Since we know that the native authors of the Chimalpopoca had codices at their disposal, and since we know that the meaning of some of the names

of Aztec barrios in Oaxaca was the same in Aztec and Mixtec (e.g., Xochimilco), it would have been plausible to read a Yucutica (Hill of the Grasshopper, i.e., Chapultepec) glyph in Aztec with the same meaning that it would probably have had in Mixtec. . . . In other words, the place glyphs in the Mixtec codices seem to have been drawn so that they could be read in several languages, a situation not dissimilar to Chinese script."

35. Durán, *The Aztecs*, p. 257.

36. Ibid., p. 257–58.

Death, Kingship, and Royal Ancestors in Buganda

BENJAMIN RAY

Most early writers on the kingdom of Buganda portrayed Buganda's rulers in the light of Sir James G. Frazer's famous concept of "divine" kingship.[1] Later anthropologists showed this interpretation to be fundamentally mistaken and put forward the view that the kingship of Buganda was essentially a political—not a religious—institution; its mythology and ritual served primarily sociopolitical ends.[2] However, much of Buganda's royal ritual and symbolism remains little understood. Frazer's views were often mistaken, but a virtue of his "ritual" approach is its integration of rites and symbols of royal death and vitality into a coherent symbolic pattern. In rejecting this pattern, social anthropologists also turned their attention away from the symbolic dimension of Buganda's royal cosmology, thus leaving largely unexplained the complex of royal ritual constituting the ideological foundation of the kingship.[3] As will become clear, Ganda rites and myths of death and homicide as well as the shrines of the royal ancestors provide a unique perspective for understanding the symbolic dimension of the kingship and hence the ideology on which it was based.

Rites and Politics of the Royal Corpse

Unless the king (Kabaka) was killed in battle or died at the hands of a princely usurper, he was allowed to die a natural death. Unlike other African kingdoms, Buganda did not practice ritual regicide as a means of "saving" the divine soul of a dying or ailing monarch from the dangers of mortal decay.[4] In the past the Kabaka's death was, however, kept secret until his ministers could secure the safety of the capital (in the face of impending anarchy) and could choose his successor, who, in turn, frequently had to kill off rival princes for the throne. When all preparations had been made, the monarch's death was publicly signaled by the beating of the royal drums. The sacred fire, which burned at the palace and symbolized royal vitality, was put out and its official attendant was strangled. Officials announced the

A Study Fellowship from the American Council of Learned Societies supported my research on the kingship and shrines of Buganda in 1972. In this connection I also wish to acknowledge the assistance of the Head of the Princes, Mr. Paul M. Lukongwa, whose permission made my work possible.

Kabaka's death by the expressions "the fire has gone out" or "the Kabaka is no longer able to fight." No one ever said the Kabaka had died. Instead, people referred to their deceased king as having "gone away" or as having "disappeared," both expressions being common Ganda euphemisms for death. In reference to the Kabaka, these expressions also recall the mythical tradition about the "disappearance" of Kintu, the sky-born founder of the kingship, who did not die but went away or disappeared into the forest at Magonga after establishing the kingdom. Indeed, Kintu's legendary disappearance became a symbolic paradigm for the death of his successors and for the architecture of their spirit shrines. Like Kintu, the Kabakas do not die; they disappear into the forest sanctuaries of their shrines.

In Buganda the purpose of the royal funerary-accession rituals was not the transference of the divine soul of the king to his successor (as Frazer's theory assumed)[5] but rather the transference of the political rights and duties of the kingship itself. In these ceremonies the body of the deceased Kabaka played a crucial role; royal accession rites followed the general Ganda funerary-inheritance ritual pattern in which the body of the deceased is an essential ingredient.[6] It is proof that the person has died, and without it the designated heir cannot perform the inheritance ceremonies that invest him (or her) with his (or her) predecessor's social role. In the royal context, the accession ceremonies require the king-elect together with his chief ministers to perform a leave-taking rite, which involves placing a new barkcloth over the royal corpse while gazing into its face and saying, "I cover it with barkcloth." Possession of the king's body was therefore a *sine qua non* for accession to the throne, especially in cases of disputed succession between rival princes. As Professor M.S.M. Kiwanuka observed, "the prince who had it [the body] would be the one who performed the funeral rites and then went through the accession ceremonies."[7]

That the royal corpse still had political as well as ritual meaning more recently is revealed by the Ganda response to the return of the body of the Kabaka Sir Edward Mutesa II from London in 1971. Mutesa had died in exile under the regime of Uganda's former Prime Minister Obote, who had abolished the kingship. When the army leader, General Idi Amin, overthrew Obote, one of his first acts was to call for the return of Mutesa's body and for a proper burial of Buganda's popular king. Although Amin was not himself a Muganda, he wished thereby to win all-important Ganda political support for his new government. When the body arrived, Ganda response was tumultuous and unrestrained. Thousands of mourning Baganda poured into Kampala, the capital, to greet the casket containing their beloved Kabaka. For five years the Baganda had lived without their Kabaka and although the kingship had been abolished, the exiled Kabaka still remained Buganda's "symbol of ultimate concern."[8] In Ganda eyes, the return of the Kabaka's body meant nothing less than the return of their historic cultural identity.

Although the celebration of the return of Mutesa's body was primarily a Ganda event, Amin used the occasion to his own political advantage. Without forewarning the Baganda, he had the body taken by helicopter directly from the airport at Entebbe to Kololo Hill in Kampala, where Uganda's independence ceremonies had taken place just nine years before. By circumventing the twenty-mile road journey through the heart of Buganda, where thousands of Baganda were waiting to greet the Kabaka's casket, Amin quickly brought the body to a place of national rather than local Ganda significance. At Kololo, Amin made a major speech before Mutesa's body, reminding the Baganda that although Mutesa had been their king, he had also been the first president of "all" Uganda. In this way Amin tried to direct Ganda loyalty beyond their Kabaka to himself as the new president. Over the radio the Kabaka's brother also appealed to the Baganda not to kill members of political parties that had not supported the Kabaka, for some Baganda were reported to be saying, "I shall give my life [you shall slaughter me] if Mutesa really died." The next day, Amin went to Namirimbe Cathedral where, despite his Muslim faith, he attended services in order to receive the salutations of thousands of joyous Baganda, "You have saved us, Dada"; "Dada, you have redeemed us"; "Long life Dada."

For the Baganda, the return of Mutesa's body clearly raised hopes for the return of the kingship itself. Now Mutesa's successor could be ritually installed, thus achieving Buganda's political "redemption." But these hopes were quickly dispelled. Soon after the funeral ceremonies at the royal tombs at Kasubi, the new government was forced to clarify the situation. It had previously urged the Ganda chiefs not to allow the appointed successor, Prince Ronald Mutebi, to place the barkcloth over his father's body. In the government's view this "would signify his virtual enthronement." But the rite had been duly performed at Kasubi. Nevertheless, the government refused to recognize the existence of a new Kabaka, "the barkcloth act being only a rite."[9] As far as the government was concerned, the Kabakaship had been buried with the late Kabaka. While complying with the government's wishes against fully installing a new Kabaka, the Ganda chiefs had Prince Ronald perform the barkcloth rite in order to make him Mutesa's official heir and thus Buganda's prince regent. If the king was dead, the dynastic line still had a chance to survive.

Coronation "Charter" of Conquest and Regicide

In the past, the royal corpse was removed after the performance of the barkcloth rite and was taken away for embalming and burial. This process lasted approximately six months; then the king went into mourning. In nonroyal contexts, the body is buried immediately after the family leave-taking ceremony, and mourning begins. In both instances, the mourning period is a time between the burial of the deceased and the installation of his successor when the descent group of the deceased lives in an anomalous situation without any jural or ritual authority. The significance of this period is appropriately expressed through symbols of reversal indicative of the "betwixt and between" status of the deceased's relatives. None of the relatives is allowed to work; their food is cooked and eaten charred and whole; they must wear old clothes; and they are prohibited from washing, cutting hair and nails, and from engaging in sexual relations.

In the royal context, the period of mourning was preceded by a series of "coronation" ceremonies at the royal shrines on Budo Hill.[10] As several authors have pointed out, the political purpose of these rites was to legitimize the chosen prince as the official successor to the throne. But, more important, their symbolic purpose was to link the princely successor to the origin traditions of the kingship in preparation for his accession. What these traditions recall is the precedent of royal succession by conquest and regicide.

The ceremonies began with a mock combat, called the "battle of reeds," between the advancing party of the Kabaka elect and the priestly guardians of the hill-top shrines. Both sides fought with elephant grass "spears" until the king's party "conquered" the defending priests and ascended the hill, thus capturing the kingship.[11] This battle reenacted previous conquests that had occurred at Budo, the last being Kintu's conquest of Bemba-Musota, the "snake" chief, who ruled the land before Kintu's arrival.[12] Kintu's victory marked the origin of the Ganda kingship and expressed its ideology of succession by conquest. Following this tradition, the "victory" of the new Kabaka's party demonstrated that the chosen prince has the right to obtain the supernatural resources of the kingship and to succed to the throne in conformity with the precedent of conquest and killing. Although succession by election of the ministers of state frequently occurred, conquest by rival princes was, until recent times, the dominant pattern. As Kabaka Mawanga was told at his installation in 1884, "Fight your enemies and conquer Buganda." According to one Ganda author, this meant "a kingdom is always conquered, not succeeded to."[13]

After the ritual battle the Kabaka-designate was taken by the priests to view the relics of the four shrines on the hill. These commemorated a succession of indigenous rulers who attained the throne by regicide. The most important shrine (and the only one now standing) is the House of Budo, which contains the jawbone of the legendary priest Budo. As if to put an end to the tradition of regicide associated with the kingship, Budo made a magic horn and gave it to prince Namugala and his brothers, saying, "If any of you becomes king and steps on the horn he will never be overthrown."[14] When Namugala succeeded to the kingship after killing his predecessor, he established Budo hill as the main "coronation" site because of the power of the horn he had implanted there in a mound, called Nakibuuka.[15] The mound is located on a promontory where Kintu slew Bemba, and it marks the grave where Bemba and his predecessors are buried. The climax of the ceremonies occurred when the Kabaka-elect and his queen sister crawled across the promontory toward the mound for their investiture. Stripped of their regal dress, the royal pair were pulled to their feet on top of the mound by Budo's chief priest and invested with new barkcloths signifying their accession. Then the chief priest gave the new king the royal spear and told him, "Go and conquer all your enemies." Grasping the spear, the Kabaka responded with the words, "I am the king to live longer than my ancestors, to rule the nations, and to put down rebellion." With this vow the king confirmed his authority to kill for the sake of his own longevity for the security of the kingship. A kingship that originated in regicide was thus to be sustained through homicide. This involved the authority not only to execute criminals and rebels but also to murder otherwise loyal subjects for ritual purposes.

The "Fowl" and the Origins of Death

At the conclusion of the ceremonies at Budo, the king went into mourning for a period of about six months and lived secluded in a specially constructed hut in accordance with the symbolic restrictions described above. When the king was informed that his predecessor had been fully entombed and buried, he ordered the drums to be sounded and decreed the end of mourning. The next day the king "hunted" and killed a gazelle, and afterward he washed and shaved to remove all traces of mourning. The hunting ceremony was performed to commemorate the legendary return of King Kimera, the third Kabaka of Buganda, who was born in the foreign kingdom of Bunyoro and returned to Buganda to reclaim the throne, hunting as he came. In a symbolic sense, this rite also signaled the "return" of the Kabaka-elect from his secluded state of mourning ("outside" the sphere of the kingship) to the final ritual stage wherein he would acquire the full rights and duties of the throne and become fully incorporated into his kingdom.

When the "hunt" was over, two men were arbitrarily seized and brought before the king. The king wounded one of them slightly with his hunting spear. This man was called the "fowl," and he was then taken away and put to death. Another human "fowl" was wounded by the king and killed at the conclusion of the installation ceremonies. After taking his enthronement vows ("If I am the real king, I will conquer my enemies"), receiving the royal sword ("With it cut judgment in truth, and anyone who rebels against you, you shall kill with this sword"), and beating upon the Mujaguzo drums, two men were brought forward and the king wounded one of them with an arrow. This man was later taken to the border of the neighboring kingdom of Bunyoro (Buganda's traditional enemy) where he was killed, and his body was burned with a fire made from the center post taken from the deceased king's tomb. According to Kagwa, this man was called the "Fat Rooster killed during the king's ceremonies."

The killing and eating of a fowl is a customary feature in all Ganda funerary-inheritance ceremonies, and it precedes the installation of the heir. The fowl is cooked over a fire made from the center post of the house of the deceased and it is eaten by the members of the family. According to Roscoe and Gorju, this is done to remind the people of the origin of death.[16] In the beginning, death was unknown when Kintu and Nambi (here represented as the first couple) departed from heaven to live on earth.[17] As they were leaving, Nambi's father, Gulu ("Heaven"), told Kintu never to allow Nambi to return, even if she forgot something, because she would risk encountering her brother, Walumbe ("Death"), who would want to follow her to earth and "kill your children." But Nambi returned despite Kintu's warning because she had forgotten to bring along grain to feed her chickens. When Walumbe saw her return, he chided her for leaving and for no longer cooking for him, since this is an unmarried sister's customary responsibility. Walumbe's accusation is also the customary charge elder brothers make at their sister's betrothal ceremonies. Walumbe then went to Buganda with his sister and asked Kintu to give him one of his daughters as a cook, but Kintu refused. Whereupon Walumbe caused the girl to die, and in this way death became the fate of the rest of Kintu's children and descendants. Walumbe's claim to Kintu's children also follows Ganda social custom, since the mother's brother has first rights to his sister's offspring. Convention prescribes that a father must give his brother-in-law a token gift when his children come of age in order to "ransom" them, lest the mother's brother claim them for himself.[18] By thus portraying death as the "mother's brother," the Baganda explain why death has the ultimate claim on human lives. In the funerary context, the eating of the funeral fowl also serves as a reminder that death's claim stemmed from a chance misdeed at the beginning of time.

Royal Homicide: Order and Vitality

Although no explanation for the substitution of men for birds in the royal installation ceremonies is explicitly given, it is apparent that these ritual murders are related to the theme of ritual homicide that dominates the concluding portion of the installation ceremonies.

These murders fall under the general rubric of *kukuza*—"strengthening," "maturing," and "protecting" the heir. In nonroyal contexts, the kukuza rite is performed by the heir by stepping over his ritual sister's legs, an act which, according to Mair, "symbolized sexual intercourse." On this and other occasions Mair reports that the purpose of the kukuza is "to produce a general beneficial effect on the process with which it is connected" and "the period which it inaugurates," in this case the accession of the new heir.[19] In the royal context, the killing of the second human "fowl" is followed by a series of subsequent kukuza murders, all of which are said to "invigorate" and "confirm" the king in his kingdom. The parallelism between the two forms of kukuza, sexual and homicidal, appears explicit: both are expressions of intrinsic power. The sexual form of kukuza is a display of intrinsic human power, while the homicidal form is a display of intrinsic royal power.

This connection between kingship and the act of homicide is confirmed by B.M. Zimbe in an interesting passage at the beginning of *Kabaka ne Buganda*. There he points out that "when an enemy was killed in battle, Baganda would say, 'I have killed you on behalf of the Kabaka' (because I have no power to kill, only the Kabaka). God (Katonda) gave the power to kill exclusively to the Kabaka. Even when killing animals, one says *kulwa Kabaka*. All things lie under the power of the Kabaka, both men and animals."[20] Accordingly, the installation killings followed a definite sequence; first the king displayed his power over the animal world by a royal "hunt," and then he displayed his power over his human subjects by a similar act, thus extending his dominion over all living beings. As we have seen, the killing of the first human "fowl" was preceded by a "hunt" in which the king killed a gazelle, while the second "fowl" was killed after the king had wounded this victim with a hunter's arrow. Another murder committed several months after the king's accession (to "invigorate" the new king) followed the same pattern. First, the king killed a leopard, one of the most ferocious nocturnal killers, and then, with his spear, he wounded a man, who was taken away and strangled. The leopard skin was later stitched together with the skin of a lion, the "king" of the daylight predators, and made into a royal carpet, symbolic of the ultimacy of the king's power.[21]

Sometime after his installation at Budo, the new Kabaka went to Nankere where he inaugurated a final orgy of killing to mark his accession. First, according to Kagwa, "he went out of his way to Bukoto in Kyadondo for hunting."[22] Then Nankere presented him with one of his sons (or relatives), who was dressed as a prince, and thus as a potential challenger to the throne. This man was killed, and the muscles of his back were used to make royal anklets to add "vigor" to the king. A whip was also made from the skin of the victim's back and used to enforce order at the king's court. Later, at Busiro the king ordered a number of arbitrary executions among the ranks of his personal servants and pages. Those who responded obediently to a series of royal commands found themselves to be the unfortunate victims of royal anger; their dutiful behavior was interpreted in various ways as a failure to properly serve the king and thus implicitly as a form of rebellion.

Although these killings were said to strengthen (kukuza) the king, it is also clear that they were statements about the nature of royal authority. As one of Mair's informants put it, these murders were assertions that "the new king had entered on his reign and acquired the power of life and death over his people."[23] They may also have had an archetypal dimension, that is, to have been repetitions of an original mythical act, for homicide like the kingship originated from a primordial act of the founder, Kintu. In the beginning, murder did not exist until Kintu, in a fit of rage, speared and killed his faithful prime minister, Kisolo, for punishing a criminal at court without the king's knowledge. "Conscience-striken, Kintu ran away and vanished," never to return.[24] Homicide thus originated as an expression of royal anger against a suspected but otherwise dutiful palace servant, exactly as portrayed in the final sequence of ritual murders when the newly installed Kabaka "angrily" killed some of his most faithful servants on the pretext of failing to serve the king. What this showed, among other things, was that only the king could distinguish appearance from reality, that is, loyalty from rebellion. Thus he held the key to political order. Hence, when the king killed his subjects, even for what appeared to be perfectly arbitrary reasons, this was a display not only of royal authority but also of order in its purest form.

From time to time, and whenever the king fell ill, the priest of the war god, Kibuuka, also ordered arbitrary killings as a form of kukuza. As Mair points out, these murders were not performed as sacrifices to appease the gods nor were they occasions to execute convicted criminals as a display of royal power. Rather, like the installation murders, they were performed as ritual "purifications" (kukuza) to "protect" the king and to "set the land aright." This connection between taking human life and strengthening the king has been noticed by several authors, but it has not been satisfactorily explained. Drawing on Roscoe's account, Frazer regarded these murders as magical ways of transferring the victim's soul-vitality to the king, thus renewing his powers;[25] but Roscoe's informants never gave this or any other explanation. Mair was unable to discover any explicit formulation about the efficacy of such murders apart from their stated purpose of protecting (kukuza) the king, and setting the land in order.[26] Richards indicates that such killings were both magical rites and displays of royal power.[27] But why this kind of display, and how could it be thought to strengthen the king and to order the kingdom?

The explanation appears to lie in the myths and rituals of the kingship. As we have seen, the installation rites assert that the kingship originated in regicide and that it was to be sustained through homicide. Murder thus constituted the foundation and strength of the kingship. All royal symbols reinforce this point. The king is referred to as the lion and the leopard, predators whose power is manifested by killing. He is also a hunter, a killer among men; and he is likened to the "queen termite" who requires the supreme sacrifice of the members of her colony on her own behalf. Indicative of this attitude is one of the popular names that kings gave to their palaces, *kanyakasasa*, "Blacksmith's Forge." It derives from the proverb "Just as the blacksmith's shop has coal burning all the time, yet no ashes accumulate, so it is with the king who always kills his people, yet they go to him."[28]

To be sure, the practice of killing subjects could be carried too far, and kings who did so were said to be cruel and soon found themselves to be the object of revolt and the victims of regicide. But if not overdone, some public display of arbitrary death was an accepted phenomenon. Although appalling to European visitors, such as the nineteenth-century explorer John Hanning Speke, who suspected that Mutesa I used human beings for rifle practice, it was an accepted, indeed, expected mode of exhibiting royal power, especially when that power seemed most threatened by sickness in the palace or on the throne. The power thus displayed was the essence of the kingship; and display renewed that essence. This was not political murder but controlled symbolic killing that belonged to the "peace" of the incumbent's reign. It contrasted with the period of anarchical political killing of the chaotic interregnum when princes competed for the throne. At court, the occasional killing of palace officials for minor offenses was an analogous symbolic display. As a high form of entertainment, it provoked outbursts of mockery and nervous laughter from other officials in the competitive palace meritocracy. At most, the unfortunate victim could thank the Kabaka for "correcting" him and at least in this way achieve a measure of redemption by dying as a tribute to royal power and authority.

Cycle of the Moon: Death and Life

If arbitrary death by royal decree served as a constant symbol of royal order and vitality, the appearance of the new moon served a similar function on the celestial plane as a symbol of cosmic vitality and order. The appearance of the new moon signified a resurgence of life after a period of darkness when the lunar rhythm was momentarily interrupted.[29] According to one Luganda account, "On the day the new moon became visible, people rejoiced, took out their magic horns and requested that their lives might be prolonged and praised their gods for having enabled them to see the new moon. The following day was Bwerende. They did not do any work that day and congratulated one another upon having been able to see a new moon and wished one another to see it again."[30] These ritual days of rest were the principal occasions when the people visited the temples to honor the gods.

At this time also, members of the royal class visited the shrines of the dynastic ancestors. At the palace, the king's "Twin" (a vase-shaped container which held part of the royal placenta and personified the king) was taken from its temple and brought before the king who unwrapped and inspected it. Afterward the Twin was exposed to the moonlight and anointed with butter. Today this ceremony is no longer performed, but I have been told that on the night of the new moon the king did not sleep in the palace with his wives but went to another hut where he spent the night alone. The next day the king observed the prohibition against work and passed the day reviewing the relics of the national gods at his palace shrines "as a sign of respect and gratitude for having been tided over another month ['moon']."[31] These ritual prohibitions against work and sexual relations suggest that originally the moon may have been thought to "die" during its dark phase, since apart from the lunar days of Bwerende, such prohibitions are associated only with periods of mourning. In any case, at the time of the new moon the idea of passage through a period of darkness and a transition that reminded the people of death was explicitly expressed. When the moon became visible again, the kingdom celebrated a renewal of life and reestablished contact with the spiritual world of the ancestors and hero-gods, thus reforging the unity of the cosmos.

Royal Shrines: History, Drama, and Pilgrimage

As the preceding statement implies, Ganda cosmology is based on a division between the world of the living and the world of the dead. Since the spiritual realm is the world of the dead, the gods (*lubaale*) are regarded as the spirits of national heroes who became gods after they died. Similarly, the kings are revered as sacred beings only after they have died, when they become spirits in the service of the kingship. After the entombment of the royal corpse, the jawbone was removed and taken to a palace shrine where it was enthroned in the concealed forest portion of the shrine. This is where the spirit of the king also went to live. The spirit then chose a new "wife" to serve as a medium, and henceforth the spirit, called the Ssekabaka, appeared and spoke to the people of the Kabaka's court.

The divine aspect of the kingship thus belonged to the sphere of the dead Kabakas (Ssekabakas), not to the living kings, as early writers believed. To be sure, the Kabakas were surrounded by numerous taboos and were accorded an enormous degree of respect; their despotic authority inspired considerable awe.[32] But, unlike other African kings, they had no divine qualities or special mystical powers. They were entirely human figures within an institution whose political dimension was completely secular. What has been overlooked, however, is that the kingship as a whole included both political and spiritual dimensions, whose division and unity conformed to the dualistic living/dead character of Ganda cosmology. This is clearly marked in the spiritual geography of the kingdom. At the center lies the county of Busiro, which was set apart as the sphere of the royal ancestors. It was governed by a chief, called the Mugema, who had responsibility over the royal funerary ceremonies, and it is where most of the dynastic shrines (*masiro*) are located. The rest of Buganda is the sphere of the living denizens of the kingdom where the living monarchs reigned.

This spiritual division also involves an important temporal dimension. The ancestor shrines belong to the past, and the territory on which they are located is regarded as the ancient "center" of the kingdom, from which it later expanded as new territory was conquered and added on. Collectively and individually, the shrines thus constitute what Oliver has called the historical "charter" of Buganda.[33] Each is a miniature "palace," whose personnel and relics maintain an unbroken continuity between the past and the present. Living at or near the shrine are the descendants of the Kabaka's prime minister and his queen sister in addition to a small retinue of local princesses and other shrine attendants, including the resident medium. Within the shrine itself are displayed a number of spears, shields, and daggers. These stand together in an upright position before the *mwaliiro*, or "altar" platform, in front of the barkcloth curtain concealing the "forest" sanctuary, where the "lion" lives. This collection of relics is especially important as a mnemonic device for remembering the history of the Kabaka's reign. Each relic has a name associated with an important historical event in the Kabaka's life. The more sacred relics are hidden from view within the forest. They include the Kabaka's jawbone and his Twin, together with the Twins of his queen sister and other royal offspring.

As the foregoing description implies, the shrines are not merely museums of a long dead past, they are also living theaters where the past may be repeatedly revived and encountered anew in the present. They are palaces where royalty may go to "attend the court" of the dynastic spirits, hence the symbolic nature of the shrine's architecture. The forest portion of the shrine represents the "other" world of the spirits and it enables them to remain in close contact with their descendants in this world, and this world with them. Within the shrine the two worlds meet precisely at the center at the mwaliiro in front of the forest and the opened curtain. The mwaliiro lies directly under the main roofbeam or the dome (of the traditional conical shrines) and it is the point of juncture between the forest and the human world. This is where the mediums sit when they become possessed by the royal spirits. Since the curtain can be opened and closed, it both reveals and conceals the spirit world of the forest. When it is opened, the front portion of the shrine becomes a stage where the spirits manifest themselves "on the heads" of their "bearers" (mediums) as they dance and flourish their spears before the seated congregation.

Such ceremonies used to occur regularly at the time of the new moon. Now they are held less frequently because of the dispersal of some of the princesses in charge of the shrines. Even though the prime minister may still be living at or near the shrine (as most of them do), he has no jurisdiction over it. He acts primarily as a caretaker, subject to the authority of the head princess, who is the descendant of the Kabaka's queen sister. This situation represents a reversal of the prime minister's political role at the palace of the living monarch, where he is the chief official. But in the ritual sphere of the dead, the women are in charge. They lead and dominate the singing, dancing, and possession, in contrast to their minor role in the political sphere, which is dominated by men. Most mediums are, in fact, women, and even those who are men are still regarded as the "wives" of the royal spirit. In the absence of any royal clan, the kings belong to their mothers' clans, and the women of these clans are said to be the mothers of the shrine. On important ritual occasions, they bring food to feed the royal spirits. Today, when there is no kingship to provide money for the unkeep of the shrines, this responsibility has also been taken up by the members of the mothers' clans.

The primary attraction of the ceremonies at the shrines is the manifestation of the Kabaka's spirit. On these occasions people come to greet it with songs and to bask in the radiance of the king. At the beginning of the ceremonies the songs beseech the owner of the house (the Ssekabaka) to invade the assembly and settle down upon the heads of their mediums and greet the people. When the spirit arrives, the audience responds with the royal greeting, "You have conquered! You have conquered! You have conquered us, indeed!" The singing becomes more animated and lively as the mediums begin to dance, crouching and thrusting their royal spears toward the seated audience. "How have you been handsome son?/How have you been cowherd?" "Sing well, the 'lion' [the spirit] is 'roaring'/Eee, the iron [the spears] made him speak at [the shrine of] Nabulagala./Convey my message to Ssalongo [the spirit]." "Let me sing for those who will 'eat' [rule over] me." As the songs emphasize, this encounter with the spirits is an event not to be missed. Several songs refer to disappointed latecomers who arrive after the curtain has closed and the spirits have returned to the forest: "They are climbing [onto the mediums], the children of Golooba at Mpinga./The elders are climbing, I shall come and see./I didn't see him. I found he had closed."

Some people also ask the royal spirits for blessings and money in the belief that they are like the lubaale gods and can materially help them. But members of the royal class who claim to know say this is a misguided (though popular) view and that the ceremonies are purely acts of commemoration, not divination, which is the purpose of the lubaale cult. In the past, however, living monarchs sometimes received advice from the royal spirits in dreams and visions, and as recently as 1954 it was said that the royal mediums sent messages of advice to Mutesa via telegram during his exile in London.

Today, in the absence of a ruling monarch the ceremonies appear to be primarily dramatic celebrations of the past by the royal class, which faces an uncertain political future. For this class, the shrines act as sacred centers, periodically drawing together groups of royalty which lack any clan or lineage unity of their own. Since the members of this class are numerous and tend to be scattered around urban areas, the shrines have acquired the character of pilgrimage sites. During most weeks there are small comings and goings of royalty, mainly princesses especially from nearby Kampala. They stay a few days near the shrine to which they are related, even when there are no ceremonies, simply to renew acquaintances and to spend some time in the country away from the city. The shrines are their country "estates," where there are vegetable and banana gardens, and where the graves of their relatives are located.

The shrines also serve as sacred centers on a broader scale, since they unite in themselves the cosmic, mythic, and historical foundations of the kingdom as a whole. The present ritual headquarters is at Kasubi, located a mile outside Kampala. This shrine, built in the traditional conical thatched-roof style, is where the last four Kabakas are buried, including Mutesa I (1854–84), who was Buganda's last and most powerful precolonial ruler. As a Muslim, Mutesa discouraged the practice of possession by forbidding anyone to become a medium of his spirit (after he died), unless he or she could show a reading knowledge of Arabic, in which Mutesa himself was literate, since he did not want to be "ridiculed." The Kasubi shrine has also become well-known to visitors from outside Uganda as one of Kampala's main tourist sights. During the busiest months of the tourist season, it draws more than two thousand visitors. Recently, the Lungfish clan of Mutesa I's father, Suna II (1824–54), completed a large new conical shrine at Wamala, a few miles north of Kasubi, with a view to its becoming the next ritual headquarters. At the inauguration of this shrine, a large number of Twins were brought in procession from their shrines in Busiro to pay their respects to Suna and his new palace. This was a rare event, unseen since the early years of this century when such processions of the dynastic Twins used to occur at each new moon. At this time the Twins were taken to the palace so that the Kabaka could greet them and thus restore his links to the sacred past as he looked forward to the future. Today, if the political dimension of the kingship no longer exists, its links to the past remain firmly established in the shrines of its dynastic ancestors, and hence its spiritual dimension still survives.

Notes

1. John Roscoe, *The Baganda* (London: MacMillan, 1911); R.A. Soxnoll, "The Coronation Ritual and Customs of Buganda," *Uganda Journal* 4 (1937); Tor Irstam, *The King of Ganda* (Stockholm: Ethnographical Museum, 1944); P. Hadfield, *Traits of Divine Kingship* (London: Watta, 1949).

2. Audrey I. Richards, "The Ganda", in Audrey I. Richards, ed., *East African Chiefs* (London: Faber & Faber, 1960); Audrey I. Richards, "Authority Patterns in Traditional Buganda," in L.A. Fallers, ed., *The King's Men* (London: Oxford University Press for the East African Institute of Social Research, 1964); Lucy Mair, *Primitive Government* (Harmondsworth: Penguin, 1964), chap. 9; Martin Southwold, "Was the Kingdom Sacred?," *Mawazo* 1, no. 2 (December 1967).

3. The watershed of this social-functional approach to sacred kingship in Africa is Evans-Pritchard's

Frazer Memorial Lecture, delivered in 1948, "The Divine Kingship of the Shilluk of the Nilotic Sudan," in E.E. Evans-Pritchard, *Social Anthropology and Other Essays* (New York: Free Press, 1962). Following this line is J.H.M. Beattie's interpretation of the royal rituals of Bunyoro, Buganda's powerful western neighbor, to whom Buganda is historically and culturally related. "Rituals of Nyoro Kingship," *Africa* 29, no. 2 (1959). Another essay by Max Gluckman, on Swazi royal rituals ("Rituals of Rebellion in South-east Africa," in Max Gluckman, ed., *Order and Rebellion in Tribal Africa* [New York: Free Press, 1960]) has touched off considerable criticism by advocates of a more "symbolic" approach. See T.O. Beidelman, "Swazi Royal Ritual," *Africa* 36 (1966). For a critical appraisal of Evans-Pritchard's original essay on the Shilluk, see Michael Young, "The Divine Kingship of the Jukun: A Re-evaluation of Some Theories," *Africa* 36 (1966). For further discussion see Benjamin C. Ray, *African Religions: Symbol, Ritual, and Community* (Englewood Cliffs, N.J.: Prentice-Hall, 1976), chap 4.

4. Traditions of this kind have been recorded in Bunyoro and in Nkore, Buganda's southern neighbor. Although Evans-Pritchard has doubted both the actual occurrence and religious motive of regicide among the Shilluk (emphasized by Frazer), regarding it as a political "fiction," what matters, as Beattie ("Rituals of Nyora Kingship," p. 138) has observed in connection with Bunyoro, "is not the question whether any kings died actually in this way, but rather the fact that this is how the kingship was thought about."

5. *The Golden Bough*, abridged ed. (New York: Macmillan, 1948), chap. 24.

6. On Ganda funerary-inheritance ceremonies, see Roscoe, *The Baganda*, chap. 4; and Lucy Mair, *An African Peoples in the Twentieth Century* (London: Routledge & Sons, 1934), chap. 8.

7. Ed., *The Kings of Buganda*, trans. of Apolo Kagwa, *Bassekabaka be Buganda* (Nairobi: East African Publishing House, 1971), p. 82.

8. F.B. Welbourn, *Religion and Politics in Uganda, 1952–1962* (Nairobi: East African Publishing House, 1965), p. 45.

9. *Uganda Argus*, 6 April 1971. Full reports of events surrounding the return of Mutesa's body were published in the *Uganda Argus* and in two Luganda newspapers, *Taifa* and *Munno*, 1–6 April 1971.

10. Accounts of the installation ceremonies vary in detail. I have drawn upon the following authors: Apolo Kagwa, *Ekitabo Kye Empisa za Baganda*, (London: MacMillan, 1952), chap. 3; Apolo Kagwa, *The Customs of the Baganda*, translation of *Ekitabo Kye Empisa za Baganda*, 1st ed., 1918, by E.B. Kalibala, ed. M. Mandelbaum Edel (New York: Columbia University Press, 1934), chaps. 3 and 6; Roscoe, *The Baganda*, chap. 7; B.M. Zimbe, *Buganda ne Kabaka* (Kampala: Gambuze Press, 1939); A.R. Cook, *Uganda Memories, 1847–1940*, (Kampala: Uganda Society, 1945); Audrey I. Richards, *The Changing Structure of a Ganda Village* (Nairobi: East African Publishing House, 1966), chap. 4.

11. The reverse occurs in the Shilluk installation "combat" in which the "kingship captures the king" (Evans-Pritchard, "The Divine Kingship of the Shilluk of the Upper Nile," p. 205).

12. Richards, *The Changing Structure of a Ganda Village*, pp. 36ff.; M.B. Nsimbi, *Waggumbulizi* (Kampala: Uganda Bookshop, 1952), chap. 1.

13. Zimbe, *Buganda ne Kabaka*, p. 81.

14. Apolo Kagwa, *The Kings of Buganda*, p. 75.

15. In 1969 one of the stately old acacia trees flanking the mound fell to the ground. This happened, I was told, when Mutesa died in exile—a fitting testimony to the loss of one of the main underpinnings of the kingship.

16. Roscoe, *The Baganda*, p. 121; Julien Gorju, *Entre le Victoria l'Albert et l'Edouard* (Rennes: Oberthür, 1920), p. 361, n.1.

17. Kagwa, *The Kings of Buganda*, p. 1: Roscoe, *The Baganda*, pp. 462–64.

18. On the Ganda concept of the mother's brother, see Mair, *An African People*, pp. 61, 80, passim.

19. Ibid., pp. 43, 248.

20. *Kabaka ne Buganda*, p. 6.

21. Together these animals represent the total animal world of herbivorous/carnivorous eaters and prey/predator beasts.

22. Kagwa, *Customs*, pp. 16–17; see also Roscoe, *The Baganda*, pp. 210–14.

23. *An African People*, p. 179.

24. Kagwa, *The Kings of Buganda*, p. 7.

25. James G. Frazer, *The Golden Bough, Part IV: Adonis Attis Osiris*, vol. 2, 3rd ed. (London: MacMillan, 1927), pp. 223–26.

26. *An African People*, p. 179.

27. "Authority Pattern," pp. 276–79.

28. Kagwa, *Customs*, p. 9.

29. This idea is found in the kingdom of Nkore and among the Swazi of southern Africa. See John Roscoe, *The Banyankole* (Cambridge: Cambridge University Press, 1923), pp. 110, 125; Hilda Kuper, *An African Aristocracy* (London: Oxford University Press for the International African Institute, 1961), pp. 76, 201–2, 208.

30. Zimbe, *Kabaka ne Buganda*, p. 13.

31. Kagwa, *Customs*, p. 9.

32. Roland Oliver, "The Royal Tombs of Buganda," *Uganda Journal* vol 23, pt. 2 (1959).

33. As Southwold points out, "ultimate authority tends to acquire sacredness" ("Was the Kingdom Sacred?," p. 21). However, Southwold sees the sacredness of the kingship exclusively in terms of its political power without recognizing its primary connection with the symbolic role of the king as the representative of the nation and with the rituals of the kingship and the shrines.

Indian Traditions—Myth and Meditation

Only in that dying, in that coming to an end, is there renewal, that creation which is eternal.

Jiddu Krishnamurti

Death as a Necessity and a Gift in Hindu Mythology

J. BRUCE LONG

It may be expedient to lose everything.
The moon says it, waxing in silence, the fruit of the heavens,
grape vine, melon vine.
Autumn upon us, the exemplar, the time of falling.
One who has lost all is ready to be born into all:
buddha moon socratic moon jesus moon
"Unless the grain falling to earth die, itself remains alone".

Daniel Berrigan, *Prison Poems*

"All things that are born, are fated to die" is perhaps the most mystifying and disturbing anomaly that a human being can experience. The recognition that the beginning of life is unknown, the end of life is unknown, and the intervening term of life is overcast by a veil of evanescence and insubstantiality gives human existence a quality of mystery that is at once fascinating and unsettling. This feeling of mystery, however, does not grow out of the mere recognition that all creatures, sooner or later, will die; its development is considerably more complex. It springs from a recognition that the nature, quality, and orientation of human life are established upon the dialectical interaction (perhaps "conflict" might be more accurate) between two ontological forces: the force of "Being," which projects the living creatures into existence at the beginning of a life-term, and the force of "non-Being," which removes those same beings at the end. The fragile, transitory, and fortuitous nature of life poses a fundamental paradox: the beings who exist in the present time did not exist before a certain point in past time, but, having come to be, will, at some point in future time, cease "to be." This paradoxical nature of creaturely existence troubles man most profoundly and, at the extreme limits of suffering, drives him to question the meaning of his existence.

The primary objective of this paper is to investigate some of the theological and ethical principles to which Hindu sages, poets, and mythographers have appealed in response either to their own inward sense of human fragility and mortality or to the pleas of their devotees and disciples for sagely guidance in meeting the unexpected difficulties of life successfully and in penetrating the mystery of human mortality.

Although the materials concerning the nature, cause, and divine-human significance of death presented in this paper do not, by any means, exhaust the data of the most ancient Hindu texts, they do seem to exemplify the sagely reflections upon the mysteries of death during the period of the religious history of India (ca. 1000 B.C.–A.D. 400). They appear to represent not so much a series of theological and philosophical statements viewed according to a pattern of historical development but rather a series of philosophical "moments" (in the Hegelian sense of the term) in the religious philosophies of ancient India concerning the question of the meaning of death when viewed within the context of the life of the universe as a totality. I will pursue this question by analyzing, in succession, a story concerning the advent of death presented in one of the *Brāhmaṇas* (i.e., Vedic liturgical manuals), a narrative account of a philosophical disputation concerning the radical cause of death in the Great Epic, the *Mahābhārata*, and a selection of materials drawn from the epics and purāṇas which represent Rudra-Śiva as the God of Death. I will conclude with a brief discussion of the various means which the sages believed to be at man's disposal for dealing with death in ways that are, at once, intellectually satisfying and experientially therapeutic and, finally, with a critical résumé of the ideas of death which seem to have played a most formative role in the development of religious thought in ancient India.

The narrative materials in the Vedic and epic literature of ancient India make two contrary claims about the nature of death and its rulership over living beings. First, the scriptures assert that death is the inescapable destiny of every creature (both sentient and nonsentient), that its rule is sovereign, and that its hold over all creatures is invincible. As one epic poet warns his listeners, "no one can escape the decree of Death, not by wisdom, nor by sacred rites nor by righteous deeds." Second, the holy texts claim that the rule of death over the creature-world is only conditional and relative, that mankind has at its disposal a variety of means to achieve immortality (*amṛta* = the state of non-death). Among these means are adherence to vows of asceticism (*tapas*), acquisition of intellectual and spiritual wisdom (*vijñāna, prajñā*), performance of sacrificial rites (*yajña* in the Vedas, *pūjā* in the epics and puraṇas), and cultivation of moral virtues (*puṇyakarma, śīla*). The full range and diversity of ideas concerning the meaning of death in epic literature can be brought into view only by holding both of these apparently antithetical views in structural opposition, and by resisting the temptation to derive a simple and univocal perspective by collapsing one concept into the other. That man is mortal and subject to a certain death and that, although death holds sway over the finite world, there is hope for escape by a few persons possessed of extra-ordinary powers of mind, will, and heart are the two ideas that define the perimeter of ancient Hindu thought concerning death.

Prajāpati as Procreator and Terminator of the Life-Process

As early as the ancient Vedic texts known as the *Brāhmaṇas*[1] (ca. 800–600 B.C.), the Divine Absolute is identified as the agent of both the initiation and the termination of the world order. Prajāpati, the Lord of creatures, who customarily is invoked as the creator, appears in one passage as the divine personification of time (*kāla*) or death (*mṛtyu*).[2]

> The Year (*saṁvatsara*) is Death (*mṛtyu*), [as Prajāpati is Grandfather Time] for by means of days and nights [i.e., the passage of time] He slays all mortal beings and they perish. He who knows the Year to be Death reaches the fullness of life before dying. The *devas* feared Prajāpati, the Year and the Ender (*antaka*), lest He should reach the end of their lives. They performed various sacrificial rites and constructed a fire-altar, praising the Creator and striving to obtain immortality but without success. Prajāpati then taught them the proper ritual and they obtained immortality (*amṛta*=not-dead). Then Death (*mṛtyu*) addressed the gods, "Surely by this means all men (*mānuṣa*) will become immortal (*amṛta*) and what share (*bhāga*) will be mine?" The gods replied, that from now on "no man will reach immortality with the body (*aśarīrāmṛto*) and that the body will be Death's portion but the spiritual (*puruṣa*) part of man might become immortal, either though sacred knowledge (*vidyāyā*) or ritual actions (*karmanā*). Those who know this or perform righteous actions come to immortal life but those who do not, return again and again to serve as food (*annam*) for Death."[3]

Prajāpati, so the sages say, exists in an irrevocable symbiotic relationship with his creation. Just as living creatures depend for their life upon food, so the gods (or, in this instance, God) require the nourishment provided by the sacrificial offerings to sustain their efforts in maintaining the cosmic order.[4] In the passage quoted above, Death is said to devour the creatures for his own support. However, given the fact that Prajāpati and Death are homologized, it is Prajāpati himself who partakes of the creatures. He must devour them periodically in order to satisfy his own hunger[5] and to acquire the energies needed to maintain the universe. He consumes the creatures as a means of preserving them from a *final* death, and, consequently, of enabling them to procreate anew.[6] Thus Prajāpati is enabled to perpetuate the life-process and to save the world and its inhabitants from the tragic destiny of either atrophy or self-destruction. Paradoxically, the only certain escape from a final and absolute annihilation leads through the gates of death to a new state of existence.

This passage from the *Śatapatha Brāhmaṇa* (the *Brāhmaṇa* of the Hundred Paths)[7] indicates that originally Prajāpati, as the divine embodiment of time (*kāla*), was both creator and destroyer of the universe. When he divided himself into two portions or cosmic functions, with the embodiment of death (*mṛtyu*) assuming the role of destroyer, the entire cosmos had to be apportioned between Prajāpati and Mṛtyu. This task was accomplished by subjecting man's physical aspect to the rule of mortality (*mṛta*) and his spiritual aspect to that of immortality (*amṛta*). Prajāpati and Mṛtyu, then, are the original pair, the precosmogonic duad—birth and death, creation, and destruction. Together they form the primal source from which all creatures arise in the beginning and the end (*anta*)[8] to which they return at the termination of a life-period.

According to Vedic scriptures, Prajāpati is simultaneously the sacrificer,[9] the sacrifice,[10] the sacrificial victim,[11] and the recipient of the fruits of the sacrifice.[12] He *is* the entire universe. As such, he experiences every phase of the life-process of the cosmos, from birth to death (and later in the tradition with the development of the idea of transmigration of the soul) to rebirth. His dismemberment on the sacrificial altar reduplicates, on the microcosmic scale, the periodic deterioration and rejuvenation of the entire cosmos. The myths and rituals addressed to Prajāpati celebrate the inescapable fact that the procreation of new beings depends upon the provision of the necessary life-forces and living space by removing a certain number of creatures from the world. Thus the myths and rituals are directives to mankind to look upon life and death as two interdependent phases of a single natural process.

The central message of this myth is that the person who perceives the mystical identification between Prajāpati, Kāla, and Mṛtyu and gives public demonstration to this knowledge by faithfully performing his sacrificial duties will survive for a full term of life.[13] Persons who succumb to a premature death, before their lifetime has run its normal course, must be presumed to have been ignorant of the ontological identity between creator (*sraṣṭā*, *dhātā*) and destroyer (*antaka*, *vināśaka*) and, as a consequence, to have failed in the performance of his ritual duties. The text declares that he who knows that time is death and that Prajāpati is the initiator and terminator of the lives of all creatures will not be subject to (premature) death.

The Origin of Death from the Wrath of Brahmā

When we turn to a text of more recent vintage in the *Mahābhārata*, we find ourselves in a drastically altered cultural milieu. Many of the ancient Vedic deities have been eclipsed by deities who have risen to prominence in post-Vedic times. In the passage to be analyzed, Brahmā has replaced Prajāpati as the agent of creation, and the agent of death has yet to make an appearance. In addition, Śiva-Mahādeva, the successor in the epic literature to the Vedic god Rudra and, according to epic mythology, the bringer of death and destruction, assumes a role more normally associated with Viṣṇu, namely, the agency of preservation (*sthiti*).

Another important cultural innovation in the epic period is that the Vedic sacrifice has begun to be supplanted, or at least supplemented, by a different mode of worship (i.e., *pūjā* = worship of tangible images of deities with offerings of fruits, flowers, incense, prayers, hymns of praise, etc.). Furthermore, the sacrificial priest, who enjoyed preeminent power in the Vedic tradition, is beginning to be replaced as the primary religious functionary by ascetics (*sannyāsis*, *yogis*, *sādhus*) who seek personal liberation from rebirth through austere penances and self-mortification (e.g., fasting, meditating, submitting the body to extremes of heat and cold).

In the myth being considered here,[14] the holy teacher Bhīṣma is instructing his student, Yudhiṣṭhira, the personification of Righteousness in the *Mahābhārata*, concerning the origin and cause of death. We learn from the teacher that the mere recitation or hearing of this story frees one from the fear (*bhaya*) of death and, in a sense, from the iron grip of death itself.

Yudhiṣṭhira, the offspring of Righteousness (*dharma-putra*), grieves over the death of his many kinsmen who had fallen on the field of battle during the internecine conflict between the Pāṇḍavas and Kauravas. Out of depths of his own feeling of desolation and despair, he cries, "Whose offspring is death? Whence comes death? Why does death sweep away the creatures of this world?" In hopes of assuaging Yudhiṣṭhira's grief, Bhīṣma, the elderly savant of the Kaurava lineage, relates a story which the sage Nārada told King Anukāmpaka when the latter was grieving over the death of his son:

> In the beginning, Brahmā created multitudinous creatures who did not know death [for death had not yet appeared]. They multiplied so rapidly that no one had room to breathe. Brahmā sought the means to reduce the number of beings but could find none. His frustrations gave way to wrath (*krodha*) and from this wrath sprang a fire of cosmic dimensions. Then Lord Śiva, in the form of Sthāṇu [a mighty column], appeared before the Creator, hoping to pacify his wrath, saying, "Know, O Lord, that my prayers to you are on behalf of the creatures of the world. Since you created them, then do not be angry with (i.e., destroy) them." Brahmā replied, "I am not angry, nor do I desire the death of all creatures. It is out of a desire to lighten the burden of the weight of the manifold creatures upon the Earth that I have brought about this destruction. The goddess Earth, oppressed by her plight, solicited my aid to rescue her from sinking into the waters of chaos by destroying the creatures. When, after reflecting a great while upon the means of destroying these increased (*vṛddha*) beings, I failed to find a way, and anger took possession of me." Sthāṇu again said, "Do not become angry concerning the need to destroy the creatures; exercise mercy and spare all of them. You have burnt them to ashes and those that have been destroyed will never return. Therefore, withhold your energy (*tejas*), replace your wrath with pity towards them, to the end that they may return to the world through repeated rebirths. Brahmā, the Grandfather of the Universe, repressed his *tejas* within Himself and then provided for both birth (*pravṛtti*) and death (*nivṛtti*) for all creatures. After he had suppressed that fire, there sprang from the pores of his body a dark maiden attired in red robes, eyes blazing-red, wearing celestial ornaments. Brahmā named her Death (*mṛtyu*) and commanded her to kill all beings "both learned and foolish" without exception.[15]

This myth poses a number of intriguing and puzzling problems concerning the nature and cause of death. First, it is unusual for death to appear in feminine form in Hindu literature. Indeed, this is the only instance known to this writer, with the exception of the appearance of death in feminine guise by the side of Yama in the *Brahmā-vaivarta Purāṇa*.[16] Moreover, the reasons given for the appearance of death are varied and, perhaps, slightly confused. Destruction of a certain number of the creatures is necessitated by the inauspicious commingling of a number of preestablished conditions: the procreation of an excessive number of beings or their tendency to live unrealistically lengthy periods of time,[17] together with Brahmā's failure to devise a means of dealing judiciously with the "population crisis." Although Brahmā claims that he is not angry, in truth he is, and it is because he cannot devise a means of delimiting his expenditure of creative energies that the creation, paradoxically, is threatened with wholesale destruction. The myth seems to be making a fine distinction between an efficacious and an inefficacious death. Whereas an inefficacious death leads to the total and irremediable annihilation of the universe, an efficacious death promotes the continued procreation of creatures and the perpetuation of the natural cycle from birth to death and thence to rebirth. The central concern of this myth is the provision of the cosmological basis by which the universe can be preserved.

Two startling paradoxes are present in this myth. First, Sthāṇu (= Śiva), who normally represents the powers of disease and death, assumes the task of pleading for the lives of the creatures. Second, in a religious tradition in which final liberation (*mokṣa*) from rebirth (*saṁsāra*) is held to be the *summum bonum* of human existence, Śiva decries Brahmā's act of reducing the creatures to ashes and thereby hindering their return to the world. The first paradox can be explained, in part, by two interrelated concepts of divinity in Hindu thought. Hindus believe that all the gods are but diverse forms of the one Formless, Eternal Absolute and, given this fact, the various powers and functions of divinity may be assumed by first one and then another god, depending upon the demands of the existing conditions. In addition, Hindus reject the idea that death brings life to an absolute and final termination. They believe rather that the extinction of the life forces (*tejas*, *prāṇa*), whether with regard to the life of a single creature or that of the entire cosmos, is but a necessary interlude between life-periods. Based on this "transitive" view of birth and death (or creation and destruction), the Highest Being would be expected to promote and direct the natural process throughout each of its separate, but interconnected, phases.

The second and more troublesome of the two problems (i.e., Śiva's insistence that Brahmā restrain his wrath in order to return a certain number of the creatures to the finite world through rebirth) might be illuminated, in part, by considering the underlying paradoxical relationship between the doctrines of Transmigration (*saṁsāra*) and Liberation (*mokṣa*) in ancient Indian thought. Hindu poets, mythographers, and philosophers assert that men are destined to undergo repeated rebirths within the realm of suffering and death because of their ignorance of the essential unity underlying and supporting the world of multiplicity. Escape from this misfortune of endless rebirths comes to that person who realizes a perfect union (or, in the case of theistic Hinduism, *blessed communion*) with the Eternal Absolute. But a crucial element in Hindu religious thought, which is often ignored by Indian and western commentators alike, is that salvation is available only to those creatures who are still living in the realm of *saṁsāra*. In other words, only human beings who are subject to rebirth can achieve liberation. Hence the very possibility of being liberated from the round of rebirths depends on the fact that a person returns to the realm of mundane existence a sufficient number of times for the spiritual conditions required by final liberation to be fully realized. Viewed in this light, Śiva's plea to Brahmā to spare the lives of the creatures, to return them once again to the temporal realm, and to provide them with an additional opportunity to work toward their salvation seems to suggest that in no other way could they hope to achieve complete salvation (*mokṣa*).

The second segment of the same myth presents some new themes and brings into sharper focus the precise nature of the forces which give rise to this conflict between Brahmā and his offspring.

> On hearing the command of Brahmā, the goddess shed bountiful tears and caught them in her folded hands. She said to Brahmā, "How could such a lady as I, created from your own essence, perform such a terrible deed? I am fearful of acts which are unrighteous (*adharma*); please give me work to do that is righteous (*dharma*). How, indeed, can I murder living beings who have harmed me in no way? Worse yet how can I bring myself to kill friends and relatives whom I love? I fear that the relatives of those who die by my hand will curse me in later times. The tears of the survivors who are sick with grief, will scorch me throughout eternity. O Lord of Creation, grant me this wish, that I may perform asceticism." Brahmā replied, "O Mṛtyu, you were created by me for the destruction of all creatures. Set your mind to the task and do not despair; you cannot do otherwise." [You will not incur blame for doing this.] Lady Death steadfastly refused to comply with Brahmā's wishes and finally retreated to a sacred place to perform asceticism. For thousands of billions of years, she underwent the most severe austerities, living upon grass and water, then upon water only, and, finally, upon air only, desiring nothing but the welfare of the creatures. . . . Finally, Brahmā appeared in that place and, again, said "Since no guilt will come to you for this act, set yourself the task of destroying the creatures. My command is unavoidable. For this act, Eternal Righteousness (*sanātana-dharma*) will abide in you." After refusing once more, she is told that the tears in her hands will assume the form of horrible diseases which will take men away once their time has come. She will inflict men with Desire (*kāma*) and Wrath (*krodha*) but will incur no iniquity because of the perfect equanimity of her actions. In this way *dharma* rather than *adharma* will be upheld. Out of a fear of Brahmā's curse, Mṛtyu agrees. And, therefore, as the end (*anta*) draws near for each person, she strikes him with Desire and Wrath and destroys his body with the diseases which solidified from her tears of grief and anger. She removes the creatures only at the appointed time (*kāla*) and thereby escapes iniquity (*pāpaṁ*). Knowing this fact [the nature of the cause of death], therefore, a person should not grieve. "For even as the five senses disappear when the person is in deep sleep, later to return to life once the sleeper awakens, even so, in the same way, the creatures, with the destruction of their bodies, go from this world into another world and return from there again *in due time*." [emphasis added]

Mṛtyu's line of defense is explicit. She can see no justification for the compulsion to perform the same dreaded deed that Brahmā himself, the Grandfather of creation, had been incapable of performing—particularly in recognition of the fact that she is a projection of his essential nature. Moreover, she feels that Brahmā's commandment demands that she pursue a course of action (i.e., murder) which, in a court of law, would be grounds for criminal sanction. From the standpoint of morality, the removing of living beings would blot her character with iniquity (*doṣam*) and she would be condemned by the surviving kinsmen, all of whom are dear to her. Her arguments scarcely require defense from the viewpoint of morality or the *dharma*-ethic. Such acts would redound to her in the form of demerits (*a-puṇyaṁ*, *pāpaṁ*) and would have an irreparably destructive effect upon the human family by progressively and permanently diminishing its numbers.

The exchange between Brahmā and his offspring, Mṛtyu, is reminiscent, in many respects, of the dialogue between Kṛṣṇa and Arjuna in the *Bhagavad Gītā* concerning the relative merits of adhering to the *dharma*-ethic of a warrior by killing his kinsmen versus following the *mokṣa*-ethic of the *yogi* by withdrawing from the world. In essence, the line of reasoning presented by Brahmā in this myth and by Kṛṣṇa in the *Gītā* is as follows: Everyone, without exception, is born to a predetermined duty (*dharma*), established by the family and caste into which one is born. The purpose of life is bound up with the fulfillment of one's own duty (*svadharma*), even if performed imperfectly. With regard to Mṛtyu's situation, Brahmā urges her to recognize that her *svadharma* requires that she remain within the realm of worldly affairs for the purpose of removing those creatures whose appointment with destiny has arrived; thereby she is to promote the orderly progression of the cosmos. Furthermore, since both birth and death are subject to the operations of time or destiny, she (Mṛtyu) should consider herself to be not the primary cause but merely the attendant occasion of the death of these creatures. Even those who die at her hands are destined to come again; their death is not a finality. For these reasons, she is enjoined to withstand the temptation to escape this onerous task by resorting to a life of asceticism and to remain committed to the course of action to which she was born. It is upon Mṛtyu's successful accomplishment of her *svadharma* that the world depends for its survival.

The central thrust of Brahmā's argument is that each creature can choose only to perform his own duty, and that human actions performed in accordance with the dictates of *dharma*, even though they may appear to be morally reprehensible, not only *do not* bring blame upon the agent but actually purify him of any iniquities incurred from previous transgressions. Apparently, Brahmā felt a need to provide Mṛtyu with a means of escaping the threat of guilt for her part in removing the creatures. This concern for her welfare is exemplified in his command that she inflict each of the creatures with the poisons of desire (*kāma*, libidinous attachment to objects of pleasure) and wrath (*krodha*, frustration over the loss of desired objects and a decrease in pleasure), and with diseases (*roga*, perhaps, in the cases of those persons who die a "natural death," nothing more than age and senility). By succumbing to the sins of desire and wrath, man enters a state of culpability and, for this reason, comes to deserve the fate of death. And, since rebirth itself is a sign of personal imperfection and culpability, Mṛtyu's act of removing them from the life-world is altogether befitting their present condition and hence is not subject to condemnation or recrimination. By interweaving the strands of various themes into the fabric of a single narrative (i.e., the need for death, origin of death, rationale for death) the mythographer has accounted for the fact of death and at the same time provided justification for its operation in the finite world.

Disputation Concerning the Cause of Death

Since the central narrative of the *Mahābhārata* concerns the story of warfare between two clans of a single family over the question of legitimate succession to the rulership over the realm of the *Kurus*, it is inevitable that questions relating to the nature and causes of Death should arise on numerous occasions and under diverse existential conditions. On one occasion a courageous warrior is wracked in mind and body with grief over the death of his friends and relatives on the field of battle. At another time, a mother and father are tested for their ability to remain faithful to *dharma* following the death of their only child. At still another time, a father whose son has died in his youth searches for a moral justification for this tragic event in order to find an escape from his grief. These and similar circumstances provoke a wide range of questions pertaining to the advent and meaning of Death within the life-realm. Such questions as the following abound in the *Mahābhārata*: What is the origin of Death? What is the ultimate purpose and meaning of Death? What kind of human meaning can the living beings derive from experiencing the death of others? Among the numerous primal causes of the advent of Death presented by the epic bards are the divine personification of Death itself, the will of God (*parameśvarecchā*), the machinations of time or destiny (*daivam, vidhi*), and a person's deeds in a former lifetime.

Human Action (*karma*) as the Primary Cause of Death

It is commonly recognized by all who are acquainted with Indian thought that the belief that a man is what he does forms one of the cornerstones of the Hindu view of man. According to this doctrine, as a man desires and wills, so he acts; his volitions and deeds in the present life predetermine his nature, character, and social status in the next. All people are therefore the sum of all their deeds.[18] As the sage declares, "Verily, one becomes good through good deeds and evil through evil deeds."[19]

One myth in the *Mahābhārata*[20] presents in a most dramatic manner the rationale for designating *karma* as the radical determinant of the time, occasion, and immediate cause of death. Once again, we find Yudhiṣṭhira grieving over the death of thousands of kinsmen and cohorts on *Kurukṣetra* and seeking a word of consolation and peace of mind from his preceptor, Bhīṣma. The aged teacher urges Yudhiṣṭhira not to squander his grief upon the death of his comrades in the knowledge that he (Yudhiṣṭhira) played no direct role in bringing about their demise. Bhīṣma begins his instruction by raising a question that will force his student to delve below the surface appearances and to become aware of the deeper and subtler causes of death, "Why do you believe your soul (*ātman*) to be the cause (*hetuṁ*) of your actions, when by nature they are dependent upon something else, given that its (i.e., *karman* or *kāla*) actions are subtle (*sūkṣma*) and beyond the grasp of the senses?" To drive his point home to the grieving warrior, Bhīṣma then recites the story of the conversation (*saṁvāda*) about the cause of death within a group composed of the personification of death, a saintly woman named Gautamī, the personification of time, a fowler (*lubdhaka*), and a serpent (*pannaga*).

> One day an elderly lady of patient and tranquil mind named Gautamī found her beloved son dead from snakebite. An angry fowler named Arjunaka brought the snake to her with a vow to kill it as revenge for its role in causing the boy's death. The woman, free of grief, replied that the serpent was undeserving of such a destiny, in that her son's death had come about by the decree of Time (*kāla*), not through the

agency of the serpent. More important, while the boy's life could not be restored by destroying the serpent, no harm would come to the fowler by sparing its life. The fowler urged the woman to be practical-minded, to dispense with such wise-sounding but empty words as these, "meant only for Perfected Ones," and to give vent to her grief by taking vengeance on the serpent. She rejected his various arguments, until, finally, the snake freed itself from the fowler's rope and contended that it had no will of its own but merely acted as an agent of Mṛtyu. It, therefore, could not be held directly responsible for the boy's death. Then, the embodied form of death appeared and declared that neither the serpent nor himself was culpable, for "like the clouds in the sky (*jaladavat*), I am subject to the authority of *kāla*." It is *kāla* that directs [*pravartanta*, lit.: stimulates, incites] all creatures to act. Both action and abstention from action are instigated by *kāla*. All things whether existent (*bhāva*) or non-existent (*abhāva*) are created (*sṛjyante*) and destroyed (*hṛyante*) by *kāla*. Finally, *kāla* arrived on the scene and began trying to absolve all of them of guilt by placing the onus of the deed upon the *karma* of the dead child himself. He contended that the child was killed as the result of his own *karma* in the past. Neither he (*kāla*) nor the serpent, nor death itself had been the primary cause (*prathamo hetuṁ*) of the child's death. The mother then confessed that her *karma* too influenced his death and that she must share in the responsibility. Then, everyone returned to his own abode free of sorrow (*viśoka*) and anger (*abhūdviroṣa*) in the knowledge that birth and death and the attainment of heaven or hell result from the fruits of each person's deeds in the past.[21]

Bhīṣma concludes the tale by assuring Yudhiṣṭhira that even as the woman's child did not die as the result of the influence of the serpent, Time, or Death but as the result of the child's deeds during a previous lifetime, so too his own kinsmens' deaths occurred as the direct result of their *karma*.

Bhīṣma's intention in relating the story is to provide Yudhiṣṭhira with an escape from the crippling effects of an overwhelming sense of personal guilt and self-denegration. The central point of his message is that man should not squander his energies in grieving over events which are beyond his control, in the recognition of the fact that all events occur as the result of deeds performed in past time, or according to the dictates of the law of *karma* or destiny (*daivam, vidhi*).

In startling contrast to the fowler who based his judgment upon evidence from the world of appearances and upon the desire for personal aggrandizement, the child's mother perceived the primary cause of her son's death to be the unerring will of Death itself. But, according to the story, even her point of view must be rejected in the end. Like the other explanations proposed, her belief that the divine embodiment of death is the cause of the death of her son fails to give an adequate accounting of the role of human action in the causation of events.

In terms of the doctrine of human action (*karma-vāda*), the child's death should be recognized as the result of the coalescence of a number of conditions, most of which are subtle and imperceptible to the human senses and mind. When the death of her son is viewed at the level of surface appearances only, the serpent, indeed, is recognized to be the immediate cause of the event. But when seen through the lens of mental discrimination (*viveka*) or intuitive insight (*vijñāna*), it is discovered that the primary causative factor (*prathamo hetuṁ*) was the child's own *karma*[22] in a previous lifetime, not the venomous bite of the serpent. Had the child's mother allowed the fowler to take vengeance on the serpent, even more unfortunate consequences would have resulted. The fowler's act of vengeance would have provoked future misfortune for his willful disruption of the orderly operations of the law of *karma*, while, at the same time, his attempt to achieve retribution for the child's death by taking vengeance on the serpent would have failed to contact the root cause.

In the course of delivering yet another lengthy discourse to Yudhiṣṭhira, Bhīṣma proclaims that the particular divine realm to which men go after death depends upon the specific rite (*karma*) or vow (*vrata*) which they perform during their lives. The most auspicious and beneficial of these vows is fasting (*anāśana*). The length of life in this world, he maintains, is determined by behavior (*ācara*), established upon the changeless and eternal foundation of Righteousness (*dharma*).[23] Those persons who live righteous lives in this world pass through death into the realm of Pure Being (*sat*), and those who live unrighteous lives enter a state of non-Being (*asat*). In response to Yudhiṣṭhira's expression of doubt that righteous deeds will not *necessarily* produce good results, the sage replies that action (*karma*) and one's essential nature (*svabhāva*) are determinative factors in bringing about the various states of affairs in human life. A person therefore is obligated to continue performing actions in full and unyielding confidence that meritorious deeds, according to the law of necessity (*nimitta*), will produce meritorious results. Bhīṣma concludes his discourse with the assertion that *karma* (or *kāla*) is the causal basis of all states of being and the primal cosmic principle which prohibits the production of inauspicious (*a-dharmika*) consequences from (*dharmika*) actions.[24]

A brief digression concerning some of the finer points of the Hindu doctrine of *karma* might illuminate some of the subtleties of this doctrine which western scholars have frequently overlooked. From the time of the Vedas, the Hindu doctrine of sacrifice (which serves as a paradigmatic model for human action in general) has been based on the notion that human action in the present sets in motion certain invisible (but extremely effective and indissoluble) forces, which, in turn, give rise to other forces in a chain reaction. Hence all human actions—good or bad—produce powerful causative forces that continue exerting an influence on subsequent situations and events long after the original impulse has disappeared from the level of phenomenal perception.

Past actions may be causative forces in shaping future actions either directly and immediately or indirectly over a period of time. A human deed or a natural event may give rise *directly* to other actions and events by coalescing all the elements and stimuli required to bring various potentialities into concrete appearance. For example, the act of repeatedly hacking the trunk of a tree with a sharp axe in the same area will fell the tree and scatter the life-forces which sustained it. In this instance, the act of cutting served as the direct cause of the falling of the tree. Moreover, that same activity may give rise to a lengthy chain of secondary conditions or effects stretching over a long period of time and a broad spectrum of space. The act of felling the tree will set in motion a lengthy and extremely complicated chain of events culminating in the decomposition of the tree and the provision of additional nutrition for the growth of other botanical organisms. Here the visible effects of the act of felling the tree would, in time, recede below the level of perceptible causes to become one among a collectivity of "attendent circumstances." Though inaccessible to human sensation, the earlier action would continue to play an active role in promoting the organic process.

To take an example from the realm of human experience, a person may suffer a profoundly disruptive failure or disappointment in early life and after the passage of some years he may fall victim to another misfortune, which, though causally linked with the previous mishap, shows no "visible" traces of that linkage. Phrased in the terms of Freudian psychoanalysis, a traumatic experience during childhood, after slipping below the level of consciousness, may reemerge at a later time to the level of consciousness and serve as a primary factor in the development of a state of neurosis or psychosis.

Considering that all human actions produce causative influences, it must be recognized that no deed, however trivial it may appear to be at the time of performance, is devoid of causative influences and often far-reaching consequences (*phala*). As Vyāsa instructs Yudhiṣṭhira, "I am convinced, O Bhārata, that acts, good and bad, are continually revolving here as a wheel, and men obtain the fruits (*phala*) of those acts, whether good or bad, that they do. One sinful act arises out of another. [Even as one meritorious act proceeds from another.] Therefore, O Tiger among Kings, renounce all evil and do not submit your heart to grief."[25]

Time (*kāla*) as the Causative Agent of Birth and Death

The ancient Vedic texts known as the *Brāhmaṇas* contain elaborate descriptions of and commentarial glosses on the sacrificial rites believed by the priests to be the most efficacious means of maintaining the cosmos in a state of relatively stable and orderly creativity. One of the central convictions upon which *Brāhmaṇical* speculation is based is that, with the passage of a year in the life of the universe, the life-powers of the world become exhausted and require regeneration. The energies that invigorate and support the world are restored, first, by fragmenting and then reuniting the body of the creator god, Prajāpati, upon the altar in the form of the sacrificial libation. In view of the care with which the priests aligned the "reconstitution" rite at the juncture between the old year and the new, it is evident that the sages perceived an ontological link between the great Soma sacrifice and the periodicity of the cosmos. At numerous points in the *Brāhmaṇas*, the cosmos is identified with the year and the sacrifice with both the year and the universe.

Kāla is one of numerous abstract pseudo-philosophical concepts which Vedic poets employed in portraying their vision of the origin and foundation of the universe. The term came into prominent use early in the Vedic tradition (in the *Atharva Veda*) and has continued until today to appeal to some Indian thinkers as a viable cosmogonic theory.[26] The concept of *kāla* has played a role in Indian thought comparable in many ways to that of related ideas in other cultures—*moira* in Greece, *maat* in Egypt, *tao* in China, *logos* in Stoicism and Christianity, and *nous* in Neoplatonism.

Kāla is personified as a cosmogonic force in the AV (XIX. 53, 54), is identified with Prajāpati, and is praised as all-creating (AV X. 8).[27] The waters and even Prajāpati himself are believed to be the offspring of *kāla*. In the later portion of the *Maitrāyaṇīya Upaniṣad* (VI. 14–16), the birth of *kāla* occurs simultaneously with the birth of the Sun. Since the Sun is the source and support of all living things and, in the *Upaniṣads*, is identified with the Brahman, *mutatis mutandi*, *kāla* is identified with the Brahman, the highest principle and the source of all that is.[28]

In the *Brāhmaṇas*[29] and in the *Mahābhārata*,[30] the poet asserts that *kāla* is the year (*saṁvatsara*) and the six seasons are his mouths (*vadanās*). It is the mouths of *kāla* which swallow up the creatures, "each in his own time." Again, in the *Maitrāyaṇīya Upaniṣad*, it is stated that *kāla* "cooks all the creatures," meaning that he ripens them with the passage of time in order to make them fit to be swallowed by death. The *Mahābhārata* reiterates the same notion by asserting that "*kāla* cooks (i.e., ripens or digests) the elements, *kāla* devours all beings."[31] *Kāla*, again, is the immutable and eternal foundation upon which the universe, with all its progeny, is established.[32] Throughout the Indian religious tradition, the scriptures assert that anyone who fails to recognize the mystical identity between *kāla* and death is destined to succumb to a premature demise.

In a word, *kāla* is believed by Hindu sages to be the mysterious and unpredictable (but inerrant) agent of birth and death within the realm of human, animal, and divine creatures, and, at the cosmic level, the power that brings about the evolution and involution of the entire universe.[33] Even in the case of those who meet what appears to be an "untimely" or "accidental" death, such persons are brought to their destiny by the inexorable operation of the Wheel of Time (*kālacakra*). Indeed, in view of the Hindu belief that *kāla* operates according to its own invincible law in creating and destroying all forms of life, with the result that "no one can ever escape that which is destined,"[34] there is no justification for viewing any death (or birth), whatever the circumstances, as accidental, untimely, or unnatural. Everything that happens, does so in its own time and in accordance with the dictates of cosmic necessity. In recognition of the invincibility of the law of *kāla*, the sages declared that *kāla* is the power of cosmic proportions that determines the beginning and the end of a life-period. Bhīṣma declares, "Death has been decreed for all created beings (*bhūtānāṁ*). When their hour (*vidhi*, *kāla*) comes round, all beings are removed by law (*dharmeṇa*)"[35] Again, the wise Saṁjaya consoles Dhṛtarāṣṭra, trapped in the bonds of grief, with these words:

> "You should not grieve over that which is inevitable, for who can escape, even by his wisdom, the decrees of *kāla*? Existence and non-existence, pleasure and pain—all are caused by *kāla*. As *kāla* creates all things, even so *kāla* destroys all creatures. *Kāla* it is that consumes all creatures: *kāla* it is that extinguishes the fire (of destruction). All states of existence, both good and evil, are caused by *kāla*. *Kāla* dissolves all things and procreates them anew.... *Kāla* is invincible and impartial ... knowing that all things ... are the progeny of *kāla*, you should refrain from losing your senses."[36]

These and similar declarations concerning the intractability of the law of *kāla* express a profound sense in the mind of the poet that the cosmos and everything in it is established upon and governed by a law that is insensitive to the demands of reason, moral action, and even spiritual wisdom. This cosmic law governing both life and death works its ways relentlessly and unswervingly, without any special regard for the station or condition of individual persons. "So it has been disposed by the Disposer (*vidhātṛ*) . . . the *daivam* (or Fate used synonymously with *kāla*) cannot be overcome by any human deed . . . so do not hope to alter *kāla*."[37] So invincible are the laws of *kāla* (syn.: *daivam, vidhi, diṣṭa*) that men are counseled to resign themselves to their inability to overcome, by their own efforts or by appeal for divine assistance, the destiny to which they are born. The sage declares, "Everything is appointed by god,"[38] for "man was created bereft of free will at the command of the Creator."[39] Obviously, in these last two passages, the sage is making a straightforward identification between *kāla* and the will of the Creator.

Finally, in the story of Ṛṣi Vipula and King Devaśarman,[40] the statement is made that day and night and the six seasons (i.e. *kāla*) are witnesses to and judges of all human deeds:

> Having committed a sin in secret, no sinner should delude himself that his transgression is known to himself alone. When a man perpetrates a sinful deed in private, both the Seasons and the Day and Night behold it as well . . . and it is *kāla* which brings that sinner to the demise which he deserves.

Time is conceived as the manifestation of the law of Fate in the form of temporality, the coming-to-be and passing-away of living beings. *Kāla* brings to pass every state of affairs within the temporal order and brings to fruition every human action, in accordance with its own inherent law of retribution. If there be any basis for speaking of human freedom in this connection, it would have to be limited to the voluntary submission to the dictates of the law of time by each person.

Śiva as Kāla and Mahākāla—Time as Destroyer and the Destroyer of Time

The religious and philosophical traditions in India seem, from earliest times, to have been marked by a struggle between two opposing views of the nature of the Divine Absolute. On the one hand, there were the so-called Transcendentalists or Universalists (exemplified by the composers of the philosophical hymns in the Vedas and by the Vedāntins) who conceived the Absolute to be an impersonal or transpersonal and an abstract cosmogonic principle (*Tad Ekam, Hiraṇyagarbha, Kāla, Skambha, Brahman*). On the other hand, there were the Personalists or Religious Theists who believed that the Supreme Reality, the primal agent of Creation and Destruction, the Cause of all causes, could be adequately conceived only in anthropomorphic terms as a personal Divine Being, possessed of all the constitutive attributes and faculties of mankind (*Puruṣa, Prajāpati, Brahmā, Viṣṇu, Śiva*).[41]

Thus far this paper has been concerned almost entirely with the nontheistic and impersonal conceptions of the cosmogonic agent. We turn now to a brief examination of the conceptions of the agent of death (and of birth) that are formulated in the thought-forms of a personalistic theism. Although a close examination of the ancient Brāhmanical literature will show that over the centuries a number of different divine and semidivine beings have served as candidates for the office of the Agent of Death (notably, Yama, Nirṛti, and in a most benign form, Viṣṇu), a study of the late Brāhmanical and the epic literature will demonstrate that Rudra-Śiva, more than any other divinity, became identified prototypically as the divine personification of the forces of decay. Therefore, after discussing briefly a few examples of the Lord of Death in the Vedic literature, we will examine the testimonies of Hindu sages concerning Śiva's assumption of this role in the *Mahābhārata* through his manifestations (*mūrtis*) as *Kāla*, *Mahākāla*, and *Bhairava*.

In Vedic literature, it is the semidivine figure of Yama, the lord of the blessed dead, who stands out from the company of the other deities as the master of the souls of the deceased. Though not a god in the strict sense, he is addressed as a semidivine king (*RV* IX. 113. 8) who exercises sovereign rule over the deceased (*yamárājñaḥ*: X 16. 9). Death is the path of Yama (I. 38. 5) and at one point Yama himself is identified unequivocally with death (I. 165. 4). His close relationship with Varuṇa (X. 97. 16) is suggested by the mention of a foot-binder (*paḍbīśa*) which he employs in harnessing the souls of the deceased before transporting them into the world beyond. Varuṇa, who in an early strata of the *Rig Veda* is the sovereign ruler over the entire universe (I. 23. 5) and the superintendent of the cosmic order (*ṛtasya gopa*), is throughout the Vedas regarded as the omniscient and omipotent embodiment of time, the divinity who determines the destinies of all the creatures and of the world itself. Again, in the *Bhagavad Gītā*, Kṛṣṇa appears in resplendent glory as the Lord of the Universe and proclaims to his prodigy, Arjuna, "I am non-death (*amṛta*) and I am death (*mṛta*), both Being and non-Being am I, O Arjuna."[42] And, again, he says "*Kāla* am I, wreaker of the world's destruction, once matured—resolved (am I) to devour the worlds."[43]

However, in the final analysis, it is Rudra-Śiva more than any other deity who assumes the role of the agent of death and the lord of the souls of the deceased in the *Mahābhārata* (excluding the *Bhagavad Gītā*) and the purāṇas. In the context of the doctrine of the triadic godhead (*trimūrti*, Brahmā, Viṣṇu, Śiva) Śiva consistently undertakes the role of world-annihilator (*lokāntaka*). In the course of instructing Yudhiṣṭhira in the art of praising Mahādeva, Vāsudeva (i.e., Viṣṇu) declares:

> The Brāhmaṇas conversant with the Vedas declare that that god possesses two forms (*rūpās*). One of these is terrible (*ugra*, *ghora*) and the other is mild (*saumya*) and benevolent (*sadāśiva*). . . . By means of the mild and benevolent form he engages in the practice of the *brahmacarya* vow. With the other form that is extremely terrible he is engaged in all phases of world destruction.[44]

In the epics and purāṇas, Śiva combines within his person all the polar elements in the universe. He is, on the one hand, the practitioner of austere asceticism (*tapasvin*, *mahāyogin*) and, on the other hand, the fearless leader of divine troops (*gaṇapati*) and killer of demons.[45] As the archetypal ascetic, he employs his ascetic energies (*tejas, tapas*) as a means of obliterating the demonic powers which threaten the maintenance of the world order. At the end of a cosmic aeon, it is Śiva, again, who annihilates the universe by the projection of those same energies in the form of a universal conflagration.

Bhīṣma, the elderly and wise preceptor of the Kauravas, invokes Śiva as the absolute embodiment of the three phases of the natural cycle:

> Thou art He that has created from thy right side the Grandfather Brahmā, the Creator of all things. Thou hast created Viṣṇu from thy left side for protecting the Created Order. As omnipotent Lord, thou hast created Rudra at the end of the Yuga and at the time of the Great Dissolution (*mahāpralaya*). Assuming the form of *kāla* of stupendous might, Rudra sprang from thy body to destroy all creatures, both mobile and immobile, as the terrible cloud *saṁvartaka* of all-engulfing fire. Verily, when the (appointed) time (*kāla*) approaches for the dissolution of the cosmos, Rudra stands to swallow up the universe.[46]

When employed in his proper role as the third member of the divine triad, Rudra appears as the one who "burns and oppresses, is sharp and fierce, is endowed with great celestial energy and is engaged in gorging on flesh, blood and marrow, [therefore] he is addressed as Rudra."[47] He is "the death which resides in the bodies of all creatures."[48] Wrath, fear, diseases and death (*krodha, bhaya, rogas, mṛtyu*) are said to be his offspring.[49] He resides within the *saṁvartaka* wave which engulfs the cosmos at the end of the World Age, for it is Rudra's mouth that "roars and burns the waters of the sea in the form of a huge mare's head."[50] Again, he appears at the end of each cosmic era in the form of an awful cloud, with a hundred thousand tongues of fire employed in the destruction of all creation.[51] He is said to be the only being who endures during the long night which follows the universal dissolution.[52] In consequence of his identification with lust (*lobha*), wrath (*krodha*), and cupidity (*kāma*) and with other diverse evils which drag men to hell, Śiva is the presiding deity during the fourth or Kali Age.[53]

He is invoked as "the astrologer of the gods" inasmuch as he directs his attention toward the motion of the Wheel of Time (*kālacakra*) which records the succession of rebirths (*saṁsāra*) and is made up of the luminaries of the firmament.[54] As the Great Yogin and the Lord of Time who deceives Time by transcending its irresistible influences,[55] Rudra is said to be the "maker of the year, the months and the seasons." It is he "who sets the Wheel of Time revolving by assuming the form of the Sun and nine planets."[56] Therefore, the one who initiates the revolution of the Wheel of Time and the one who halts the progression of Time is one and the same agent of cosmic activity.

According to the scheme of epic mythology, Rudra-Śiva, in his fierce and destructive aspects, appears to be related to Time as a cosmogonic principle at two levels of being. First, He is *kāla*,[57] the embodiment of mundane temporality, the Wheel of Time, which projects into being the myriad of ever-reincarnating souls which constitute the moral world of *dharma*. Second, he is, in essence, *Mahākāla*,

Great Time as eternity or timelessness. In the form of *Mahākāla*, he both establishes and dissolves the boundaries of the finite time of human and cosmic life—hence his name, "the destroyer of time" (*kālasaṁhāra*). As the scorching fire of eternal wisdom, he liberates men from the chains of finitude, consumes the karmic residue of their ignorance, and transports them beyond the cycle of birth, existence, and death and into the boundless realm of Eternal Bliss. Tāṇḍi, a famous devotee of Śiva, in the course of singing praises to Śiva's majesty, says of this god, "Thou art death (*mṛtyu*), thou art the Lord of the dead (*yama*), thou art fire as consumer of oblations (*hutāśana*), thou art time (*kāla*) and thou art endless time (*mahākāla*)."[58]

Thus Rudra-Śiva is a multifarious kaleidoscopic deity who is at once fierce and calm, malevolent and benevolent, erotic and austere, kinetic and inert, a deity who commingles within his person all the opposites in the universe. He is the divine embodiment of the entire world process, expressed in the perpetual fluctuation of creation and destruction. As the embodiment of time, he symbolizes the forces of disintegration and death, just as in the form of the Lord of ascetics (*mahāyogin*), with phallus always erect, he represents the powers of regeneration and reintegration. Śiva is the source of all the contraries, including good and evil. Those persons who bring this truth to full realization within the depths of their being and live according to its dictates will overcome death and come into possession of immortality.

The Means of Triumphing over Death

The mythic and didactic orations in the *Mahābhārata*, which are delivered in response to questions concerning the origin, nature, and purpose of Death, seem to have developed around two different philosophical doctrines: death is the inescapable destiny of every living creature and cannot be avoided by any means whatsoever; and death is not invincible and can be overcome by various means which, theoretically, are available to all men. Although the sacred literature provides little or no evidence that the question of human mortality and the possibilities of achieving immortality were debated by sagely teachers and dialecticians in a public forum during the epic period, it stands to reason that the question of death and the means available to human beings for dealing with it in a meaningful way would have ignited the interest and imagination of the great thinkers of the time and would have provided the basis of philosophical disputations which doubtlessly occurred in hermitages, religious schools, and royal courts. It seems probable (though not demonstrable on the basis of the texts which we have at hand) that these two assertions about death would have served as the extreme philosophical positions between which the participants in any disputation would have defined their positions. If this claim is true, then we must hold the two assertions about death together in a dialectical tension in order to derive a true picture of the intellectual struggle over the question of death which transpired in the ancient tradition.

We now return to the question which, no doubt, occupied a central place in the thinking of the epic sages: What is the extent of the rule of death over the creature realm? On what basis, if any, can mankind hope to find an antidote or antidotes to death? And, finally, what is the nature of such antidotes, provided they do exist?

On the one hand, the texts assert that "Death removes every living creature—Devas, Dānavas and Gandharvas—without exception."[59] Death is the gateway through which every living thing must pass. Even the entire universe is passing away and, in time, will dissolve completely. But the Hindu belief in the transmigration of souls provides man with a word of encouragement, even as he confronts the certainty of death in the midst of life. Kṛṣṇa counsels his ever-attentive student, Arjuna, "And even if you think it [the embodied self] is continually [re-]born and constantly [re-]dies, even so you grieve for it in vain. *For death is a certainty for him who has been born and birth is a certainty for him who has died. Therefore, for what is unavoidable, thou shouldest not grieve.*"[60] Birth and death follow one another as the tracks follow a moving wagon. The sagely Vyāsa, compiler of the *Mahābhārata*, confirms the inescapability of death by reciting the story of the sixteen virtuous kings who, though they performed sacrifices, gave gifts to Brahmans, and ruled according to *dharma*, in the end "fell prey to death."[61]

On the other hand, the myths assert the contrary belief, that death is not the inescapable destiny of all beings and that man has been provided with various means of breaking its hold. Even though men cannot hope realistically to avoid the actual event of death (although there are instances in the epics and purāṇas where persons of extraordinary moral or spiritual powers have escaped death altogether), they can escape the sentence of "death in life" (i.e., living in continual fear of death) by reciting or listening to stories about the origin of death and its purpose within the cosmic scheme. The sages assure their listeners that those who listen with pure and receptive minds to such salutary tales will acquire a knowledge of the means of "living a good life" and "dying a good death." As Vyāsa declares to Yudhiṣṭhira, "I will relate to you the priceless story of the origin of death. Having heard it, you will be freed from grief and the grip of the chains of attachment. It is a powerful story which extends the duration of life, destroys grief and promotes general welfare. It is an efficacious story, capable of defeating multitudes of enemies; of all things, it is, by far, the most salutary. Indeed, it is equal [in efficacy] to the study of the Vedas."[62] (Take note of the fact that in this statement Vyāsa promises not immortality but an extension of the term of life.)

In Vedic literature,[63] the somewhat modest claim is made that a person can expect to survive and flourish for the duration of a full lifetime by acquiring mystical knowledge of the High God and by performing faithfully all the injunctions of Holy Law (*dharma-śāstra*). In the later literature, the sages make the more ambitious promise that he who performs auspicious deeds (*puṇya karma*) and the efficacious rites of sacrifice can hope to escape an inauspicious death by traversing the Way of the Ancestors (*pitṛyāna*) and returning to earth again in a higher state of existence.[64] On the other hand, those who, while still in this world, purify their minds and bodies through concentration (*dhyāna*) and the perfection of spiritual knowledge (*prajña*, *jñāna*) can expect to travel the Way of the Gods (*devayāna*) to the world of Brahman, "from which there is no coming back."[65] Even the gods themselves must perform sacrifices and practice asceticism in order to free themselves from the clutches of death.[66]

According to the *Bhagavad Gītā*,[67] those persons are freed from death who have relinquished (*tyakta*) all desire and all activity arising from desire by "finding the Self within the self" and "being satisfied with the Self alone."[68] That person who destroys the impulse to perpetuate his lifetime in the mundane world of time and space, who renounces attachment to the world "which is Death itself," and fixes his mind only upon God can escape the vicious cycle of coming-to-be (*pravṛtti-bhāva*) and passing-away (*nivṛtti-abhāva*).[69]

Many other myths in the *Mahābhārata* and in various purāṇas support the claim that men in every world-age (including the *Kali* Age) possess the means to defeat death and to gain immortality. In the myth of "The Man Who Overcame Death"[70] both Sudarśana and his wife, Oghavatī, pass the test of moral fortitude to which Yama had put Oghavatī by trying to seduce her in the guise of an uninvited guest. They demonstrate their righteousness by performing what one western scholar has called "The Act of Truth,"[71] the "singleness with which the performer or some other person used by the performer as a dynamic reference, fulfills his personal duty (*dharma*)." Again, according to the popular legend of Sāvitrī, the heroine ultimately persuades Yama, the God of Death, to release her husband from the clutches of death, by virtue of the steadfastness of her moral resolution, the strength of her asceticism, and the depth of her wisdom.[72] And the young student Naciketas remains so persistent in his determination to learn the profound mysteries of the realm of death that Yama finally consents to grant him the powers of mystical insight.[73]

In a number of instances, a person is liberated from the terrifying and inescapable noose of Yama, the Lord of the Dead, by an unswerving devotion to God. The most noteworthy examples are Mārkaṇḍeya,[74] a devotee of Śiva, who escaped Yama by clinging tenaciously to the *liṅgam*, and Prahlāda,[75] a devotee of Viṣṇu, who withstood the onslaughts of temptation and ridicule from his father and antagonist, Hiraṇyakaśipu, and even Yama himself, by remaining steadfastly devoted to Viṣṇu. Too numerous to mention are the instances of Yogis in the epics and purāṇas who nullify the power of Yama (and, in some instances, of Śiva himself), by means of the singleminded cultivation of self-denial, fasting, and austere penances. By means of *tapas*, Dhruva (the Pole Star) is said to have set his foot upon Yama's head and to have cursed him to suffer the fate of a Śūdra for one hundred years.[76] Even the ferocious demon Rāvaṇa, the embodiment of all the evil forces in the universe, defeated the God of Death by means of his powerful austerities (*tapas*).[77]

Conclusion

In this rapid survey of the Vedic and post-Vedic literature one central point stands out. In at least two of the myths treated here (the Prajāpati myth and the Brahmā myth), the sages reject without serious consideration the idea that the world could continue to function effectively without the removal of the old and worn-out creatures by the divine representative of death. Death is recognized by all the sages without exception to be a legitimate and indispensable component of the cosmic scheme and a rightful recipient of a proper share in the world's bounty.[78] At numerous points in the literature, there appear subtle hints that death and evil (or sin = *pāpaṁ*) may be causally related in the sense that the advent of one may have given rise to the other.[79] But in the final analysis, all the myths are in agreement that without the entry and continued operation of death in withdrawing from the temporal world those creatures whose terms of life have matured, and thereby providing living space for new beings, the universe soon would suffocate under the weight of its own superfluous progeny. In order to promote his proper functioning, death is provided with the physical aspect of mankind as his nourishment. With these facts in mind, the Hindu texts advocate that man view death as an occasion that calls for celebration, rather than mourning. The person of perfect wisdom sees death as being both a necessity and a gift.

The existence of death in the finite world therefore is recognized by all Hindu sages (theists and nontheists alike) as an integral phase of the natural process. The nontheists tend to view death as an inescapable necessity and identify it with the machinations of time, destiny, or human action, without reference to any transcendental Being. The theists, on the other hand, identify the event of death, regardless of its immediate cause, as the expression of the omniscient will of a gracious deity, who grants death as a boon to the world for the orderly progression of the parade of creatures. Furthermore, the mythologies of both Viṣṇu and Śiva are informed by a deep conviction that the birth and death of living beings are only the spontaneous manifestations of the Deity's "divine play" (*deva-līlā*). Viewing the entire drama of the cosmic process *sub specie aeternatatis*, one discovers that creation and destruction, at all levels of the universe, are nothing more than two phases of a divine game that is being carried out on a playing field of cosmic proportions.

When we view the Vedic and epic myths concerning death at a glance, we discover that birth and death are invested with an ambivalent (i.e., relative or conditional) value. Indeed, the most characteristic Hindu view of life and death *is* the relative view. Hindu mythographers envision life and death not so much as distinct ontological entities, eternally separated from each other in a state of polar opposition, but rather as complementary and interpenetrative phases of one and the same natural process. Hence, in the terminology of classical Yoga, that person whose consciousness has become stabilized by the insight that it is the very nature of things to come-to-be and pass-away, will cease to find any occasion either for rejoicing over birth or grieving over death.

> For death is a certainty for him who has been born,
> and birth is a certainty for him who has died.
> Therefore, for what is unavoidable thou shouldst not grieve.[80]

The mythic and didactic materials in the ancient Indian literature which we discussed here seem to suggest that although few if any persons can hope to escape the sentence of death, there are numerous means accessible to all human beings for transcending and ultimately triumphing over the experience of grief which is provoked by the loss of a kinsman or a comrade or by the anticipation of one's own death. The sense of a personal loss and the attendant feelings of physical, mental, moral, and spiritual impotence which inevitably follow in the wake of such an experience can be dissolved and replaced by a commitment to a position of resignation to, if not an affirmative acceptance of, the inevitability of death for all creatures. In a word, by achieving the level of consciousness which reveals death to be both a cosmic necessity and a divine gift, a person may, with steady and tranquil mind, elude the iron grip of death and pass through the "narrow gate" into immortality.

Notes

Abbreviations

Ait. Brh.	*Aitareya Brāhmaṇa*
AV	*Atharva Veda*
BĀU	*Bṛhadāraṇyaka Upaniṣad*
BG	*Bhagavad Gītā*
Bhāg. Pur.	*Bhāgavata Purāṇa (also known as Śrīmad-Bhāgavatam)*
Chānd. Upan.	*Chāndogya Upaniṣad*
Jaim. Brh.	*Jaiminīya Brāhmaṇa*
Kauṣ. Upan.	*Kauṣītaki Upaniṣad*
Mait. Saṁh.	*Maitrāyanī Saṁhitā*
Manu	The Laws of Manu (= *Manu Smṛti*)
Mat. Pur.	*Matsya Purāṇa*
MBh.	The *Mahābhārata*
Rām.	The *Rāmāyaṇa*
RV	*Rig Veda Saṁhitā*
Śat. Brh.	*Śatapatha Brāhmaṇa*
Śvet. Upan.	*Śvetāśvatara Upaniṣad*
Tait. Brh.	*Taittirīya Brāhmaṇa*
Tait. Upan.	*Taittirīya Upaniṣad*
Tāṇḍ. Brh.	*Tāṇḍya Brāhmaṇa*

1. *Śat. Brh.* X 4.3.1–10. Consult vol. 43 of the *Sacred Books of the East* (F. Max Müller, General Editor, Oxford: Clarendon Press, 1879–) for this text. Cf. *Śat. Brh.* X 1.3.1–7; *Mait. Saṁh.* I 6.2; *Tait. Brh.* I 1.10.1.

2. *Śrīmad-Mahābhārata*, critically edited by V.S. Sukthankar et al. (18 vols., Poona: Bhandarkar Oriental Research Institute, 1933–66), I 189.1–9 in which Prajāpati, identified here with the Brahman as the Guardian of the universe, is the being to whom the celestials resort for shelter when Yama, the Lord of the Dead, ceases to carry out his appointed task of bringing a certain number of creatures to death as a means of protecting the universe from becoming overcrowded by an excess of creatures.

3. Cf. *Tait. Upan.* III 7–10 wherein a relation of mutual support is established between the world and the Brahman, with each nourishing the other. Knowledge of this fact allows one to be eaten by Brahman "without being consumed."

4. *Tāṇḍ. Brh.* VI 7. 19; VIII 8. 14; *Śat. Brh.* II 5.1.3.

5. See *BĀU.* I 2.1ff. where "Hunger" is identified with death and is said to have been the primal, pre-cosmogonic principle from which the entire world system developed.

6. *Tāṇḍ. Brh.* XXI 2.1; *Tait. Saṁh.* II 4.4 [1].

7. The *Brāhmaṇas* are ritualistic manuals containing instructions to the officiating priests on the proper mode of performing various sacrifices, together with elaborate interpretations of the esoteric meanings of the symbolic images, ideas, and actions which constitute the various rituals. Chronologically, the *Brāhmaṇas* stand between the collections of Vedic hymns (ca. 1200–1000 B.C.) and the early *Upaniṣads* (ca. 800–700 B.C.).

8. In addition to conveying the sense of end, limit, or conclusion in a chronological frame, the Sanskrit term *anta* also implies an axiological consummation, i.e., the point at which something reaches maturity, completion, or fulfilment. Cf. the term Vedānta (= *Veda-anta*) designates the philosophy which represents both the chronological termination and the spiritual perfection of the Vedic tradition. Compare also the Greek term, *telos*, which bears this same double meaning. See P. Tillich, *The Protestant Era* (Chicago: University of Chicago Press, 1957), p. 28.

9. *Ait. Brh.* VII 8.2; *Tait. Brh.* II 1.2.1.

10. *Tāṇḍ. Brh.* VII 2.1.

11. *RV* X 90; *Śat. Brh.* XI 1.8.5.

12. *Śat. Brh.* X 2.2.1.

13. See Franklin Edgerton's article, "The Fountain of Youth," *Journal of the American Oriental Society* 26, no. 1, (1905): 1–67, in which the author argues that in Hindu thought, *amṛta* (immortality) is conceived not as an endless extension of ordinary human life in a supraterrestrial realm but as a long and satisfying existence in this world, filled with health, wealth, numerous progeny and general well-being.

14. *MBh.* [Crit. Ed.] XII. 248.12–27; 249.1–22; 250.1–42. Alternate version: VII, App. I, no. 8, 11.35–249. The textual version of this myth is so lengthy and verbose that I have presented a brief paraphrase.

15. The same situation appears in slightly different form in the *Bhāg. Pur.* (III 12.1–20) where the cosmos at first is threatened with extinction when the "mind-born" sons of Brahmā persist in their performance of the vows of asceticism in lieu of procreating the beings needed to promote the life-process. Afterward, the cosmos is again threatened by the production of an excessive number of Rudras, who, as sons and projections of Rudra (who himself was an offspring of Brahmā's wrath) "with their blazing glances consume the four directions together with me [i.e., Brahmā]."

16. I 8.9 ("Mṛtyukanyakām"), ed. Hara Prasad Sastri, 4 vols. (Poona: Ānandāśrama Sanskrit Series, no. 102, 1935).

17. The term *vṛddha*, which appears in the alternate version in the *Droṇaparvan* can mean either "increased in numbers" or "advanced in years."

18. Consult M. Bloomfield, *The Religion of the Veda* (New York: Putnam, 1908), p. 259 for a summary statement concerning the Hindu doctrine of *karma*.

19. *BĀU* III 2.13. *puṇyo vai puṇyena karmaṇā bhavati pāpaḥ pāpeneti.* Cf. *BĀU* IV 4.5, and *Manu* 11.4.

20. *MBh.* XIII 1.10–73 [Crit. Ed.] This legend serves a crucial function in the epic by providing a moral justification for the use of warfare in establishing and maintaining the Eternal Law (*sanātana-dharma*). Warfare is justified by appealing to the argument that death, under all circumstances (including death in the midst of battle), is the direct result of the *karma* of each person during a previous lifetime.

21. *MBh.* XIII 1.64: *akarodyadayaṁ karma tanno' rjunaka codakam/ praṇāśaheturnānyo'* a *asya vadhyate' yaṁ svakarmaṇā//.*

22. Consult the lengthy oration which Draupadī delivers to Yudhiṣṭhira during the exile in the forest concerning the essential nature of *karma*: *MBh.* III 33.1–58.

23. *MBh.* XIII 148–50. Cf. *AV* XIX 53, 54 in which *kāla* is said to be the witness and judge of all human actions.

24. The apparent confusion in this story between *karma* and *kāla* as the direct cause of death arises from the tendency of Hindu mythographers to identify the law of time and human action and to view them as expressing a single universal law.

25. *MBh.* XII 32.20–21: *athāpi loke karmāṇi samāvartanta bhārata/ śubhāśubhaphalaṁ ceme prāpnu vanīti me matiḥ// evaṁ satyaṁ śubhādeśam karmaṇastatphalaṁ dhruvam/ tyaj tad rājaśārdūla maivaṁ śoke manaḥ kṛthāḥ//.*

26. See N.N. Bhattacharyya, *History of Indian Cosmogonical Ideas* (New Delhi: Munshiram Manoharlal, 1971), esp. chap. 10.

27. Consult A.B. Keith, *Religion and Philosophy of the Veda and the Upanishads*, vols. 31–32 of HOS (Cambridge, Mass.: Harvard University Press, 1925), p. 444; A.A. Macdonell, *Vedic Mythology* (Strassburg: Trübner, 1897), p. 120. Cf. *MBh*. I 1.187–91; 3.147–49; 47.15–29; 59.32–33 for examples of this use of *kala* in epic literature. It is interesting to note in this connection that the *Kālāmukhas* (the face of Time), an extreme sect of the *Kāpālikas*, themselves a subsect of the *Paśupata-Śaivas*, were so called because of their belief that, for the attainment of heaven, one must eat food from a skull, besmear the body with ashes of a corpse, consume the ashes and perform a variety of ascetic vows. See G.S. Ghurye, *Indian Sadhus*, 2d ed. (Bombay: Popular Book Depot, 1964), p. 48ff., and Haripada Chakraborti, *Asceticism in Ancient India* (Calcutta: Punthi Pustak, 1973), pp. 165–66.

28. Cf. *Svet. Upan.* where *kāla* is included in a list of cosmogonic powers (along with nature, necessity, chance, matter, and spirit) as representing various rival theories of causation. The composer of the text concludes that *kāla*, as temporal process, is subservient to the Brahman, here identified with Rudra.

29. *Jaim. Brh.* 1.12.

30. *MBh*. XIII 43.10; 148.40; 1.187–90. For epic views of *kāla*, consult B. Barua, *A History of Pre-Buddhistic Indian Philosophy* (Delhi: Motilal Banarsidass, 1970), pp. 198ff, (reprint of 1921 ed.).

31. *MBh*. I. 1.188: *kālaḥ pacati bhūtāni kālaḥ saṁharati prajāḥ.*

32. MBh. XII 231.25. Cf. XII 244.2 where *kāla* is identified as the "sixth" (phenomenon) which governs and organizes the five elements. According to the so-called *Mokṣadharma*, "*kāla* matures all things by itself within itself. But none of the creatures here [in this world] knows that in which *kāla* is matured." In this same text (267.3–10) it is said that *kāla* procreates the universe from the five gross elements.

33. *AV* XI 53, 54. Cf. Isadore Scheftelowitz, *Die zeit als schiksalsgottheit in der indischen und iranischen religion (Kāla und Zurvan)*, Beiträge zur indischen sprachwissenschaft und religiosgeschichte, vol. 4 (Stuttgart: Kohlhammer, 1929), pp. 54ff. for a discussion of the Hindu doctrine of *kāla* and the Iranian concept of *zurvan*.

34. *MBh*. XII 32.10, 11.

35. The editors of the Crit. Ed. containing the legends of Mṛtyu (*Adhyāyas* 52–54 of the *Droṇa-parvan*, Bomb. Ed.) judged this section to be a later addition and placed it in Appendix 1. 8 (240–43).

36. *MBh*. I 1.186–90.

37. *MBh*. IX 62.77 (Southern Ed.); 61.68 (Bombay Ed.): *evaṁ vidhātrā vihitam . . . daivaṁ puruṣakareṇa na śakyam ativartitum . . . kṛtantam anyathā kartuṁ ne'cchet so'yam//*. Cited in E.W. Hopkins, *Epic Mythology* (Strassburg: Trübner, 1915), p. 75. Cf. *MBh*. II 56.17; 57.4.

38. *MBh*. V 159.14ff.

39. *MBh*. V 39.1; *anīśvaraḥ . . . Dhātrā tu diṣṭasya vase kṛto'yam.*

40. *MBh*. XIII 43.4ff.

41. The distinctions between these two conceptions of the Absolute came into sharp relief in the Advaita-Vedānta of Śrī-Śaṅkarācārya (ca. eighth or ninth century A.D.) and the Vaśiṣṭha-Advaita-Vedānta of Śrī-Rāmānujācārya (ca. twelfth century A.D.). Whereas Śaṅkara differentiated between God characterized by attributes (*saguṇa-Brahman*) and the Eternal Absolute devoid of attributes (*nirguṇa-Brahman*), Rāmānuja identified the Eternal Absolute as Brahman qualified by attributes (Brahman-Śrī-Nārāyaṇa-Viṣṇu) and rejected the notion of a traitless Absolute altogether.

42. *MBh*. IX 18–19.

43. *MBh*. XI 32.

44. *MBh*. XIII 145.3–6.

45. Among Śiva's more famous acts of destruction are the following: Dakṣa's horse-sacrifice, the demons Balāsura and Andhaka; Kāma, the god of passion and lust; the triple fortress of the Asuras; the eyes of Bhaga; the teeth of Pūṣan; the arms of Sūrya and various animal-demons—the tiger (*vyaghra*), elephant (*gaja*), and buffalo (*mahiṣa*); *māyā*; and, finally, the universe itself.

46. *MBh*. XIII 14.182–84.

47. *MBh*. XIII 145.7–10.

48. *MBh*. XIII 145.20.

49. *MBh*. XIII 14.413.

50. *MBh*. XIII 141.20.

51. *MBh.* XIII 17.79.

52. *MBh.* XIII 17.146.

53. *MBh.* XIII 17.146.

54. *MBh.* v. 59.

55. *MBh.* v. 48.

56. Consult *MBh.* XIII 17.38, where Śiva is to be the ruler over the nine planets.

57. The persistence of the practice of identifying *kāla* (as time or death) with Rudra-Śiva is clearly evidenced by the exegesis of the term *kāla*, both in its denominative and its derivative forms (*kālāya namaḥ*, "Glory be to Kāla") in the *Paśupata Sūtram*, the primary sacred text of the ancient school of Śaivism called *Paśupatas* or *Lakuliśas*. In 11.23 it is said: "Here this 'Kāla' is equivalent to Maheśvara [i.e., Rudra-Śiva]. Why? Because ... He dissolves the states of existence (*kālas*) belonging to individual beings by separating them from bodies, senses and objects, etc., known as *kāla*. So it is said, 'Rudra is remembered as *Kāla* because He dissolves this (entire) world containing both the moveables and immoveables from Brahmā to a bark.'" Haripada Chakraborti, *Paśupata Sūtram with Pañchārtha-Bhāṣya of Kauṇḍinya* (Calcutta: Academic Publishers, 1970), p. 117.

58. *MBh.* XIII 14.

59. *MBh.* VII 52.15.

60. *BG* II 27; emphasis added.

61. *MBh.* VII 55–70.

62. *MBh.* VII 52.23–24 (P. C. Roy) in Crit. Ed., App. I, no. 8 (42–44).

63. See the section of this paper dealing with the myth of Prajāpati as death. Cf. *Śat. Brh.* X 4.3.1–10.

64. *RV* X 2.7; X 88.15; *AV* XV 12.5–6.

65. Consult *Chānd. Upan.* V 10.1–6; *BĀU* VI 2.15ff.; *Kauṣ. Upan.* I 1.2–3; *BG* VIII 23.

66. *Śat. Brh.* XI 4.3.20; *Tait. Brh.* III 11.8.5ff.

67. II 16, 57, 70.

68. *BG* II 17.

69. *BG* II 16.

70. *MBh.* XIII 2.34ff. [Crit. Ed.].

71. W.N. Brown, "The Basis for the Hindu Act of Truth," *Review of Religion* 5 (1940): 36–45.

72. *Mat. Pur.*, chaps. 211–14.

73. *Kaṭha Upan.* I 1.11.25. *MBh.* XIII 71–72, 84.

74. Located in the *Skanda Purāṇa*.

75. *Viṣṇu Pur.* I 17–20; Cf. *MBh.* XII 160.26–28; 124.19–63 *Devībhāgavata* IV 10.33–40; 15.36–71; *Bhāg. Pur.* VII 1–10.

76. *Bhāg. Pur.* VI 3.2; IV 12.30; I 14.15.

77. *Rām.* III 44.28. Cf. *Rām.* V 78.12–13; VI 35.21 for brief descriptions of the battle between Rāvaṇa and Yama, the God of Death.

78. Compare the demand for a rightful share on the occasion of Dakṣa's sacrifice by Rudra-Śiva after Dakṣa, his father-in-law, had refused Śiva an invitation to the ritual because of the "demoniac" features of his style of life, appearance, and behavior: *MBh.* VII 173.42ff.; Xa 17f.; XII App. I. 28 [Crit. Ed.].

79. *MBh.* I 189.1–9; XII 248–50.

80. *BG* II. 27.

"The Death That Conquers Death": Dying to the World in Medieval Hinduism

DAVID R. KINSLEY

In a variety of ways and contexts the Hindu tradition affirms that to meditate on death is efficacious in the religious quest for salvation. In the devotional writings and hymns of different Hindu saints from varying *sampradāyas* (sects), in cultic and ritual settings, such as those of the Pāśupatas, Kāpālikas, and some aspects of Tantrism, and in certain mythological figures, the Hindu religious tradition declares that to die to the world while living is to win spiritual rebirth.

Dying to the World in Nonritual Settings

The Marathi saints Nāmadeva (1270–1350) and Tukārāma (1598–1650), devotees of Viṭṭhala (or Vitobhā), Viṣṇu, are typical *bhaktas* (devotees). They declare that spiritual destiny lies in devoting the entire life, in love and adoration, to God. Redemption consists in serving and participating in the Godhead, in living in or vis-à-vis the fundamental reality of the Divine Presence. To live in God implies a surrender of the self, or the ego, a giving up or letting go of the world of material well-being, a dying to the world of "me" and "mine." Tukārāma puts the matter succinctly: "Sainthood can be acquired, says Tukā, only at the cost of life. He who is not prepared to sacrifice his life, should not brag of spirituality."[1] To think about death is to meditate particularly on one's own inevitable decay and passing away and thus to render oneself open to immortality in the transcendent and eternal presence of the Godhead. To meditate on one's own death is to see oneself from the perspective of eternity as an eternal lover of God. It exhausts the attachment to friends, family, and self and forces one to acknowledge his final dependence on God.

> When I consider that, at the end of my life, I shall have to depart alone; when I think that my mother who bore me in her womb for nine months will cruelly stand aside; when I find the futility of the affection which sisters and brothers bear towards me; when I find that children and wife shall stay away when my body will be burning upon the funeral pile; when I contemplate how friends and relatives shall leave me in the cemetery and walk away; I then begin to shed tears; my throat chokes; I find that darkness reigns everywhere; my only resort is Thy feet, says Nāmadeva.[2]

Implicit here is the teaching that it is spiritually efficacious to think about death, a teaching that is explicit elsewhere in Nāmadeva's hymns and in the writings of Tukārāma.

> We should always think of death, says Nāmadeva, in whatever pursuit we might be engaged. As when a thief is being carried to the hanging place, death is approaching him at every step; as when a man is plying his axe at the root of a tree, its life is diminishing every moment, similarly, whatever we may be doing, we must suppose that death is always approaching us.[3]

> Old age comes and tells a tale in the ear that Death will soon pounce on the body. Why should not the mind grow alert at such a message? . . . In no time shall the last scene take place. . . . Think of the family deity, says Tukā, and leave away empty words.[4]

> You see the burning of other people's bodies. Why does it not make you alert? Cry after God without fear, before death has caught hold of you. Death is verily a price which the body has to pay. . . . Why do people vainly seek after various paths? When death comes upon you, it shall not allow you to move an inch.[5]

The devotee is attentive to God: he is "alert" to the inevitable limitations of his physical existence and consequently "alert" to God, in whom there is eternal life.

The saint, finally, is one who has sacrificed himself (or is willing to sacrifice himself), one who has died to the world and has been reborn in God. Tukā says:

> If we want to enjoy God, we should lop off our head from our body, and hold it in our hands. We should set all our belongings on fire, and should not look behind. We should be as bold, says Tukā, as a fly, which falls straight into a flame.[6]

> No room has now been left for sin and merit, or for happiness and misery. . . . *Death has occurred during life* and the distinction between Self and not-Self has disappeared. . . . There is now no room for caste or colour or creed, or for truth and untruth. . . . When the body has been sacrificed to God, says Tukā, all worship has been accomplished.[7]

The "mantra," "to die while living," the admonition to surrender lust for and attachment to the phenomenal world that binds inextricably to a limited existence, is repeated elsewhere. In the hymns of Gorakhnath and the songs of the Bauls of Bengal salvation involves the discovery of an inward freedom, the discovery of an immortal essence, the discovery, in the imagery of the Bauls, of "the man of the heart."

> O Siddha, wander not to other places; within thy body resides the Essence, the Truth. Seek the one who speaks; *die while still alive*, by reversing the process; rise into heaven by natural ease; whereby you will not have to suffer at the hands of Death and you will go across.[8]

> Between the doors
> of birth and death,
> stands yet another door,
> wholly inexplicable.

He who is able
to be born
at the door of death,
is devoted eternally. . . .

Die before dying,
die living.[9]

He who lives with the knowledge of death, who knows his attachments to the world must end in suffering and sorrow, prepares himself to set free the "man of the heart."

Those who are absorbed
by the flavours of feelings,
and are wholly living
with the knowledge of death,
have won their foes—
pride and envy,
lust and anger,
ignorance and greed.[10]

In Gorakhnath and the Bauls, as in yoga generally, spiritual freedom involves "reversing the process" (Gorakhnath) or "walking against the wind" (Haridas Baul). Yogic technique aims at reversing the evolution of *prakṛti*, whose instinctual tendency is to evolve to grosser or heavier forms, to differentiate and particularize itself into concrete forms that obscure the inward freedom of *puruṣa*. The yogi, by means of various techniques, seeks to withdraw his senses from the phenomenal world, thus isolating himself and cutting himself off from participating in prakṛti's wild dance. He dies to the world, as it were, by "going against the stream."[11] To die while living is to be unattached to a world of matter that inexorably leads to physical decay and death, to stand aloof and free whether one acts or does not act.

Those who are dead
and yet fully alive
and know the flavours
and feelings
in loving;
they will cross the river.
Gazing at
the stream of life and death,
they seek integrity.
They have no wish
for happiness at all.
walking against the wind.

They kill lust
with lust
and enter the city of love
unattached.[12]

The devotional songs of Rāmprasād and other Bengali Śāktas also articulate the theme of dying to the world in order to gain spiritual rebirth or freedom. Rāmprasād, in a hymn reminiscent of Nāmadeva's, anticipates his own death and realizes that his only refuge is trust in Kālī.

> Consider this, my Mind, that thou hast none whom thou mayest call thine own. Vain are thy wanderings on the earth. Two days or three, then ends this earthly life; yet all men boast that they are masters here. Time's master, Death, will come and overthrow such masterships. Thy best-beloved, for whom thou art so terribly concerned, will she go with thee? Nay; rather, lest some ill befall the home, she will sprinkle with cowdung the house where thou hast died.
>
> Rāmprasād says: When Death shall seize me by the hair, then, Mind, do thou cry *Kālī*, *Kālī*, and vain will be Death's purposes.[13]

The devotee of the goddess, particularly the devotee of Kālī, surrenders to her by giving up a grasping, clutching hold on the world of "me" and "mine." He dies to himself and in the striking imagery of the following hymn creates within himself a burning ground where Kālī may dance.

> Since thou lovest burning-grounds, I have made my mind a burning-ground, that the Dark Goddess, Dweller amid the dead, may dance there always. Nothing remains in my mind, Mother, save flames of funeral ever burning. Against thy coming, I have scattered ashes everywhere.
>
> Flinging beneath thy Feet him who is Time's Great Period and Conqueror of Death, come, Mother, dancing come, and, though my eyes are shut, I shall see thee.[14]

Dying to the World in Cultic and Ritual Settings

It is perhaps in the context of ritually dying to the world that some of the cultic practices of the Pāśupatas, Kāpālikas, Aghoris, and Tāntrikas should be understood. Pāśupata *sādhana* clearly aims at renunciation of the world. Liberation—union (or communion) with Śiva—demands physical, mental, and emotional renunciation of the world. In the *Pāśupata-sūtra* and Haradatta's *Gaṇakārikā*, Pāśupata sādhana is outlined as progressing through four stages, to the final liberation, which is the fifth stage. These stages are the marked, unmarked, victory, cutting, and cessation. For each stage there is an appropriate place, procedure, and attainment.[15] The appropriate place for sādhana in the cutting stage is the cremation ground (*Pāśupata-sūtra*, V. 30). The intention of this aspect of Pāśupata sādhana seems clear. Before achieving final union with Śiva, all ties to the phenomenal world must be cut, and the most appropriate place to do this is the cremation ground, where attention is constantly directed to the transience of the physical body and the final end of all attachments to the physical world.[16] Surrounded by death in the place of death, those aspects of reality that end in the fires of the cremation ground become distasteful. Further, continual confrontation with the funerals of others leads to the anticipation of one's own death; attachment to the world and the ego is cut and union with Śiva, the conqueror of death, is sought.

Although dwelling in a cremation ground may not have been part of a formal pattern of sādhana for the Kāpālikas and Aghorīs, they are typically pictured as dwelling in cremation grounds. It may be assumed that the intention of living in cremation grounds had for these sects the same (or a similar) intention it had for the Pāśupatas, since both the Kāpālikas and Aghorīs sought through various practices and techniques to renounce the world.[17] The symbolism of death and decay is further reinforced among the Kāpālikas by their attire. Kāpālikas are consistently described as wearing garlands of skulls or bones, covering their bodies with ashes from the cremation ground, and using a skull as a begging bowl.[18]

Cremation grounds are also seen as "auspicious" or appropriate places for sādhana in some aspects of Tantrism. In the *Karpūrādi-stotra* the *sādhaka* is expressly invited to meditate on the image of Kālī in the cremation ground.[19] He is to confront the mistress of death in her favorite haunt and by so doing surrender himself to her all-pervading and redemptive power.[20] Skull altars and seats for meditation in a circle of skulls,[21] typical in Bengal, probably serve to some extent as surrogates for cremation grounds in Tantrism.[22]

The Pāśupatas, Kāpālikas, Aghorīs, and Tantrikas (particularly Vāmācāra Tantrikas), as is well known, are looked on with some suspicion by the Hindu orthodox tradition. In many texts they are considered heterodox—their "odd" behavior is often given as proof—or at least dangerously aberrant.[23] Those practices that suggest a ritualized dying to the world, however, often have precedents in the orthodox tradition itself, and as such should not be taken as insignificant, peripheral oddities vis-à-vis the main currents of Hindu spirituality.

The *āśrama* system affirms the importance in the Hindu tradition of renouncing the world by physical removal and undertaking various ascetic practices aimed at mental and emotional isolation from the social-physical world. In the *vānaprastha* stage ritual suicide is permitted by some authorities. If the forest hermit is sick, cannot perform his duties, feels that death is near, or has the desire to secure release from *saṁsāra*, some authorities say he may undertake the *mahāprasthāna*, the Great Journey, walking to the north without eating or drinking until he dies.[24] The mahāprasthāna, and other forms of ritual suicide, such as drowning oneself at holy places or falling from a cliff, appear to be literal rituals of dying to the world.

The symbolism of dying to the world is also clear in the fourth āśrama, *saṁnyāsa*. The appropriate rituals for entering this stage as given in orthodox texts clearly depict a ritualized initiatory death and rebirth. After giving away all his possessions the saṁnyāsin-to-be performs his own *śrāddhas* (funeral ceremonies).[25] After these rituals are completed he shaves his head, clips his nails, and takes a bath.[26] He stays up all night and the next day he performs several Vedic *gṛhya* rituals, after which he burns all his sacrificial instruments in the sacrificial fire. He is then instructed to "deposit the fire in himself" (a ritual self-sacrifice, perhaps) and bid farewell to his family and relatives with the words, "to me belongs no one nor do I belong to any one."[27] Having ritually died to the world, he should now meditate on the vileness of the human body and the transitory nature of all things,[28] wander naked or with only a single piece of cloth to cover him, live in an uninhabited place or house or in a burial ground, and seek to achieve a state of mind that transcends the pairs of opposites (e.g., *dharma-adharma*, purity-impurity, truth-falsehood).[29] He should, according to the *Saṁnyāsa-upaniṣad* (13), deal with his body "as if it were dead."[30]

The theme of initiatory death, of dying to the world in order to transcend it, is also revealed in texts of a Tantric nature that are not specifically associated with any particular sampradāya or any particular *saṁskāra* or āśrama. Ritual worship as described by the *Kālikā-purāna* includes four stages: preparatory acts, meditation, worship proper, and concluding acts. The aim of these rituals is worship of, by identification with, the divine. In the worship proper the sādhaka had identified himself with the various gods and goddesses and thus worships himself, a typical Tantric theme. In the second stage, meditation, the sādhaka achieves ritual identity with the divine by spiritual death and rebirth. The ritual procedure for accomplishing this deification is as follows: The sādhaka, seated within a *maṇḍala* he has previously drawn (or imagined), forms the *mudrā* of the tortoise (the symbol of the foundation of the cosmos and of ascetic withdrawal) and undertakes *prāṇāyāma* (breath control). He then performs *bhūtaśuddi*, the ritual (mental) destruction of his *jīva* and body, effecting his own death. The sādhaka first imagines his life-principle (jīva) passing out of himself after having been identified with various elements: fire, wind, water, and finally space. As the subtlest of elements, space (*ākāśa*), the life-principle leaves the body through the *brahmarandhra*, the aperture in the crown of the skull. The sādhaka then meditates (or imagines) the destruction of his body (or more properly, his corpse, since he has just "died"). The body passes through desiccation (*soṣaṇa*), burning (*dahaṇa*), removal of the ashes (*bhasmaprotsāda*), and finally the "shower of *amṛta* (nectar)," in which the "old body" is completely washed and made wholly pure. The adept then re-creates the world, which came to an end in the previous ritual of bhūtaśuddhi, and in re-creating it he identifies himself with the entire cosmos—and with those beings or presences that govern, protect, and pervade it —with the words, "This is me" (55.36–37).[31]

Insofar as the maṇḍala serves as the sādhaka's place of ritual dissolution and re-creation, and insofar as his mantras and mudrās effect his own ritual death, the maṇḍala serves as a stylized cremation ground and the sādhaka's ritual words and gestures serve as a symbolic śrāddha ceremony. The adept in these rituals oversees his own death, ritually destroying himself, ceremonially annihilating the old, bound, finite creature, who is less than divine and immortal. Or it is possible to say when the cremation ground is used for sādhana the cremation ground becomes the magic circle in which transcendence of the human condition is effected. In these cases the environment reinforces the intention of the ritual, which is to die to the world, and thus acts as a maṇḍala, a special, auspicious, or magic ground where spiritual victory may be achieved.

The Paradigmatic, Evocative, and Provocative Roles of Śiva and Kālī in Dying to the World

Dying to the world as the gateway to freedom seems to be the paradigmatic role or the evocative and provocative effect of certain strains in the mythology of Śiva and the primary "lesson" to be perceived in the iconography and mythology of Kālī.[32] In these two "presences" the Hindu mythological tradition dramatically affirms the efficacious nature of confronting the void—the dark emptiness that follows Nāmadeva's anticipation of his own death, the chaotic abyss that creeps up on man in his sickness and old age, threatening to engulf him, reducing him to dust and ashes. Śiva and Kālī dramatically and unambiguously force their devotees' attention to the fleeting, painful dimensions of life, inviting those who glimpse them to consider the inevitable destiny of phenomenal reality.

The world seems predictable, stable, and manageable—a place where one can feel "at home" and shape with confidence and security a capsule of happy well-being. The world appears to be a tolerable place if each person upholds his dharma. And there is, to be sure, an appealing warmth to the regulated, protective ideal of the social order as perceived in the history of Indian culture.

Finally, however, this world (only one among countless worlds) will succumb to the cosmic rhythms of Śiva's dance and be consumed in fire. Spun into existence in his dance of creation, it will cease to exist when Śiva's dance takes on a new, frighteningly powerful step and be choreographed out of existence. Śiva's whirling arms and kicking foot, his tousled hair, the ring of fire within which he dances convey, to him who adores the great Dancing God, the ephemeral nature of the world. From the perspective of Śiva's cosmic dance, this world, and the individual biography, are fragile, fleeting, and phantasmagoric.

Śiva himself provides an additional model (or models) for those devotees who see beyond the dazzling display of *māyā*, divine magic, or *līlā*, divine play, that pervades the creation. Isolated in yogic meditation on the summit of Mount Kailasa, withdrawn and cut off from the creative processes, Śiva represents the yogi who "goes against the stream," who dies to the phenomenal world of prakṛti in order to revel in *mahāsukha*, the great happiness of liberation from all finite contingencies. The destroyer of Kāmadeva, the god of sexual desire, Śiva is the paradigm for renunciation of the world and its entanglements in quest of final and complete liberation.[33]

One of Śiva's favorite haunts—the locus of his dance of destruction—is the cremation ground, where he is surrounded by ghosts, goblins, and ghouls. Covered with ashes from the cremation ground, naked or seminaked, garlanded with a necklace of skulls, Śiva provides models for several of the cultic or ritualistic actions already mentioned. And although Śiva appears to be inauspicious and threatening to the ordered, carefully tended garden of "civilized" well-being in the phenomenal world, he represents redemption to his devotees, who know they must die to the world in order to participate in his grace.

Your sport is in burning grounds, O destroyer of Smara;
 Pisācas (who eat the flesh of human beings) are your companions;
ashes from a funeral pyre are ointment for your body;
 and your garland is a string of human skulls—
though your character and your name as well may be wholly inauspicious,
yet, O gift-bestower, to those who call you to mind you
 are the supreme symbol of fortune.[34]

Similar themes are found expressed by Kālī worshipers: to confront, meditate, or dote on the goddess Kālī is to become "alert" to the realities of suffering, decay, and death.[35] By becoming a child of the Black Mother one confronts one's mortal, ephemeral nature and the final destiny of one's body and ego in the fires of the cremation ground. She is typically described in Bhāratcandra Rāy's *Annadā-mangal-kāvya* (eighteenth century) in which she appears with an army of demons and ghouls to rescue Sundar, the hero of the story, who is about to be executed.

> And amidst them all, the goddess—her long and matted hair flowing wildly, she laughed her long and maddened laughter, her third eye scarlet, moving like a disc in her head, her greedy tongue protruding long and loose; she shone with brightness more vertiginous than the sun or fire; she ground her huge hard teeth, her lips drawn back, and streams of blood ran down from her lips' sides; corpses of children swung as earrings from her ears, and on her breast there hung a string of severed heads, with wild and awful faces. Her garland was the intestine of the demon, her girdle one of demons, her ornaments of bones. In lust for blood and flesh the jackals circled round her, and the earth trembled with their howling. She trampled heaven, earth, and hell, crushed them beneath her feet . . . ; her feet were on the breast of prostrate Śiva, lying in meditation-trance with closed eyes.[36]

Kālī is a particularly dramatic and appropriate representation or mythological embodiment of māyā, prakṛti, and *kāla* (time). As such she presents to those who meditate on her a glimpse of the phenomenal world as it really is, fleeting and constantly in flux. Her voluptuous figure, her prominent breasts, heavy hips, and nudity suggest the dark allure of māyā's bewitching magic,[37] but her overall presence and her preference for the cremation ground enable one to tear the veil of māyā and perceive the void that lies behind the phenomenal world. She represents, that is, māyā as seen from the "other shore" of enlightenment or freedom; she represents the "shrew" who lurks behind the seductive mask of the phenomenal world.[38] Essentially māyā is that which prevents seeing the world as it really is; it is the superimposition of a finite, ego-centered understanding onto the world. Māyā is the way things seem: beautiful, bewitching, predictable, eternal. Kālī subverts a māyā-induced feeling of at-homeness in the world by calling attention to the inevitables of life: suffering, decay, and death.

Kālī's disheveled hair, her wild dancing, and her thirst for blood convey the idea of prakṛti. Prakṛti, the phenomenal world that binds man to not-knowing, binds him to physical limitations and traps him in the mesh of saṁsāra. Redemption lies in checking the inherent urge to multiply, diversify, and solidify. Redemption lies in withdrawing from the blind rush of prakṛti, from the whirligig of saṁsāra, by courageously going against the stream. Kālī expresses unambiguously the suffering to which that stream leads.

Kālī also embodies time, dramatically conveying the truth that decay is inherent in all things, that life is fleeting and threatened by disease, old age, and death. As the mistress of time she appropriately lives in the cremation ground, impressing on her devotees the truth that she is all-consuming, sparing nothing and no one, leveling all to ashes in the fires of her dwelling place. Her weird, uncanny laughter mocks those whose orientation in the world is based on the shifting sands of the ego, whose eyes are blinded and ears blocked to the sights and sounds of death and suffering, whose noses are stopped against the stench of decay. Her raised and bloodied cleaver is ever poised to stop the charade of the ego-centered life, and nothing will stay her hand except a recognition of the world as it really is, knowledge and anticipation of one's fragile mortality, and a dying to the phenomenal world.

Kālī's appearance reflects her redemptive power. Her girdle of severed arms suggests the end of grasping, her nudity and unbound hair suggest the freedom of liberation, and the prone Śiva (Mahākāla) beneath her feet suggests the triumph over the binding limitations of the phenomenal self that is bound by decay and time. Her two right hands making the mudrās (gestures) of "fear not" and boon-conferring[39] suggest her devotee's fearlessness before her bloodied sword that now has nothing to cut or kill. For those who drink deeply of the Dark Goddess and who have consequently died to the world there *is* nothing to fear. Having died to the world they are free from the fear of suffering, decay, and death. They have extinguished the fires of the clutching ego and now lie content, beside the prone Śiva, beneath her dancing feet in eternal bliss.

Conclusion

> My Mind, why so fretful, like a motherless child? Coming into the world you sit brooding, shivering in the dread of death. Yet there is a Death that conquers death, the Mightiest Death, which lies beneath the Mother's Feet. You, a serpent, fearing frogs![40]

Man's confrontation with his own mortality, his meditation on and acceptance of his limited, physical existence, prepares him to perceive his destiny and ultimate dependence on, or participation in, an "other," transcendent dimension of reality. To think about death, particularly one's own death, makes one "alert," as Tukārāma says, to the presence of God. To anticipate death, furthermore, is to imaginatively die to the world, to be provoked to discern a world or a way that is not grounded in one's own ego-centered being. And to die to the world is to be reborn within a new possibility, a new frame of reference, a new cosmos, to have transcended the "old man." In the context of bhakti, yoga, Tantrism, saṁnyāsa, or devotion to Śiva or Kālī, dying to the world explodes the habitual world of self, family, and dharma. To imagine one's funeral, to watch the funerals of others, to perform one's own śrāddha, to imaginatively expel one's life force and reduce one's body to ashes, to confront or meditate on, or devote oneself to Śiva or Kālī, to make of oneself a cremation ground for their redemptive dances, to die while living, is to be redeemed from the habitual clinging to self that encapsules man in a world of limited possibilities, all of which inevitably involve pain. It is to undergo, in the words of Rāmprasād, the "Death that conquers death."

These examples teach that for life to be redemptive one must ritually, imaginatively, or subconsciously anticipate one's decay and death. In a sense living itself must, at some point, consciously become a ritual of dying and death in order for new possibilities to be perceived and realized. Traditional Hindu funeral ceremonies (i.e., the śrāddha) do not carry one across the ocean of saṁsāra, they do not provide a means of crossing the turbulent stream of rebirth. To transcend the endless round of saṁsāra, to reach the other shore, one must die *while* living. Anticipating death is the first step in the spiritual quest. It provokes an inward dying to the world, and it (ideally) provokes nausea with the world and a yearning for final liberation.

Notes

1. R.D. Ranade, *Pathway to God in Marathi Literature* (Bombay: Bharatiya Vidya Bhavan, 1961), p. 269, Abhanga 677.
2. Ibid., p. 150, Abhanga 24.
3. Ibid., p. 154, Abhanga 90.
4. Ibid., p. 223, Abhanga 1914.
5. Ibid., p. 223, Abhanga 1006.
6. Ibid., p. 258, Abhanga 3414.
7. Ibid., p. 269, Abhanga 3171; emphasis added.
8. Mohan Singh, *Gorakhnath and Mediaeval Hindu Mysticism* (Lahore: Mercantile Press, 1937), p. 45; emphasis added.
9. Gosāin Gopal in Deben Bhattacharya, trans., *Songs of the Bards of Bengal* (New York: Grove Press, 1969), p. 65; emphasis added. See also p. 64.
10. Haridās, ibid., p. 67.
11. Mircea Eliade, *Yoga: Immortality and Freedom*, trans. Willard R. Trask (New York: Pantheon, 1958), pp. 270ff.
12. Haridās, in Bhattacharya, p. 68.
13. Edward J. Thompson and Arthur Marshman Spencer, trans., *Bengali Religious Lyrics, Śākta* (Calcutta: Association Press, 1923), no. 51, p. 62.
14. Ibid., no. 68, pp. 70–71. See also no. 84, p. 83, and Jadunath Sinha, *Rama Prasada's Devotional Songs: The Cult of Shakti* (Calcutta: Sinha Publishing House, 1966), no. 167, p. 89.
15. Haripada Chakraborti, trans., *Pāśupata Sūtram with Pañchārtha-Bhāṣya of Kauṇḍinya* (Calcutta: Academic Publishers, 1970), p. 186; David N. Lorenzen, *The Kāpālikas and Kālāmukhas: Two Lost Śaivite Sects* (New Delhi: Thomson Press, 1972), pp. 185–86.
16. The importance of meditating on the body and on all attachments to the phenomenal world as transient is made clear in Kauṇḍinya's commentary. In a typical Buddhist analysis he demonstrates how

all attachments to the phenomenal world must result in sorrow, since the entire phenomenal world is constantly in flux and in the process of decaying and dying. See his commentary on *Pāśupata-sūtra* V. 35 (Chakraborti, p. 179).

17. The best work on the Kāpālikas is Lorenzen's *Kāpālikas and Kālāmukhas*. Lorenzen makes it clear that the overall intention of Kāpālika sādhana is renunciation of the world and union with Śiva, despite the general interpretation of them found in the works of their opponents, who caricature the Kāpālikas as primarily (or solely) practitioners of black magic. See also Eliade, pp. 299–301, 419–20. For the Aghorīs see Henry Balfour, "The Life History of an Aghorī Fakir," *Journal of the Anthropological Institute* 26 (1897): 340–54; H.W. Barrow, "On Aghoris and Aghorapanthīs," *Proceedings of the Anthropological Society of Bombay* 3 (1893): 197–251; William Crooke, "Aghori," in Hasting's *Encyclopaedia of Religion and Ethics*; and Eliade, pp. 296–301, 419–20.

18. Lorenzen notes that many aspects of Kāpālika sādhana have their paradigms in Śiva himself and that these practices are performed by Śiva in the context of his expiating the sin of killing a *brāhman* (he decapitated Brahmā's fifth head). In order to cleanse himself of the crime Śiva had to perform the penance of wandering about declaring his sin, carrying Brahmā's skull, covering himself with ashes, and begging his food. The Kāpālikas refer to their ritual practices as the *mahāvrata* (the "great vow"). The sādhana of the mahāvrata, Lorenzen suggests, is efficacious for the Kāpālikas in two ways: by imitating Śiva's actions they become "ritually 'homologised'" with Śiva (p. 80), and by undergoing penance for the greatest crime, killing a brāhman, while being innocent of such a crime, they acquire immense merit (p. 77). Although I do not wish to ignore or underestimate the expiatory, imitative, or meritorious aspects of the Kāpālika sādhana, it does seem clear that these ritual acts and paraphernalia also function as reminders of the transience of all phenomenal things and, in fact, may be understood as a ritual dying to the world (which is perhaps implied in Śiva's expiation itself). Living in the cremation ground, futhermore, does not seem to have been part of the mahāvrata.

19. *Karpūrādi-stotra*, vss. 7, 8, 15, ed. and trans. Arthur Avalon [Sir John Woodroffe], *Hymn to Kali (Karpuradi-stotra)*, 3rd ed. (Madras: Ganesh, 1965), pp. 67, 69, 84. Kṛṣṇānanda Āgamavāgīśa, comp., *Bṛhat Tantrasārah* (Sanskrit), 2 vols. (Calcutta: Basumatī Sāhitya Mandir, 1341 B.S. [1934]), 1:374, the *dhyāna mantra* of Śmaśāna-kālī from *Kālī-tantra*.

20. Arthur Avalon, ed., *Principles of Tantra: The Tantratattva of Śrīyukta Śiva Candra Vidyārṇava Bhattacārya Mahodaya*, 3rd ed. (Madras: Ganesh, 1960), pp. 164, 766. The theme of acquiring "victory" is central in both these passages that speak of sādhana in the cremation ground, and it seems clear that "victory" means victory over fear, particularly the fear of death.

21. For photographs of a skull altar and a Tantric "seat" surrounded by skulls, see Nik Doublas, *Tantra Yoga* (New Delhi: Munshiram Manoharlal, 1971), pp. 23, 95.

22. The significance of skulls in Indian religion clearly goes beyond their association with death and decay. Skulls have magical power; they are the source of strength, intelligence, and power of men and as such are important ritual paraphernalia. See Robert Heine-Geldern, "Kopfjagd und Menschenopfer in Assam und ihre Ausstrahlungen nach Vorderindien," *Mitteilungen der anthropologischen Gesellschaft zu Wien* 67 (1917): 1–65, and Eliade, p. 420.

23. Wendy Doniger O'Flaherty, "The Origin of Heresy in Hindu Mythology," *History of Religions* 10, no. 4 (May 1971): 271–333.

24. Pandurang Vaman Kane, *History of Dharmaśāstra* (Poona: Bhandarkar Oriental Research Institute, 1941), vol. 2, pt. 2, pp. 922–25.

25. According to Kane (ibid., p. 958) the actual performance by the saṁnyāsin-to-be of his own funeral ceremonies as part of his ritual of leaving the world is typical only of medieval texts, for example, *Smṛtyarthāsara*, *Smṛtimuktāphala* (of Vaidyanātha), *Yatidharma-saṁgraha*, and *Nirṇayà-sindhu*.

26. Several of these ritual practices are also performed in the *dīkṣā* ceremony, a clear theme of which is dying to the profane world and being reborn into the sacred. See *Satapatha-brāhmaṅa* III 1.2.1–2.3.30.

27. Kane, vol. 2, pt. 2, pp. 958–59.

28. For example, *Manu-smṛti* VI. 76–77, *Yajñavalkya-smṛti* III. 63–64, and *Viṣṇu-dharmasūtra* 96. 25–42. See Kane, ibid., p. 938.

29. Kane, ibid., p. 939.

30. Ibid., p. 942.

31. K.R. Van Kooij, *Worship of the Goddess According to the Kālikāpurāṇa*, pt. 1, *A Translation with an Introduction and Notes of Chapters 54–69* (Leiden: Brill, 1972), pp. 14–17. This ritual structure, in abbreviated form, is found elsewhere: *Agni-purāṇa* 33.29–40 and *Garuda-purāṇa* 12. In the *Mahānirvāṇa-tantra* (v. 92–104) a ritual very similar to that of the *Kālikā-purāṇa* is aimed at destroying "a black man . . . the embodiment of all sin" (v. 98) (Arthur Avalon, trans., *The Great Liberation* [*Mahānirvāṇa-tantra*], 4th ed. [Madras: Ganesh, 1963], p. 103). In Sakalakirti's *Tattvārthasaradīpika*, a fifteenth-century Jain text, a vivid account of imaginative or meditative death and rebirth is given (R.G. Bhandarkar, *Report on the Search for Sanskrit Manuscripts in the Bombay Presidency for the Year 1883–1884* [Bombay, 1887], pp. 110ff; cited in Eliade, pp. 209–10).

32. Although only Śiva and Kālī will be discussed here, it is clear that other deities may also function in these roles, although not in such unambiguous ways. Although Yama, the Hindu god of the dead, should present a good example of this, he does not, probably because he is also known as the first man in Hindu mythology and thus plays the role of a "culture hero," a guide and protector of the dead. He may be described as fearful, but not as consistently as Kālī, for example. In Buddhist Tantrism his fearful presence is much less ambiguous. This may be because his role as the first man is not known or is minimized in Buddhism. The goddess Chinnamasthā (the severed-headed one), known in both Hinduism and Buddhism, is a "lesson" for those who would die to the world. She is typically shown having severed her own head from her body; she holds the head in one hand and the sword in the other. Chinnamasthā, however, is a fairly insignificant deity in Hindu mythology compared with Śiva or Kālī.

33. Śiva himself, of course, participates in saṁsāra from time to time, wholeheartedly, and his association with the *liṅgam* is a constant reminder that his vitality underlies all of creation. See Wendy Doniger O'Flaherty, "Ascetism and Sexuality in the Mythology of Śiva," *History of Religions* 7, no. 4 (May 1969): 300–37; 9, no. 1 (August 1969): 1–41.

34. *Mahimnastava* 24, W. Norman Brown, ed. and trans., *The Mahimnastava, or Praise of Shiva's Greatness* (Poona: American Institute of Indian Studies, 1965), p. 17. See also M.A. Dorai Rangaswami, *The Religion and Philosophy of Tevāram* (Madras: University of Madras, 1958), bk. 1, p. 402.

35. For the history and a more detailed interpretation of Kālī, see David Kinsley, *The Sword and the Flute—Kālī and Kṛṣṇa, Dark Visions of the Terrible and the Sublime in Hindu Mythology* (Berkeley: University of California Press, 1975), pt. 2.

36. Edward C. Dimock, ed. and trans., *The Thief of Love: Bengali Tales from Court and Village* (Chicago: University of Chicago Press, 1963), pp. 128–29.

37. These features are evident in most contemporary images of Kālī and are specifically described in her most popular form as Dakṣiṇa-kālī. See Āgamavāgīśa 1, 310–11.

38. A vision Ramakrishna had of māyā conveys dramatically the significance of Kālī as māyā seen from the "other shore." In his vision he saw a beautiful pregnant woman emerge from the Ganges. She lay down on the bank and gave birth to a child. She caressed and suckled the child fondly. Then suddenly she was transformed into a horrible hag. She grasped the child in her jaws, crushed and swallowed it, and returned to the waters of the river (M. [Mahendranath Gupta], *The Gospel of Sri Ramakrishna*, trans. Swami Nikhilānanda [New York: Ramakrishna-Vivekānanda Center, 1942], pp. 21–22).

39. Āgamavāgiśa, 1, 310–11.

40. Rāmprasād, in Thompson and Spencer, no. 42, p. 57.

Indian Traditions—Ritual Practice

"Some children love to watch the cremations," Rud said: "The skull is usually the last thing to be burned. Sometimes it collapses with a loud pop, like a balloon bursting. When that happens, the children clap their hands."

Alexander Campbell, *The Heart of India*

Sapiṇḍīkaraṇa: The Hindu Rite of Entry into Heaven

DAVID M. KNIPE

With few exceptions, the Hindu rites at the time of death and the procedures for cremation (*antyeṣṭi*) are fairly uniform throughout the regions of India. Similarly, the series of rites for the departed (*śrāddhas*), where it has been retained, is performed according to traditional archaic standards. The basic structures of the antyeṣṭi and the śrāddha rites proceed from vedic models, models prefigured in the saṃhitās and brāhmaṇas, detailed in the gṛhyasūtras, and then conveyed with continuing elaboration in two thousand years of dharmaśāstra literature. This conformity in ritual across vedic, epic, purāṇic, and āgamic periods, and on into modern practice, is remarkable considering that the answer to the question, "Where does a Hindu go when he dies?," had varied considerably within each one of these periods.[1]

Perhaps the question should be rephrased, "*Who* is a Hindu after death?," because the reply then would necessarily articulate the complex of stages that the deceased traverses between earthly expiration and eventual acceptance among his ancestors.

I shall examine the rite of *sapiṇḍīkaraṇa*, the moment of entry of the deceased into the world of the ancestors (*pitaraḥ*—literally, the Fathers, *pitṛ* in the singular), and the series of bodily constructions and dissolutions the deceased undergoes before becoming established in the world beyond. Contemporary practice of the post-cremation śrāddhas, as performed by some traditions in Varanasi (Banaras), Uttar Pradesh, will be an ancillary focus of discussion,[2] and attention will be accorded the history and structure of the rites in the literature of the ritual tradition of Hinduism.

Of all the complex stages in the Hindu rites of death and dying, the most arresting moment comes at the sapiṇḍīkaraṇa, the time-filled action of blending the deceased with his forefathers, of transforming the vulnerable, disembodied spirit (*preta*) of this world into the secure pitṛ of that other world. The sapiṇḍīkaraṇa, or *sapiṇḍana* as it is sometimes called, is a "creating of the *sapiṇḍa*" relationship, that is, an establishing of the ritual bond between the generations of those (living) who *offer* and

I wish to acknowledge here my thanks to the American Institute of Indian Studies for extending to me a Senior Research Fellowship, 1971–72; to Banaras Hindu University, with which I was affiliated for a year; and especially to my research assistant, Shri Satyanarayan Pandey, for his most valuable aid.

those (deceased) who *receive* the *piṇḍa*, a symbolic meal of food pressed into a ball. The rites before death have their own mixture of tough and tender realism. The preparations after death are hurried and shocked, followed swiftly by the stark vigil of cremation, an occasion, perhaps, for reverie and insight. Then the successive days of piṇḍa offerings are a recovery and recuperation for the mourning family, even as the temporary body of the deceased is symbolically constructed in the rites. But the moment of transition—however elaborate and sumptuous a rite it may be for the wealthy, or however brief and poorly performed it may be for the masses—is one of profound religious awareness. It is one of the great spiritual dramas of man. And yet it is one of the least studied aspects of Hinduism.

New Bodies for the Emigrant Dead

The non-Hindu who examines the system of postcremation śrāddhas, that is, the prescribed offerings for the nourishment and promotion of deceased ancestors, might conclude that priorities somehow have been muddled. If the basic Hindu doctrine of transmigration (*saṃsāra*) is operative (and the dharmaśāstra literature never suggests its suspension), then rebirth in another terrestrial existence is an eventual concomitant of death. The self (*ātman*) is known to discard the body of each lifetime and then collect itself toward a new one (*Bṛhadāraṇyaka-upaniṣad* 4.4.3–4), commuting as readily as a caterpillar from leaf to leaf or an artifact of gold formed in the hands of a smith. It takes on new bodies as effortlessly as a man puts on new clothes (*Bhagavadgītā* 2.22). Moreover, a new body after death is as natural a transformation for the self as the changes a child's body undergoes in becoming an adult (*Yājñavalkya-smṛti* 20.49).

But if transmigration of the imperishable self is thus assured, why is a great company of deceased ancestors still existent in some extraterrestrial world? Further, if the inescapable laws of *karman* stand effective, how can it be that these ancestors subsist in continued dependence on the ritual activities of their descendants? Is it the case that the simpler, unsophisticated vedic desire to prevent the dissolution of an afterlife for the deceased has prevailed? Did the pre-upaniṣadic fear of repeated death institute procedures for the ritual maintenance of ancestors in the "other" world, procedures that later demonstrated the peculiar capacity of death rites generally to resist change? The doctrines of transmigration and liberation transformed the whole of ancient Indian speculation and practice, but the rites accorded the ancestors bear a stamp of rigorous antiquity. They appear to endure beside the newer sentiments of saṃsāra and mokṣa.

The poets of the Ṛgvedic hymns did not frequently chant on death and the afterlife. Most of their funerary verses are collected in an early section of the tenth maṇḍala; these hymns to Yama, Agni as the cremation fire, and the ancestors are just as obscure as those on other subjects addressed to other beings. But among the prominent features is a concern that the deceased obtain a new body for his life in a new home among the Fathers in heaven (Agni *kravyād*, "eater of flesh," having consumed the old one).[3] *Ṛgveda* 10.14.8, for example, directs the deceased to join Yama and the ancestors in the highest heaven, where he will unite in radiance with a body. Another hymn has the deceased proceed to the third celestial "light," there to unite with a body (10.56.1). Sometimes it is Agni who is requested to supervise this unison of the departed with his new life and new body (10.16.5; 10.15.14).

Nothing of the deceased's former body, mind, or spirit remains below, according to the *Atharvaveda* funeral liturgy,[4] which shows specific concern that all traces of the dead body be consumed in the pyre. Whether Agni acts to translate to heaven the life-principle alone (variously called *manas*, *asu*, *ātman*, *prāṇa*), or whether the dead body is itself somehow transmuted into the celestial one, is unclear. Two intriguing references in this same *Atharvaveda* liturgy seem to indicate that a single limb surviving the pyre can become the entire celestial body.[5] One may gauge the religious values inherent in burial and expectation of rebirth in rites associated with the soil: the bone fragments are collected from the pyre in a jar, buried in preseeded ground, and carefully nourished with milk and water.[6] The liturgy for that classical rite of the gṛhyasūtras, which in medieval and modern times has largely been replaced by Ganges or other river burial of the bone fragments or ashes, involves part of the *Ṛgveda* 10.18 burial hymn.

Yet another fate of the corpse lies in the vedic-upaniṣadic notion of the redistribution of cosmic elements. The well-known ritual circulation of elements that undergirds the saṃsāra expressions of the upaniṣads (e.g., the journey of the self [*puruṣa*] after death in the five-fire doctrine in *Chāndogya-upaniṣad* 5.4–9) has prefigurations in the final maṇḍala of the *Ṛgveda*. In 10.16.3 the deceased on the pyre is ritually dismissed to the cosmos, his eye to the sun, his life-breath (ātman) to the wind, his body to the plants. He is thus projected back into the three-leveled world according to the cosmic law (*dharman*).[7] This is an obvious reversal of the cosmogonic process outlined in the *puruṣasūkta* (*Ṛgveda* 10.90.13), where the sun is born from the eye of the sacrificial god, Puruṣa, the wind from his breath (prāṇa), the moon from his mind.

In the powerful prayer that concludes the *Vājasaneyi-saṃhitā*, the one about to die declares: "Now my breath (*vāyu*) is the immortal wind, this body is ashes" (40.15ab). *Śatapatha-brāhmaṇa* 14.6.2.13 raises the eschatological question precisely: What becomes of the self (puruṣa) of the dead man after all of his components have gone back to their respective elements?[8] The answer could only be sought in the brāhmaṇical doctrine of sacrifice itself, wherein the victim (e.g., the horse in the great two-year drama of the horse-sacrifice, the *aśvamedha*) is collective space-and-time, reintegrated, consecrated, immolated, and offered as the manifest cosmos that Puruṣa, the sacrifice-person, first became.[9] This sense of ritual reunification, of a return to the beginning when space-and-time is clean and all unused, is perpetuated at the personal, microcosmic level in the "final offering," the antyeṣṭi, the cremation-sacrifice that recapitulates cosmogonic totality and potentiality, and dramatizes death as the matrix for a new being.

It appears that, in matters of death and continuation, "all ways are the Queen's ways." In this respect, modern India has conserved the vedic heritage. If questioned about the fate of a recently deceased person, Hindu villagers today could summon more or less vague and successive replies, all with scriptural, folk-literary, or proverbial supports, to indicate that the departure was in the direction of some immediate terrestrial rebirth or cosmic dispersal reminiscent of the classical return to the five elements,[10] or transmission to heaven, or an unhealthy lingering in the locales of life, death, and the cremation site. This simultaneity of presence of the deceased in varied, even contradictory situations appears to be more the norm than the exception in the history of religions.

Having reviewed these vedic conceptions of human mortality and afterlife, we must now examine the mature system of postcremation śrāddhas. In the ritual tradition of Hinduism ceremonies during the first ten or eleven days after death are known as *nava-śrāddhas*, their principal function being the ritual construction of a temporary body for the deceased.[11] It is no longer the case, as it was in Ṛgvedic eschatology, that a complete new body awaits the deceased in heaven. He requires exact assistance of the living in order to emigrate from this world to that higher one, to pass from the dangerous condition of a disembodied spirit[12] to the secure role of pitṛ among his own pitaraḥ. In order to negotiate that passage he must have a proper body (or series of bodies) and regular nourishment. According to some authorities,[13] this requires a full year of daily ritual activity from the day of death until the day of the sapiṇḍīkaraṇa and release from "pretahood." It is understandable that efforts were made to condense such a demanding calendar, and sapiṇḍīkaraṇa in its modern form generally occurs on the twelfth day after death, that is, at the end of a symbolic year. Another cause for abbreviation is that perpetual concerns regarding ritual purity and pollution are better served by a shorter period of ritual impurity (*sūtaka*) borne by the family of the deceased during the mourning period. So inauspicious are the cremation and pre-sapiṇḍīkaraṇa rites that many ritual texts covering the rites of passage (*saṃskāras*) omit the funeral ceremonies altogether. Others, like the *Prayogaratna*, append a separate manual on the subject. Some texts point out, not imprudently, yet another reason for moving the sapiṇḍīkaraṇa to within a few days of the cremation: were the eldest son, or other relative serving as the sacrificer (*yajamāna*) for the deceased, to die during the course of the year, the preta would be stranded by the truncated ritual.

One must appreciate here the fact that *jñānakāṇḍa* (the texts dealing with liberating knowledge) and *karmakāṇḍa* (the texts dealing with rites) have disparate concerns and priorities. The *Vedānta-sūtras*, which are concerned with knowledge, proceed from the ambiguities of upaniṣadic statements on perishable and imperishable constituents of being and describe the soul as wrapped in the intangible, subtle aspects of the elements during its journey from material body to body. This distinction of the intangible body (*sūkṣma-* or *liṅga-śarīra*), which survives cremation, from the tangible body (*sthūla-śarīra*), which is eliminated by cremation, is always set in a soteriological discussion. The spirit with its subtle body that is the continuing "mark" of individuality, transcending death upon death, will finally lose even that *liṅga* when it merges with *bráhman*.[14] Thus the soul in its subtle vehicle, escaping from the heart upward through the cranium,[15] has an ultimate residence in view. There is no concern in the vedānta texts for the ritual necessity of constructing an intermediate body.

The ritual texts and other smṛtis, on the other hand, do not focus on the long-range mokṣa ideal. Their preoccupation is with the immediate task of transmitting the spirit of the deceased to his place among the ancestors. Their method, consistent with the brāhmaṇical sacrificial schema, has recourse to the ancient *mantra*s and ancient offering procedures. The smṛtis do not all agree on the nature and longevity of the intermediate body or, in fact, the number of bodies that the preta requires,[16] but they are uniform in their understanding of the creation as a *ritual* task. As far as this temporary body for the preta is concerned, it is no less than a replication of cosmogony and the primordial sacrifice-person. Modern dharmaśāstra literature appears to have lost sight of this central drama. There are, classically, sixteen śrāddhas to be performed prior to the sapiṇḍīkaraṇa. Man (puruṣa), like Puruṣa-Prajāpati and like the whole of space-and-time, is sixteenfold, according to a *Śatapatha-brāhmaṇa* account of creation (11.1.6.1–36), and remarkably, the pre-sapiṇḍīkaraṇa *śrāddha* system of re-creation seems to follow suit. Although temporary and intermediate, this new body is nonetheless the fruit of sacrifice and, as such, a microcosm spun anew.

On the first day after death the sacrificer bathes and dresses, then creates a single tennis-ball–sized mass of cooked white rice[17] (called piṇḍa) and, at a quiet place near a river or temple tank, and perhaps with the assistance of his family priest and a special priest acting as the watchful presence of the deceased, places it on a tiny altar of loose earth no more than half an inch high. This rice-ball represents the preta (i.e., the spirit of the sacrificer's father), endowed only with its briefest, subtlest body, and is therefore accorded all the honors of worship: incense, flowers, a tiny ghee lamp, and white threads as symbolic clothing. Most important, a small clay cup of water containing sesame seeds is poured out onto the ball. Each day this procedure will be repeated with a single ball of rice as the preta on the altar. The cups of water offered, however, increase by one each day until there are ten on the final day. And each day of the rites results in a new portion of the preta's intermediate body, the head being created on the first day, then in succession the neck and shoulders, the heart and torso, the back, the stomach, the thighs and bowels, the lower legs and skin, the knees and hair, the genitals, and, on the tenth day of the offerings, the preta receives digestive powers so that the sufferings of hunger and thirst now experienced by the "body of nourishment" duly created may be allayed by continued offerings of piṇḍas and water from the living.[18]

In contemporary practice it appears usually to be the wealthy and the devout who fulfill this entire sequence of offerings. All such rites are performed "according to one's capacity." The results are the same, Banaras paṇḍitas will admit, if offerings are made only on the first, third, and seventh days, or on the tenth day only.[19]

A less expensive form of attention to the deceased in these ten days, however, is not abbreviated. That is the custom of hanging two clay pots by strings from a peg in a *pīpal* tree near a river or a temple tank, one pot containing water for the deceased, who lingers in or near the tree until the rite of sapiṇḍīkaraṇa, and in the other pot a ghee lamp to light the way for the preta. Early each morning the sacrificer bathes, then refills the hanging water pot with river or tank water from his bath. On the tenth day, when the subtle body disappears in favor of the newly ritualized intermediate body, the pots are taken down and smashed.

This ends the ten-day period of ritual impurity suffered by the mourning household. The sacrificer and all the male members of the family will bathe and be shaved by barbers, and they will return home purified of death's defilement. Technically, according to later ritual authorities, the nava-śrāddhas during this defilement period were not true śrāddhas at all. Only now with purity regained on the eleventh day can the first *ekoddiṣṭa* (rites for a single deceased person),[20] with the requisite feeding of invited brāhmaṇas who represent the company of the ancestors, take place. No deceased ancestor (and certainly no brāhmaṇa surrogate nowadays!) would consent to be entertained as guest in a house of defilement.

There is not space here to detail the "mixed" śrāddhas of the eleventh day, a day that may, in the more elaborate postcremation śrāddha schedule, involve as much as a ten-hour sequence of a half-dozen major events, including the establishment of the deceased in sixteenfold time and sixteenfold space, the worship and ritual payment of a priest who has served during the nava-śrāddhas as a ritual surrogate for the deceased, the feeding of eleven brāhmaṇas, and such occasionally performed rites as the *nārāyaṇabali.* In some parts of India the giving away of a cow, a substitute for the ancient bull-sacrifice, may also be performed on the eleventh day.[21]

Since the sapiṇḍīkaraṇa was originally a year subsequent to cremation there was time to observe twelve (lunar) monthly piṇḍa offerings in the ekoddiṣṭa pattern. These plus a three-fortnight offering (after one-and-a-half months), and offerings on days immediately prior to the first, sixth, and twelfth months made a total ritual year of sixteen. Variant texts allow for an intercalary month, still observing the sacred totality of sixteen. Thus in collapsing the anniversary śrāddha to the twelfth day, only the eleventh day remains to celebrate these sixteen offerings. The modern rite dispenses in this fashion with a whole "year" of sacrifices in about two hours, using sixteen cooked-rice piṇḍas plus 360 barley piṇḍas for the requisite daily rites. Somewhat more artificial is the other carryover from the sixteenfold *soma* pattern, the placement of the preta in a line of sixteen deities, all of whom receive elaborate worship from the sacrificer. These include Viṣṇu, Śiva, Yama, Soma, Agni, and Mṛtyu.

The nārāyaṇabali, in its full form a rite of tremendous power, is designed to promote the deceased, after the sapiṇḍīkaraṇa, to the Vaikuṇṭha heaven of Viṣṇu. It involves a *Viṣṇu-tarpaṇa* with milk and water, and a sixteenfold worship of the preta in the company of Brahmā, Viṣṇu, Maheśa (Rudra), and Yama, utilizing the sixteen verses of the *puruṣasūkta.* Simultaneously, *havana*s of ghee and grains are made in the offering fire.[22]

But the dramatic focus of the eleventh day comes with the worship and ritual payment of the priest who has served as ritual surrogate for the dead. This is one of the most extraordinary roles in all of Hindu ritualism. The priest is a *mahāpātra*, a brāhmaṇa who performs the necessary role of silent, watchful stand-in for the preta. It is an unenviable priestly function. Connections with the defilement of death have brought mahāpātras as a class, at least in many parts of north and central India, to a low and ill-regarded status, cut off from the Sanskritic traditions of the priestly caste. Because they perform all too well the ritual presence of the deceased, making claims on the finances and emotions of the living, who must ritually maintain them, they are dismissed as a greedy, cantankerous, illiterate lot. For the common man they perform whatever passes for the nava-śrāddhas. For the elaborate rites of the wealthy, however, the mahāpātra is the continued presence of the preta, observing every detail of the rites promoting the preta to the ancestors. He is permitted to say or do nothing whatever. But when he receives all the lavish *dakṣiṇā*s in the form of gold, utensils, bed, linens, clothes, food, and paraphernalia intended to maintain the deceased and satisfy his every need for the coming year, the mahāpātra always begs, cajoles, and argues for more. And more he receives, lest the deceased take offense.

The eleven brāhmaṇa guests on the eleventh day are all mahāpātras. This feeding of brāhmaṇas who represent the ancestors is a focal point of the ancient śrāddha system. However, the increased fear in later times of the defilement of death, even *after* the ten-day period of recognized impurity, created a scarcity of willing brāhmaṇa guests, and the low-status mahāpātras, today invariably poor despite an occasional windfall in the demise of a wealthy patron, make themselves available, and therefore despised, for the ritual task. The number eleven is not idle, for they represent the eleven Rudras, and therefore the deceased's ancestors. (On the following day, twelve days after death, the deceased is ritually joined to his ancestors.)

The Triple World of the Immigrant Dead

Thus far the rites have focused on the deceased in his vulnerable preta condition. First, he has been the vague ghost in the tree. Then, in his more demonstrable presence as mahāpātra, he has made claims on the living for his continued support. And he has brought a company of ancestors, in the form of invited brāhmaṇas, to come and sit for a ritual feast. From where have these ancestors arrived? As early as the *Ṛgveda* (e.g., 10.15.1) there is understood to be a tripartite hierarchy of the Fathers (pitaraḥ). From the cremation fire the deceased ascends to the triadic *lokas*, earth, midspace (atmosphere) and sky (heaven), according to the *Atharvaveda* funeral hymn.[23] This ascension through the trileveled cosmos is precisely dependent on the ritual activities of the living: the ancestors are in fact *brought into being* in the three worlds by offerings.[24]

Further, the upward mobility of the ancestors is complemented by the fact that they are mortal. Unlike the gods, the Fathers are themselves subject to repeated death (*punarmṛtyu*),[25] a conception that the epics and purāṇas perpetuated in higher drama with a world view in which these very lokas themselves died periodically.[26]

More to the point of homogeneity of the Fathers, however, is the identification of three generations of deceased paternal ancestors with three classes of deities residing in the three levels of the cosmos. An individual's deceased father (pitṛ) is to be found among the eight Vasus in the earth (pṛthivī), the Vasus being presided over by Indra or Agni or both. A deceased grandfather (*pitāmaha*) is a temporary resident of the midspace (*antarikṣa*) where the eleven Rudras, under the leadership of Rudra himself, are located. And a deceased great-grandfather (*prapitāmaha*) is in the company of the twelve Ādityas in heaven (*svarga*), where either the god Varuṇa or Aditi, their mother, rules.

These three closest generations of the ancestors thus inhabit the three-layered cosmos in close association with the gods. They are, in fact, "on call" precisely like the deities who are invoked for sacrifices, and when, for example, eleven brāhmaṇas are required to attend the sixteen ekoddiṣṭa rites (now condensed to the eleventh-day rite), the "grandfathers" leave their midspace home in the form of "the Rudras" to accept the piṇḍa offerings. Similarly, the "fathers" appear as the eight Vasus, with that number of living surrogate brāhmaṇas taking part.[27] These three paternal generations are the recently deceased, the powerful immigrants to the three worlds who exist in symbiotic ritual connections with their living descendants. They require sustenance for their continuing journey to the unmanifest, the ocean of dissolution that lies beyond these three worlds. And the living have need of these celestial intermediaries for health and long life, for wealth and progeny.

Significantly, these three ranked but cohesive generations contrast with those gone before as well as those coming after. If the preta undergoing a symbolic year of nava-śrāddhas may be said to exist in the dawn of death, the full power of day belongs to the unit of his Fathers with the Vasus, Rudras, and Ādityas, while death's twilight is the phase of the three preceding generations, the remote dead. The remote dead (a sacrificer's great-great-grandfather and *his* father and grandfather), although still venerable and nominally included in the sevenfold sapiṇḍa lineage with the sacrificer and the intermediate triad, are distant and relatively inaccessible. They are, in fact, on the frontiers of dissolution to other life forms, where the doctrine of saṃsāra, however contrastive with purāṇic chronologies for an individual's sojourn in heavens and hells, seems not so disjunctive after all. These remote dead require scant ritual attention from the living since their physiological presence is necessarily diminishing. Graphically, Manu and the purāṇas call them *lepabhāgin*s, because they receive not the full piṇḍa or the full water cup, but only the remnants, the "wipings" (*lepa-*) of the hand *after* he has served the basic (nearer) triad in *pārvaṇa-śrāddha*.[28] The purāṇas extend to them an emotional benefit of the doubt by referring to them collectively as the *nāndīmukha-pitaraḥ*, "Fathers having faces of joy," as distinguished from the *aśrumukha-pitaraḥ*, the father, grandfather, and great-grandfather, "having faces of tears."[29] Whether the happiness of the further triad, vis-à-vis the nearer triad's grief, has to do with its distance *from* the fact of death or its proximity *to* prolonged heavenly rewards, rebirth, *or* liberation is a matter of some significance, but one that the purāṇas douse more with shadow than light. Such collectivities allow little margin for individual merit or demerit, and would appear to presume a common destiny for the generations.

To return to the Fathers in the three worlds, it is necessary to look again to the sacrificial schema of the *Śatapatha-brāhmaṇa* to understand the underlying cosmography of death and rebirth. The funeral hymn, *Ṛgveda* 10.15.1, declares that the Fathers (pitaraḥ) enjoy soma (a sacred inebriating drink). As in the general sixteenfold symbolism or in the connections of the śrāddhas to lunar phenomena, there is the strong presence of the soma sacrifice. Soma, pressed three times daily—morning, noon, and evening—is offered to the Vasus, the Rudras, and the Ādityas, respectively.[30] In the section of the *Śatapatha-brāhmaṇa* that concerns the ritual construction of the fire-basin (6.5), the cosmos is ritually assembled by the sacrificer following the model of the gods: first, on the bottom, is the earth, originally made by the Vasus, and now recreated by the sacrificer. Second is midspace and third is heaven, originally created by the Rudras and the Ādityas, respectively. "He [the sacrificer] then completes the fire-altar [=the cosmos] by a fourth, the Viśvedevāḥ," representing the four quarters of space. Thus the ātman (6.5.3.5) of Agni, at once Puruṣa/Prajāpati/the sacrificer, is composed of the three worlds plus a transcendent fourth.[31] (See Figure 1.)

This pattern is ancient, and highly significant. *Ṛgveda* 10.125 knits together the essential components in a hymn that precisely connects the sacred utterance (*Vāc*, cf. bráhman) to the sacrifice for ancestors. It is ritual speech that carries the Vasus, Rudras, Ādityas, and even the transcendent fourth, the Viśvedevāḥ, to the (śrāddha) sacrifice, and ritual speech that carries soma to them. Most important, it is ritual speech that "brings forth the pitṛ," even to the highest level (vs. 7), by which the transcendent level of the Viśvedevāḥ, the realm of the remote, long-gone ancestors may be understood.[32] This early vedic conception is perpetuated in the gṛhyasūtras and in such texts as the *Viṣṇudharmaśāstra*, thus assuring liturgical longevity in the ritual manuals of classical and medieval India. *Kāṭhakagṛhyasūtra* 50.10 addresses the ancestors in earth, midspace, heaven, and the (transcendent) ocean with the ritual utterance "*svadhā*!"[33] in a series of prayers equating Vāc and immortality (*amṛta*) with the sacrifice of life-strength (*ūrj*), which is the essential, saplike "vigor" of the piṇḍas and water. Here again is the continuity with the ancient soma rites: cooked-

4	Transcendent	Viśvedevāḥ	Remote ancestors
3	heaven	Ādityas	great grandfather
2	midspace	Rudras	grandfather
1	earth	Vasus	father
			son

Figure 1. The correspondence of cosmic, divine, and human triads, completed by a transcendent fourth. At the point of the sapiṇḍīkaraṇa, the deceased, or preta, moves from the level of "son" to the level of "father" and is thereafter dependent upon his son as sacrificer of offerings.

rice balls are not soma, but their powers in the context of the soma-mantras are life-sustaining to the point of re-creativity.

From these and other vedic contexts it can be seen, turning to the sapiṇḍīkaraṇa, that the prior worship of the Viśvedevāḥ is *not* simple recognition of "the All-Gods," as is the contemporary paṇḍitas' explanation. Rather it is the *ritual presence* of the remote ancestors who are dispersed to the four quarters of the transcendent region beyond these worlds. They are worshiped first, their representation being to the immediate right of the sacrificer's right knee as he sits facing south. (See Figure 2.) Directly in front of him is a row of four leaf-plates, which now receive four large cooked-rice piṇḍas. Two low earth-altars are prepared directly before the sacrificer's right knee, a small one to receive the *preta-piṇḍa*, an elongated mass of cooked rice, and a larger one to receive a row of the three round piṇḍas of the Fathers.

After making numerous offerings to the east-west row of all four generations, the sacrificer takes up the preta-piṇḍa and places it on the western altar. Then he takes up the piṇḍa representing the preta's father (his own grandfather) and places that on the closest place before him, the other two piṇḍas following away from him in a north-south line. He now recites mantras from the *Ṛgveda* (including the last three verses of the *Ṛgveda*, 10.191.2–4) and the *Vājasaneyi-saṃhitā* (twice repeating 19.45–46), these mantras stressing the unity and equality of the ancestors. As he recites he blends the water cups of the Fathers into that of the preta, reciting

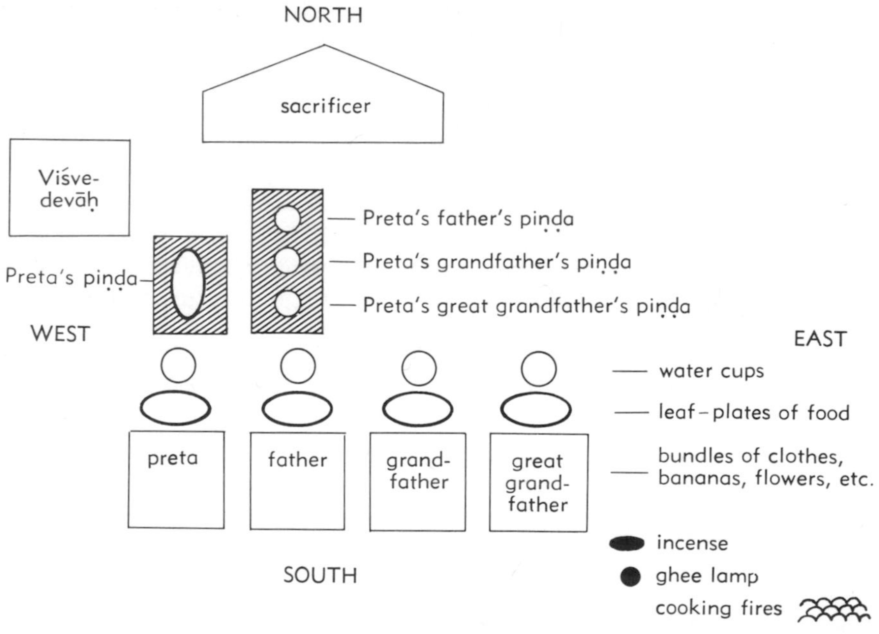

Figure 2. Sapiṇḍīkaraṇa, just before the ritual blending of the deceased (preta) into his three paternal ancestors by his son (sacrificer).

the names of the ancestors along with his deceased father's and declaring that he unites them. Then cutting the preta-piṇḍa into three slices he blends each slice into one of the three piṇḍas of the ancestors, reciting the name of each, and the act of uniting each with the deceased. "Go to your father (grandfather, great-grandfather)" are the words he addresses to each slice of the preta-piṇḍa as it mixes with its ancestral counterpart. Finally, the three are blended into one, and in *that moment* the deceased has passed from the preta to the pitṛ stage and has joined the revered company of the ancestors at home in the three worlds, his father and grandfather having advanced to new levels and divine groupings in the cosmic and ritual hierarchy, and his great-grandfather having been regenerated into the realm of the remote dead as one of the Viśvedevāḥ.[34]

Another conflation of vedic-Hindu liturgical practice and probable indigenous folk religion occurs in a ceremony that sometimes concludes the sapiṇḍīkaraṇa. The *Prayogaratna* and some other manuals direct the sacrificer to the border of his village where he should throw the piṇḍas into "the Gaṅgā" (meaning the local river), then return home to bathe and present offerings to the Viśvedevāḥ.[35] This closing sacrifice to the Viśvedevāḥ seems to have been replaced in many regions by offerings to crows, the crow having widespread folkloric associations with the souls of the dead. Not only the collective remote ancestors but perhaps also the preta may be personified by the crow. At the Rāmakuṇḍa in Nāsik, a special śrāddha site for western India, the crow may clearly be seen as yet another commanding presence of the deceased. When the sacrificer, upon concluding the sapiṇḍīkaraṇa, goes outside of the ritual pavilion he carefully lays out on a leaf plate the special piṇḍa intended for a crow, then waits to observe reactions from the first crow to approach. If the piṇḍa is accepted and eaten immediately, all is well, but if, as is sometimes the curious case, the crow struts about the piṇḍa with disinterest, if not hesitation or naked aversion, the sacrificer and mourners understand that the deceased is declaring to them his dissatisfaction and they then must remember how and where they have failed him.

In conclusion, the period of the brāhmaṇa texts (*Aitareya*, *Kauṣītaki*, *Śatapatha*, and so on) was the crucial one for myths, rites, and symbols of death and rebirth. It was then that the application of the Puruṣa-Prajāpati cosmogonic model to an *individual's* postcremation passage was first conceptualized and concretized liturgically, and there that the cosmically renewing potency of the soma rites and mantras was first brought to bear on human regeneration and perpetuation. The ritual world view of early vedic religion could abide through several strenuous periods via the directives of the sūtras and śāstras for individual funeral and ancestral rites, with remarkably little tampering from the innovative doctrines, theologies, and cosmographies that gradually eroded the official, institutional structures of vedic religion. Although the concern shifted from the early vedic desire for a state of perpetual nondeath or immortality to the dilemma of saṃsāra and the ideal of mokṣa, the intention of the śrāddhas survived, and the understanding of the passage of the deceased as a cosmogonic progression, with an individual's salvation dependent on the correct ritual activity of his descendants, permitted these archaic ceremonies for the dead to continue to the present day.

The continuity of life forms and the mutual responsibility of the living and the dead for one another are borne out by the often repeated liturgies. The sacrificer, as he offers food and water to his Fathers, addresses them directly, contractually, hopefully:

> This life-strength is for *you*, this "*svadhā*" is for *you*!
> Eat and drink! Do not allow *us* to perish![36]

Notes

1. By "vedic" is meant the period of composition and compilation of *śruti* from the *Ṛgveda* (ca. fourteenth century B.C.) to the early upaniṣads (ca. sixth century B.C.). The śrauta-, gṛhya-, and dharma-sūtras succeeded in the next half millennium. The gṛhya- and dharma-sūtras were the anchors of dharmaśāstra to the vedic substratum. The first centuries of the present era witnessed completion of the two epics as well as beginning production of the legal-ritual smṛtis (*Manu*, *Yājñavalkya*, and so on). The period of composition of the purāṇas and āgamas begins before the middle and extends to the close of the first millennium. Although production of the legal-ritual smṛtis dwindled by the seventh and eighth centuries, the writing of commentaries (ṭīkās) and annotated digests (nibandhas) based on the whole of dharmaśāstra and the vedic mantra traditions had just begun. Numerous ṭīkās and nibandhas were produced up until the eighteenth century. One such digest among those of current authority in Banaras, where it was composed by Nārāyaṇa Bhaṭṭa in the sixteenth century, has an extensive section on *antyeṣṭi* and *śrāddha*. This is the *Prayogaratna*, cited occasionally below.

2. Narratives of observed rites that are included here with historical and interpretive materials do not presume, of course, to represent typical or exemplary ceremonies. Rites of the same name taking place in Poona, Calcutta, Madras, or, for that matter, in Banaras as well, although structurally and functionally the same, could display a wide variety of details due to vedic and śāstric traditions, sectarian persuasions, class, caste, and economic status, or to employ that phrase of convenience in all ritual manuals, due to "local custom."

3. Excepting, of course, possible references to direct inhumation such as *Ṛgveda* 10.18. Cremation evidently became, and remained, normative for all but exceptional funerals during the vedic period. On the exceptions, see Willem Caland, *Die altindischen Todten- und Bestattungsgebräuche* (Amsterdam, 1896; reprint, Wiesbaden, 1967), pp. 85–98.

4. 18.2.24; cf. the *Kauśika-sūtra* utilization of these *Atharvaveda* stanzas, 82.29 and 85.26.

5. 18.2.26; 18.4.64. This brings to mind the later purāṇic belief that a bone or fragment of the deceased's body will bring him mokṣa or astronomical periods of time in heaven if it is thrown in the Ganges. Cf. *Viṣṇudharmasūtra* 19.10–12. The cremation rite at Banaras always concludes with the sacrificer flipping the last unburned fragment of the body into the Ganges.

6. The *asthisañcayana*, or bone-gathering rite, described as part of the burning-ground (*śmaśāna*) procedures in *Śatapatha-brāhmaṇa* 13.8.3.1ff.

7. Not, as later authorities presumed, according to his "merit." In pada c, *āpo*, the "waters," can be construed as the poet's reference to the atmosphere or midspace, located beyond *dyu*, the sky, and *pṛthivī*, the earth. On diffusion to the elements, cf. also *Ṛgveda* 10.58.7.

8. Speech (*vāc*) to Agni, *prāṇa* to the wind (*vāta*), the eye (*cakṣus*) to the sun (*āditya*), the mind (*manas*) to the moon (*candra*), the ear (*śrotra*) to the quarters (*diśaḥ*) of heaven, the body (*śarīra*) to the earth (*pṛthivī*), *ātman* to midspace (*ākāśa*), body hair (*loman*) to plants (*oṣadhī-*), head hair (*keśa*) to trees (*vanaspati-*), blood and semen (*lohita* and *retas*) to the waters (*āpaḥ*).

9. Cf. *Aitareya-brāhmaṇa* 2.6.13; *Śatapatha-brāhmaṇa* 13.5.2.13–16; *Śāṅkhāyana-śrautasūtra* 16.6.3–4; *Bṛhadāraṇyaka-upaniṣad* 1.1.1–2.

10. Sanskrit *mahābhūtāni.* According to *Aitareya-brāhmaṇa* 3.3 the ātman *is* the five great elements. Cf. *Taittirīya-upaniṣad* 2.1; *Praśna-upaniṣad* 4.8. In popular belief, there is, and was anciently, a vague homology between *bhūta*, "element," and *bhūta*, "ghost, malevolent spirit"; both words derive from the past passive participle of *bhū-*, "be"; thus bhūta, "become, gone; being, existing, present."

11. Technically, the śrāddhas of the "new" (*nava*) or recently deceased are those of the first ten days, while the "mixed" (*miśra*) śrāddhas include remaining rites up to the sapiṇḍīkaraṇa. Thus, in the modern ritual calendar, *miśra-śrāddhas* are crowded into the eleventh day. Some authorities, however, count the eleventh day, too, among the nava-śrāddhas.

12. The same word *preta* also indicates "dead body" in the ritual texts. Literally, "gone out, departed," preta in the sense of the dead occurs in the *Śatapatha-brāhmaṇa* (e.g., 10.5.2.13), but not in the saṃhitās. Cf. in the śrāddha sections of *Śāṅkhāyana-gṛhyasūtra* (4.2.7; 4.3.5–6) and *Pāraskara-gṛhyasūtra* (3.10.49–55) the distinction of the preta prior to the sapiṇḍīkaraṇa.

13. The rites for a single deceased person are collected under the rubric *ekoddiṣṭa*, pertaining to "one" (*eka*) only, to distinguish these śrāddhas from those for *groups* of ancestors previously deceased. The paradigmatic form of śrāddha, which the ekoddiṣṭa adopts mutatis mutandis, is the *pārvaṇa-śrāddha*, which is celebrated for the father, grandfather, and great-grandfather on the paternal side of the sacrificer's ancestry.

14. Śaṅkara, in his commentary on 3.1.1, describes the *sūkṣma* aspects of the elements as "seeds" of the next *sthūla-śarīra.* Cf. *Vedānta-sūtras* 1.4.2–3; 4.2.1 ff. Śaṅkara cites *Bṛhadāraṇyaka-upaniṣad* 4.4.1–4. On the *liṅga*, see *Maitrāyanīya-upaniṣad* 6.10 and the vaguer references in *Katha-upaniṣad* 2.3.8 and *Śvetāśvatara-upaniṣad* 6.9. In vedānta literature *ātivāhika* is an epithet of the liṅga (śarīra). This word becomes in the purāṇas a reference to the subtle and immediate body that requires no ritual construction.

15. Thus the still current practice of breaking the skull of the corpse after it has burned on the pyre for an hour or two. The ātman in its *sūkṣma-śarīra* might otherwise be unable to exit through the *brahmarandhra* suture at the crown of the skull. On this upaniṣadic eschatological physiology, see *Chāndogya-upaniṣad* 8.6.6 and *Kaṭha-upaniṣad* 2.3.16; cf. also *Aitareya-upaniṣad* 1.3.12, the *sīman* or *vidṛti* being the door by which the ātman *enters* the body.

16. In addition to the ātivāhika (the "carry-over" body) that appears to compare with the vedāntic sukṣma-śarīra, the purāṇas employ terms for intermediate śarīras (*bhogadeha, pretadeha, yātāniya*) that express particular functions. In purāṇic belief the automatic subtle body enveloping the spirit escapes from the corpse but then must itself be replaced by a ritual body, more physical in nature, so that offerings of food and water can be enjoyed and utilized by the preta. Then, after sapiṇḍīkaraṇa, yet a third body becomes the spirit's vehicle to heaven and hell to "endure" the rewards and punishments due to previous karman. (Again the symbolic year appears when the purāṇas speak of the twelve-day journey of the soul to reach the kingdom of Yama.) Thus in the ten days of piṇḍa offerings following death, the ātivāhika body, composed of fire, wind, and space (*tejas, vāyu, ākāśa*) but *not* of the other two elements, earth and water (*pṛthivī, āpaḥ*), daily shrinks away to nothingness in size and strength. For references to the purāṇas and nibandhas, see P.V. Kane, *History of Dharmaśāstra*, vol. 4 (Poona, 1953), pp. 265–66, and Dakshina Ranjan Shastri, *Origin and Development of the Rituals of Ancestor Worship in India* (Calcutta, 1963), pp. 58ff.

17. Sesame seeds (*tila*) are an essential ingredient, and the boiled rice may also contain milk, ghee, honey, sugar, and so on.

18. Authorities vary in recounting this ten-day physiological assembly. Nārāyaṇa Bhaṭṭa's *Prayoga-ratna*, ed. by Vasudeva Sharma, 2nd ed. (Bombay, 1937), *Antyeṣṭipaddhati*, pp. 12–13, gives details. Cf. also p. 27. Incidentally, among the *saṃskāras* (vedic-Hindu rites of passage), it is remarkable to note the parallel structures of these post-cremation śrāddhas and the rites at birth (*jātakarman*). In each case, following the day of birth/death there are ten days of offerings of rice, sesame, and so on, ten being a homology to the human gestation period of ten (lunar) months. It may well be the case, then, that the completion of the temporary body on the tenth day is an intentional *re*birth expression. In the case of both sets of rituals the twelfth day marks the resumption of offering fires, the completion of purification and the transition out of the great time (twelve days representing the twelve-month year) into routine ritual time.

19. From the gṛhyasūtras on through the whole of dharmaśāstra the number of *nava-śrāddhas* prescribed varies considerably, but a predilection for certain odd-numbered days, among days one to eleven after

cremation, persists. Cf. Nārāyaṇa Bhaṭṭa, *Prayogaratna*, p. 11, on these nava-śrāddhas that cumulatively remove *pretatva*, the condition of "pretahood."

20. See n. 13.

21. Often detailed in purāṇic descriptions of the afterlife is a twelve-day journey of the preta to the kingdom of Yama, prior to the punishments and rewards that await the deceased in the various *narakas* and *lokas*. To cross the dread netherworld river Vaitaraṇī the deceased must hold on to the tail of this cow that has been sacrificed (given). Without elaboration Nārāyaṇa Bhaṭṭa calls the *vṛsotsarga* the most important part of the śrāddhas.

22. Cf. *Prayogaratna*, *Antyeṣṭipaddhati*, p. 14.

23. 18.4.5, 78–80; cf. *Kauśika-sūtra* 87.8.

24. *Śatapatha-brāhmaṇa* 2.6.1.1–3; subsequent vss. (4–7) make it clear that a threefold system of the Fathers, homologized to the three-fire schema, ranks them hierarchically according to the substances that they themselves had offered while they existed in life (*soma*, cooked food, or nothing at all being their offerings). This is an intriguing prefiguration of upaniṣadic eschatology: ritual activity (karman) in life bears results—advantages and disadvantages—in the mobile ranks of the ancestors.

25. *Śatapatha-brāhmaṇa* 2.1.3.4: *amṛtā devā . . . martyāḥ pitaraḥ*. Cf. 2.1.4.9.

26. In the world view of periodic dissolution (*pralaya*) the number of "heavens" had proliferated far beyond the original triad.

27. See, e.g., *Prayogaratna*, pp. 17–18, the Vasus Dhruva, Adhvara, Soma, Āpa, Anila, Anala, Pratyūṣa and Prabhāsa being the pole-star, sky, moon, water, wind, fire, dawn and light, respectively. Cf. *Manu* 3.189 on the relationship of the pitaraḥ to the brāhmaṇas in śrāddhas.

28. *Manu* 3.216; *Matsyapurāṇa* 18.29; and so on.

29. Cf. Kane, *History of Dharmaśāstra*, 4:528–29.

30. *Śatapatha-brāhmaṇa* 4.3.5.1. "Vasus, Rudras and Ādityas are the three classes of gods." Cf. also 1.3.4.12.

31. For a discussion of the transcendent fourth beyond the triads, see my article, "One Fire, Three Fires, Five Fires: Vedic Symbols in Transition," *History of Religions* 12 (1972): 28–41. *Chāndogya-upaniṣad* 3.1–10 provides an example of the expansion of this triad to a pentad, with the addition of a transcendent pair, the Maruts (with Soma as deity) and the Sādhyas (with Brahmā as deity), at the fourth and fifth levels respectively. Horizontally, with orientation in plan, the five classes are in the east, south, west, north, with the Sādhyas at the center or zenith. Further, the five are associated, again in the correct ascending order, with the sequence of the four vedas, and bráhman, the sacred utterance itself, completing the pentad at the zenith.

Similarly, the septadic cosmography of the purāṇas reveals, like the vedic-Hindu pentad, an interior structural triad (e.g., earth, midspace, heaven), although now with *two* interstices opening up each segment of the triad instead of one only. The macro-microcosmic correspondences that evolve in purāṇic Hinduism (mythology, cosmogony, eschatology) and in tantric *yoga* (the seven *cakras* as seven lokas, and so on) are relevant to our understanding of the septadic *sapiṇḍa* structure.

32. This hymn is rearranged, probably for liturgical benefits in the rites, in *Atharvaveda* 4.30, where the juxtaposition of speech-born soma and the rebirth of the pitṛ is more clearly indicated.

33. *svadhā* is both the ritual utterance and the offering to the pitaraḥ; traditionally, it is said that the *devas* enjoy hearing "*svāhā*," the benediction accompanying offerings to them, as the Fathers delight in hearing "*svadhā*." Cf. *Ṛgveda* 10.14.3.

34. It is difficult to convey the power of this and related rites for the dead without visual materials. A color videocassette of the antyeṣṭi and śrāddha rites is available from the South Asian Language and Area Center, Univ. of Wisconsin, Madison. This is Program 15, "Death and Rebirth in Hinduism," of my series, *Exploring the Religions of South Asia* (Madison, 1975).

35. *Antyeṣṭipaddhati*, p. 20. An apparent mystical connection between the Viśvedevāḥ, sacrificial remnants, and the beings of animals and birds may be seen in *Aitareya-brāhmaṇa* 3.31.

36. *Kāṭhakagṛhyasūtra* 50.11; emphasis added.

Parsi Zoroastrian Myth and Ritual: Some Problems of Their Relevance for Death and Dying

CYRUS R. PANGBORN

The social scientists have made students of religion aware of the human penchant for elaborately ritualizing the transitional experiences of life. Fraught with danger because the transitions may not be successfully negotiated, these experiences are crises. The rituals are designed to provide the corporate (not to mention divine) aid needed by individual persons for moving through childhood into adolescence, from youth to full maturity, finally from life to death and, perhaps, to new life altogether. These are the rituals we call rites of passage.

The Zoroastrian Parsis[1] share with all others of the human race the heightened feeling associated with passing from life to death and many of their ritual acts are not sufficiently different to set them apart from other religious communities. Some specific concerns, however, are focal points for the intense feelings of the Parsis. It is those that strike the non-Zoroastrian as unusual or atypical that I shall describe.

The Parsi rituals associated with death should begin before the last breath is drawn and continue, according to defined frequency, until the respectful memory in which descendants held the deceased has faded. The usual summary of these rites retains few of their curious features except, notably, the use of the *dakhma* (Tower of Silence) for the deposition of corpses. More descriptive accounts, however, reveal the intense anxiety occasioned by death. The dead and the living survivors alike are threatened by evil, and anxiety is felt for both. But, as other writings show, every single death also kindles afresh another fear among Parsis—the fear of their corporate extinction.

The cultic ceremonies designed long ago to allay fears for the soul of the dead and the welfare of the living may be presumed efficacious. On the other hand, it may be that these archaic rituals promote fears and anxieties among contemporaries that have no basis in present-day Parsi experience. That, however, is another question. If the ceremonies are effective in accommodating the total range of anxiety, then they must be deemed acceptable, even if a more economical response could allay fears on a smaller scale. The fear of Parsi extinction is a different matter. The Parsis, as well as observers, agree that the cultus is not presently an effective solvent for this problem. But whereas the orthodox regard the cultic regulations for religious observance and daily life as ineffective only because they are not rigorously followed, critics believe that it is precisely because the rules are too well applied that Parsi survival is problematical. The question of which argument possesses greater merit need not be settled here. My concern is to show that the cultus which provides the rites for assuaging the fear of death has not been effective in dealing with the burgeoning anxiety engendered by the prospect of corporate extinction.

Tracing Anxiety to Its Source

An understanding of why Parsis do what they do to deal with their fears, whether effectively or not, depends on knowing the considerations which originally gave rise to fear. Thus the inquirer asks if the source could have been Zoroaster, the founding prophet of the faith; and noting that protection of basic natural elements from pollution is a central concern of funeral ceremonies, he turns to the *Gathas*, the hymns of the founder-prophet, to find the germ of contemporary concern for the holy purity of fire, air, earth, and water. There are only five surviving *Gathas* of the many credited to Zoroaster by tradition. But these at least, although containing admonitions enjoining stewardship, yield no clues that would make him accountable for his later followers' notions about innumerable ways of cultically corrupting the physical bases of life. Nor is the *Yasna*, a priestly composition postdating Zoroaster but including his five *Gathas*, of any decisive importance for the inquiry. In the *Videvdat*, however, Zoroaster's morally sensitive concern for the gifts of nature has been transformed into obsessive anxiety about pollution of sacralized elements.

The *Videvdat*, the first ecclesiastical law book of the Zoroastrians, was another priestly contribution to their canonical scriptures, the *Avesta*, all—the *Gathas* alone excepted—in a language called simply Avestan. Characterized by Karl F. Geldner as "the Leviticus of the Parsis,"[2] the *Videvdat* is a compendium of profanations to be avoided, which, if not avoided, must have their effects canceled by rites of purification, penance, and atonement. Here, then, appear for the first time the rules for preventing the pollution of earth by dead bodies, having the dog gaze upon the dead during funeral rites, and disposing of corpses by exposure in a dakhma. These are only a few of the many prescriptions for which Zoroaster's authority was claimed, but which in all probability were more congruent with aboriginal beliefs and cultic practices swept away in his reform and then reintroduced by the Median Magi.

Native Persian culture, including religion, languished during the half-millennium of foreign rule after 330 B.C. Then the accession to power in A.D. 220 by the Sassanids, who claimed hereditary continuity with the Achaemenids, provided the opportunity for a renaissance that included the transcription of whatever could be remembered (about one-fourth) of the *Avesta* by priests many generations removed from those who had composed it.

The renaissance continued for Zoroastrianism even after the Muslim conquest brought defeat to the Sassanids in A.D. 641. But restrictions on non-Muslims made a group of Zoroastrians restive; they decided to seek refuge elsewhere and eventually reached India in the eighth century. Others endured their disabilities and wrote in the then-vulgate language of Pahlavi such works as the *Dinkard*, *Nirangistan*, and *Dadistani-i-Dina*. Much of this dates from the ninth century and provides not only extended commentary on the *Videvdat*'s prescriptions but also a much expanded treasure of theology, mythology, legend, and eschatology.

Non-Muslims in Persia continued to suffer political disabilities for centuries, but Muslim religious fanaticism had abated by the fifteenth century so that Persian and Parsi Zoroastrians reestablished communication. Thus the Parsis became joint heirs, with the Persians, of the Pahlavi literature and the possessors as well of a series of letters called the *Rivayats*. Dating from the early fifteenth through the eighteenth centuries, these were written by Persians in response to questions from the Parsis who feared that in their isolation they might be forgetting or pragmatically adapting, and therefore corrupting, the faith as it obtained in Persia.

Suffice it to say that from the early nineteenth century, the Parsis have been guided in all things essential by the same body of scripture, commentaries, and tracts as have the native Persian Zoroastrians. And although much of the literature may be of the Pahlavi period, the basic lineaments of thought and practice have been consistently Avestan. Thus such Parsi deviations as occurred before the *Rivayats* were acquired and by choice have not been corrected are too minor to require Mary Boyce to qualify her dictum that "Zoroastrianism is characterized by immense conservatism. Essentially and in details, therefore, the later religion is unchanged from that of ancient Iran."[3]

The Myth as Context for Ritual

Thus the anxieties that the death rituals are designed to allay have their ideological basis not so much in anything known to have been taught by Zoroaster as in the remythologized soteriology of the later Avestan period. The *Gathas* presented a relatively unadorned picture of life after death. It would be the souls that survive this life, since they are created immortal and, at birth, are pure and innocent. The souls of men who choose *Ahura Mazda* and walk by choice in his ways of truth and righteousness (or, as the Zoroastrian "Golden Rule" puts it, by *humata*, *hukhta*, and *hvarshta*—good thoughts, good words, and good deeds) as taught by Zoroaster, will successfully negotiate the crossing from this world to paradise. The image of a bridge, called *Chinvat*, is used to aid in conceptualizing the transition. Judged by their own consciences, the righteous will be helped across by Zoroaster and so enter into the bliss and felicity of heaven, *Garo Demana*. But the wicked, likewise so judged, will fall into perdition and misery, a fate lasting at least until some final resurrection at the end of history.

From this simple plot, the later *Avesta* developed (or reconstructed) an elaborate scenario in which *Fravashis* have prominent places. Fravashis are the prototypal heavenly beings or spirits to which the souls of men correspond. Having their origin in eternity or prehistory, they come to earth by choice, each to serve as a human soul's "higher double."[4] Apparently entering into the person, the Fravashi serves its analogue, the soul, as its lifetime guardian, guide, and admonisher. At death, "the Fravashi . . . remains hovering over the soul."[5] For three days it remains on earth, then it accompanies the soul through Judgment and during its ascent through the lower heavens (the new lower levels ancillary to Garo Demana that were supplied by post-Gathic imaginations). In the event that the soul has been wicked, the Fravashi parts company with it, returning to highest heaven while the soul goes instead to hell, *Drujo Demana*.

The subsequent activity of the Fravashi and its corresponding soul appears to be variously conceived. On the one hand, there is the traditional belief that Fravashis in general, whether of souls now in heaven or of souls yet unborn, "wield great power in both the worlds, rendering great help to those who invoke them, and [in the case of those who have already made their descent as doubles for living souls and have returned] keeping watch and ward about the abodes in which they once had lived."[6] They delight in being remembered by the living and "seek their praise and prayer, sacrifice and invocation."[7] They are thought to descend for the last ten days of the Zoroastrian year, the rituals of which period are dedicated to them and to all departed souls. But failure to attend to them is to invite their curse and lose their blessing. Departed souls, according to this conception, do not return once they are across the bridge, since they are bending their efforts toward reaching highest heaven, and the grateful prayers of the living help them in their ascent just as they please the Fravashis. On the other hand, in popular thought, distinctions are often blurred and the functions of the Fravashis and departed souls confusedly conceived. Then, says Dhalla, "The intermingling [of the forms of ancestor-worship] becomes so complete that the souls and not the Fravashis are supposed to come down to the rituals even on the days originally consecrated to the Fravashis."[8]

Many heavenly characters in the Avestan and Pahlavi mythopoeic elaborations of the drama of death have no place now in the script. Modern Parsis have found the stage crowded with minor characters too numerous to remember and too suggestive of polytheism to be credible. The Avestan texts used as funeral liturgy, however, perpetuate by invocation the belief in several of the ancient dramatis personae, particularly the angels (*yazatas*) of judgment: *Mithra* (the judge, known also as *Meher*), *Rashnu* (angel of justice), *Ashtad* (angel of truth), and a fourth yazata, *Sraosha* (the enemy of night's darkness, temptation, and all evil, and the guardian of obedience and discipline), who remains with a righteous dead person as the divine helper and protector of his soul into the fourth day and until Chinvat has been crossed and Mithra and Rashnu have rendered judgment. To Sraosha, therefore, are addressed the prayers and litanies of the death ceremonies for those days.

When account has been taken of the current tendency toward demythologizing the soul's pilgrimage after death, there remains a puzzling residue of belief in the need of extraordinary aid from divine agents. Why should such aid be so important if, as Parsis also say, the passport to paradise is reasonable fidelity in life to the ideals of good thoughts, good words, and good deeds in response to divine love and grace? The resolution of apparent discrepancy depends on distinguishing between theoretical claims and de facto realities. The funeral rites—which are what Parsis *do*—remain virtually unchanged despite the pruning of the traditional mythology. Here is a clue that the world of the *Videvdat* may not have been left far behind after all.[9] The dangers threatened by the demonic "opposite numbers" of the angelic forces apparently remain as real as ever in the Parsi imagination. The name of the fear is pollution.

The Rites for the Dead

The rituals of protection begin if possible even before the moment of death. Relatives, and the dying person too, if able, should recite a *patet* (a confession of sin) and, especially, the *Ahuna-Vairya*, a short prayer believed to be Gathic in origin. It is commonly believed that "if this prayer is repeated properly even once in the correct rhythm and intonation, and with a clear understanding of its meaning, it is equal in efficacy to the repetition of a hundred other hymns put together."[10] Thereafter, no one is ordinarily allowed to touch the body except professional body-bearers, who are to cleanse their own bodies by formal baths employing *gomez* (consecrated bull urine) before and after, and to wear special white apparel while performing their duties.[11] The *Sachkar* ceremony (of bathing with gomez and water, and dressing the corpse) is described as "elaborate" and of a nature demanding "great fortitude."[12] It is accompanied throughout by prayers, and completed when the *Sudreh* and *Kusti* (white undershirt and woven string girdling the waist—the external symbols of Parsi identity) have been put on and the body covered by used but freshly laundered white garments.

When the bearers have shifted the body to a low stone slab and described three circles around it with a metallic instrument, such as a nail, they temporarily retire. Twice during the shrouding of the body a dog is brought in to view the corpse. It is supposed to be four-eyed—that is, to have two eyelike spots above its eyes—but lack of a dog with such marks is the mother of frequent substitutions of any dog available. Modi cited six speculative reasons for the *sagdid* ("the sight of a dog"), and refrained from asserting the validity of any of them.[13] The usual explanation, however, is the one favored by Rustomjee, to the effect that a dog is "infallible" in detecting whether or not the corpse is really and finally lifeless.[14] This "viewing" is repeated at the beginning of each of however many of five periods (*Gahs*) of the Zoroastrian day pass before transfer of the body to a dakhma.

Fire, the Zoroastrian symbol par excellence, is brought in after the first sagdid. Fed by scented sandalwood, it is kept kindled by either priest or layman, until departure for the dakhma. The fire tender usually also recites prayers from the *Avesta*.

The principal ceremony is performed during the last hour that the body is in the *bungli*. The two bearers return and place an iron bier next to the body. Two priests then begin the *Geh-Sarna*, the recital of the *Gathas*. When they pause midcourse, the bearers lift the body over the bier; the priests complete the recital. Once more the dog is brought in. Then assembled male relatives and friends proceed past the body and bow in respectful salute. The bearers cover the face of the deceased, strap the body to the bier, and deliver it to other bearers outside for final carriage to the dakhma. These bearers, who must work in pairs—one or more according to the weight to be carried—are of another class; their only business is that of rendering this nearly final service. The males who wish to follow do so in pairs and only if dressed in white. The body is put down outside the dakhma and another sagdid is performed. The company pays a last respectful look, and the initial bearers return to carry the bier inside the tower, where the body is then undressed and left partly if not entirely exposed for drawing the attention of vultures. The clothes are thrown into a pit to decompose.

Outside, the prayers first spoken when the person was dying or had just died are repeated. All those present, after bathing any uncovered portions of their bodies with gomez and water, depart. After returning to their homes, it is expected that they will do what those who did not participate in the final procession have presumably done already—take an ordinary bath and resume their normal activities. Meanwhile, all participating bearers have been engaging in the rituals of their own purification.[15]

But this summary account is misleading as it stands. Reference must be made to concerns besides those humanitarian and hygienic. For example, there is the *paiwand* (a cloth such as a handkerchief or cotton tape), which must be held by two persons—the bearers who prepare the body, the two persons who must always be in attendance by a corpse until the final ceremony, the bearers who carry the body to the dakhma, and the pairs of persons joining the final procession. The usual explanation, that pairing and the use of the paiwand "create a view of sympathy and mutual help,"[16] obfuscates but does not conceal the survival of fear engendered by the *Videvdat* that

> corporeal defilement is just as much an abomination to Ahuramazda as the moral one; both are fully alike and equally punishable. Through contamination with unclean things, *e.g.*, a dead corpse, which is possessed by Ahriman [the evil spirit], this enemy of cleanliness acquires just as much domination over men, as through the perpetration of wicked deeds, and in consequence, the laws in reference to the purity of the body have just as much weight as those in reference to the purity of the soul or to the moral deeds.[17]

Dastur Dabu, although more influenced by occultism than many Parsis, was not far from representing a common concern when he explained that a corpse

> is corrupt flesh, radiating a type of emanation (*Nasush*) which is supposed to defile the etheric aura (*Khureh*) of a living being touching it. This is termed *Rimani*. . . .
>
> It is strictly forbidden to touch or carry a corpse single-handed. Two persons connected with *Paevand* are required. . . . If one touches it alone, the dual magnetic forces of defilement would be jointly located at his heart. But if two men (with Paevand) work in unison, the centre of *Rimani* would be within the cord.[18]

In any case, the confusion of the material with the spiritual shows in the notion of the *Karp* or astral body. As noted earlier, ceremonies continue into the morning of the fourth day of (or third day *after*) death, because the soul remains in the world for three nights before proceeding to Chinvat. The ceremonial fire and a light are kept burning at the place where the body had lain, and priests lead prayers at the beginning of each gah. A special ceremony called the *Afringan* is performed each night and another called the *Uthamna* on the morning of the fourth day. The effort is mainly to beseech and even strengthen Sraosha so that he "will be able to save his [the departed's] soul from the hands of the demons for the three days."[19] Meanwhile, during the first half-hour the body lay in the dakhma, the sun and the supplementary action of the vultures helped the soul and its spiritual body, the Karp, to come out from the physical body.[20] The heat of the ceremonial fire then protects the soul and Karp until they rise from the earth for a "new location in God's unbounded Universe."[21]

The inventory of prescriptions and proscriptions is still incomplete. The corpse when first laid out must not be in a position for its head to point northward because, according to tradition, the north is the direction from which proceed "all kinds of dangers and evils [including] mental."[22] *Juddins* (non-Zoroastrians) may view the body before it is first bathed by bearers but not afterward; nor are they to join in the procession to the dakhma or touch any Zoroastrian until the dakhma ceremonies are completed, lest the protection afforded the believers by their prefuneral purificatory ceremony be vitiated.[23] Even the language of the rituals is prescribed—as is the case for all Zoroastrian ceremonies—and this despite the fact that only the exceptional priest knows the Avestan and later Pahlavi period languages enough to translate what he first learned by rote and is now reciting. To translate texts into the vernacular for liturgical use "would be revolting," according to one highly authoritative priest;[24] at the very least, the ritual in translation could not "retain its mystic attraction and convincing efficacy."[25]

The most pressing obligations, before any worshipful post-dakhma rituals are performed, are to cleanse the slab on which the corpse first lay and any utensils that may have touched the body at home or bungli. The agents are gomez and water, with the number of washings varying from one for gold to six for stone—the more porous, in other words, the more the cleansing required. Contaminated porcelain, however, and wood or clay as well, cannot be salvaged.

For the next three days, abstinence from meat and from cooking in the house where death occurred is generally observed. At the five gahs of each of these days a prayer of thanks to Sraosha (the *Sravosh-baj*)[26] and the prayer of repentance (the *Patet*) are said, along with the traditional gah prayers (one for each particular period), by two or more priests and the relatives. The Afringan ceremony, repeated at each nightfall, increases the honor paid to Sraosha by requiring the artifacts of fire, a metallic tray, water, and flowers, a special seating arrangement, and the priests' recitation of additional textual material, mainly Avestan. The family may wish also that certain higher liturgical services, useful for any occasion of need for aid from the heavenly hierarchy, be performed at a fire-temple coincidentally with the domestic rites. The Uthamna ceremony occurs after 3:00 P.M. on the third day. It is much like those of the other gahs except for announcing the donations relatives and friends will make to charity as memorials to the deceased. The soul, having thus received the protection and support of Sraosha for three days, proceeds to Chinvat for the judgment it will receive on the following morning.

Before dawn of the fourth day, the last and most ambitious of the funeral ceremonies, the *Cheharum*, should be performed. It consists of four *Baj*, the first addressed to the yazatas, Rashnu and Astad;[27] the second, to *Ram-Khvastra* (the yazata of rarified air through which "the soul of a good pious man passes away to the higher regions"[28]); the third, to *Ardafravash* ("the spirits of all the departed souls whose rank the particular deceased . . . has joined"[29]); and the fourth or final, to Sraosha, in gratitude for the protection he has given the soul during its ordeal.

There are still *Afringan-baj* ceremonies to be performed during the next gah of this fourth day. They will be expected again on the tenth day, the thirtieth day, then monthly, and after that, annually. The annual observances continue as long as the living descendants are willing and able to pay the fees for their performance. The presumption is that the arrangement is mutually rewarding. A soul, pleased by the righteousness of "dear sons," can "rest in peace and tranquillity," and the living may find themselves in turn assisted with "an invisible helping hand."[30]

Skeptics may regard the anxieties which the ceremonies attempt to vanquish as arising from notions lacking validation from Zoroaster, reason, or nature; and there are members of the community, especially among *behdins*, who think just that. But, as noted earlier, the ceremonial answer seems equal to the magnitude of the problem as the majority view it, and the needs of particular persons, deceased and living, are apparently met. It is otherwise with respect to the fear of corporate extinction.

The Threat of Parsi Demise

This old fear undoubtedly arose when Persia fell to the Greeks and remained under a rule not strictly indigenous until Pars again supplied the ruling dynasty in the

Sassanid era. At that time, however, it was only the religion, not the people, that languished. Hence the earliest analogue to the Parsis' present plight was occasioned by the Muslim conquest of Persia and final victory in A.D. 641.

Parsis differ when identifying the time of greatest trouble, but almost all affirm that the flight to India was occasioned not only by Muslim pressure to convert but also by the threat of death if they did not.[31] Actually, the history of the times as far as Zoroastrians are concerned is sketchy and difficult to authenticate. What has apparently locked the tradition of persecution firmly into the store of Parsi memories, making the fact if not the date important, is a Persian-language poem, *Kisseh-i-Sanjan*, composed by a priest of the Gujarati community in about A.D. 1600. It is the story of how that community came to be, according to the cumulative oral traditions of the time.

The Persian experience might still be recalled as a romantic example of heroism and its pain forgotten were it not that the Hindu provincial rulers, who had given the Parsi pilgrims asylum, were overwhelmed in the late fourteenth and early fifteenth centuries by Muslim rulers already in India and ever seeking to increase the area of their hegemony. Once again the ancestors of today's Parsis are remembered as having found their lives as well as their faith in jeopardy. But another obscure era followed, and not until after the late seventeenth century, when a significant number of those disheartened by their fluctuating fortunes under the Moguls had begun their migration southward to the developing settlement of the English that is now Bombay can the threads of the story be picked up again.

Today, of course, the Parsis do not fear external persecution. But the memory of past instances is recalled to make real the fear of extinction for whatever reason, and this in the hope of persuading the living to man the barricades against the latest strategy of the prince of demons—racial suicide.

The problem, judging by the number and temper of pamphlets, tracts, articles, and chapters of books devoted to it, is serious and multifaceted. The Bombay Parsis who prospered, first as ambitious employees of English entrepreneurs and then as entrepreneurs themselves (so that theirs was the bellwether community of all Indian Parsi communities well into the twentieth century), are now suffering economic decline and demotion to lower rungs on the Indian social-political ladder.[32] With the economic pinch has come postponement of marriage and thus smaller families, not to mention increasing incidence of what is almost apostasy for males—bachelorhood by choice. The practice of endogamy is part of the syndrome.[33] At the same time that the Parsis are shrinking in number, the youth are exercising more independence in choosing their own mates; finding fewer fellow Parsis to choose from, they tend more and more to marry exogamously or to honor endogamy in the breach by not marrying at all. The divorce rate, too, has risen sharply since 1936. Still other causes of concern, apparently justified by recent corroborating studies, are the signs among Parsis of deterioration in general health and a high incidence of genetically transmitted vulnerabilities.[34]

The net result of all interrelated factors is a steady decline in the Parsi population of India,[35] and most notably of its largest community, in Bombay, where the death rate is approximately 50 percent higher than the birth rate.[36] The danger of extinction is real and the intense concern about it is understandable.

Proposed Solutions

The concern is expressed again and again not only by respected and articulate leaders of the Parsi community but also by many whose only ostensible credentials appear to be their convictions and access to a printing press. In either case, views are more polarized than marked by moderation. Thus, at one extreme, counsel stresses rededication to the whole scriptural, theological, and cultic tradition, faithful cultic observance and retention of the liturgical languages (otherwise dead), respect for priestly authority, more religious education for the laity, strict endogamy, exclusion of prospective converts, and support of familiar types of charitable trusts and benevolence as means of promoting the Parsis' education, health, and social welfare. In contrast is the agenda of the reformers. They would depend almost exclusively upon the *Gathas* for foundations, and upon their interpretation in the light of modern knowledge for current guidance (thus denying the authority of the late Avestan and Pahlavi traditions). They would reform the cultus—by translating the liturgical texts, eliminating the elements of ritual deemed archaic, abandoning altogether such ritual acts as purport to supply religious remedy for physical pollution, and utilizing modern science to clarify and separate the traditionally and confusedly overlapping categories of hygiene, morality, and religion. There appears to be no demand for abandoning the hereditary principle with respect to the priesthood, but the reformers are generally in agreement that there can be no revision of the cultus without thoroughgoing reform of priestly education, the functions of the priestly office, and compensation for the profession. They would, in most cases, tolerate exogamy and endorse conversion to the faith. And, finally, they are concerned to devise new institutional agencies to combat the decline in fortunes and restore the Parsis' individual and corporate self-respect and well-being.

Illustrative of the reformers' position is the advice of the sociologist P.A. Wadia that the community cease trusting in

> teachers who make a deliberate effort to teach dogmatics, to glorify the dead past and to instill in the minds of the young ideas which have become discredited. . . . It is infinitely better to leave boys and girls alone in these matters than to start them on ideas that can only breed a false religious pride . . . and . . . incline them to superstition and bigotry.[37]
>
> Our own ancestors in India freely mingled by marriage and otherwise with the people of the land; and it was because we mingled that we managed to survive. Can we today by a different policy, a policy of rigid exclusivism and in-breeding . . . hope to survive?[38]

> Can our small community . . . with religious beliefs which do not penetrate beyond the surface . . . reasonably look forward to the future with courage and confidence? . . . self-righteous pride will not convert us into the strong ones of the Lord.[39]

Similarly, Umrigar, a behdin, has argued that it is "petty" to insist that prayers be recited in a dead language, that corpses be disposed of only in dakhmas and to the accompaniment of "expensive religious ceremonies," and that the community's doors be closed to prospective converts.[40]

When the argument is taken up by a person of some influence among Parsis, but of amateur standing as a writer, criticism can be blunt and pungent, as Dara J.D. Cama's evaluation of traditional ritual:

> Indulging in Rituals, ceremonials, and occult performances (popularly known as Priests' codes) which are supposed to ensure varied happiness here and in heaven, is to substitute [for] the God of Righteousness . . . the idol of reward.[41]
>
> Even in these days of eau-de-cologne soaps and bowel wash with potent disinfectants, we fall back upon the subtly-purified and mantra-infected urine of a bull for purifying our interior and exterior. A good Zoroastrian needs no washing and purifying of his soul. Nothing pure needs to be purified.[42]

Judging, however, by the tone of frustration in reformist literature, orthodox traditionalism—represented principally but by no means exclusively by the priesthood—is retaining its at least nominal authority over the Parsi community. As Dabu has written, in justification of leaving customs intact:

> Ceremonies are the pillars of Zoroastrian Faith. . . . If one is after fault-finding no custom or usage is foolproof or faultless.[43]
>
> Parsis' . . . racial characteristics are hereditary, and preservation of their blood from getting mixed with that of other races is a necessity. . . . The admission to the Parsi community is impossible as an alien cannot change his blood . . . and . . . may not have the same reverence for fire in the Parsi Temples.[44]

Another venerable *ervad* (priest), the Dastur at Udvada (site of the oldest fire-temple in India), has located in divine and therefore eternally valid revelation the authority for traditional views:

> Our religion is the religion sent to us by Ahuramazda. Conversion and faith in Religion of Revelation are incongruous. God has given us our Religion under His own Laws of making up an appropriate set of beliefs of His own Choice and man takes birth in an environment best suited for him to carry out the allotted mission in life. Just as a man cannot change his parents he cannot change his religion. . . . It is our Prophet and our Ancestors who have put us in charge of our divine heritage. . . . Our Ancestors suffered a good deal . . . to preserve, promote and defend this divine heritage and pass it on to a succession of generations. We pray to God to help us fulfil our allotted mission.[45]

The word of an influential behdin on the issue of mixed marriages and their threat to the religion was widely circulated in 1970 for the support it gave to a custom of long standing.

> We emphatically maintain that our religion and culture deserve to survive and not be frivolously frittered away. . . .
>
> Our boys were the first to set the bad example. Due notice was not taken of it by our community, in the belief that children born of a Parsi father . . . would after all be Parsis and admissible in the Parsi fold. Then Parsi girls followed the evil example. . . .
>
> We maintain that mixed marriages are condemnable for Parsis.[46]

Although it is common to argue that traditions once based on revelation and religious insight are also validated today by science and common sense, Rustomjee and others are satisfied that the benefits of traditional cultic observance are discernible and need no scientific explanation or demonstration.

> The "Sudreh" [the identifying undershirt] has a magnetic effect upon the body, when it is worn next to the skin. . . . That effect is discernible by the soul. . . .
>
> [It] helps to ward off the malefic influence of the inclement elements outside man. . . .
>
> It will thus be noticed that man's full purpose of life is achievable through the force of the symbology of his sacred garment. . . .
>
> Let us [also] therefore treat our valuable symbol, the "Kusti," [the sacred girdle] our fortifying power, our help against the onslaught of evil . . . as . . . the protective spiritual weapon which can stand by us, giving us the hope of salvation for our soul.[47]

Conclusion

The myth and ritual that compose a cultus are living bread if they rescue life from banality and transmute death by explaining it as requisite to life's renewal. Zoroastrians have found their cultus functional in this sense for many centuries and thus without need of essential change. Like all people, they might face perils visible and material, invisible and spiritual, and not without fear and trembling; but anxiety met its match in the hope and assurance engendered by time-honored forms of belief and cultic observance. In this century, however, declining fortunes and diminishing numbers have become a concern of the whole community. The establishment finds the basis for infidelity in the doubts and skepticism encouraged by modernity and, in turn, the cause of Parsi acceleration toward extinction. The accused have not been at pains to deny that funeral rites in particular have their efficacious relevance, but they have replied that it is for want of reform measures in general that the community is dying.

Doubtless there are many nonreligious factors, favorable and unfavorable, having their bearing on the issue of survival. But the traditionalists and reformers alike believe that if their advice were taken, all the factors favorable to the preservation of the faith and the community would be called into play. Meanwhile, neither of the opposing convictions about what ought to be allays anxiety about what is.

Communities of immigrant Zoroastrians in other hemispheres may evolve strategies of survival that prove successful. But in India, where the largest community of Zoroastrians has its home, if no stratagem old or new stems the present trend, the vultures may wheel ominously in the air, with no feast in sight.

Notes

1. Parsis are the Zoroastrians whose ancestors migrated from Persia and took refuge in India rather than convert or suffer the disabilities of being "infidels" to the Muslim Arabs who imposed on the land their religion as well as their rule. Today, this Indian community, centered principally in the cities of Bombay and Poona and the state of Gujarat, constitutes about four-fifths of the world's approximately 120,000 Zoroastrians. Its practices, therefore, may be regarded as essentially normative for the faith.

The name, *Parsi*, like *Persia*, derives from *Pars*, the name of the province from which came the first rulers strong enough to create the nation state of Persia and, after that, an empire, in the sixth century B.C.

2. "Avesta Literature," *Avesta, Pahlavi, and Ancient Persian Studies*, first series, ed. Karl J. Trübner and Otto Harrassowitz (Byculla: Bombay Education Society's Press, 1904), p. 8. See also Maneckji Nusservanji Dhalla, *History of Zoroastrianism* (Bombay: K.R. Cama Oriental Institute, 1963); A.V. Williams Jackson, *Zoroaster* (New York: Columbia University Press, 1898); Dosabhai Framji Karaka, *History of the Parsis*, 2 vols. (London: MacMillan, 1884); J.H. Moulton, *Early Zoroastrianism* (London: Williams and Norgate, 1913); and R.C. Zaehner, *The Dawn and Twilight of Zoroastrianism* (New York: Putnam, 1961) for detailed analyses of Zoroastrian origins during the first millennium B.C., the adoption and transformation of the religion by Median priests (the Magi), and the composition and fate of the *Avesta* up to the time when Cyrus the Great's Achaemenid empire (founded in 550 B.C.) fell to the Greeks in 330 B.C.

3. "Zoroastrianism," in *Historia Religionum*, vol. 2, *Religions of the Present*, ed. C. Jouco Bleeker and George Widengren (Leiden: Brill, 1971), p. 211.

4. This term is used by Dhalla, *History of Zoroastrianism*, p. 237. See also pp. 234ff.

5. Khurshed S. Dabu, *Message of Zarathushtra*, 2d ed. (Bombay: New Book Co., Private Ltd., 1959), p. 64. Dabu, in 1971, was the oldest active priest in Bombay and the Dastur (high priest) of Wadiaji *Atash-Beheram* (the highest of three grades of fire-temples).

6. Dhalla, *History of Zoroastrianism*, p. 239.

7. Ibid., p. 240.

8. Ibid., p. 243.

9. Thus I.J.S. Taraporewala, a Parsi widely respected for his blend of piety and critical common sense, could write, "No nation can maintain its spiritual life on such washings . . . and upon such an obsession of 'the Demon of the Corpse,' and of the other demons, such as we read of in the Vendidad [Videvdat]," and still describe and justify contemporary rites for the dead the liturgical content of which remains virtually unchanged since the time of its prescription. *The Religion of Zarathushtra*, 2d ed., rev. (Bombay: Bombay Chronicle Press, 1965), pp. 71, 59–63.

10. Ibid., p. 33.

11. Framroz Rustomjee, "Zoroastrian Ceremonies for the Disposal of the Dead" (pamphlet), 2d ed., (Colombo: Nadaraja Press, 1965), p. 3. This is not as it was described in 1922 by Modi, author of the definitive work on Parsi ceremonies, who said that "some near or dear one" did the bathing and dressing between the moment of death and the arrival of the body-bearer. Meanwhile, relatives might embrace the deceased, but thereafter, the body was "supposed to fall under the influence of Druj-i-Nasush, i.e., the evil influence of Decomposition." Anyone then touching the body, except the bearers, was required to take a "sacred bath . . . under the directions of a priest." Jivanji Jamshedji Modi, *The Religious Ceremonies and Customs of the Parsees* (Bombay: British India Press, 1922), p. 55. But Rustomjee's account agrees better with later custom according to which the corpse is transferred by ambulance to a *bungli* (funeral cottage) near the dakhmas before the ceremonial bath. This custom of using one of the several memorial

bunglis erected on Malabar Hill, Bombay, by philanthropic Parsis, has all but replaced the no longer affordable provision of a special room at home for no other purpose than accommodation for the dead and the ceremonies prior to bearing the body to a dakhma. In 1968, as a sample and average year, the bunglis were used for 999 persons, while services were held in homes for only 17. (See *Report for the Year 1968*, by the Trustees of the Parsi Punchayet Funds and Properties, Bombay, p. 30.)

12. Rustomjee, "Zoroastrian Ceremonies," p. 3.

13. *Religious Ceremonies*, pp. 58–61.

14. "Zoroastrian Ceremonies," p. 5. This contemporary rationalization might be expected from one who has no special reputation as a historical authority, but it is an occasion for real surprise to find the renowned Modi omitting from his list of possible reasons for the *sagdid* the *Videvdat*'s own explanation, to the effect that the four-eyed dog prompts *Nasu* (the corpse demon, feminine in gender) to fly away. Perhaps the omission illustrates that latter-day tendency toward mythopoeic economy I have already mentioned.

15. Ibid., p. 4, and Taraporewala, *The Religion of Zarathushtra*, p. 60n., agree that the bearers' clothing has to be discarded and never worn again. Clothing worn by family and friends during the rites may be cleansed and reworn, although not again for "religious purposes." Modi, *Religious Ceremonies*, p. 73.

16. Modi, ibid., p. 64.

17. John G. Rhode, "Comparison of the Laws of Ormuzd with the Laws of Jehova," as extracted and translated from Dr. Rhode's German (Bombay, 1879) by K.R. Cama, *The Collected Works of K.R. Cama*, vol. 2 (Bombay: K.R. Cama Oriental Institute, 1970), p. 61.

18. *A Hand-book of General Information on Zoroastrianism* (Bombay: P.N. Mehta Educational Trust, 1969), p. 43.

19. Modi, *Religious Ceremonies*, p. 78, quoting from the *Shayast la Shayast* (of the Pahlavi period) as translated in *Sacred Books of the East*, vol. 5 (1880), chap. 17, 3, pp. 382–83.

20. See Dr. M.D. Karkhanavala, an Ervad (priest) quoted in a pamphlet originally written by Nasserwanji Byramji, "Reference to a Model of a Tower of Silence," in 1899, and reprinted "With added Opinions of Present High Priests of Bombay" (Bombay: Jehangir M. Engineer, August 1964), p. vii.

21. Rustomjee, "Zoroastrian Ceremonies," p. 6. *Karp* is the Pahlavi form of an earlier Avestan word meaning "form" or "appearance." Rustomjee rendered it *Keharpa*, as do a number of contemporary Parsis. This, however, is "a very corrupt spelling," says Hanns-Peter Schmidt, Professor of Indo-Iranian Studies at UCLA, for whose letter of counsel and correction on this and other linguistic and historical points I am deeply grateful.

22. Modi, *Religious Ceremonies*, p. 56.

23. Rustomjee, "Zoroastrian Ceremonies," p. 2.

24. Interview with Dr. Firoze Meherji Kotwal, Principal of M.F. Cama Athornan Institute (school for priests' sons and the training of those wishing to exercise their hereditary prerogative to train for the priesthood themselves), at Andheri, Bombay, 14 October 1971.

25. Interview with Dr. Jal F. Bulsara, a *behdin* (layman) and sociologist who from 1930 to 1941 was Secretary of the Bombay Parsi Panchayat, 21 October 1971.

26. A *baj* is a brief ceremony consisting of "words or prayers religiously recited in honor of particular beings, such as the yazatas . . . and Fravashis . . ." with offerings sometimes accompanying the recital. Modi, *Religious Ceremonies*, p. 354.

27. Ibid., p. 83.

28. Modi, *Religious Ceremonies*, p. 84. See also Rustom Masani, *Zoroastrianism* (New York: Macmillan, 1968), p. 106.

29. Modi, ibid., pp. 84–85. Another interpretation would make Ardafravash "the personification of the *fravashis*"—in other words, a kind of collective yazata. See Mary Boyce, "Zoroastrianism," p. 227.

30. Modi, ibid., pp. 85–86.

31. Taraporewala has stood almost alone as a challenger of this oft-parroted tradition. He is convinced that the Zoroastrian masses readily converted once given the occasion for choosing between their own decadent religion and the still fresh ideals of Islam, and that the period of persecution is to be placed later, in the ninth century, when the Muslims' evangelism had deteriorated into coercive fanaticism. *The Religion of Zarathushtra*, pp. 70–73.

32. See P.A. Wadia, *Parsis Ere the Shadows Thicken* (Bombay, 1949), pp. 4–9, for documentation of a marked slippage of Parsis from the professional and business ranks into the ranks of unskilled labor and the unemployed.

33. See n.38.

34. Sapur Faredur Desai, *A Community at the Cross-Road* (Bombay: New Book Co., 1948), pp. 87–112. Desai cited tuberculosis, respiratory diseases, mental illness, and retardation as endemic among Parsis. For details on divorce, see p. 38 A; postponement of marriage, p. 39; the 40 percent increase in number of unmarried adults, p. 44; smaller families, p. 73.

35. See Eckehard Kulke, *The Parsees, A Bibliography on an Indian Minority* (Freiburg: Arnold-Bergstraesser Institute, 1968), p. xxi. His inquiry yielded population figures of 110,000 Indian Parsis in 1951 but only 100,600 ten years later—a loss of almost 10 percent.

36. K.D. Umrigar, "Are the Parsis Dying Out?," *The Illustrated Weekly of India*, 29 August 1971, p. 33. Bombay's Parsis number about 70,000 of a Maharashtran community which declined from 77,542 in 1961 to about 75,000 in 1971.

37. Wadia, *Parsis*, pp. 77–78.

38. Ibid., p. 140. There is no unanimity of opinion as to when endogamy was adopted by the Parsis as a wall of protection for the Zoroastrian faith. The orthodox think it was chosen by deliberation at the time of the Parsis' arrival in India, but liberals think the practice developed later, acquiring the authority of dogma only after it had become standard practice.

39. Ibid., p. 141.

40. Umrigar, "Are the Parsis Dying Out," pp. 33 and 35.

41. A behdin businessman, in an untitled pamphlet written as a letter to his uncle in Ahmedabad and sent in published form to the Trustees of the Bombay Parsi Panchayat for their enlightenment (Bombay, 15 November 1965), p. 2.

42. Ibid., p. 4.

43. Khurshed S. Dabu, "Ceremonies for Dead," *Parsiana* 3, no. 12 (October 1967): 17.

44. Dabu, *Message of Zarathushtra*, pp. 15 and 17.

45. Hormazdiar Kaiyoji Mirza, "On Conversion and Converts in Zoroastrianism," *Parsiana* 6, no. 10 (August 1970): 33.

46. Firoze C. Davar, "Parsis and Racial Suicide," *Jame-e-Jamshed*, 29 August 1970. The professor's article, in this Parsi, Gujarati-language newspaper, was reprinted four times—twice in the newspaper itself, once in the *Memorial Volume* of the Golden Jubilee of the Memorial at Sanjan and the Birth Centenary of the Late J.J. Vimadalal, 1971, and once as a pamphlet from which the quotation was taken (Bombay: Dinar Printery, n.d.), pp. 3, 4, 5.

47. Framroz Rustomjee, "Distinguishing Symbols of the Parsis," *Parsiana* 7, no. 3 (January 1971): 18, 19–20, 21.

A Japanese Buddhist Perspective

If the body dies, it does no harm to the mind, but if the mind dies, one can no longer act as a man even though the body survives.

Yoshida Shoin, *Zenshu*, I, VIII, 299

Practicing Dying: The Samurai-Zen Death Techniques of Suzuki Shōsan

WINSTON L. KING

Suzuki Shōsan lived from 1579 to 1655, was trained in the profession of samurai, and took an active part in the wars of unification under Tokugawa Ieyasu (1542–1616). Although the unification was largely completed by 1603, he stayed on in Tokugawa service—having been awarded a small fief—until about 1620, that is, until a few years after Ieyasu's death. Then at the age of forty-one he gave up the profession of samurai—giving his inheritance to a nephew rather than to a son—and became a Zen monk. He was allowed to keep his layman's name. His biographer notes: "He asked the abbot Tai Gu for a new [monk's] name. Tai Gu declined, saying, 'Your religious accomplishments carry great weight with the public; can anyone think of making up a name for you? So after considering the matter, your old [given] name is good.' Hence he was known as Shōsan."[1] He had been interested in Zen (of the Sōtō variety) as a samurai and had pursued his interests as time allowed. Now as a monk he became a kind of peripatetic teacher, traveling from hermitage to hermitage and remaining in each one for a time, as moved by inclination and request. He was called Teacher (i.e., spiritual master) by the many who sought his advice and by about fifty men who considered themselves his disciples.[2] He wrote some short practical treatises on Zen Buddhist practice and many of his epigrams and sermonettes have been preserved.

But even though he gave up his profession of samurai at a relatively young age and became a Zen monk, he remained a samurai swordsman in spirit always, as well as in his interpretation of Zen practice. This samurai Zensmanship was neither strange nor strained, of course, in view of the long and intimate historical-cultural associations of Zen tradition and the profession of samurai, which began with the national dominance of the militaristic Hōjo regime in the thirteenth century. In D.T. Suzuki's words, Zen "never actively incited" the samurai to carry on their profession, but "it has passively sustained them when they have for whatever reason once entered it"[3]—and, it might be added, became traditionally known as the proper training for the warrior class.

This is not the place for a full-scale discussion of the classic pattern of samurai training, but since it was the subculture in which Suzuki Shōsan was nurtured, and since it exercised a dominant influence on his approach to Zen, it will be helpful to notice a few relevant features of the discipline. In a passage reminiscent of Hakuin's delineation of the proper use of the kōan Suzuki writes:

> The fighter is to be always single-minded with one object in view: to fight, looking neither backward nor sidewise. . . . He is therefore not to be encumbered in any possible way, be it physical, emotional, or intellectual. . . . A good fighter is generally an ascetic or stoic, which means he has an iron will.[4]

This, of course, is descriptive of the moment of combat when all doubts, thinkings-about, and distractive emotions are cast aside; the fighter's total visceral-physical strength is fused into one supreme effort and concentrated in the sword itself. But such an intensity of combat power can arise only out of a basic preparation of the heart and mind as well as of the sword arm and its skills. The good samurai was required to be *always* ready for instantaneous combat; his senses and total psychosomatic set were to be geared to the slightest indication of danger and to spring into either defensive or offensive action, as the occasion might require, on the spur of the moment. But this is not the totality of the matter; at the deepest level combat-readiness is identical with death-readiness. Although the samurai was not actually always faced with a mortal combat situation, or in danger of imminent death, he must train himself for the moment of combat by living always and intimately with the thought of death:

> The idea most vital and essential to the samurai is that of death, which he ought to have before his mind day and night, night and day, from the dawn of the first day of the year till the last minute of the last day of it. When this notion takes firm hold of you, you are able to discharge your duties to their fullest extent. . . . Think what a frail thing life is, especially that of a samurai. This being so, you will come to consider every day of life your last and dedicate it to the fulfillment of your obligations.[5]

Again, from the same source and in the same spirit we read:

> Bushido means the determined will to die. When you are at the parting of the ways, do not hesitate to choose the way to death. . . . Some may say that if you die without attaining the object, it is a useless death, dying like a dog. . . . [But] in case you die without achieving the object, it may be a dog-death—the deed of madness, but there is here no reflection on your honor. In Bushido honor comes first. Therefore, every morning and every evening, have the idea of death vividly impressed in your mind. *When your determination to die at any moment is thoroughly established, you attain to perfect mastery of Bushido.*[6]

Perhaps it was in this spirit of Bushido, "the way of the warrior," that Suzuki Shōsan spoke when he defined the "essence of Buddhism": "Two or three old women came and asked him about the essence of Buddhism. The Teacher said: 'I do not know anything that I can teach you.' After a little while he said suddenly: 'You will die. You will die. Never forget the fact of dying and say the Nembutsu.' "[7]

Quite obviously when a man describes the essence of Buddhism to be the perpetual remembrance of his own death, or at least finds such a remembrance to be an eminently viable way into the practice of Buddhism, the general Buddhist truth of the impermanence of human life has received a powerful and specifically experiential confirmation in that man's life. Even if one did not previously know that Suzuki Shōsan had been a samurai it could almost be guessed from such a statement as this one—as well as many others in which "practicing dying," that is, being aware of the imminence of death, is a persistent theme.[8] And in an autobiographical passage he vividly indicates how practicing dying became part of his consciousness at an early age and how important it was in his interpretation of Zen:

> One day a certain monk said: How does one arouse and produce the power of Ni-ōh?
>
> The Master said in answer: Just by practicing dying. From the time I was a young man, by continually leaping into the midst of enemies of great strength, I was constantly practicing dying. Thus I could enter into [this death practice] soon. On one occasion I attacked these two or three men who had spears. I was pierced in my body and while experiencing death without [actually] dying, and throwing my body into this struggle, I struck off their heads, broke their spears and thus was not defeated. So while learning to die in various ways, I came to know this power of Ni-ōh. [7a, 128, p. 176]

This passage indicates how central the samurai experience and spirit were to Suzuki Shōsan's existential mode, both as man and as Zen practitioner. His experience of the pains and fear of death, while still in life, was a kind of direct, personal revelation of the Buddhist truth of impermanence and suffering. Also, his samurai training had taught him how to go straight forward (toward some goal or other), regardless of the prospect of death. To him the lesson of this was twofold: Death was to be negatively conquered by deliberately facing it and *choosing* by an act of imagination to feel its cold piercing breath perpetually on the back of his neck—even in the midst of security and good health, and despite the natural human desire to put death-thoughts far away and live in present enjoyments. On the positive side, such experiences had given him confidence in the power of the steadfast mind and will to go on beyond the fear of death and to seize the prize regardless.

But before I discuss in detail the conversion of Suzuki Shōsan's warrior-philosophy into a viable spiritual discipline it will be interesting to probe further into his existential concern. The source of his concern to achieve an efficacious spiritual discipline seems thoroughly Buddhist: the fear of rebirth in lower levels of existence, and the desire to end the whole process of rebirth. However much contemporary Zen may be reticent on the matter of rebirth, or however much Suzuki Shōsan may have "misunderstood" Zen in this respect, there can be no doubt that he believed in rebirth and was concerned to escape it by achieving the death of the mind or of ordinary selfhood. He refers to rebirth frequently in a taken-for-granted way.

> Even if such a one obtains the reward of heaven[ly birth], he may suddenly fall into hell. Therefore, though just now for a little, one's mind is virtuous, soon it will be an evil mind. In any case, if the root of mind is not cut off, rebirth will not be cut off. . . . If

> but a very little of intellection remains, you will receive rebirth according to the world of that thought.

And he warns those whose minds are dominated by the passions: "As for such an one as is addicted to this evil way, who repeats it over and over, existence will not always be in the *human* realm" [7a, 57, p. 155]. Nor can the conclusion be escaped that when he speaks about himself he is not being merely metaphorical:

> The teacher said: "I do not know what sorts of things a Buddhist should do, but I know only that I am a bad man. If you should become my friend, and should [frequently] come and go, I would tell you that my mind is a place wherein dwell hungry ghosts and beasts. I am truly aware of nothing better than this. You think that I am pretending to be humble, but I know I am continuously sinking into hell." [7a, 57, p. 154]

With this apparently genuine interest in escaping rebirth goes his correlate concern, to die a good death. But what is a good death? In the samurai tradition it is dying a brave, honorable, unafraid death, even though no apparent purpose is served by it; it is meeting death head-on without flinching in body or heart. Converting this to the Zen spiritual idiom, a good death is a physical death already prepared for by the "destruction of the mind"—of individualized selfhood—which requires, of course, courage and skill. *Then* physical death is of no consequence and can be faced freely as a deliberately willed action, even though it is forced on everyone by the circumstances of human frailty. Suzuki Shōsan desires to prepare for this kind of good death.

Sometimes he is confident that his samurai experience of meeting death face to face has adequately prepared him for the inevitable:

> Without the spirit of valorous determination, of what little avail will be the spirit of the ordinary man at the moment of death! . . . In developing this mind quickly, as I did, I thought that it might be passed on quickly to everyone, but not even one person was able to receive it! Therefore it appears to be something that is very hard to attain to by practice and a very hard thing to be passed on to others. [7a, 81, p. 163]

However, anxiety is sometimes expressed concerning whether he has truly carried over the genuine intrepidity of the samurai into its Zen-spiritual form and whether he has conquered the fear of death as a genuine samurai-Zen person ought to have done:

> If it be asked whether I am a cowardly samurai since I no longer kill living beings in this manner, I simply cannot answer. Since giving up the taking of life I have proceeded with ascetic disciplines. Even if I do not study this "complete virtue" with anybody [a master?], I have a feeling of uneasiness concerning this matter of not dying freely. By training in various ways I can understand this principle of "freely dying." [7a, 72, p. 161]

Whether the "can" in the last sentence indicates realized experience or hope that it *will* be the case is not clear. But it seems to be more the latter, as in this passage:

"Because I am a man who does not want to die, even if I be killed no matter what I do, without thinking about it I train myself to thrust my neck forward so that I shall die of my own desire" [7a, 57, p. 154]. This is perhaps Suzuki Shōsan's best figure for training: to make the inevitable, the predetermined, fact of his own physical death into a freely willed act at the same time. This is more difficult to do than to be a samurai fighter readying himself for possible death in the next encounter. The samurai must not think about the possibility of life—or death—at the moment of encounter; he had been taught that the properly death-ready warrior most often escaped death, whereas the fearful or life-desiring one often died in combat. But the potential free spirit must come to terms with the final physical death that comes to every person by sword, sickness, or old age. And Suzuki Shōsan's figure of speech takes cognizance of this. Every person perpetually stands before the executioner's block, where the sword of ultimate death will descend without fail. No kind of bravery or training can prevent it. One's only freedom is mental, somewhere "within" the inexorable physical event, here signified by the power to stretch forth his neck of his own free will to receive the downstroke of the inevitable sword.

Why then is it that Suzuki Shōsan, sure as he sometimes is that he has developed a mind of "valorous determination" sufficient for the hour of death, at other times has an uneasiness about not dying freely? Is it because he has had no final satori breakthrough experience? Or because he is, like Hōnen Shōnin, aware of his weaknesses, feels those "hungry ghosts and beasts" prowling constantly within, and senses that the desire for life still has a hold on him? Perhaps these questions cannot be definitely answered; but further analysis of Suzuki Shōsan's interpretation of "practicing dying" in a Zen manner may cast light on this matter. And there are autobiographical statements bearing on the same point.

Precisely why Suzuki Shōsan turned from a samurai calling to the Zen monkhood may not be clear. Perhaps it was a moral revulsion against killing; this might be inferred from the previous quotation about whether he had become a "cowardly" samurai. Or perhaps with Ieyasu dead and the country unified under the Shogunate he felt that his samurai work was done. Yet one so thoroughly impregnated by the samurai spirit cannot be viewed as profoundly revolted by it; still other passages suggest that he recommended the actual use of a kind of samurai-Buddhist technique for battle itself. It may be that he became interested in "killing the self," rather than others, even though this could be done honorably in the samurai tradition. Toward the end of his life, he counseled a young samurai who wished to become a monk to remain a samurai because it would be spiritually more valuable. He does not speak in terms of repentance and grief over his own past.

Obviously, the transition from samurai to Zen monk was not radical. The close rapport between Zen and the martial arts has already been alluded to. And Suzuki Shōsan had learned about and even practiced Zen in the course of his career as samurai, so that his two careers were organically related. In any case, both Buddhism and the samurai tradition were deeply impregnated with the notion of the transiency of life and the nearness of death. The samurai, by virtue of being a samurai, was already more than half "converted" to Buddhism, and converted in a deeply existential way, because of the samurai gut-level feeling for, and of, death. That this lesson was deeply imprinted on Suzuki Shōsan's consciousness is evident from his earlier noted definition of the essence of Buddhism as the remembrance that one will die. And not only once did he say this, but the awareness of impermanence and of his own impending death as an integral part of that impermanence seems to have been at the core of his advice to anyone and everyone bent on following the Buddhist way. Thus, to a nun about to go on a pilgrimage: "As for this body, it is a body which will certainly perish. Keep always in mind the illusory-dream, the bubble-and-shadow nature of phenomena. Consider [for instance] the floating flowers and falling leaves. Certainly you should [always] be observing such things. Do not ever forget that the last hour is right now" [7b, 84, p. 222].

What then is the situation of a samurai, already "half-converted" to Zen, who actually turns to Zen? How would a "full" conversion take place? The death-awareness and death-readiness of the samurai, no matter how genuine, are merely the raw material of the Zen experience that must be transformed into a spiritualized death-readiness. There must be a destroying of the life-desiring, ego-centered thrust into new existences, a "making the calculating mind die," and a "rooting out the entire mind that has been at work since eternity."[9] The Zen Great Death is this death, not the physical death; the Great Death, thus, makes the prospect of physical death secondary and unimportant and an individual who has experienced it is physical-death-ready far more deeply and positively than the samurai can ever be, though the samurai's death-readiness opens up the possibility of that deeper awareness to him.

It is possible to speculate about Suzuki Shōsan as follows: He was a man who by experience was trained in death-readiness and personally aware of death-like pains—while still living. Yet his concern about death and his ability to die "freely" (the death-as-executioner figure of speech) were still with him. Here is his existential kōan; herein is the raw material for the angst-filled Great Doubt, whose dissipation in satori will enable him to die freely and be completely death-ready in all senses and at all levels. Can the Zen death-vocabulary and discipline bring his potential to full fruition?

Suzuki Shōsan seems to have accepted the Zen death-vocabulary as valid. He says that the passions are to be "extinguished," and "always practicing dying there can be nothing but an easy death" [7a, 87, p. 165]. (Obviously the first death is spiritual and the second is physical.) Again he speaks of "extinguishing the intellectual[istic] understanding" and becoming "earth-like," that is, relatively insensible to anything but the meditative object, as a way of "eliminating the self" [7a, 57, p. 155]. He warns that if the "root of mind is not cut off, rebirth cannot be cut off"; if even a little intellection remains, one will be reborn in the mode which that intellection embodies.

We may finally note another set of passages. In one of his most vivid figures he speaks of "doing [the self] to death" by meditation [7a, 42, p. 151]. And in other places he smoothly blends the samurai and Zen essences. Thus, in two statements that would surely have gladdened the heart of Hakuin Zenji had he read them, Suzuki Shōsan portrays the proper attitude of the spiritual warrior bent on exterminating the ordinary heart-mind:

> You must tauten the heart-mind, fix the eyes, set the teeth firmly, fasten your attention intently on samsaric factors, and make the heart-mind ready for death at any moment. You are a single horseman in the midst of a thousand, or even ten thousand enemy horsemen, who must guard and control the heart-mind. Thus holding the heart-mind firmly, it comes to maturity; and then making it an emptiness, one can use it in everything freely. [7b, 84, p. 221]
>
> One day a man asked him: "How does one use the 'free-floating mind' of which you speak?"
>
> The Teacher answered: "It is the heart-mind which is about to enter the tiger's mouth. Again, it is the disposition to advance step by step [as does the swordsman] with the eye fixed [on his opponent] for the final blow. If this frame of mind be lacking such a heart-mind is useless for anything.[10]

And yet again he distinguishes, in somewhat the same manner as did Hakuin a century or so later, between Jōdo nembutsu and Zen zazen, with a seeming preference for the latter:

> On a certain day he spoke thus: "One must learn zazen as it is done in the usual way of Zen enlightenment. In the Jōdo sect the 'mind of faith' is raised up by chanting the nembutsu; and in the Zen sect the original nature of No-conception, No-thought is produced. There, firmly fixing one's eyes, one causes the rising of the courageous and concentrated mind by means of his training. Otherwise, defeated by the passions, he will have no steadiness in zazen." [7a, 76, p. 162]

But having said this we may go on to say that though the samurai-warrior imagery is clear throughout, and though he may be called a "Zen" priest or monk and accept the general mode of Zen practice, that acceptance is by no means routine or total. There were several serious qualifications and criticisms of Zen as Suzuki Shōsan perceived the matter. One objection is methodological:

> One day he said to a woman: "The mind of a woman is also the Buddha mind. The passionate mind, just as it is, is the mind of enlightenment. It is only the mode of its use that is different. Therefore firmly disciplining the mind-heart you should practice Ni-ōh zazen."
>
> Then a certain man said: "Truly then Nyorai zazen is a bad thing is it not?" The Teacher said in response: "No, it is not bad. However, this Nyorai zazen is not useful to give the beginner; it is a skilled technique." [7a, 106, p.171]

Nyorai zazen has as its typological image the usual seated meditating Buddha. But Ni-ōh zazen, Suzuki Shōsan's special samurai-type invention, takes as its guiding image—and perhaps even visual meditative base—the two fierce warrior gods or kings who guard the entrance to many Buddhist temples in Japan. In Suzuki Shōsan's opinion this vigorous motif was best fitted for the beginning, and lay, meditator, for it was more in keeping with the realities of his existential situation than the passive-silent Buddha imagery. The Ni-ōh image mirrors the fierce struggle against passions, the readiness to meet the threat of ever-lurking physical death, and the iron determination to kill off the usual self that is the hallmark of the successful meditator, particularly in the context of secular life.

And, parenthetically but importantly, Suzuki Shōsan was highly critical of the usual Zen of his day. Hajime Nakamura puts it as follows:

> Shōsan Suzuki (1579–1655), a *samurai* by origin, advocated what is called the Zen of the Two Kings. The gist of his teaching is to practice Zen with the spirit of the Two Kings, the fierce and the brave. "In these days," he preaches, "it has been overlooked that the Buddhist Law is saturated with great strength of prowess and solidity. It has come to be soft, gentle, disinterested, and good-natured, but none has trained himself to bring forth the spirit of a vengeful Ghost. Everyone should be trained to be brave, and to become a vengeful Ghost of Buddhism."

He notes further that "there was a positive repulsion" in Suzuki Shōsan, "against the seclusionist and self-satisfied attitude of the traditional Zen sect." And he quotes Shōsan as saying somewhat plaintively: "There is none who advocates applying it [the law of Buddha] to matters of mundane existence. Am I the *first to advocate* this?"[11]

His preference for Ni-ōh practice must be integrated into this context. (And of course it was also quite in keeping with his samurai approach to meditation.) It is also in this same context of impatience and dissatisfaction with monastery zazen —or at least some current interpretations of it—that he is speaking in some other passages. In one he inveighs against what he considers to be a false, inverted, withdrawn-from-the-world conception of Zen No-mindedness:

> They work at a form of zazen that is like an empty insect-case. They think the real No-thought, No-mind is to be completely dull and silent, in a state of thinking of nothing at all. This is a great mistake. This sort of use of the practice will diminish one's capacities; one may become ill, even insane. The Buddha-dharma of No-thought No-mind . . . can be used everywhere. No-thought No-mind is to be used when one is sad, when one is joyful, indeed on every occasion. [7a, 70, p. 160]
>
> Nowadays there are many who, falling into "Nothingness views" do harm to people. Saying, "We have the Original Emptiness" they maintain impassive faces. Now this is "existent reality" in excess. [7a, 112, p. 172]
>
> Indeed when there is no-conception, No-thought, one relates to *everything*. [7a, 112, p. 172]

He seems to be saying, in the best Zen activist tradition of Hui Neng, the Sixth Patriarch, that a No-mindness interpreted as mental blankness or emotional impassivity can neither serve the ordinary man in daily life nor is it productive of the true death of the ordinary mind. If the ordinary mind is to be "killed" it must not be "killed" by abstracting *from* it, but in the midst and by means of its own activities.

However, Suzuki Shōsan's criticisms of Zen are more fundamental than this. He is not addicted to any one method for accomplishing the Great Death. The particular method is of little account in itself, since "there are at least ten thousand ways of practicing the discipline of the Buddha" [7b, 72, p. 160]. And with specific reference to the Nyorai and Ni-ōh varieties he elsewhere suggests that the two are really much the same inwardly, despite outward differences. The essential thing in all cases is the rousing up of the spirit of courage—to do the self to death [7a, 81, p. 163].

Thus it is not surprising later on to find him recommending a variety of swords for dealing death to self—especially including the Zen-despised nembutsu. He certainly did not find the Zen kōan either an indispensable or perfect spiritual sword. The kōan itself, when practiced in the Kufu manner—a total intensive struggle toward its solution until either meditator or kōan yielded—could become a heavy burden and even produce what it was designed to destroy, attachment—in this case to the kōan itself:

> As for completing a kōan by training in the Kufu manner, it is said "It is like one who, having picked up a chest of 1,000 *chin* weight, cannot put it down; or like one who is searching for a necessary article which has been lost. If he does not succeed in the search he is required not to relax his mind from his purpose, and thus in this situation he will produce evil attachment and discrimination. Attachment will become devilish and a sickness. The discriminative mind will come to be outside himself."[12]

Another passage seems to indicate an attack against the kōan method itself. In response to a man who had come seeking some special word of wisdom from him, a Zen master, Suzuki Shōsan disclaims any transcendent wisdom (he is only an old "Zen beggar") and reverses the direction of the questioning:

> Again the Teacher said: "You appear to be someone who has a grasp of Buddha Dharma. So please show me what you have."
>
> The man said he knew nothing.
>
> Said the Teacher: "No, no! There must be one thing." He said severely: "Show me at once."
>
> Then the man said: "By a monk I was given [as a kōan] the story of Jōshū's 'Go wash your begging bowl!' I am on the point of achieving satori."
>
> Said the Teacher: "There are what are called the Three Jewels and consequently the monk becomes a jewel for the people of the world. But if, contrary to what we should expect, he gives a useless thing, he harms people."

The "useless thing" is quite obviously the kōan. And he went on to say: "Now it is not that there is not a penetration of a kōan, but even if one does penetrate [a kōan] he cannot stop the hungry ghost and beast mind-heart" [7a, 57, p. 155]. Here is the nub of his objection to kōan Zen. The kenshōs produced thereby do not seem to fully deal with the continuing existence of the hungry ghost-beast–ridden mind of the meditator. That is, they have not put to death the passion-self, or perhaps better, self-attachment to passion, no matter how much the kōan is "penetrated"—

a favorite Zen phrase. Hence the Great Death has turned out to be no death at all, only pseudo-death taking the form of the dull-empty mind and the impassive face.

The kōan-induced kenshō had not done the ghost-beast–ridden mind to death in the soul of the practitioner. Approaching physical death with its train of rebirths still remained, breathing coldly down his neck; it had not yet been vanquished by the death of that self which rejects death. The meditator was not yet ready for the freely chosen, freeing death.

In this connection the question must be raised as to whether he indeed intended to reject the Zen experience of satori (kenshō) altogether, as being totally ineffective to accomplish the death of the self-mind. In one passage he speaks differently about satori itself: "One day speaking to the crowd he said: 'Giving "satori" easily to the beginner and "awakening" him in a short time is a great sin. Nowadays there are many of this sort. This is something to be feared'" [7a, 103, p. 170]. The quick satori, a sudden, one-stroke samurai destruction of the karma-laden, rebirth-producing mind, may not be as easy as it seems to some Zen practicers. Again he says in the same general context, with specific reference to the shout of enlightenment, that is, words said upon sudden satori and viewed as an authentication of it:

> There is no special means. The "enlightened statement" and the like are useless. Just as a poison drug may become a medicine and [in reverse] a medicine become a poison, so the enlightened statement many times may become a danger. More than "enlightenment-gaining shouts" or anything else, [it is essential] just to train with a bold courageous spirit. The old song says: "The satori that is not a satori is [the real] satori. The satori that is a satori is a mere dream-satori." Indeed the satori that is a satori is an uncertain thing. I like the satori that is *not* a satori. Hōnen's own Nembutsu Ōjō was a non-satori satori. [7c, 5, p. 236]

And yet again:

> On the occasion of the evening talk a priest asked: "At the time of zazen, without thinking of a kōan [ko soku] or saying the Nembutsu, is it not good just to exert one's power vigorously?" The teacher said: "One should [indeed] use all [of his powers] vigorously and if he thus exerts his energies let it be on just one thing—kōan, dhāranī, or Nembutsu. Without letting his energy flag, let him do this. Now certainly, if one desires to make his powers come alive, he should fasten his eyes on Bodhidharma's picture and do zazen." [7b, 135, p. 179]

Suzuki Shōsan's basic concern is the cultivation of a bold and courageous spirit that samurai-like faces the problem of the destruction of that self attached to life. Any device that can be successfully used in such a spirit is allowable, be it Zen kōan, all-schools dhāranī (mantric-magic repetition), or the Pure Land Nembutsu. The mode of its use is far more important than what is used. Interestingly the Zen master Hakuin was to say the same thing a century later with specific reference to the Nembutsu: "Whether one sits in dhyanic meditation, chants sutras, repeats mantric incantations, or uses the *nembutsu*, working, and working thus, one comes to where 'before' and 'after' are cut off. . . . How then, though there are differences in practice and discipline, can there be difference as regards attainment."[13] However, there is this difference: In the end Hakuin found the kōan far more successful in producing clear definite satori than the nembutsu; Suzuki Shōsan preferred the nembutsu even for himself.

Finally, in this context, an even more fundamental question must be raised, even though it cannot be answered with certainty: Does Suzuki Shōsan, in finding the nembutsu equal to, and in his own experience and teaching preferred to, the kōan, thereby completely reject the sudden enlightenment doctrine that goes along with kōan use? He often seems to imply that the ghost-beast mind can be destroyed. He is at least confident that samurai-like, ready-for-death determination will overcome it and produce the "free-floating" or no-mind state spoken about by Zen. But, as noted, in his own experience the doubt of easy-sudden death to that mind seems to linger on despite his early-begun practice of death. Thus he writes: "Even though from the time of his youth one has an intention, a deep desire burning like fire in his heart, and practices until the age of 80, the [full] opening [of truth] will not have been revealed" [7c, 13, p. 240]. And again: "And even if one does achieve true enlightenment, there is no final fulfillment for 5 or 10 long ages" [pt. 1, p. 10].

And further—though this may be because he was constantly advising laymen who were beginners in meditation—he seems to envision only the gradual eradication by some continually practiced method against the tenacious life-force rather than some grand, once-for-all breakthrough into the transcendence of the Great-Death, Great-Life experience of Daie-style Zen.[14]

In this section I turn to the specific techniques Suzuki Shōsan urged on his hearers for their spiritual advancement. Two features stand out: first, he is at great pains to address himself to lay people and their problem of finding a way to destroy the ghost-beast mind in the midst of daily secular activities; and second his directions for the use of his preferred, though perhaps not exclusive, instrument, the nembutsu, fully embody his samurai militancy turned Buddhist-spiritual. For him the nembutsu repetition is a sword by which one ever cuts away at the cord that binds a person to ongoing saṁsāra.

Perhaps it is his feeling that Zen practice tends to be separated from common life, good only for the withdrawn monk, that turns him away from the traditional kōan use. Thus he writes, with seeming reference to the kōan-type device, that "farming itself is Buddha-work. *You need not especially seek out some mental device,* for every one's body is the Buddha-body and every mind is the Buddha-mind. So your [every] action is a Buddha-action" [7a, 98, p. 168]. And he is much concerned lest the higher states, such as realization of Original Emptiness or No-Mind, should be separated from ordinary human existence:

> The mind of the ordinary man is comprised of just this existent reality. So, if one does not train by means of this ordinary mind, what training can there then be?... In general, existent mind that seeks Buddhahood separates itself from existence; and the "no-mind" that has the understanding that all is the mind-state of "Original Emptiness" is *not* separated from existence. [7a, 112, p. 172]

For Suzuki Shōsan the mark of true No-mindedness—resulting from the death of the attached mind—is its applicability to all circumstances and items. No-thought, No-mind can be used on everything, even the materials of joys and sorrows. But though this is in line with Hui Neng's denunciation of mirror-wiping Zen, which seeks to achieve a mindless, thoughtless trancelike vacuity of consciousness, Suzuki Shōsan makes his directions for the practice of no-mindedness more specifically lay oriented than Hui Meng did. For example, he counseled farmers that their work was Buddha work, or that it might become Buddha work. "But meanwhile, rousing up the power of your vow, you can exhaust your karmic hindrances by the work of farming if with every stroke of your hoe you say: 'Namu Amida Butsu, Namu Amida Butsu'" [7a, 98, p. 168]. He also has specific recommendations for those in other vocations, some ethical, some technical. The dancer who is anxious to develop the No-thought, No-mind quality is urged to unify mind with action, to become the one whose part is being played [7a, 72, p. 160]. Suzuki Shōsan goes on to say that if he cannot show the dancer how to achieve Buddhahood in dancing, "my virtue is incomplete." A hunter seeks his counsel also, perhaps with tongue in cheek:

> In this connection someone said to me: "For a long time I also have been a devoted hunter. Show me how to become a Buddha by *killing*." And I had this to give him for a lesson. What I said to him is this: "Every time you kill a bird and it spins around and around, its wings turning helplessly, crying 'Kya-kya,' does it seem *amusing* to you to kill? When you yourself are about to die will this then be delightful to you? If you yourself can die cheerfully you [will] have become a Buddha. 'To become a Buddha' is to die with an easy mind. Therefore, every time you kill, every time you snap and break the bones, because there is a learning to die over and over again, you should be able to die yourself, smiling with pleasure. This is the man who is the *true* killer." [7a, 72, p. 161]

In one other passage he is portrayed as giving advice to a still practicing samurai:

> One day a samurai came and asked about the manner of saying the nembutsu. The Teacher explained, saying: "While you are engaged in carrying out the duties of a samurai, as you stand confronting enemies who are prepared to defend themselves, leap into the midst of them concentratedly repeating 'Namu Amida Butsu, Namu Amida Butsu!' Thus you may repeat the 'leaping nembutsu' so as to be able to freely enter into their midst." [7c, 36, p. 248]

In neither of the two latter cases does Suzuki Shōsan counsel his hearers to forsake their occupations. It may be implied in the advice to the hunter that a nonkilling occupation would be better. Perhaps this advice mirrors his own course of thought in forsaking the profession of samurai; in the text it is followed by the earlier-quoted passage in which he replies to the suggestion that he has, in turning to the Zen monkhood, become a "cowardly" samurai. But in the other case both Suzuki Shōsan and the samurai take for granted that even a samurai who *faithfully* performs his chosen or inherited vocation can achieve Buddhist no-mindedness and work toward his own salvation—the destruction of the ghost-beast disposition. And he actually counseled another samurai not to leave his profession for the monkhood.

I turn finally to Suzuki Shōsan's specific discussion of the nembutsu as a spiritual sword for killing the rebirth-bound selfhood. That he esteemed the nembutsu highly cannot be doubted: "Now even though it is a bad thing to put into words, you think that the nembutsu is for the unskilled. But the repetition of the two words 'Nen Butsu' *is* thinking of the Buddha . . . therefore by the assiduous doing of the nembutsu one's various mental functions must be eliminated." And he finds it useful himself:

> Even Hōnen left behind him in documents three pages as a testament saying that he knew no means of enlightenment other than the nembutsu. I too find it good to employ this practice. *This is the first and only way of practice that is not a defective one.* When the great bell is struck and sounds "gon-gon" within one's heart, he should strongly recite "Namu Amida Butsu, Nama Amida Butsu": and thus evil action will not be able to present an appearance for even a little. By means of doing this continually the destruction of conceptualization will take place.[15]

On one occasion it is reported that "the Teacher was *always* saying the nembutsu" for which he was reproached by a senior priest, probably of Zen persuasion. But the Teacher retorted that the nembutsu was surely as good a practice as the Zen "Hōge chaku, hōge chaku.[16]

The use of the nembutsu as recommended by Suzuki Shōsan seems to have been a Zennish-kōan sort in which the samurai readiness-for-death is dominant. He presents as his own interpretation—"Though I have never heard this from the ancient traditions, this occurs to me now"—five types of nembutsu-saying: Meritorious action, in which the repetition is an encapsulated way of honoring all the Buddhas and reciting all the scriptures; penitence and confession nembutsu; nembutsu of cutting off, in which evaluative thinking (good thinking, evil thinking) are cut off "with the sword of the nembutsu"; preparing-for-death nembutsu, in which one thinks of each moment as the last one in his life; and the tranquil nembutsu, one of "non-obstruction by the 10,000 things" of this life, gentle as the soughing of the wind in the pines—a most uncharacteristic version for an ex-samurai! But clearly the third and fourth would be his favorites [7c, 36, p. 248].

Suzuki Shōsan is also very specific, in a non-Pure Land manner, about the goals the practicer of the nembutsu should set for himself: "As to setting up the Pure Land or Amida [as image or idea] and [by means of these] seeking birth in the Pure Land, if one makes this his aim, this too is possession by a devil" [7b, 39, p. 201]. Or again, after extolling the nembutsu as a means of "subjugating the disease of the passions" and evading thought concepts, he goes on to say: "But that man who uses the nembutsu, thereby seeking the pleasures of the Pure Land Paradise and seeking life after death—he will keep on adding extensively to his rebirth karma. This sort of man lusts after death alone" [7b, 84, p. 221]. Elsewhere, using a division different from the five-type schema:

> Even in the recitation of the nembutsu there are two [sorts of] actions: That one by which one hopes to become a Buddha by means of reciting the nembutsu is a work [leading to] rebirth; but in reality the truly right work is in hoping to extinguish all of the passions by means of the nembutsu. [7a, 87, p. 165]

In another passage, he says:

> "You too, as though becoming earth without thought, should practice the nembutsu discipline."
>
> Then the man asked: "This discipline. What sort of thing is it?"
>
> The Teacher answered: "It is a matter of getting rid of the self."
>
> Again [the man] asked: "As though of insensate earth. What is the meaning of that, would you please tell me?"
>
> The Teacher answered: "To completely discard intellectual understanding, any fanciful ideas you may carry in your breast, to extinguish the intellectualistic understanding by repeating 'Namu Amida Butsu, Nama Amida Butsu,' to blot out the reason, to become of one piece with emptiness—thus becoming earth-like—this we call the discipline that attains Buddhahood." [7a, 57, p. 155]

He recommends attaching the nembutsu to the breath rhythm: "Meanwhile, abandoning everything, repeating 'Namu Amida Butsu, Namu Amida Butsu' as you draw your breath back and forth [like a saw], and always practicing dying [of the self] . . . you must use only a vigorous nembutsu; a weak nembutsu repetition will not do" [7a, 87, p. 165]. Indeed Hōnen gave us the truly right prescription for nembutsu practice:

> When a certain man asked Hōnen about the desire for the next life, Hōnen replied: "With respect to the desire for the next life, one must repeat the nembutsu with the mental attitude of one who is just about to have his head cut off."
>
> This is a *good* teaching. If one does not repeat the nembutsu in this way he cannot exhaust his clinging to the self. [7a, 125, p. 176]

In conclusion, Suzuki Shōsan is completely Zen-samurai oriented; the great goal of all Buddhist techniques is the death of conceptualized thinking and the destruction of the ghost-beast heart-mind of every person. But on three points he differs from contemporary practice: his way is for every person—not just the monk—and therefore must be integrated with the farmer's hoeing and the dancer's dancing; the kōan is not the best adapted means in this, or perhaps any, context to produce rebirth-ending enlightenment; and enlightenment, whatever it is, is not something that can be secured in a flash by a sudden satori. It is rather a lifelong quest for which the thought-killing use of the nembutsu is best adapted. Thus his method of nembutsu use seems Zen in practice; but his expectations are more in the spirit of Pure Land Buddhism: one faithfully, persistently continues to use a chosen means of salvation (the nembutsu) but does not expect a final conclusive breakthrough "revelation."

There is no better conclusion than Suzuki Shōsan's own autobiographical and evaluative statement about his meditative experiences to the young samurai who wishes to become a monk:

> Again, after this, when I was 60 years old, at dawn [one day] at the time of the tiger [3–5 A.M.] I was suddenly gripped by the mind of the Buddha [who said], "All beings in the three worlds are regarded by me as an only child." Truly at that moment when I looked at the situation of the ants, suffering and enjoying life, the desire that by some means or other they would be saved penetrated to the very marrow [of my bones]. But this state of mind too was lost after three days. However, even now this is of value. From that time on there has arisen [in me] some small mind of compassion.
>
> Nor am I without a kenshō type of experience. This too [came] when I was 61 years old. On August 27th, at the dawning of the 28th, I effortlessly parted from samsāra and assuredly encountered Original Nature. On that occasion there was only "nothing, nothing" and I was in a frame of mind that just wished to dance and dance. Indeed at that time even if you had cut off my head, I would have thought "Truly this is nothing, nothing at all." Some thirty days passed like this and [then] I thought: "No this kind of thing [i.e., experience] is not suitable for me, for it can be only an activity which uses a single capacity." So then I cast it away from myself and returning and taking up my own real self, I thrust that [same old] death back into my bosom and practicing vigorously carried on my discipline. As I expected, *all such experiences are false* and this bag of dung called Shōsan remains hidden [i.e., is not properly dealt with in such experiences]. Again, after this, [having] the very same awareness as Fuke, I walked along the way [having his state of awareness] but a distance of perhaps three miles [i.e., a very little way]. This has been of great benefit to me. There rose in me the strong desire to devote myself life after life and world after world to the [full] attainment of Fuke's [level of awareness]. Furthermore, even though I too, just as I have said above, have moved along step by step in completing my disciplines, and having cast aside even kenshō, have returned to what I really am and worked and worked at my practice, even now this bag of excrement can't give itself up.[17]

Yet this hardy spirit who confessedly had many lives yet to go before he reached "home," and who steadfastly refused to believe that any of his self-destroying efforts had completely severed the bonds that bound him to rebirth, did consider that he had done most of what could be done in his present life: "Having continued my life up to this present day, my spiritual discipline has almost been completed" [7c, 13, p. 242]. And his biographer's epitaph is fitting for an ex-warrior who had pursued the Zen goal for many years with a samurai's intensity of total concentration of all his powers: "Then at the hour of the monkey on the 25th day of June (1655), he died with pleasure. He was 77 years old and had been in the monkhood 36 years" [pt. 1, p. 13].

Notes

1. SS I, p. 4. All references to Suzuki Shōsan's own writings and to his biography are from *Suzuki Shōsan Dōnin Zen Shū* [*Collected Writings of Suzuki Shōsan*], ed. Suzuki Tetsushin, 2d rprt. ed. (Tokyo: Sankibo Busshorin, 1962). References in the text are to this edition.

2. Hajime Nakamura, *Ways of Thinking of Eastern Peoples* (Honolulu: East-West Center Press, 1964), in various references always refers to him as a priest, but priest-monk, or monk-priest might better describe him. As noted, the term shi, teacher or perhaps spiritual master, is usually applied to him in the texts.

3. D.T. Suzuki, *Zen and Japanese Culture* (Princeton: Princeton University Press, 1970), pp. 61–64. Tokiyori, a regent of the Hōjō family, was the first of his family to adopt Zen.

4. Ibid., p. 62.

5. Ibid., p. 72. Quoted from the *Hagakure*, a samurai "primer" begun in the seventeenth century.

6. Ibid., p. 73; emphasis added.

7. The mode of notations for this and most of the following references is: SS II, 7a, 161, p. 185, signifying, part II, section 7, subsection a, paragraph 161, page 185. All references hereafter are from part II unless otherwise indicated. All translations were made under the guidance of Professor Fujiyoshi Jikai of Hanazono College, Kyoto, but my wife and I take responsibility for any mistakes.

8. The phrase translated here as "practicing dying" is literally "work for and practice death" or "dying" (shijo o shishū, sometimes simply shishū) or "death practice" or "training for death." The image and experience intended by this phrase seems to be the actual and present sense of dying such as Suzuki Shōsan had when pierced by his enemies' spears. Hence the active-present form "practicing dying" is used here.

9. D.T. Suzuki, *Zen Buddhism* (New York: Doubleday, 1956), p. 138.

10. 7c, 5, p. 236. *Shin* or *Kokoro* is here translated, and sometimes elsewhere, as heart-mind. This is better than the usual "mind." It is the visceral mind, so to speak.

11. Pp. 495, 382, 507, respectively.

12. 7b, 39, p. 201. A *chin* or *kin* equals about 1 to $1\frac{1}{3}$ pounds.

13. Suzuki, *Zen and Japanese Culture*, p. 84.

14. Daie (1089–1163) refused to recognize early-received satori-like kōan resolutions as genuine. He pushed his disciples long and hard, each on his initial kōan; when it was finally resolved, that was the *full* attainment—in contrast to Hakuin who worked for early satori and subsequent development.

15. 7a, 57, p. 155. Cf. words of Shan-tao of Tang China (A.D. 618–907): "The sharp-edged sword is another name for Amitābha. An invocation of the name absolves from sin." Quoted in Nakamura, p. 495; emphasis added.

16. 7a, 162, p. 185. This means "Throwing down," throwing away preconceived ideas.

17. 7c, 13, p. 240–41. Fuke (ninth century), an eccentric Zen monk, contemporary and possibly critic of Rinzai. "Founder" of the Fuke sect in China.

Biblical and Judaic Traditions

But one could ask: Why should one affirm one's essential being rather than destroy one's self? The answer to this must be that the person becomes aware of his infinite value.

Paul Tillich

Human Mortality as a Problem in Ancient Israel

WOLFRAM HERRMANN

The Israelites' conception of death and the underworld has been described many times.[1] In a recent monograph L. Wächter treated the questions thoroughly and comprehensively.[2] It is, however, still desirable to consider how death and afterlife are related to each other in the successive epochs of Israelite history, and how each pictures the sense of life in the face of death from its own particular perspective.

It is not my intent to carry out the totality of this work here. Rather, the goal of the following exposition is to contribute to it by focusing on the period of ancient Israelite history in the eighth century B.C., before the rise of classical prophecy. Initially the manner in which people attempted to deal with the fact of death must be examined. It is not enough to trace how death was experienced at the level of feeling; how death was comprehended as a matter of belief must be investigated as well. What is more, the answer to the question of the "Why" of dying can be found. But the traditional body of material, from which one can infer the answers being given to this question, is extremely limited and, furthermore, does not allow a direct grasp of the answer. It can be assumed, however, that the material had a much greater importance in the feeling-for-life of the ancient Israelites than the extent of the literary deposit implies.

First, I shall examine briefly some of the evidence that reveals the ways dying was spoken about in ancient Israel and the attitudes toward the universal fact of impending death. This will highlight the importance of the problem.

There is ample literature that reveals how death and dying were part of Israelite thought and experience. According to the Joseph story, when Jacob found that his son Joseph, whom he had believed to be dead, was alive, he made the comment that he would gladly die.[3] This comment is understandable given the context. Such an attitude acknowledges the inevitability of death, but, after an experience of great good fortune, death is greeted confidently. Beyond this there is evidence of both downright contempt for death and an actual longing for death.[4]

Since the literary heritage of Israel is characterized by Yahwistic belief, death is often related to Yahweh's exercise of sovereign power. Some documents trace both life and death back to Yahweh,[5] and others mention that Yahweh lets a man die or kills him.[6] A short passage of special importance in this connection is found in Exodus 4:24–26, where it is related that Yahweh attacks Moses, intending to kill him because he has not been circumcised. Yahweh's right to exercise power over death is further amplified when it is said that he turns death away[7] by saying to a man that he shall not die.[8] The same idea has been expressed in the tradition of the awakening of the dead which is found in the Elijah and Elisha legends.[9] But it should be noted that the prevention of death and the awakening from death both signify only a prolongation of life. Mortality remains.

Since it was believed that the death of an individual could be attributed to Yahweh and that Yahweh could freely exercise his judgment regarding the end of life, it was also recognized that he could inflict death on a man who had transgressed. Just as the death penalty existed in the sphere of law in serious cases, so death was frequently regarded as a divine punishment for sin.[10]

Even if, as is apparent, death is subject to Yahweh's exercise of power, the fate of death was greeted by the Israelite not with joy but with fear. The fact that man had to die was seen as oppressive.[11] The words of the Amalekite king Agag give indirect testimony to the fact that death was perceived as bitter.[12] Such bitterness could merely be moderated.

How strongly people could be affected by the death of other persons they esteemed or loved is exemplified by the lamentations of David over Saul and Jonathan.[13] The lament of David over his son Absalom is especially touching.[14] The book of Jeremiah contains words of the dirge as they doubtless had been employed from the oldest times,[15] words that make apparent the pain felt at the loss of a loved one.

A conclusion based on the observations made thus far is that the Israelite viewed death as an inevitable human destiny;[16] death is "the way of all the earth."[17] Such an admission sounds decidedly fatalistic; and man's resignation to this fate is all the more hopeless since he does not even know the time of his death. But then the question of the origin of such a destiny must arise. People did not simply accept death—even though they were disturbed by fear—they also posed the question as to why people are subjected to death and why, unlike the gods, they are not entitled to eternal life. Moreover, such a question is to be expected, because it already existed among the other peoples of the ancient Near East.

The Adapa myth from Mesopotamia is concerned with this question.[18] It undoubtedly deals not just with the personal fate of the wise Adapa, who appears as the central figure in the myth; Adapa should be understood as a prototype of mankind, or, even more generally, as a prominent figure whose fate has operated on behalf of mankind. The decision of one individual becomes the destiny of all.

A brief summary of the myth: Ea had created the wise Adapa, but had not given him eternal life. Once upon a time, as Adapa was fishing on the sea, the south wind upset his boat. In a rage he shattered the wings of the south wind with his voice. The father-god Anu heard about the incident and summoned Adapa before him. Ea gave Adapa exact rules of behavior to take along on this journey because he was afraid that Anu wanted to kill Adapa. When he appeared before Anu, Adapa had to report his activities. Since two gods interceded for Adapa, Anu calmed himself and decided that, since Adapa knew the secrets of heaven and earth, he should become completely like the gods and should receive eternal life as well. Therefore Anu had bread of life and water of life placed before him. Following the advice of Ea, Adapa refused both. Anu was astonished at this and had him brought back to earth. Adapa had missed the unique opportunity of procuring eternal life for mankind.

G. Roux[19] treats the possible interpretations of the myth in detail and seeks to find the motives for the actions of the main characters. He concludes that our logic may take us too far from the point of the myth: "Perhaps the ancients were not troubled by our logic. Perhaps this obscurity was desired by the redactor of the myth. The story of Adapa has something of the Sibylline in it. Like many folk stories it includes, it seems, an 'enigma' which we may discuss at length of an evening . . . and which we are still discussing."[20] At the end of his essay. Roux gives an interpretation of the myth that does justice to it, and into which the features previously mentioned fit well: "Like Etana, like Gilgamesh, he has let slip by the unexpected opportunity which was offered to him. In this myth, the 'fundamental pessimism of the Babylonians' has once again found expression."[21]

In the extensive Gilgamesh tradition, the problem also plays a role. Gilgamesh, because the approach of death seems to put the meaning of existence itself in question, seeks to acquire eternal life. He finally obtains the possiblity of such life in the form of an herb that guarantees eternal youth. He wants to take it with him to Uruk and to cultivate it there so that he and his people will continually have access to it. Unfortunately he loses it and has to return without having attained his goal. He and his people remain mortal.

The Gilgamesh tradition was widespread in the ancient Near East. Archaeologists have found traces of it not only in the Sumero-Babylonian area, but also in northern Mesopotamia, Asia Minor, and Palestine. The problems with which it deals were therefore familiar to residents of the Syro-Palestine area. Still, in this area an independent mastery of such questions was sought, and this is demonstrated by a part of the Aqhat legend from Ras Shamra.[22]

[She lifts up her voice and] cries:
  "Hearken, I pray thee, [Aqhat the Youth:
A] sk for silver, and I'll give it thee;
  [For gold, and I'll be] stow't on thee;
But give thou thy bow [to me;
  Let] Yabamat-Liimmim *take* thy *darts*."
But Aqhat the Youth answers:
"*I vow yew trees* of Lebanon,
  I vow sinews from wild oxen;
I vow horns from mountain goats,
  Tendons from the hocks of a bull;
I vow from a *cane-forest* reeds:
  Give (these) to Kothar wa-Khasis.
He'll make a bow for thee,
  Darts for Yabamat-Liimmim."

Then quoth the maiden Anath:
"Ask for life, O Aqhat the Youth.
Ask for life, and I'll give it thee,
  For deathlessness, and I'll bestow't on thee.
I'll make thee count years with Baal,
  With the sons of El shalt thou count months.
And Baal when he gives life gives a feast,
  Gives a feast to the life-given and bids him drink;
Sings and chants over him,
  Sweetly serenad[es] him:
So give I life to Aqhat the Youth."
But Aqhat the Youth answers:
"Fib not to me, O Maiden;
  For to a youth thy fibbing is *loathsome.*
Further life—how can mortal attain it?
  How can mortal attain life enduring?
Glaze will be poured [on] my head,
  Plaster upon my pate;
And I'll die as everyone dies,
  I too shall assuredly die.
Moreover, this will I say:
My bow is [*a weapon for*] warriors.
  Shall now females [*with it*] to the chase?"
—[Loud]ly Anath doth laugh,
  While forging (a plot) in her heart:
"Give heed *to* me, Aqhat the Youth,
  Give heed to me for thine own good.
[. . .] I'll meet thee in the path of arrogance,
  [Encounter thee] in the path of presumption,
Hurl thee down at [my feet *and trample*] thee,
  My darling great big he-man!"[23]

In this section, as in the Gilgamesh tradition, the starting point is that man does not have immortality, but that immortality can be offered to him by the gods or by a divinity. At first glance, the episode cited here seems to deal only with the personal fate of Aqhat. When, however, in a later part of the story, a general sterility of the fields begins because of the death of the youth, his fate attains a broader meaning. It is apparent in the conversation between Aqhat and the goddess Anath that men do not have immortality, because the offer of immortality once made to them had been spurned. This is similar to the Adapa myth. The argument here, however, seems to be remarkably enlightened in that the reason given for the rejection of the offer is that man is inescapably mortal, and that therefore any divine offer of immortality can only be a deception.

After these observations, derived from the written legacy of the other peoples of the ancient Near East, I can return to the Old Testament and consider at what points in the Israelite literature thoughts about the origin and cause of death, as they existed in the environment, were incorporated. An independent, aetiological narrative, which raises the question of why man is mortal and then provides an answer, does not exist in the Old Testament. Nevertheless, there are various contexts in which some indications relevant to the matter can be found.

First, Genesis 6:1–4 should be cited. This short passage, which many like to title "The Origin of the Giants," breaks down into two parts which seem, on the basis of the wording, independent of one another, verses 1–3 and verse 4. With respect to the content both parts belong together, since in both the subject of the conjugal union of divine beings with human women is discussed. However, the result of the action is different in each case. In verse 4 the sexual union between gods and women results in the generation of the mighty heroes of antiquity, an observation that does not need to be discussed further here. Of much more significance for this study are verses 1–3. In these verses it is said that the sons of the gods were pleased with the human women because of their beauty and chose wives from among them, and that Yahweh then established the life span of men at one hundred and twenty years. The reason for placing this limitation on the length of human life is that the union between gods and women constituted a transgression of the boundary line between the world of the gods and that of men. Thus the basic reason is ethical in character. But a reason derived from experience is also given: "Because he also is flesh" (verse 3a). Flesh is transitory, mortal. Moreover, the setting of a life span that is of limited duration is clearly based on the supposition that, until that time, life was not conceived of as limited, or at least not so narrowly limited. Evidently man was originally given the possibility of participating in eternal life exactly like that of the gods. This supposition is also supported by the negative statement of verse 3a.* This sentence is best rendered as follows: "Thus said Yahweh: My spirit will not be strong in man forever." If the spirit of Yahweh bestows life on men and animals—the Israelite view[24]—then clearly the view expressed in verse 3 is that the life-producing spirit of Yahweh is not to be in each individual man for all eternity; rather it is to be taken away at the proper time. Thus eternal life is denied to man. The correctness of this view is confirmed by the explicit designation of man as "flesh," that is, as transitory being, and by the limitation of man's life to one hundred twenty years.

It has long been recognized that there is no genuine Israelite tradition contained in verses 1ff. and verse 4. On the contrary, there are remnants or reverberations of a mythology with which Israel became acquainted in its surroundings. It is possible that the myth already contained the forbidden transgression of a boundary and the resultant setting of limits to human life, but this is unlikely. In its present form, verse 3 originated with the Israelite narrator.

Thus the fact is that the Israelites, in order to answer the question about the limitations of human life, referred back to a Canaanite myth; they did not create a separate narration because one already known provided information about the primeval period of the human race. At a decisive point, however, the mythical

* A technical defense of the interpretation of the verb on which the subsequent translation of the Hebrew statement is based has been omitted by the translator. Readers who are interested should consult the original German text.

account was transformed and thereby made a part of the Yahwistic belief. The rejection of eternal life for man goes back to a decision by Yahweh based, on the one hand, on the fact that the human body cannot be allotted eternal permanence; more important, the mortality of men was also understood as a punishment meted out through divine intervention.

It must also be taken into account that, for the Israelite, the setting of a limit of the life span at one hundred twenty years was not considered to be a limitation in contrast to an unending permanence of life, but rather as the curtailment of a much longer life span originally attributed to the men of primeval time in Genesis 5 and 11:10–32. These passages are, of course, to be classified as from the source *P* (a relatively late, priestly text), but it is generally assumed that they contain ancient traditional materials. Here, then, is a transformation in a broader sense that the myth underwent when it became a part of the Israelite way of thinking.

In the Canaanite myth, the gods' action in preventing man and the half-gods born from them from obtaining eternal life was evidently motivated by the fear that the number of half-gods could become overwhelming and consequently mankind could invade their domain and acquire their powers; but, in the context of the Yahwistic belief, the decision was understood to be a punishment for the transgression of a boundary line that had to be strictly maintained. In both cases, the justification for this measure was not questioned. There was no indication that since the initiative had originated with the sons of gods, they therefore should at first, or at least in addition, be held responsible; such logic does not do justice to the matter and should not be expected. The starting point was, above all, the question of the human situation. The human situation was explained through myth and, in the Israelite cases, emphasis was on the responsibility of man in relation to his god.

Finally, some observations based on the narrative of Paradise and the Fall in Genesis 2–3 must be taken into account. Here also is not an independent aetiology, but only a few sentences inserted into a larger context and made to serve a more general purpose. It is agreed in most Old Testament studies that this passage contains a series of traditions which have, in this context, been integrated into a more coherent unity. The recognition that several aetiologies are involved suggests that there is here an aetiology for the fact of human mortality which, after all, is an important component of any aetiology of "mankind."

In order to delineate the units significant for the present discussion, it is necessary first to recognize the existence of literary components. The observations that point to a division of the Yahwistic material into two sources—observations first made at the end of the last century and continuing to receive support today—may no longer be rejected out of hand.* Moreover, it is certain that, in the source stratum in which man's banishment from the tree of life is discussed, the source of the banishment is a human error, in particular, an intrusion into the sphere of the gods. The underlying concept is that originally man had the possibility of access to a tree whose fruit bestowed immortality. When man no longer observed the boundary

*A technical discussion and evaluation of recent scholarship concerning these sources has been omitted by the translator. Readers who are interested should consult the original German text.

separating him from the world of the gods, they became afraid that man could also take the final step and acquire eternal life, a possession they claimed for themselves alone. In order to prevent this, they drove him out of the garden of the gods in which he had lived up to that time and provided for the guarding and blockading of the way there. Thus man is mortal and was not able to acquire immortality.*

We certainly do not stray from the meaning of the passage if the gods are spoken about in the plural, since the verses in question bear a strong mythological stamp. The tree of life and its fruit that grants immortality, the garden of the gods, the cherubim (divine mixed creatures), and the flashing, flaming sword are mythological motifs. It is therefore possible that the "nomadic source material" contained traces of an obviously Canaanite myth which concerned itself with the same question being considered in Israel, and which therefore was willingly adopted.

As was the case in Genesis 6:1–4 it is again confirmed that, in Israel, when assertions were made about basic facts of human existence, ideas from the surrounding world were adopted and served as integrated components in the oldest materials of Israelite tradition. They were, to be sure, adapted to the Yahwistic belief, but their factual content remained valid, because in them the disrupted relation to god and the resulting transitoriness of man was acknowledged as an answer to the question of the why of human mortality. There was a transformation in the material, however, for now man was confronted with a single acting subject in the divine realm. Yahweh planted the garden as a place of residence for man, whom he had created. It was the violation of his command that caused man to be driven out of the garden, so that he no longer had access to the tree of life. The conclusion is similar to that of Genesis 6:1–3. The Israelite knew he was responsible to Yahweh, and he deduced that it was because of an initial lapse that he did not attain immortality, or lost it again; that is, he deduced that man is mortal.

Genesis 6:1–2 is also concerned with human error, the transgression of the boundary between humanity and divinity; this same emphasis is expressed in chapters 2 and 3, through the reference to human guilt. It is not possible to know with complete certainty the extent to which the extant portions of the narrative describing the situation belong to the source stratum *N* (the "nomadic" source). However, that which was important for the Israelite of historical times and therefore still has theological importance for us today emanated from both source strata *J* (the Yahwistic source) and *N*. In these sources the rigors of human existence as well as man's transitory nature and his inability to attain eternal life are given their origin in his grasping for the fruit of the tree of knowledge. Guilt consists in human transgression of the pertinent divine prohibition, in lustful desire to grasp divine powers. The threat of 2:17b is properly related to 3:22b if we assume that "you will die" means simply "you will be mortal."

The question arises whether the attempted desire to understand the reasons for mortality represents an intellectual achievement unusual because of its concern with

*A critical examination of various scholarly views concerning the relationship between the narrative dealing with the tree of life and that dealing with the tree of knowledge has been omitted by the translator. Readers who are interested should consult the original German text.

that issue, which could only be attained under conditions particularly suited for it and from a point of view still to be recognized. Such a possibility cannot be rejected, and the possible arguments for and against it must be investigated. The source strata of the Pentateuch, to which the evidence treated here must be attributed, are dated by Georg Fohrer[25] at the end of the ancient Israelite period, about 800 B.C. Moreover, he regards these sources as representative of a conscious reaction of nomadic circles in Judah against the joyous acceptance of the indigenous culture expressed in source *J*.* Since the time of David a strong spiritual contact existed between the Israelite north and the Judean south, and since this contact was intensified during the reign of Solomon and was again reaffirmed by the Omrides, the traditional materials bearing mythological characteristics probably originated primarily in the north, where Israel lived in closer contact with the Canaanite population. But this rather general statement will have to be satisfactory, because we cannot speak more exactly about where and when the relevant myths were introduced into Israel. This means, however, that the time when the convictions expressed here were generally adopted by the tribes of Israel was a very ancient period, and that these convictions later moved to Judah. But if the myths dealing with the problem of why man does not possess immortality were integrated into the thought world of Israel at a relatively early time and were made aetiologically serviceable in the way described, then there are no readily discernible differences between the manifestations and perceptions of death in the written Israelite materials and those in the answers incorporated in the Canaanite myths that were taken over and given different emphases. It is not only possible, but highly probable, that the same men who had known death as an inevitable destiny derived from a divine source, and, at the same time, had feared this destiny, sought to understand why their god had ordered life in this way. They did not close their eyes to reality; they recognized human guilt and responsibility before a divine sovereign.

The ancient Israelite, where he sought an answer to the question raised by the transitory nature of man, lived from the mythical material of his world. This myth-world also taught him that the universal fate of death could be broken through and abolished. In ancient Israel there were two men placed into the world of the gods—according to the belief of Israel into the world of Yahweh—and in this way were granted eternal life. These men were Enoch,[26] who was known from the primeval period, and Elijah,[27] who at the end of the ancient Israelite period was elevated to great importance, whose "heavenly journey" is depicted in strongly mythological colors. Certainly in this conception there is a special preference (as in the case of Utanapischtim, the Mesopotamian hero of the deluge) that came only to a few and was not attained in general. Such a conception made mortality much more difficult to bear, but in so doing, it prepared the ground for the emergence of other solutions.

[*translated by James R. Price*]

*A technical discussion of the sources has been omitted by the translator. Readers who are interested should consult the original German text.

Notes

1. A. Bertholet, *Die israelitischen Vorstellungen vom Zustand nach dem Tode* (Tübingen, 1914); G. Quell, *Die Auffassung des Todes in Israel* (Leipzig, 1925); G. von Rad, "Der Tod im Alten Testament," *ThWB* 2 (1935):848f.; G. von Rad, "Alttestamentlichen Glaubensaussagen vom Leben und vom Tod," *Allgem. Ev.-Luth. Kirchenzeitung* 71 (1938):826–34; H. Schmid, "Tod und Totenreich im Alten Testament," *RGG* 6 (1962), cols. 912f.; H. Ringgren, *Israelitische Religion* (Stuttgart, 1963). Full footnotes may be found in the original publication of this article. See "Das Todesgeschick als Problem in Altisrael," *Mitteilungun des Instituts für Orientforschung* 16 (1970):14–32. In this adaptation the notes have been abridged.

2. *Der Tod im Alten Testament* (Berlin, 1967).

3. Gen. 46:30.

4. Judg. 5:18; 8:21.

5. Deut. 32:39; 1 Sam. 2:6.

6. Gen. 38:7, 10; 1 Sam. 2:25; 1 Kings 17:20; Exod. 14:25–28.

7. Exod. 10:17.

8. Judg. 6:23; 2 Sam. 12:13.

9. 1 Kings 17:17–24; 2 Kings 4:18, 37.

10. Gen. 6:7; 7:4, 22f.; 18:23f.; 20:3, 7; 38:7, 10, 24; Exod. 22:24; 32:27f.; Num. 11:1, 33; 16:26, 30–33; 21:6; 25:8f., 18; Deut. 32:22–25; Josh. 5:4–6; 7:25; Judg. 9:54–56; 20:13; 1 Sam. 2:25, 33f.; 12:25; 26:10; 2 Sam. 12:14, 18; 21:1–9; 24:10, 15.

11. Gen. 20:8; 26:7; 32:11; without the use of the verb "to fear," Gen. 12:12f.; 20:11; Exod. 2:15; Judg. 6:22f.; 13:22; 1 Sam. 5:11; 27:1.

12. 1 Sam. 15:32; cf. Gen. 37:35; 42:38; 44:29, 31.

13. 2 Sam. 1:19–27.

14. 2 Sam. 19:1f.

15. Jer. 22:18; 34:5.

16. Gen. 3:19; Num. 16:29; 2 Sam. 12:23; 14:14.

17. 1 Kings 2:2.

18. Cf. *Ancient Near Eastern Texts Relating to the Old Testament*, edited by James B. Pritchard (Princeton: Princeton University Press, 1969), pp. 101–3; hereafter *ANET*.

19. "Adapa, le Vent et l'Eau," *Revue d'Assyrologie* 55 (1961):13–33.

20. Ibid., p. 31.

21. Ibid., p. 33.

22. *ANET*, pp. 72–99.

23. The translation of lines 16–45 of 2 Aqhat is that of H.L. Ginsberg in *ANET*, pp. 151–52.

24. Gen. 2:7; Pss. 104:29f.

25. *Introduction to the Old Testament*, translated by David Green (Nashville: Abingdon, 1968), pp. 143–92.

26. Gen. 5:24.

27. 2 Kings 2:11.

The Holocaust and the Kiddush Hashem in Hassidic Thought[1]

PESACH SCHINDLER

Whenever the subject of *Kiddush Hashem* (Sanctification of God's Name) came under discussion during the Holocaust, Maimonides' classic summary[2] of the various means by which the Jew may fulfill the commandment of the Sanctification of God's Name was invoked. Rabbi Shimon Huberband, Rabbi Menahem Zemba, and Hillel Zeitlin[3] in the Warsaw Ghetto all paraphrase Maimonides, applying the term Kiddush Hashem to any Jewish victim of the Holocaust. "As Maimonides ruled: 'A Jew who is killed, though this may be for reasons other than conversion, but simply because he is a Jew, is called Kaddosh.' "[4] Maimonides, however, clearly reflects the consensus in the Talmud, cautioning against the indiscriminate application of Kiddush Hashem by death alone in the event that the Jew has a choice. The Jew is bidden to sanctify God's Name in life, especially when the enemy offers no choice but death.[5] Moshe Prager, a Holocaust researcher, focusing on religious responses, defines Kiddush Hashem within the Holocaust context.

> What is *Kiddush Hashem*? Dr. Burg made reference to both passive and active forms of *Kiddush Hashem*. This is not exact. What actually determines [Kiddush Hashem], is the very focus of the conflict. If one wishes to really understand the Ghetto, one must determine: What does the enemy want from me? If the enemy demands my honor, then my honor bids me to sacrifice life for honor. . . . However, the moment the enemy clearly insists: "I demand your life," then a sense of honor compels me to fight for my life.[6]

This broader concept of Kiddush Hashem, contextually tied to the objective of the foe, moved Rabbi Yitzchak Nissenbaum[7] to coin the phrase "*Kiddush Hahayim*," Sanctification of Life, as the way to Kiddush Hashem.[8]

Although Kiddush Hashem was reinterpreted in terms of Kiddush Hahayim, the Holocaust odds ran high in favor of some form of Kiddush Hashem terminus in death, rather than life. Here as well, the Holocaust added a new dimension. In Jewish martyrology of the past, the Jew had the option of choosing life, most likely by rejecting Judaism. The martyr of the Holocaust, without life options before him, and counter to the expectations of his murderer, did indeed choose the manner in which he would accept and prepare for his death. Freedom of choice between one's life or religious faith was converted to the option of "going to one's death degraded and dejected, as opposed to confronting [death] with an inner peace, nobility, upright stance, without lament and cringing to the enemy.... This new option ... became another attribute of *Kiddush Hashem* during the Holocaust."[9]

Hassidic responses of Kiddush Hashem are interpreted on the background of both the Kiddush Hahayim manifestations, especially as these were reflected in spiritual-passive resistance and physical resistance and, presently, Kiddush Hashem, the manner in which death was faced.

One notes the *zekut* (privilege) motif in anticipation of offering one's life for Kiddush Hashem. The Ostrovzer Rebbe, Rabbi Yehezkel Halevi Halstuk, confronted the Nazis in Zusmir in *tallit* and *kittel* during the winter of 1943, prior to being shot, and declared: "For some time now have I anticipated this *zekut* [of Kiddush Hashem]. I am prepared."[10] The Koloshitzer Rebbe, Rabbi Hana Halberstam, in 1914 anticipated his own death during the Holocaust in the fall of 1942. Hassidic tradition relates how this Rebbe, at the age of thirty, prayed at the grave of Rabbi Elimelech of Lizensk: "May the Almighty grant, that I be privileged to die for *Kiddush Hashem*."[11] Ahron Zeitlin describes an aged Hassidic Rebbe whose only son was murdered in the Holocaust. The night prior to a planned rescue of the elder Rebbe, the son appears in a dream to his father, depicting the "infinite holiness" of those who died for Kiddush Hashem in the Holocaust. The following morning the Rebbe refused to be rescued, lest "he be denied the privilege of *Kiddush Hashem*." The following day, the Rebbe joined other Jews being assembled for their final destination.[12] The Shidlowitzer Rebbe, Rabbi Haim Rabinowitz, comforted the people packed in the cattle wagons without food and water on a four-day trip to the death camp. "Fellow Jews, do not fear death, To die for *Kiddush Hashem* is a great privilege."[13]

Proper *hakanah* (preparation) and *kavanah* (absolute concentration), prior to the performance of a *Mitzvah*, is essential, as well, prior to the act of Kiddush Hashem. In discussing the significance of Kiddush Hashem, the Koidenover Rebbe, Rabbi Alter Perlow, in the Vilna Ghetto retold the Hassidic legend of the "Zaslover Martyrs" who died for Kiddush Hashem. Their souls came to the *Ba'al Shem Tov* pleading for *tikun* (restoration), since their thoughts during the act of Kiddush Hashem were not pure.[14] The Piazesner Rebbe taught in the Warsaw Ghetto: Those who fail to praise God in death, will neither be aware of Him in the world to come.[15] Rabbi Mendele Alter, the brother of the Gerer Rebbe, was among a group of Jews ordered to undress in Treblinka during the summer of 1942. Realizing that these were his last moments the Rebbe pleaded desperately for a glass of water. A Jewish guard usually noted for his cruelty to fellow Jews was touched by the plea. He provided the water under the impression that the Rebbe wished to quench his thirst before death. Instead, the Rebbe used the glass of water to cleanse his hands, as an act of purification prior to Kiddush Hashem, urging: "Fellow Jews, let us say the *widui* (the confessional) prior to death."[16] The Brezner Rebbe, Zaloshizer Rebbe, Matislaker Rebbe, and Stoliner Rebbe[17] are among a number of Hassidic leaders who led Jews in their final *widui* as preparation for Kiddush Hashem.

The attitude developed before Kiddush Hashem also determined the manner in which death was actually confronted. The Kiddush Hashem reports of the Brezner, Grodzisker, and Zaloshizer Rebbeim reflect their calming influence on the terrified victims, as they themselves faced death with dignity.[18] In each of these instances the final request included the wearing of a *talit katan* or *talit* (form of prayer shawls) at the time of death. Other descriptions of Kiddush Hashem actually include instances of confronting death with the *hitlahavut* (ecstasy), appropriate to the fulfillment of the final and ultimate Mitzvah.[19] With a Torah scroll in his hands, Meir Ofen, a Kabbalist and a Hassid of the Dzikover Rebbe, led hundreds of Jews during their march to the mass grave, reciting from Psalms 33:1, "Rejoice in God, righteous ones!"[20] The Grodzisker Rebbe, Rabbi Yisrael Shapira, in an inspiring message before entering the gas chambers in Treblinka, urged the Jews to accept Kiddush Hashem with joy. He led them in the singing of *Ani Ma'amin*.[21] The Dombrover Rebbe, Rabbi Haim Yehiel Rubin, prayed the Sabbath service, his last, with great fervor, sang the Sabbath meal songs, and led twenty Jews in a Hassidic dance prior to death in graves dug by themselves.[22] The Spinker Rebbe, Rabbi Yitzchak Isaac Weiss, danced and sang in the death wagons to Auschwitz, especially the prayer "*Vetaher libenu leabdekha be'emet*" (Purify our hearts so that we may serve You in truth).[23] *Esh Kodesh* observes that he who is murdered in Kiddush Hashem

> does not suffer at all . . . since in achieving a high degree of ecstasy, in anticipation of being killed for the sake of sanctifying His Name, blessed be He, he elevates all his senses to the realm of thought until the entire process is one of thought. He nullifies his senses and feelings, and his sense of the material dissolves in this process. Therefore, he feels nothing but pleasure.[24]

The mutual interrelationship between God and the Jewish People, throughout, is evident in the Kiddush Hashem motive. The Slonimer Rebbe cites the *Zohar* in observing that God dyes His garments in the blood of the martyrs who died for Kiddush Hashem.[25] The Piazesner Rebbe contrasts the suffering as punishment for sins and the suffering for Kiddush Hashem. The latter is aimed not only at the individual physical Jew; the consequences of the suffering affect his very faith and way of life. In such instances (as exemplified by the Kiddush Hashem in the Holocaust), "it is we alone who suffer with Him."[26] *Em Habanim Semehah*[27] points to a similar interrelationship between Kiddush Hashem, "sanctified by thousands and tens of thousands, [is the cause of the] weakening of the *kelippot* (shells), enabling the gates of *Eretz Yisrael* to open." In turn, the realization of Israel's return to Zion will serve to "magnify and sanctify the Name of God."[28]

Kiddush Hashem was also manifested in Kiddush Hahayim (Sanctifying the Name of God in Life). Such responses took the various forms of modest physical resistance, a pattern of spiritual and passive resistance, and *mesirat nefesh* (uncompromising personal sacrifice), in order to assist others in times of crisis. Rabbi

Nehemya Alter set the tone at a meeting of rabbis in Lodz, insisting that Kiddush Hashem may take various forms. However, crucial to the act is "not to degrade ourselves before the *goyim*."[29] Kiddush Hahayim dictates that the Jew face death, and live his life in dignity, cognizant of the Divine component present in man. Dignity in response to attempted acts of physical and spiritual degradation was dramatically demonstrated in Lublin toward the end of 1939. The German commander had forcibly assembled the Jews in an empty field on the outskirts of the city and ordered them in jest to sing a Hassidic melody. Hesitantly, someone began the traditional melody "*Lomir zich iberbeten, Avinu Shebashomayim*" (Let us become reconciled, Our Father in Heaven).

> The song, however, did not arouse much enthusiasm among the frightened masses. Immediately, Glovoznik [the commander] ordered his hooligans to attack the Jews since they refused to fully comply with his wishes. When the angry outburst against the Jews continued, an anonymous voice broke through the turmoil with a powerful and piercing cry, "*Mir velen sei iberleben Avinu Shebashomayim.*" We will outlive them, O Father in Heaven! Instantly, the song took hold among the entire people, until it catapulted [the people] into a stormy and feverish dance. The assembled were literally swept up by the entrancing melody full of *dveikut* (ecstatic devotion), which had now been infused with new content of faith and trust.[30]

The intended derision was turned into a disaster for the bewildered Nazis, forcing the commander Glovoznik to order a halt to the paradoxical spectacle. The Zelichover Rebbe, Rabbi Avraham Shalom Goldberg, while hiding in Zelichov, in June 1942, responded to the increasingly despondent fellow Jews who shared his secret cover: "We must remain hidden, perhaps it will save the life of but one Jew. Every Jew who remains alive, sanctifies the Name of God amongst many. He is indeed a man of courage, because he will not submit to the Nazis and will not extinguish his precious life."[31] The Piazesner Rebbe touches on the necessary interrelationship between those who die for Kiddush Hashem and the implication of Kiddush Hahayim for those who remain alive. Directing his remarks to those in the Warsaw Ghetto whose spirits have fallen, the Rebbe cautions:

> We have always been bidden to control ourselves against temptations and evil inclinations as implied by [the teaching] "Who is strong? He who controls his [evil] inclinations."[32] And presently we have been given an additional responsibility: to control ourselves against dejection and depression, and to support ourselves in God. True, this is very, very difficult, since suffering is too much to bear, may God have mercy. However, at a time when many Jews are burned alive sanctifying God, and are murdered and butchered only because they are Jews, then the least we can do, is to stand up to the test and with *mesirat nefesh*, control ourselves and support ourselves in God.[33]

Rabbi Menachem Zemba may have summarized the Kiddush Hahayim motif during a zealous plea for resistance before the Warsaw Ghetto uprising in April 1943.

> Thus, by the authority of the Torah of Israel, I insist that there is absolutely no purpose nor any value of *Kiddush Hashem* in the death of a Jew. *Kiddush Hashem* in our present

situation is embodied in the will of a Jew to live. This struggle for aspiration and longing for life is a *mitzvah* to be realized by means of *nekamah* (acts of revenge) *mesirat nefesh* and in the sanctification of the mind and will.[34]

Hallowing and sanctifying the Name of God is rooted in Hassidism and permeates its teachings and mode of life. In its efforts to achieve *tikun* in this world as a preparation for *tikun* in the upper world, Hassidism sought "to overcome the separation between the holy and the profane. . . . Everything wants to be hallowed, to be brought into the holy, everything worldly in its worldliness. . . . Everything wants to come to God through us . . . to let the hidden life of God shine forth."[35] Although Buber viewed Hassidism as "the only mysticism in which time is hallowed,"[36] Hassidism actually elaborated on Judaism's principle of "Venikdashti betok bnei Yisrael" (I shall be sanctified amidst the children of Israel).[37]

Kiddush Hashem in Hassidism assumes various guises attainable ultimately in death, as well as in life. Interpreting the verse, "Because of You, we are killed all the day; we are considered sheep for slaughter,"[38] the second Komarnor Rebbe, Rabbi Eliezer Zvi Safrin, echoed the *Midrash*: "There is not another nation who is prepared to sacrifice its soul for *Kiddush Hashem*, blessed be God, as is evident among Israel."[39] According to Hassidic tradition the Baal Shem Tob offered the last two hours of his life as a gift to God, "a true sacrifice of the soul [*mesirat nefesh*]."[40] The traditional view of Kiddush Hashem as the supreme test of faith, which allows every Jew to reach heights of sanctity, was noted by Rabbi Shneur Zalman of Liadi, and incorporated into the Habad school of Hassidic thought. "Even the simplest of Jews, and sinners in Israel, generally, sacrifice their lives for *Kiddush Hashem* and [in the process] undergo terrible suffering, so as not to deny the One God."[41]

The zekut motive is also evident in Hassidic thought. Rabbi Levi Yitzchak, when discussing "the purpose of all creation," observes: "Thus, every Jew [is prepared to] be killed for *Kiddush Hashem*, happy in the privilege of sanctifying, by his own means, the Name of Heaven."[42] Rabbi Nachman of Brazlav petitions the "Master of the Universe, to grant me the privilege, in Your compassion, to sacrifice my life for *Kiddush Hashem*, in truth, at any time."[43]

Hassidism expounded that man in the service of God should perform all of his deeds with mesirat nefesh. Rabbi Yaakov of Polnoya draws the following instruction from the saying of the Sages:

> Who is wise? He who learns from every man.[44] Even to the extent that he learns from a prohibited act. [For instance] when he sees someone in the act of cohabiting with an animal, [may he apply the following lesson]: if this one endangers his life (since the law of the land prescribes the death penalty for such an act), yet does not hesitate for even one moment, because of the physical pleasure derived—how can he (who observes the act) not fail to sacrifice his life in the service of God, which is an eternal, spiritual delight![45]

Rabbi Aaron of Karlin taught: "*Es kon nit zein emes afilu ein tnua ketanah, un mesriat nefesh*" (The slightest act cannot be sincerely performed without *mesirat nefesh*).[46]

Hassidim often use the terms Kiddush Hashem and mesirat nefesh interchangeably.[47] In order to dedicate one's soul to God, the soul had to be gradually sensitized and prepared to make the offering. To die for Kiddush Hashem, according to Rabbi Nachman Kossover,[48] is the ultimate in human altruistic behavior, since "he who is ready to die for God, does so because he loves Him, and not as a reward."[49] Rabbi Israel of Rizin interpreted Leviticus 1:2 as follows: "Only he who brings himself to the Lord as an offering, may be called man."[50] Rabbi Moshe of Kobrin anticipated that man would eventually replace the Temple sacrifices as the ultimate expression of devotion to God. "Lord of the World, we, we shall bring ourselves to You in place of the offering."[51] Mesirat nefesh in this tradition helped prepare the ground for the Kiddush Hashem responses noted in the Holocaust.

The related Kiddush Hashem motifs of zekut, hakanah, and *hithlahavut* (ecstatic response to a religious act), as well as the acceptance of death with dignity and honor, were all part of a complex interlocking pattern reflecting a special relationship which would be effected and realized between the Jew, the Jewish People, and God, via Kiddush Hashem. The Maggid of Zlochov applied the kabbalistic formula of the human deeds which have an impact on the cosmos to the concept of Kiddush Hashem.[52] This symbiotic relationship between man and the cosmos is dramatized in Hassidic tradition. The Baal Shem Tob visited the bereaved Jewish mother of a boy who was killed in Polnoya,

> a victim of "*alilat sheker*" (false accusation), and who very much sanctified the Name.... He [the Baal Shem Tob] comforted her, saying: "You should know that all of the worlds which were opened for Isaac at the time of his binding, were also opened [for the boy] when he was killed."[53]

The Kiddush Hashem impact may also reverberate in the regions of the *sefirot*, resulting in a repositioning of the various symbolic terms which represent God's mystical qualities. Rabbi Yitzchak Isaac of Komarno, a devout Kabbalist, isolated mesirat nefesh and Kiddush Hashem as the factors enabling the Jew to elevate the Divine manifestation of *Malkut* (the "kingdom" of God)[54] to the level of *Binah* (the "intelligence" of God).[55]

Another kind of interrelationship between the Jew and his Creator through Kiddush Hashem had been noted by the Matislaker Rebbe.[56] An identical observation is recorded of the Gerer Rebbe. "Why is man afraid of dying? Does he not then go to his Father!"[57] In a similar vein, Rabbi Moshe Leib Sassov was seen dancing on a vessel threatened by a terrible storm. When his teacher Rabbi Schmelke inquired as to the reason for the unexpected exuberance, Rabbi Moshe responded: "I am overjoyed at the thought that I shall soon arrive in the mansion of my Father." "I shall join you then," said Rabbi Schmelke.[58]

Kiddush Hashem is also related to redemption. In the letter of the Baal Shem Tob to Rabbi Gershon Kitover, reference is made to instances of Kiddush Hashem in the communities of Zaslov, Sibotke, and Danowitz: "All gave their lives for

Kiddush Hashem and sanctified the Name of Heaven, thus responding to the test. Due to this virtue, our Messiah will come."[59] The prolonged *Galut* (exile), and its intensification, can be reversed. Its tikun "consists of self-sacrifice for *Kiddush Hashem*, along with *mesirat nefesh*, with all our heart and soul,"[60] taught the Komarnor Rebbe.

Despite the evident readiness of Hassidim to die for Kiddush Hashem with mesirat nefesh when put to the test, "the very purpose of creation of man is that he observes the Torah and its commandments, 'and live by them,' but 'not die by them,'[61] except when the time has come to leave this world."[62] Good deeds of man represent the raw materials which sanctify both the upper and lower worlds. They serve to counter the phenomenon of death according to Dov Ber of Mezritch.[63] In his prayer requesting God to allow him the privilege of experiencing Kiddush Hashem, Rabbi Nachman of Brazlav straddles a thin line between Kiddush Hashem articulated in life and that expressed in death. On the one hand, Rabbi Nachman pleads: "May I truly be prepared to die any death and to suffer every pain and torment for the sanctification of Your great Name."[64] Yet, significantly, in the balance of the prayer, Rabbi Nachman clearly makes reference to a vicarious Kiddush Hashem death experience, stopping short of death itself. He prays for the ability

> to portray within my mind all of the deaths and torments, in a realistic likeness . . . until I actually sense the pain of death and torment, as if in fact I would be killed or tortured for the Sanctification of Your great and holy Name, to the very point when my soul shall practically expire. . . . This would make it necessary to overcome [the final death process] and to diminish those thoughts in order that I not die prematurely, God forbid.[65]

Rabbi Simcha taught that a Jew involved in the process of life, as a partner of God in creation, bears witness to God's greatness. Therefore, "when a Jew dies, a member of God's chosen People, the Lord takes the loss to heart, since this accounts for one person less to glorify and sanctify His Name."[66] The Baal Shem Tob viewed his own efforts at miracle healing "only for *Kiddush Hashem*."[67] The Kotzker Rebbe emphasizes Kiddush Hashem as Kiddush Hahayim. Interpreting the verse "You shall be men holy to me,"[68] the Kotzker taught: "Let your holiness be human, and may your human acts be holy. This is the holiness demanded from man. God has no need for angels in heaven."[69] The other world is not to be sought as an escape from the responsibilities of life on this world. Said Rabbi Naftali of Ropshitz: "No Jew can possibly inherit the world to come except by means of this world."[70]

Notes

1. Reprinted from *Tradition* 13, no. 4 and 14, no. 1 (1973), excerpted from my dissertation (see List of Contributors).

2. Moses Maimonides, "*Maamar Kiddush Hashem*," *Iggarot Harambam* [The Letters of Maimonides]

(Jerusalem: Mosad Harav Kook, 1960), pp. 29–65. Also Maimonides, "*Mishneh Torah, Sefer Hamadah,*" "*Yesodei Hatorah,*" chap. 5, pp. 1–11.

3. *Kiddush Hashem: Katabim Mime Hashoah Mctok Hagenazim shel Arkion Ringelblum Begetto Warsha* [Writings from the Days of the Holocaust from the Hidden Ringelblum Archives in the Warsaw Ghetto], edited by Nahman Blumenthal and Joseph Karmish (Israel, 1969), pp. 23–24. Henceforth *Kiddush Hashem.* Hillel Seidman, *Yoman Getto Warsha* [Diary of the Warsaw Ghetto] (New York: *The Jewish Week*, 1957), p. 221. Henceforth *Yoman Seidman.* Mordechai Lansky, *Meme Hayehudim Begetto Warsha* [The Life of the Jews in the Warsaw Ghetto] (Jerusalem: Yad Vashem, 1961), p. 209. Huberband, Zemba, and Zeitlin were all close to Hassidism. Huberband's maternal grandfather was the Hassidic Rebbe of Chencin in Poland. (*Kiddush Hashem*, p. 11.) Rabbi Menahem Zemba, a key religious leader in the Warsaw Ghetto and among those who encouraged physical resistance (*Yoman Seidman*, pp. 95, 221), was significantly influenced by the Hassidic school of Kotzk. Zeitlin, noted scholar, writer, and mystic, spent the final days of his life in the Warsaw Ghetto studying the Zohar, prior to his death in Treblinka. Hillel Seidman, "Hillel Zeitlin," *Morgan Journal*, 26 January 1947. Also a brief essay "Hillel Zeitlin" in *Yoman Seidman*, pp. 294–98.

4. *Kiddush Hashem*, p. 23. A search of Maimonides' works and consultation with scholars failed to reveal such a source.

5. "*Maamar Kiddush Hashem,*" p. 60. See Talmud Sanhedrin 74a, citing Leviticus 18:5, "You shall keep My laws and My norms, by the pursuit of which man shall live," interprets this as: "You shall live by, and not die by them." "*Maamar Kiddush Hashem,*" p. 55. Meir Dvorzeski and Yosef Gutfershten, *Jewish Resistance During the Holocaust: Proceedings of the Conference on Manifestations of Jewish Resistance* (Jerusalem: Yad Vashem, 1970), pp. 129, 380. Henceforth *Proceedings: Resistance Conference.*

6. Reference to Dr. Yosef Burg, Minister of Welfare, The State of Israel, who addressed the 1968 *Conference* cited. Moshe Prager, *Proceedings: Resistance Conference*, p. 119.

7. President of the Religious Zionist Mizrachi movement in Poland before and during the early Holocaust period. Died in the Warsaw Ghetto, 1943.

8. "It was then that the vacuum of the Ghetto was filled with Rabbi Yitzchak Nissenbaum's profound dictum, 'This is the hour of *Kiddush Hahayim*, and not of *Kiddush Hashem* by death. The enemy demands the physical Jew, and it is incumbent upon every Jew to defend it: to guard his own life.'" Nathan Eck, *Hatoim Bedarke Hamawet* [Wandering on the Roads of the Dead] (Jerusalem: Yad Vashem, 1960), p. 37. See also Shaul Esh, "Kiddush Hahayim Betok Hahurban," *Molad* (Israel), nos. 153–54 (1961): 106–99.

9. Meir Dvorzeski, "Haamidah Behayeh Yom Yom Begeta'ot U'wemahanoth," *Proceedings: Resistance Conference*, p. 128.

10. Menashe Unger, *Sefer Keddoshim* (New York: Shulsinger Brothers, 1967), p. 36. See also "Delegat Shildert Letzie Minuten Fun Ostrovzer Rebben," *Morgen Journal*, 3 June 1946, p. 3.

11. Unger, *Sefer Keddoshim*, p. 342.

12. "A Maisse Mit A Rebben Un Zein Zuhn," *Morgen Journal*, 12 July 1946, p. 5.

13. Y.M. Kersh, "Brief fun Churef-Gevorene Yiddishe Shtet un Shtetlech," *Forward*, 11 July 1946, p. 8.

14. Unger, *Sefer Keddoshim*, p. 374, citing Joseph Fuchsman, an eyewitness.

15. *Esh Kodesh* (Jerusalem: Wa'ad Haside Piazesne, 1960), pp. 97–98. Henceforth, *EK.*

16. Moshe Prager, *Eleh Shelo Nikne'u*, vol. 1 (Bnei Brak, Israel: Netzach, 1963), pp. 157–58. As recorded by an eyewitness, Rabbi Abraham Shmuel Binyamin Sofer.

17. The four were, respectively: Rabbi Nahum Yehoshua Halevi Pechenik, in an open grave in Sarne, Poland. Unger, *Sefer Keddoshim*, p. 84. Rabbi Shem Klingsberg, in the main square of Plashov, Poland. His final prayer included: "May it be Thy Will that I have the privilege of atoning for all Jews." Ibid., p. 152. Rabbi Yehezkiah Fisch, ibid., p. 233. A day before his arrival in Auschwitz he exclaimed with a joyous clap of his hands: "Tomorrow we shall meet with our Father!" A note was discovered among his books found in the Matislaker Ghetto with the inscription of the prayer to be recited prior to Kiddush Hashem via death. *Eleh Ezkerah*, vol. 4, p. 75. Rabbi Moshe Perlow, in the Stoliner Ghetto. Unger, *Sefer Keddoshim*, p. 272.

18. Ibid., p. 84. Rabbi Eliezer Horowitz, ibid., p. 101. Ibid., p. 152. Dignity in response to crisis was the theme of the Slonimer Rebbe, Rabbi Shlomo David Yehoshua Weinberg, in a message to his Hassidim delivered in the winter of 1940. Drawing on the teaching of the Riziner Rebbe, Rabbi Israel of Rizin

(died 1850), the great grandson of Rabbi Dob Ber, the Slonimer prepared his Hassidim. "The son of the King, who is an inseparable part of his father the king, does not change his character under any condition, no matter how depressed. Though he may be degraded and despised . . . at the nadir [of life], he must yet know and recall always, that he is the son of a king." *Zikron Kadosh* (Jerusalem: Yeshibat Bet Abraham, 1967), pp. 12–13. As told by an eyewitness, Moshe Weinberg. See *EK*, p. 158, for identical *ben melek* motive.

19. Maimonides, "*Maamar Kiddush Hashem*," p. 58.

20. Mordechai Eliav, ed., *Ani Ma'amin* [I Believe] (Jerusalem: Mosad Harav Kook, 1969), pp. 23–24.

21. Unger, *Sefer Keddoshim*, pp. 103, 110; Rabbi Yitzchak Herzog, *Haolam*, 4 April 1946. *Ani Ma'amin*, in this instance, refers to the twelfth of Maimonides' *Thirteen Principles of Faith* reinforcing the belief in man's ultimate redemption. "I firmly believe in the coming of Messiah; and although he may tarry, I daily wait for his coming."

22. M.A. Ger, "The Dombrover Rebbe Tanzt Mit Zeine Hassidim," *Der Tag* [The Day] 3 March 1946, p. 2.

23. *Hassidut Spinka Weadmoreha*, Jerusalem, 7, 10. Also Unger, *Sefer Keddoshim*, p. 309.

24. *EK*, pp. 8–9. The Rebbe supports the point by citing various medieval Rabbinic sources dealing with the subject of Kiddush Hashem.

25. Unger, *Sefer Keddoshim*, p. 280. See also *Zikron Kadosh*, p. 5.

26. *EK*. pp. 191–92.

27. *Em Habanim Semeha*, a key primary source for this research authored by Rabbi Yissachar Shlomo Teichthal, a leading Hassid of the Munkacher Rebbe and *dayan*. The manuscript is an attempt to explain the Holocaust, then in progress, in terms of the religious Jew's neglect of *Shivat Zion*. The work was written and completed in Budapest three months before the Nazi occupation of that city. The author was subsequently transported to Auschwitz where he met his death. Henceforth *EHS* (Budapest: Zalman Katz Katzburg, 1943).

28. "The power of the *kelippah* is dependent upon the *Galut*. With the abolishment of *Galut*, the *kelippah* will also be abolished." *EHS*, p. 214. According to *Kabbalah*, the kelippot are the prisons in which the holy sparks are confined against their will. Ibid., p. 15. We have here the profound concept of Kiddush Hashem in death eventually leading to Kiddush Hashem in life, within the context of the Jewish People in its Homeland. This is a form of tikkun central to Hassidic thought.

29. L. Feingold, "Megai Haharegah," *Ani Ma'amin*, p. 23.

30. As told to Moshe Prager by an eyewitness, Dr. Warman, the chairman of the *Yudenrat* in Lublin. Moshe Prager, "The Hassidic Movement During the Holocaust," *Sefer Habesht*, ed. Y.L. Cohen Maimon (Jerusalem: Mosad Harav Kook, 1960), pp. 269–70. Kiddush Hahayim was reflected in the manner which potential humiliation was transformed into an elevating and religious experience.

31. Unger, *Sefer Keddoshim*, p. 181.

32. *Mishneh Abot* 4:1.

33. *EK*, p. 169. Kiddush Hashem in death assumes meaning in the manner which those who remain alive achieve Kiddush Hahayim.

34. Issar Frankel, *Yehide Segulah* (Tel Aviv: Alef, 1955), p. 212.

35. Martin Buber, *The Origins and Meaning of Hasidism* (New York: Harper & Row, 1960), pp. 180, 181.

36. Ibid., p. 239.

37. Leviticus 22:32 reads: "You shall not profane My holy Name, that I may be sanctified in the midst of the Israelite people, I the Lord who sanctify you." Expounding on the background of the Talmudic discussion (*Sanhedrin* 74) concerning Kiddush Hashem, Rashi notes: "And one must sanctify the Name, this is the meaning of 'Venikdashti' [That I may be sanctified], namely, 'shemoser nafsho al ahabat yozro' [that he gives over his soul because he loves his Creator]." Rashi in Talmud *Sanhedrin* 74a. In Leviticus 22:32, Rashi further defines the ultimate Kiddush Hashem as martyrdom. "And when he gives over his soul let he be prepared."

38. Psalms 44:23.

39. H.Y. Berl, *Reb Yitzchak Isaac Mekomarno* (Jerusalem: Mosad Harav Kook, 1965), p. 190. See also Tanhuma "Tezaweh," p. 5. According to *gimatriya*, numerical code word play, popular among mystics,

the numerical value for the Hebrew letters in the phrase "Because of You, we are killed all the day," is equal to the numerical value of "Israel" (541).

40. Martin Buber, ed., *Tales of the Hasidim*, trans. Olga Marx (New York: Schocken, 1947), vol. 1, pp. 83–84. Compare with *Shibhe Baal Shem Tob*, p. 161. Actually it was his disciple, Rabbi Pinhas of Koretz (died 1791), who interpreted his master's offer to the Angel of Death: "Ani mohel leka otan shte sha'ot, welo ta'aneh oti" (I relinquish for you these two hours, and desist, pray, from further torment) as a final precious gift of life to God. "My teacher, the Baal Shem Tob, realizing the imminence of his death, exclaimed: 'Lord of the Universe, I make thee a gift of the remaining hours of my life.' This is true martyrdom for the sake of the Lord." Pinhas of Koretz, *Nofeth Zufim* (Warsaw: 1929), p. 11.

41. *Likute Amarim: Tanya*, pt. 1, chap. 18, p. 22. Tishby has documented the unique teaching of the *Habad* school of Hassidic thought, whereby there is hidden in "the right space of the heart" of every Jew (irrespective of his degree of Jewish observance or level of intellectual attainment), an equal amount of natural respect and love for the Divine and holy. The Kiddush Hashem phenomenon prevalent among all strata and elements in Jewry, reflects this collective view of the relationship between the Jewish People and God. I. Tishby, "Hassidut" (Hassidism), *HaEnziklopedia Haibrit*.

42. That is, Kiddush Hashem assumes the characteristic of a privilege rather than an obligation. *Kedushat Levi* (Munkatch, 1939), 69b.

43. *Meolamo Shel Rabbi Nahman Mebraizlav*, ed. David Hardan (Jerusalem: The World Zionist Organization, 1971), pp. 62–63.

44. *Mishneh Abot*, 4:1.

45. *Toldot Ya'akob Yosef* (Brooklyn, N.Y.: Yosef Weiss Publishers, n.d.), 19b, 26b.

46. *Beit Ahron* (Brody, 1873), p. 157.

47. Berl, *Rabbi Yitzchak Isaac Mekomarno*, pp. 238, 308, 309. See also *Likutei Amarim: Tanya*, pt. 1, chap. 18.

48. A disciple of the Baal Shem Tob, died 1775.

49. Louis I. Newman, ed. and trans., *Hasidic Anthology* (New York: Schocken, 1963), p. 438.

50. *Tales of the Hasidim*, vol. 2, p. 59.

51. Ibid., p. 168.

52. Rabbi Yechiel Michal of Zlochov, a disciple of the Baal Shem Tob, died c. 1786. The formula usually is stated: "Betaruta deletata, itaruta le'eylah" (With that which impacts below, one impacts above). The statement appears routinely in Kabbalah and Hassidic thought. (See *Toldot*, 4b; for a variant formula see *Kedushat Levi*, 23a.) See *Tales of the Hasidim*, vol. 1, p. 149.

53. Reference to Genesis 22:1–19. This episode was subsequently transformed into the forerunner and prototype of Kiddush Hashem. (See Shalom Spiegel's definitive documentation of the Akedah theme in Jewish martyrdom, *The Last Sacrifice* [New York: Schocken, 1969].) Shibhe Baal Shem Tob, p. 132.

54. The tenth in the series of ten sefirot.

55. The second in the hierarchy of sefirot. As a result of man's sinful pattern the manifestation of Malkut had fallen from its previous higher sphere. This represents a form of *Hillul Hashem* (the desecration of God's Name), the very antithesis to Kiddush Hashem. Only mesirat nefesh and Kiddush Hashem can restore ("tikun zeh") Malkut to its original position. This represents a form of tikun central to Hassidic response.

56. See n. 17.

57. *Tales of the Hasidim*, vol. 2, p. 311.

58. Newman, *Hasidic Anthology*, pp. 67–68.

59. *Igeret Hakodesh*, *Shibhe Habesht*, p. 169.

60. Berl, *Reb Yitzchak Isaac Mekomarno*, p. 238.

61. Leviticus 18:5. The interpretation of "live by them, but not die by them," is originally noted by Rabbi Ishmael, in Babylonian Talmud *Sanhedrin*, 74a.

62. *Toldot*, p. 113. Rabbi Yaakov Yosef refers to death under normal, natural circumstances.

63. *Torath Hamagid*, ed. Yisrael Klapholz, vol. 1 (Tel Aviv: Pe'er Hasefer, 1969), pp. 166b, 167a. Especially significant is the following reference: "That which is written, 'You shall be holy' [for I, the Lord your God, am holy. Leviticus 19:2], may be interpreted as follows: When you sustain the ideas

referred to as 'holy,' as we know, then you too will be holy—modeled after the Name of God. Thus, you will not encounter death . . . to wit, when you are alive, you will not be considered like the dead, God forbid."

64. *Meolamo Shel Rabbi Nahman Mebrazlav*, p. 63.

65. Ibid. The implication is: Absolute terminus of life forever prevents man from further sanctifying God's Name. Life is necessary for repeated Kiddush Hashem. This concept is a favorite of the Psalmist, "What use would my death be, if I went down to the grave? Can the dust praise You? Will it declare the truth?" (Psalms 30:10). "The dead cannot praise the Lord. Nor any who descend to silence" (Psalms 115:17). "I do not wish to die, but to live, and I shall tell of the works of God" (Psalms 118:17). A simulated experience of Kiddush Hashem, without sacrificing one's physical existence, is also noted in the teachings of the Hassidic master Rabbi Elimelek of Lizensk. "Thus we deliver our souls to [sanctify] His great Name, Blessed Be He. Man should always imagine that he truly sacrifices his soul in order that he may achieve the unity of His great Name. (*No'am Elimelek*, This is the meaning of the verse 'And when the time approached for Israel to die' (Genesis 47:29), He [Jacob] so completely devoted his soul [to the sanctification of God] that he was indeed close to death" Lemberg 1874, 24d). Both teachings imply a form of Kiddush Hashem without destroying life.

66. Rabbi Simcha of Parsischa. Newman, *Hasidic Anthology*, p. 49.

67. *Shibhe Baal Shem Tob*, p. 151. An implied facet of Kiddush Hahayim. For further treatment of the manner in which Hassidism viewed miracles as the glorious manifestation of the Divine in this world, see Yitzchak Alfasi, "Hasagot al Enoshiut U'moftim B'yisrael," *Sefer Habesht*, pp. 112–29.

68. Exodus 22:30.

69. Eliezer Steinman, *Shaar Hahasidut* (Tel Aviv: Hoza'at Sefarim Neuman, 1957), p. 236. See also Menahem Mendel of Kotzk, *Emet We'emunah* (Brooklyn, N.Y.: Ahavat Hakadmonim, 1971), p. 133.

70. *Shaar Hahasidut*, p. 261.

Islamic Traditions

The happiness of the drop is to die in the river.

Ghazal of Ghalib

Death and Dying in the Qur'ān

ALFORD T. WELCH

The Qur'ān is unique in the history of religions in recording the birth of a major religious tradition. It dates from the last twenty years or so of the Prophet Muhammad's lifetime and reached its final form within an equal period of time after his death in 632 C.E. It contains numerous references to historical events in the life of Muhammad and his contemporaries, and from the beginning to the end it responds to the historical situation—the needs, concerns, and struggles in the early Muslim community. It is thus the historian's primary source for tracing the rise of Muslim faith and practice. Yet problems of exegesis and interpretation abound, especially regarding the major themes and teachings of the Qur'ān, partly because of the difficulty of establishing an exact chronology of the text.

Popular Muslim beliefs about death and what happens to a person when he dies continue to be based more on later tradition than on the explicit teachings of the Qur'ān. An elaborate system of Muslim beliefs about the nature of death, the process of dying, and the events of the grave immediately following death developed in the early centuries following the death of Muhammad. Orthodox Muslims reached general agreement regarding the order of events, the identity and roles of the various celestial and infernal beings who greet the deceased, extract his soul, interrogate him about his faith and works, and even create a state of bliss or punishment within the grave.[1]

As interesting as an examination of this development may be, I will pursue a more limited task, providing a summary picture of the major Qur'ānic teachings on death and dying.[2] This survey will indicate the complexity and diversity of Qur'ānic ideas on this topic and also provide some perception of the Qur'ānic imagery and symbolism involving death.[3]

Death in the Context of Creation and Resurrection

The Qur'ān portrays close relationships between the concepts of death and life, death and creation, and death and resurrection (sometimes called a "new creation"), so that the complex of ideas involving creation, death, burial, and resurrection constitutes one of the major Qur'ānic death themes. One of the best examples of this blending is found in Sūra 23:12–16:[4]

> We created man from an extraction of clay;
> Then We placed him as a sperm-drop in a safe receptacle;
> Then We fashioned the sperm-drop into a clot;
> then We fashioned the clot into a lump;
> then We fashioned the lump into bones;
> then We clothed the bones with flesh;
> then We made him into a new creation.
> So blessed be God, the fairest of creators!
> After this you will surely die,
> And on the Day of Resurrection you will surely be raised up.

Death and Creation

Although the Qur'ān does contain references to the "six days of creation" and also to several versions of the creation and temptation story of Adam in the Garden, by far the majority of its references to creation speak of the procreation and birth of the individual and the forming of the child in the womb, rather than the creation of the first man and the origin of the human race. This predominant Qur'ānic view of creation and its integral relationship to death are seen in the relatively early Meccan passage, 56:57–62:

> We have created you (*khalaqnākum*); so why do you persist in unbelief? Have you considered the sperm that you emit? Do you create it yourselves, or are We its Creator? We have decreed death for you, and no one can stop Us from replacing you with other beings like you, nor from producing you (*nunshi'akum*) again in a form unknown to you. You know only of the first production; so why do you not reflect?[5]

But God does not just create man and bring about his death; rather God is the source of life renewal, as this representative passage makes clear: "He is the one who gave you life (*aḥyākum*), then He will cause you to die (*yumītukum*), then He will give you life (*yuḥyīkum*) (again)" (22:66/65).[6] In 30:40/39, this same theme occurs in the context of a rebuke against unbelievers who worship idols: "It is God who created you (*khalaqakum*), then provided for you, then He will cause you to die (*yumītukum*), then He will give you life (*yuḥyīkum*) (again). Can any of those whom you associate (with God) do any of these things? Glory be to Him! May He be exalted high above those they associate (with Him)." Another explicit assertion that other gods are impotent in these matters occurs in 25:3/3–4: "Yet, they have taken to themselves gods besides Him who create nothing but are themselves created, and who have no power to harm or help themselves, and no power over death (*mawt*) or life (*ḥayāt*) or resurrection (*nushūr*)!"[7]

Consequently, a basic premise of all Qur'ānic teaching concerning death becomes evident: in his omnipotence God determines the span of a man's life; he creates man and also causes him to die. In the following passage, 26:75–82, part of a sermon by Abraham, God's power over man's death is seen in the wider context of man's complete dependence on God from the time of birth to the Day of Judgment:

> He said: "And have you considered what you and your forefathers have been worshipping? They are all enemies to me, except the Lord of all Being, who created me and Himself guides me and gives me food and drink, and who heals me whenever I am sick, and who makes me die and then gives me life, and who, I hope, will forgive me my sins on the Day of Judgment."

This intrinsic role of God in man's existence is also vividly portrayed in 80:17/16–22; the unbelievers are reprimanded for failing to acknowledge the signs of God's power, and, in addition to a clear statement that God creates man from "a sperm-drop," the interesting suggestion is made that God himself not only causes man to die but also buries him.

> Woe to man! How ungrateful he is!
> From what did He create him?
> [He creates him] from a sperm-drop and
> then forms him and makes his path easy for him.
> Then He causes him to die and buries him.
> Then, when He wills, He raises him.

This passage suggests another important relationship in Qūr'ānic death views—man's return to the soil. In Sūra 20:55/57, in a sermon by Moses, God says: "Out of the earth[8] have We created you, and We will return you into it and then bring you forth (*nukhrijukum*) from it a second time." Here the idea of the creation of the first man from dust is combined with the idea of general resurrection, resulting in the somewhat illogical statement that people are brought forth from the earth twice. The theme of man growing out of the earth also appears in a sermon by Noah: "And God caused you to grow (*anbatakum*) out of the earth, then He will return you into it, and bring you forth (from it again)" (71:17f./16f.). Here the "growing out of the earth" refers to creation. This motif goes back, of course, to the expulsion of Adam and his wife (who is never named in the Qur'ān) from the Garden, when God says in 7:24f./23f.: "In the earth shall you dwell and have pleasure for a while. ... Therein you shall live, and therein you shall die, and from it shall you be brought forth."[9]

Death and the New Creation

The passages quoted above also indicate a close relationship between death and resurrection, sometimes referred to in the Qur'ān as a "new creation." Several verses of uncertain date contain historical allusions to disputes between Muhammad and the Meccans, in which the doctrine of resurrection is ridiculed by the unbelievers, who say: "What, after we have become bones (*'iẓām*) and broken bits (*rufāt*), will we really be raised up again as a new creation (*khalq jadīd*)?" (17:49/52, 17:98/100). Muhammad himself is scoffed at in 34:7–8 where it is recorded that the unbelievers say: "Shall we show you a man who will tell you that when you are utterly torn to pieces then you will be made a new creation? Has he invented a lie in the name of

God, or is he mad?" The consequence of such ridicule is made clear in a judgment scene in 56:46/45–48 where it is stated that those who will be damned at the Last Judgment are the ones who "persisted in the great sin of saying: 'What, when we are dead and become dust (*turāb*) and bones, shall we indeed be raised up? And our forefathers also?'"

The quickening of the dead is also portrayed in the Qur'ān in the symbolism of God's reviving of the dead earth with rain: "And it is God who sends down water (*mā'*) out of heaven and thereby revives the earth after her death (*mawtihā*). Surely in this is a sign (of the resurrection) for those who listen" (16:65/67). This motif is even more explicit in 35:9/10: "It is God who sends the winds which raise the clouds. Then when the clouds rise, He drives them to the dead land (*balad mayyit*) and thereby revives (*aḥyaynā*) the earth after her death. This is how the resurrection (*nushūr*) will occur."[10] Even more vivid is the Medinan passage 22:5 where the various Qur'ānic themes of creation, death, and resurrection are brought together. Here the two earlier views of creation are combined in a systematic portrayal of God's power over man's life and death. Also in the same context the rain is seen as impregnating the barren earth and making it fertile:

> Men, if you doubt the resurrection (*al-ba'th*), then remember (the following) that should make clear to you how things are: We created you from dust (*turāb*), then from a sperm-drop, then from a blood-clot, then from a lump of flesh, formed and unformed. Then We cause those whom We choose to remain in the wombs for a given period. Then We deliver you as infants and We rear you until you reach your prime. And some of you die (early),[11] while others are made to live to a miserable old age in which all your knowledge becomes ignorance. And you observe the earth as lifeless, but then We send down water upon it, and it throbs, then swells and delivers all kinds of beautiful plant life.

The rain impregnates the lifeless earth and makes it fertile, just as the "sperm-drop" is the source of man's life, causing the woman (here, mother earth) to "throb, then swell, then deliver beautiful . . . life."

It appears, then, that the complex of ideas involving creation, death, and resurrection began developing in the early Meccan portions of the Qur'ān as a cyclical, life-death-life theme. Some contexts involving this theme are difficult to interpret, for instance the question in 10:31/32: "Who brings forth the living from the dead and brings forth the dead from the living?" In 30:19/18 this rhetorical question is answered, but meaning is still not certain: "It is He who brings forth the living (*al-ḥayy*) from the dead (*al-mayyit*), and brings forth the dead from the living, and He revives (*yuḥyi*) the earth after her death. This is how the resurrection (*nushūr*) will occur." This statement supports the assumption that the first part of both verses refers to the resurrection. In the Medinan passage 2:28/26 an additional element is introduced, suggesting that the reference may be to the creation of the individual from lifeless matter: "How do you disbelieve in God, considering that you were dead and He gave you life, then He will make you dead, then He will give you life, then unto Him you will be returned?" Here the cycle is death-life-death-life. Still, the ambiguity in some of these contexts supports the conclusion that, according to the scheme of things in the Qur'ān, the cycle of human life and death is an integral and recurring part of the timeless cycle of nature, over which God has complete control.

Sleep and the Nature of Death

Death and Sleep

The problem of determining the Qur'ānic view of the nature of death is closely related to two other questions: the relationship between death and sleep, and the existence of the soul. Faced with the timeless mysteries of life and death, the Qur'ān adopts the ancient notion of likening death to sleep and waking to resurrection from the dead, as in 25:47/49: "It is He who has made the night to be a mantle for you, and sleep for a resting, and has made the day for a rising (*nushūr*)."[12] The night is a garment that covers a person while he is sleeping; sleep is a sign of death, and dawn (when the person awakens) is a sign of resurrection (*nushūr*), which is to be the final Awakening.[13] Sleep and death are again paralleled in 6:60f.:

> It is He who *takes you* by night and He knows what you do during the day; He raises you up again by day[14] so you may complete your appointed term. You will all return to Him, and then He will tell you what you were doing. He is omnipotent over his servants. He sends guardians to watch over you until, when any one of you is visited by death (*al-mawt*), Our messengers *take him*. They never fail (in their duty)! [emphasis added]

The same verb, *tawaffā*, appears both for "taking" man in sleep and for "taking" him in death, indicating a close relationship between sleep and death. Note that it is God (literally "he") who "takes" man in sleep (literally "by night"), while his "messengers" (*rusul*) "take" man at death. Should the conclusion thus be drawn that the Qur'ānic teaching is that God "takes" man in sleep but that his messengers (possibly the angels) "take" man at death?

A preliminary answer to this question is provided by 39:42/43, the clearest and probably the most important verse in the Qur'ān on this topic: "God *takes* the souls (*al-anfus*) at the time of their death, and those which have not died (He takes) in their sleep. He retains those against whom He has decreed death, but releases the others until an appointed term. Surely in this are signs for those who reflect!" According to this verse, God "takes" the souls both "at the time of their death" (*ḥīna mawtihā*) and also "in their sleep" (*fī manāmihā*). This appears to contradict the equally explicit statement in 6:61 that it is God's "messengers," and not God himself, who "take" man at the time of death. Conclusions regarding the agent or agents of death must be reserved until after the discussion of the *tawaffā* passages below. The more important distinction between these two texts is the occurrence of the term *al-anfus* (translated above as "the souls") in 39:42/43, suggesting that some entity actually leaves the body at death and in sleep. Whether or not the Qur'ān teaches this is a crucial question that cannot be answered strictly on the basis of the death-sleep passages.[15]

The Agonies of Death and the Existence of the Soul

An important verse for determining the Qur'ānic view of the nature of death and the existence of the soul is 6:93, which contains another crucial use of the term *anfus* in the context of a picturesque description of death. This verse dates from the early Medinan period and probably refers (at least in the first part of the verse) to the Prophet Muhammad's Jewish opponents:[16]

> Who does greater evil than the one who invents falsehood against God, or says: "I have received a revelation," when he has received none, or the one who says: "I will send down something like what God has sent down?" If you could only see the wicked ones when they are in the *agonies of death*! And the angels are stretching out their hands: "*Give yourselves up*! Today you will receive the punishment of shame for the lies you have been saying against God, displaying arrogance against His signs!"

Key elements in this verse include the involvement of the angels in the death of man and the absence of any reference to judgment between the time of death and the punishment of the wicked ones. More significant, however, for determining the Qur'ānic view of the nature of death is the expression "agonies of death" (*ghamarāt al-mawt*), the meaning of which is closely related to the interpretation of the command by the angels *akhrijū anfusakum*, which has been translated "Give yourselves up!," but which could also be rendered "Give up your souls!"[17]

The term *nafs* and its plurals *anfus* and *nufūs* are usually reflexive pronouns when they occur in the Qur'ān, as in 12:54 where the king says: "Bring him to me! I will take him to myself (*li-nafsī*)." In some contexts, these terms could be interpreted as referring to some entity within man, as in the Qur'ānic statement that involves both the *nafs* and death (*al-mawt*): "every *nafs* will have a taste of death" (*kullu nafsin dhā'iqatu-l-mawt*), which occurs three times, in 3:185/182, 21:35/36, and 29:57. Here, "every *nafs*" could be (and often is) interpreted as "every soul"; however, the contexts in which this phrase appears, and the predominant (if not exclusive) Qur'ānic usage of the term *nafs*,[18] suggest that it is better to interpret "every *nafs*" in these three verses as "everyone" or "every person," as in Bell's translation of 21:35/36: "Every person is subject to death, and We try you with evil and good as a test, and to Us are ye made to return."[19]

Unlike these contexts and others in which the term *nafs* can be interpreted either as "soul" or (preferably) as referring to the person as a whole, 56:83/82–87/86 is one passage in which the term *nafs* does not occur, but which seems to say that some entity leaves the body through the throat at the time of death: "Why, but when *it* leaps to the throat of the dying, and that hour you are watching—and We are nearer to him than you, but you do not see Us—why, if you are not at Our disposal, do you not bring *it* back, if you speak truly?"[20] This passage, which must be interpreted with interpolations for any translation to be meaningful, seems to mean: If you think you have power over death, then when you are sitting beside a dying friend at the moment of death when the soul (or spirit) is leaving the body and reaches the throat, why do you not stop the soul from leaving the body, or, if it does leave the body, force it to return?[21]

Thus, in spite of the overwhelming majority of cases in the Qur'ān where man is regarded as a whole being, in some few passages the Qur'ān does affirm the ancient Greek (and, by the time of the Prophet Muhammad, Jewish and Christian) concept that the essential self or soul leaves the body at the time of death.[22] Therefore, the command *akhrijū anfusakum* in 6:93 above could be translated and interpreted: "Give up your souls!" And the statement "God takes the *anfus*" in 39:42/43 could be translated: "God takes the souls." However, in both cases the interpretation in accordance with the Qur'ān's predominant teaching is that *anfus* refers to the "selves" or the "individuals" as wholes rather than to some separate spiritual entity within man.

If the command *akhrijū anfusakum* in 6:93 is interpreted as "Give up your souls!," then the expression "agonies of death" (*ghamarāt al-mawt*) could refer to the "tearing out of the soul," as this expression is often interpreted.[23] In accordance with this view, the first two verses of Sūra 79 are often regarded as referring to the "agonies of death" in 6:93. The first verse in Sūra 79, *wa-n-nāzi'āti gharqan*, is thus interpreted to mean the tearing out of the souls of the wicked,[24] and the second verse, *wa-n-nāshiṭāti nashṭan*, is regarded as referring to the gentle drawing out of the souls of the righteous.[25] Dawood translates these two verses: "By those who violently snatch away men's souls, and those who gently release them," and the title of this Sūra, *An-nāzi'āt*, he vividly renders "The Soul-snatchers." However, this interpretation is far from certain, as is obvious from the variety of translations. Bell, for instance, translates the same verses: "Drawing full stretch, hustling and bustling," and (in a footnote) interprets them as referring to Meccan business life.[26] Regardless of the interpretation given to the command of the angels *akhrijū anfusakum* in 6:93, there is no explicit indication in this verse or elsewhere in the Qur'ān that the "agonies of death" involve the tearing out of the soul, as this expression later came to be interpreted. A more likely meaning of *ghamarāt al-mawt* is simply "pangs of death" or "death throes."

It is clear in the texts discussed in this section that death is like sleep. In the same way that a person does not cease to exist in sleep, so also he does not cease to exist in death. And in the same way that a person "comes back to life" when waking from sleep, so also will he be revived at the great Awakening. An apparent discrepancy exists between the concept of death being like sleep, in that the soul leaves the body in death as gently as it does in sleep (at least this is the implication in 39:42/43) and the concept of the "agonies of death" in 6:93. However, all Qur'ānic references to suffering at the time of death involve unbelievers only. A possible interpretation may be that only the unbelievers will suffer the "agonies of death," while the believers' death will be like sleep.

Those Who "Take" Man at Death

The question of the identity of the agent or agents of death in the Qur'ān was raised in the preceding section. The term *tawaffā* (to take, to call in) occurs almost exclusively with the specific meaning "to take at death." (In two contexts cited above, 6:60f. and 39:42/43, this term means "to take" both in death and in sleep.) The verb *tawaffā* occurs in the following categories of contexts, in which the deceased is "taken" by: God, the angel of death (*malak al-mawt*), the messengers (*rusul*) of God, the angels (*malā'ika*), and death itself (*al-mawt*). The term also appears in prayers in which the petitioner requests that he be "taken" among those who believe.[27]

In over half of the twenty contexts of *tawaffā* in the Qur'ān, God himself "takes" man at death, as in 10:104 where this concept characterizes the dīn of Muhammad: "O men, if you are in doubt concerning my allegiance (dīn), I do not serve those you serve apart from God, but I serve God who will *take you*, and I am commanded to be one of the believers." In 16:70/72 God's control of man's origin and destiny are mentioned together: "It is God who created you and then will *take you*."[28] The oft-recited prayer in 3:193/191, "Our Lord, forgive us our sins and acquit us of our evil deeds, and *take us* among the pious" also refers to God as the agent of death.[29]

With the wealth of vivid pictures of what awaits man at death, it is surprising that the loathsome Angel of Death (*malak al-mawt*) appears in the Qur'ān by name only once, in 32:10/9–11, in a context remarkable for its lack of color: "They say: 'What, when we lie hidden in the earth, will we then become a new creation?' Indeed, they disbelieve in the encounter with their Lord! Say: 'The Angel of Death, who has been given charge over you, will *take you*. Then to your Lord you will be returned!'" Little information is offered concerning the Angel of Death, but the strongest impression is that his "taking" of the deceased relates closely to "the encounter with their Lord" (*liqā' rabbihim*).[30] Certainly the vivid details of later, popular belief concerning the Angel of Death, such as the "seizure of the spirit" (*qabḍ ar-rūḥ*), are not present in this passage.[31]

The "messengers" (*rusul*) of God are said to "take" man at the time of death in 6:61, which states: "Then, when death (*al-mawt*) comes to one of you, *Our messengers take him*, and they do not slip!" In 7:37/35 these "messengers" interrogate the unbelievers at the time of death:

> Who does greater evil than the one who invents falsehood against God or rejects His signs? Their fate (*naṣīb*) from the book will greet them, so that when *Our messengers* come to them and *take them*, they say: "Where are those you used to call upon apart from God?" And they will reply: "They have gone far from us." Thus, they bear witness against themselves that they had been unbelievers!

Here the phrase "their fate from the book" (*naṣībuhum min al-kitāb*) could be interpreted as referring to the judgment, and, if the sequence of events in the verse were strictly followed, then the messengers of God would "take" the unbelievers after the judgment; in such case, these *rusul* would not be "the angels of death" at all, but "angel guards of hell."[32] However, a comparison of this passage with other *tawaffā* passages indicates that the "fate from the book" in 7:37/35 is a metaphorical reference to death (which is the inevitable "fate" of every person, the date being recorded in the heavenly book) and is parallel to the expression "when death comes to one of them" in 6:61. Thus, these "messengers" are "angels of death."[33]

In the four contexts in which those who "take" man are specifically said to be angels (*mala'ika*), the term "death" (*al-mawt*) does not occur. The only *tawaffā* passage in which angels are said to "take" both believers and unbelievers is 16:28/30–32/34 (a context that is clearly not a unity in its present form—verses 30f./32f. are thus omitted here):

> Those whom *the angels take* while they are wronging themselves will then offer submission: "We have not been doing evil!" (The angels will then reply:) "No! surely God knows what you have been doing! So enter the gates of Jahannam, to dwell therein!"... To those whom *the angels take* while they are doing good, they will say: "Peace be upon you! Enter the Garden (*al-janna*) for what you have been doing."

According to verses 28f./30f. the angels "take" those who are "wronging themselves" (*ẓālimī anfusihim*) and then question them regarding their deeds. The purpose of this interrogation is more obvious in the parallel passage, 4:97f./99f., where the initial statement is repeated almost verbatim, and then the angels ask: "In what state were you?," to which the deceased reply: "We were miserable in the earth." The point of both contexts is that unbelievers will be questioned at death regarding their deeds on earth, and in both cases Jahannam (cf. Gehenna) is promised as the place of final abode. According to 16:32/34, those whom the angels "take" while "doing good" (*ṭayyibīna*) are not questioned at death, but are greeted with the salutation of peace (*salām ʻalaykum*) and are apparently sent immediately into paradise (literally "the garden," *al-janna*). These notions are not expressed in 4:97f./99f., nor is there an exact parallel anywhere else in the Qur'ān. Although these contexts seem to say that the angels usher the deceased to their final abodes immediately at the time of death, and the judgment before God is not mentioned, these passages have later been interpreted as referring to a state of punishment or bliss within the grave during the interval between death and resurrection.

In two other *tawaffā* passages, 8:49/51–51/53 and 47:27/29, where the angels are said to "take" the hypocrites, it is also clear that these *malā'ika* are "angels of death." In both contexts the angels "take" the unbelievers (not so named in 47:27/29) "beating their faces and backs." In 8:50f./52f., in addition to the beating they inflict on the unbelievers at the time of their death, the angels also appear to administer the punishment: "Taste the punishment of the burning! That is for what your hands have forwarded, for which God is never unjust to his servants!" These angels must be seen as the same as those in 16:28f./30f. and 4:97f./99f.; once again, the judgment before God is not mentioned. Thus, in the Qur'ān there seems to be no clear distinction between the punishment of the unbelievers at the time of death and their eternal punishment or "second death" in Jahannam.[34]

What is the significance of these *tawaffā* passages for determining the Qur'ānic view of death? Those involving the Angel of Death (*malak al-mawt*), the "messengers" (*rusul*) of God, and the angels (*malā'ika*) as agents of death could be harmonized, without doing injustice to the text, by regarding the messengers of God as angels and inferring that the Angel of Death has helpers.[35] But these passages are not so easily harmonized with those stating that God himself "takes" man at death. A literal interpretation of these *tawaffā* passages would result in a clear contradiction in the text of the Qur'ān. This apparent discrepancy is resolved by interpreting these passages as an example of what the Biblical scholars call "corporate personality." In Qur'ānic studies this concept would refer to several cases in which certain actions for which God is held to be ultimately responsible are sometimes said to be performed by certain of his agents, while in other contexts the same actions are said to be performed by God himself.[36] What is certain is that even when other agents are said to "take" man in death, the Qur'ān consistently makes clear that they are acting for God and in no way do they detract from God's omnipotence concerning man's life and death.

The Second Death

Parallel to the concept of a second life or "new creation" is a second death, an eternal death which, like the punishment inflicted at the time of the first death, is suffered only by the unbelievers. The godfearing, on the other hand, are promised "a secure position among gardens and springs" where they will be "robed in silk and brocade," will enjoy "dark-eyed, wide-eyed" maidens, will be able to call for every kind of fruit, and also "will not taste death, except for the first death" (44:51–56). The same theme occurs in 37:58f./56f. in a rhetorical question asked by believers and understood to have an affirmative reply: "Will we not die, except our first death, and will we not be punished?" Over against the pleasures of paradise, the Qur'ān portrays a second death in various dramatic settings, as in 40:11, where the damned call out: "Lord, You have caused us to die two deaths and twice You have raised us to life. Now we confess our sins. Is there any way out?" In 43:77 the tormented unbelievers go a step further and plead with the "ruler" of hell[37] to finish with them, in what is apparently a plea for annihilation so they can escape the tortures of eternal punishment: "And they will call out: 'Mālik, ask your Lord to finish with us!', and he will reply: 'No, you must remain.'" The plea for annihilation is clearer and the reply is more specific in 25:11/12–14/15:

> No, they deny the Hour [of resurrection]! We have prepared a blaze for those who deny the Hour. When it sees them [approaching] from afar, they will hear it raging and roaring. And when they are cast, chained together, into some narrow place therein, they will plead for destruction then and there. [But they will hear the reply:] "Plead not today for a single destruction! Plead for one oft-repeated!"[38]

The damned have been resurrected to a new life only to receive unbearable punishment from which they seek release; that is, they seek a second death. This idea appears specifically in 35:36/33 where they are told that they will not be permitted to die and that their punishment will not be eased: "Surely those who reject [God] will receive the fire of Jahannam. No term will be determined for them so that they could die, nor will its punishment be lightened for them. Thus do We reward every ungrateful one!"[39]

This concept is amplified further in other passages where the damned are said to exist in a state that is neither death nor life, as in 20:74/76: "Surely, he who returns to his Lord [at the judgment] as a sinner, for him is Jahannam, in which he will neither die nor live"; and in 87:10–13: "Indeed, the admonition will be accepted by those who fear [God]; but it will be rejected by those most unfortunate ones who will enter the Great Fire, in which they will then neither die nor live!" This same picture is portrayed vividly in one of those poignant Qur'ānic judgment scenes, in which an obstinate unbeliever appears before the Throne hoping for reprieve, but instead receives the hellfire: "Before him is Jahannam, where he is given to drink boiling slimy water [or oozing pus] which he gulps but cannot swallow; and death comes upon him from every side,[40] and yet he cannot die. Before him is a chastisement unrelenting" (14:16f./19f.). Thus, for the damned there is to be a second death, a death that is not death, for the dying who cannot die.[41]

The Traditional View of Death and the Events of the Grave

It is the orthodox Muslim belief that when a person dies and the body is placed in the grave, two black-faced, blue-eyed angels named Munkar and Nakīr visit the grave and interrogate the deceased concerning his beliefs and deeds in life.[42] Then, while still in the grave, the deceased receives comfort or punishment (depending on the answers given) at the hands of these two who are called "the two interrogators."[43] At a Muslim funeral a mourner may approach the corpse as it is about to be laid in the tomb and whisper instructions for answering these questions. These instructions are called "the instruction of the deceased" (*talqīn al-mayyit*), and the questioning is called "the trial of the grave" (*fitnatu-l-qabr*).[44] Popular beliefs and the teaching contained in the various creeds and manuals differ somewhat regarding the precise roles of the various celestial and infernal beings which greet the deceased at death or visit his tomb during the interval (*barzakh*) between death and the day of resurrection. The following representative account appears in a tradition recorded by as-Samarqandī on the authority of al-Barā' ibn 'Āzib and reported to be from Muhammad.[45]

When a believer is approaching death, angels (*malā'ika*) with white faces descend to him and seat themselves before him. At the moment of death, the Angel of Death (*malak al-mawt*) arrives and takes the soul, which comes forth "flowing as easily as a drop from a waterskin," and he presents it to the angels, who wrap it in a shroud with sweet-smelling aromatics and take it up to the seventh heaven.[46] Its record is written in 'Illiyūn[47] and then this soul is returned to the body in the grave, where the deceased is questioned by Munkar and Nakīr. After answering the questions successfully, the deceased hears a herald call out the good news that he is a believer and is to receive the comforts of the Garden (*al-janna*) while he is in the grave, which expands "as far as the eye can reach."[48]

On the other hand, when an unbeliever is approaching death, angels with black faces descend to him and seat themselves before him. The Angel of Death arrives at the time of death and takes the soul, which has been scattered throughout all the body, pulling it out "like the dragging of an iron spit through moist wool, tearing the veins and the sinews"; he presents it to the angels who put it in a hair-cloth and "the odor from it is like the stench of a decomposing carcass." It is taken to the gate of the lowest heaven, but is not admitted, and its record is written in Sijjīn.[49] Then the soul is returned to the body in the grave and the deceased is questioned by Munkar and Nakīr. When he cannot answer the questions successfully, the deceased hears a herald call out the bad news that he has been rejected and is to be tormented in the grave (in which a door is opened letting in heat and smoke from Jahannam, and the tomb contracts "so that his ribs are piled upon one another").

Although this account is based on Qur'ānic terms (*malak al-mawt*, *sijjīn* and *'illiyūn*, *al-janna*, and *jahannam*), both the order of events and the numerous details represent a later development. The terms *munkar* and *nakīr* do appear in the Qur'ān, but not as proper names. In the Qur'ān the term *munkar* means evil or "disapproved" deeds, and the term *nakīr* means "disapproval." There is no evidence to indicate that the "two interrogators," Munkar and Nakīr, are related to the Qur'ānic usage of these two terms.

Conclusions

Consideration of the chronological order of the various death themes in the Qur'ān adds significant insight into their meaning. The earliest references to death in the Qur'ān occur in nature metaphors and similes that appear in "sign" passages, which are relatively early Meccan but cannot be dated precisely.[50] These passages include the idea of man's death being like the death of the earth, which God revives with rain, and the symbolism of man growing out of the earth, then being returned to it, and then being brought forth again. According to the conception expressed in these passages, man's life and death are very much a part of the cycle of nature and of the overall divine economy of nature, so that it is part of God's plan to cause individuals to die so they can be replaced with others, as in 56:60f.: "We have decreed death for you, and no one can stop Us from replacing you with other beings like you, nor from making you to grow again in a form unknown to you."

The dominant theme of God's omnipotence concerning the span of man's life from birth through death, burial, and resurrection also emerges in these early contexts. The life-death-life complex involving creation, death, and resurrection forms an integral part of the Meccan portions of the Qur'ān, dating from the time when Muhammad was struggling against the powerful economic and religious forces of his native city, striving to convince his pragmatic, polytheistic neighbors of the reality of the Resurrection and Judgment, and of God's sole omnipotence over the affairs of man and nature. In addition to these rather abstract ideas regarding death in the various "sign" passages, the Meccan portions of the Qur'ān also contain vivid portrayals of the eternal death of the damned, that "second death" in which the unbeliever is suspended forever in a state of agony on the verge of death, yearning for annihilation, but being unable to die.

The question of the existence of the soul and its relation to death, and the idiom of man's being "taken" at death and in sleep, either by God himself or by the angels, do not arise in the earlier portions of the Qur'ān, but appear only in a later development. Those passages that may be interpreted as referring to some entity within man that leaves the body in sleep and in death clearly date from the time when Muhammad and the infant Muslim community were coming into close contact with the religious ideas of the Jewish community of Medina.

The *tawaffā* passages in which angels appear as agents of death also belong to this same period, along with references to the mortality and death of other prophets, statements concerning violent death and martyrdom, and legal dictums regarding murder, retaliation, and capital punishment.[51] Although some of these themes are clearly related to the legislative needs involved in establishing the new Muslim community in Medina, O'Shaughnessy seems to be correct in seeing a heightened concern about death during Muhammad's Medinan years when the Prophet reached the age when his own death became an imminent possibility.

> At the very least, then, it may be said that the fear of death is a Medinan theme and that it was in the forefront of Muhammad's thinking during the last decade of his life. . . . This preoccupation with death on Muhammad's part at this stage of his career was altogether normal and to be expected. At the time of the Hijrah in 622 he was approximately fifty-two years old—an age at which a man's achievement and reproductive life are coming to an end and at which death is a more definite possibility that cannot be easily set aside. For Muhammad in particular the Hijrah marked the close of a period of rejection and the beginning of acceptance and broadened leadership—and he would naturally regret having them cut off by death.[52]

The Qur'ān does not provide a uniform, systematic treatment of death and dying, and this has prompted some scholars to question whether the Prophet himself had any comprehensive view of this subject.[53] It is true that the larger theological and philosophical issues involving death are only hinted at in the Qur'ān, and that it was left to the later commentators and theologians to systematize Qur'ānic statements into a Muslim theology of death.[54] But the Qur'ān should not be ignored. For the pious Muslim, who has tended to base his beliefs about death more on the later views of theologians and philosophers than on the teachings of the Qur'ān, and for the Western historian of religious thought, who has largely ignored the Muslim scripture, the Qur'ān remains an almost untapped source of ideas on this vital subject that concerns us all.

Notes

1. The orthodox Muslim views on this subject are discussed in some detail in the *Kitāb ar-rūḥ*, 3rd ed. (Hyderabad: al-Ma'ārif al-'Uthmāniyya, 1357 A.H./A.D. 1938–39), by Ibn Qayyim al-Jawziyya (d. 751/1350), a student of the great Ḥanbalite theologian Taqī ad-Dīn ibn Taymiyya (d. 726/1326). This work is arranged around twenty-one questions, of which questions four to fourteen (pp. 49–112) deal with the process of dying, the inquisition by angels at the time of death, and the punishment of the grave. Duncan B. Macdonald, "The Development of the Idea of Spirit in Islam," *Acta Orientalia* IX (1930–31): 318–28, summarizes parts of this work, but omits most of the questions that deal specifically with the topic of this article. Macdonald's summary is based on the second edition, published in Hyderabad in 1324/1906.

2. Passages dealing with the mortality and death of the prophets, the martyr's death, legal statements regarding killing and retaliation, and other miscellaneous contexts involving death are not specifically treated in this article. For a discussion of these topics, see the excellent study by Thomas O'Shaughnessy, *Muhammad's Thoughts on Death* (Leiden: Brill, 1969).

3. The following Qur'ānic concordances and reference works have been used in this study: Michel Allard et al., *Analyse conceptuelle du Coran sur cartes perforées*, 2 vols. and a file of 431 cards (Paris: Mouton, 1963); Rudi Paret, *Der Koran: Kommentar und Konkordanz* (Stuttgart: Kohlhammer, 1971); and Gustav Flügel, *Concordantiae Corani Arabicae* (Leipzig, 1842; often reprinted).

4. In all Qur'ānic references in this article the verse number according to the Cairo standard edition is given first, followed by the Flügel verse number, after a diagonal, where they differ.

5. The statement "We have decreed death for you" (*naḥnu qaddarnā baynakumu-l-mawt*) in 56:60, and the expression *faqaddarahu* in 80:21, translated below as "then forms him," are often interpreted to mean that the time and nature of each individual's death are "predestined," a later theological meaning of the verb *qaddara*. For this view, see Bayḍāwī, *Beidhawii Commentarius in Coranum*, ed. H.O. Fleisher (Leipzig, 1846), II, 308, and Zamakhsharī, *Tafsīr al-kashshāf* (Beirut: an-Nashīr Dār al-Kitāb al-'Arabī, 1947), IV, 703.

6. Note that in 53:44/45 the order is reversed: "He makes to die and He makes to live." Bayḍāwī, I, 500, explains this difference in order, saying that when the statement "He makes to live" comes first, it refers to the creation or birth of the individual, but when it comes last it refers to his resurrection. See O'Shaughnessy, pp. 29–35, where it is argued that the Qur'ānic life-death-life passages are influenced by the Syrian Christian use of Deuteronomy 32:39.

7. The term *nushūr* actually means a "rising" or "rousing." See below and Richard Bell, *The Qur'ān: Translated with a critical re-arrangement of the Surahs* (Edinburgh: T. & T. Clark, 1937, 1939), p. 346.

8. Literally "it" (*hā*), referring to *al-arḍ* (the earth) two verses above in 20:53/55.

9. This pronouncement by God is not to be interpreted as a curse on Adam, as the parallel passage in Genesis 3 is sometimes interpreted by Christian (but never Jewish) commentators, as a prooftext for the doctrine of Original Sin. In Genesis 3 it is the earth, and not man (Hebrew: *ādhām*), that is cursed. Neither of these views appears in the Qur'ān, where nature is seen as a sign of God's blessing and benevolence, and Adam is seen as God's messenger (or prophet) who cannot be cursed.

10. This same theme occurs in 30:24/23: "And of His signs He shows you lightning, for fear and hope, and He sends down water out of heaven and He revives the earth after her death"; and in 30:50/49: "So behold the signs of God's mercy, how He quickens the earth after her death. Surely He is the quickener (*muḥyi*) of the dead (*al-mawt*), and He is powerful over everything!" In O'Shaughnessy, pp. 46–49, the Qur'ānic passages involving revival from dust and bones are discussed with parallels in Syrian Christian literature. Regarding the Qur'ānic picture of God's sending down rain (literally "water," *mā'*), with which He brings life to the earth, compare 21:31: "Do the unbelievers not see that the heavens and earth were one mass and then We tore them apart, and that it was from water (mā') that We created all life."

11. Bayḍāwī, I, 627, explains that *man yutawaffā* (some are taken) in this context means that they die before reaching the prime of life. The passive form of *tawaffā* occurs with the meaning "to die" also in 2:234, 2:240/241, and 40:67/68.

12. See above, where *nushūr* is translated "resurrection."

13. Pir Salahud-Din, whose lucid, interpretive translation, *The Wonderful Koran* (Eminabad, Pakistan: Raftar-i-Zamaza Publications, n.d.), is based largely on the interpretations of the classical commentators, translates this verse: "It is He who made the night a mantle for you. He has made sleep a sign of death, and has made the day a sign of Resurrection."

14. Literally, "He raises you up in it," referring to awakening in the morning, but with the connotation of resurrection, which is to be the final Awakening.

15. Conclusions regarding the relationship between sleep and the nature of death in the Qur'ān are thus given at the end of the following section.

16. See Bell, *Qur'ān*, p. 124.

17. For instance, O'Shaughnessy, p. 67, adopts the latter translation, following A.J. Arberry, *The Koran Interpreted* (London: Allen & Unwin, 1955), p. 160. This same interpretation is followed by the most authoritative German translation, Rudi Paret, *Der Koran: Übersetzung* (Stuttgart: Kohlhammer, 1962), p. 113, and also by E.E. Calverley, "Doctrines of the Soul (*Nafs* and *Rūḥ*) in Islam," *The Muslim World* XXXIII (1943):254. Bell, *Qur'ān*, p. 124, however, translates: "Out with yourselves!"

18. One context in which *nafs* appears to refer to some entity within man is 79:37–41: "As for him who was proud and preferred the present life, surely Jahannam shall be his refuge! But as for him who feared the standing (*maqam*) before his Lord, and who forbade the soul (*an-nafs*) its caprice, surely al-Janna (the garden) shall be his refuge!"

19. Bell, *Qur'ān*, p. 307. Bell also has "Every person is subject to death" in 29:57, but "Everyone is subject to death" in 3:185/182.

20. This translation is taken from Arberry, except that the pronoun "it" has been used in place of "soul" for the understood subject of the verb *balaghati* (fem. sing. of "to leap") and the fem. sing. pronominal suffix *hā* in the verb *tarji'ūnahā* (bring it back), which are usually interpreted as referring to the feminine noun *nafs*.

21. O'Shaughnessy, p. [illegible], cites parallels to this idea in early Christian literature.

22. The idea of the separation of the soul from the body is well attested to in later Muslim theology. Ibn Qayyim, p. 190, affirms that the term *rūḥ* never appears in the Qur'ān with the meaning "soul," although this usage is common in later traditional literature. See also Macdonald, "Idea of Spirit," p. 326. Ibn Qayyim's answer to the question: "Does the soul (*rūḥ*) die when the body dies?" (pp. 40–45) is that for the soul death means only separation from the body. For a concise statement of the orthodox Muslim view regarding *nafs*, see Bayḍāwī, I, 23.

23. This interpretation is adopted by Bayḍāwī, I, 300, who says that the statement in 6:93, "And the angels are stretching out their hands," means "in seizure of their spirits (*arwāḥ*)." He then amplifies the command *akhrijū anfusakum* to mean: "give them to us from your bodies." For a discussion of these ideas in modern Muslim devotional literature, see Constance E. Padwick, *Muslim Devotions: A Study of Prayer-Manuals in Common Use* (London: S.P.C.K., 1961), pp. 273–78.

24. Bayḍāwī, II, 383, says this verse means that the "angels of death" (*malā'ikatu-l-mawt*) will tear out the spirits (*arwāḥ*) of the unbelievers. See also Bell, *Qur'ān*, p. 633. The same interpretation is given in Zamakhsharī, IV, 692. It should be noted that the plural form "angels of death" never occurs in the Qur'ān.

25. Bayḍāwī, II, 383, says this verse means "they draw out (*yakhrijūna*) the spirits (*arwāḥ*) of the believers." The same interpretation is given in Zamakhsharī, IV, 692–93.

26. *Qur'ān*, p. 633 and n. 1. See also Pir Salahud-Din, p. 595. In the Qur'ān the term *nāza'a* consistently means "to quarrel," as in 4:59/62: "Believers, obey God and obey the Messenger (Muhammad) and those in authority over you. If you should quarrel (*tanāza'tum*), then refer the matter to God and the Messenger." See also 3:152/145; 8:43/45; 8:46/48; 18:21/20; 20:62/65; 27:67/66; and 52:23.

27. In one other *tawaffā* passage, 4:15/19, no agent is named: "When any of your women commit indecency, call four of you to witness against them, and if they so witness, then detain them in their houses *until death takes them*, or until God appoints a way (for dealing) with them." Here death itself "takes" the women. This idiomatic way of saying "until they die" is similar to the expression "until death faces one of them," which occurs three verses later in 4:18/22. Bayḍāwī, I, 393, states that the term *tawaffā* contains the ideas of "causing to die" and "completing a full term" as well as the usual meaning "to take (at death)."

28. See also the discussion of 39:42/43 and 6:60f. above. For other references and a brief discussion, see O'Shaughnessy, pp. 39–40.

29. Similar prayers asking to be "taken" among the righteous occur in 7:126/123 and 12:101/102. Cf. also the contemporary prayers given in Padwick, pp. 274–75.

30. Although this "encounter with their Lord" (*liqā' rabbihim*) is usually interpreted as a reference to the Last Judgment, Zamakhsharī, III, 509, suggests that this expression means only "the attainment of the end" (*al-wuṣūl ilā-l-'āqiba*).

31. See n. 23. Commenting on 32:11, Bayḍāwī, II, 119, explains *yatawaffākum* (he will take you) to mean "he will take your souls (*nufūs*)"; and Zamakhsharī, III:509, mentions the opinion of some that this expression means "he will take the spirits (*arwāḥ*)."

32. See Bell, *Qur'ān*, p. 140, nn. 2, 3; p. 618, n. 3; and p. 668, n. 3.

33. Where 6:61 reads: *ḥattā idhā jā'a aḥadakum al-mawtu tawaffat'hu rusulunā* (until, when death comes to one of you, our messengers take him), the parallel passage in 7:37/35 reads: *ḥattā idhā jā'at'hum rusulunā yatawaffawnahum* (until, when our messengers come to them, they take them). In the first context the verb *jā'a* (comes) refers to death (*al-mawt*), whereas in the second context it refers to the *rusul* (messengers) of God; still the *rusul* in these two passages must be the same—that is, "angels of death."

34. For an excellent summary of the relationship between "death angels" (*Todesengel*) and "punishment angels" (*Strafengel*), and also the relationship between these Qur'ānic concepts and similar ideas in the Bible, see Paul Arno Eichler, *Die Dschinn, Teufel und Engel im Koran* (Leipzig: Klein, 1928), pp. 104–10.

35. This explanation is given by Bayḍāwī, I, 294, and Zamakhsharī, I, 455.

36. For example, the act of recording man's good and evil deeds is attributed both to God and to various celestial beings (or beings variously designated in the Qur'ān as *rusul*, *ḥāfiẓūn*, *mu'aqqibāt*, and *raqīb*). Also, the role of casting the condemned unbelievers into the hellfire (Jahannam) is ascribed both to God and to his *malā'ika* (angels) and the *khazana* (keepers) of Jahannam. These issues and their implications for Qur'ānic exegesis in general are discussed in chaps. 14 and 16 of my unpublished dissertation, "The Pneumatology of the Qur'ān: A Study in Phenomenology" (University of Edinburgh, 1970).

37. The term *mālik* (ruler, master) in 43:77 is consistently regarded by the Muslim commentators to be the name of the chief of the angels who are the keepers of Jahannam, the hellfire. The term also appears in 3:26/25 and 1:4/3 where it clearly refers to God; this can hardly be the case, however, in 43:77.

38. Bayḍāwī, II, 35, explains the term *thubūr* (destruction) as "a death from which there is no rising again." In explaining this verse, he cites 4:156/159: "We shall certainly roast them at a fire so much that their skins are completely burned, then We (we?) shall give them other skins so they may continue to taste the chastisement."

39. Cf. also 2:161f./156f. where this punishment is said to be "God's curse and the curse of the angels," and the damned are promised that "their punishment will not be lightened, nor will they receive respite." These verses suggest the possibility that the first person plural subject in the verse quoted in the preceding note may refer to the angel guards of Jahannam, although this would be a rare case since the first person plural in the Qur'ān virtually always refers to God as the "speaker."

40. Bayḍāwī, I, 498, explains this statement as meaning that death will move in upon him from every place in his body from the roots of his hairs to his toes.

41. See O'Shaughnessy, pp. 15–16, for a discussion of "living death" in the Qur'ān.

42. Belief in Munkar and Nakīr and the "punishment of the grave" (*'adhāb al-qabr*) are affirmed in al-Ash'arī's *Ibāna* and *Maqālāt*, translated in Richard J. McCarthy, *The Theology of al-Ash'arī* (Beirut: Imprimerie Catholique, 1953), p. 250, and A.J. Wensinck, *The Muslim Creed* (Cambridge: Cambridge University Press, 1932), pp. 164–66. See also A.J. Wensinck, "Munkar wa-Nakīr," *Encyclopaedia of Islam*, III, 724.

43. See the theological work *Baḥr al-kalām fī ʿilm at-tawḥīd* [Sea of Discussion on the Science of Theology] by Abū al-Muʿīn an-Nasafī (d. 508/1114), translated in Arthur Jeffery, *A Reader on Islam* (The Hague: Mouton, 1962), pp. 436–38.

44. See Padwick, pp. 278–79. In Bell's translation of 21:35/36, cited earlier in this article, the term *fitna* is translated "test": "Every person is subject to death, and We try you with evil and good as a test (*fitna*), and to Us are ye made to return."

45. Translated in Jeffery, *Reader*, pp. 208–10.

46. Cf. Luke 16:22: "The poor man died and was carried by the angels to Abraham's bosom."

47. This term occurs in Sūra 83:18–21. For a discussion of the possible meanings, see Arthur Jeffery, *The Foreign Vocabulary of the Qur'ān* (Baroda: Oriental Institute, 1938), p. 165.

48. That is, a door is to be opened in the side of the tomb, through which breezes and a sweet aroma flow in from al-Janna. In some contexts "doors of mercy" (*abwāb ar-raḥma*) are mentioned—see Padwick, p. 274.

49. See Sūra 83:7–9 and Jeffery, *Foreign Vocabulary*, pp. 215–16.

50. O'Shaughnessy, pp. 77–78.

51. Ibid., pp. 79–82.

52. Ibid., pp. 78–79.

53. See ibid., p. 35, and Hartwig Hirschfeld, *New Researches into the Composition and Exegesis of the Qoran* (London: Royal Asiatic Society, 1902), pp. 41–42. The latter, although now dated, was a landmark in Qur'ānic research that influenced Richard Bell's studies of the Qur'ān.

54. A caution should be sounded against the tendency to fall into the error of misrepresenting the Qur'ān, either by assuming a uniformity on a given topic where in fact differences exist, or by reading into the Qur'ān extraneous ideas, or doctrines developed in later Muslim theology.

Muḥarram Rites: Community Death and Rebirth

EARLE H. WAUGH

Every year during the month of Muḥarram, the Shīʻa community of Islam enacts rites connected with the death of Ḥusain, the son of ʻAlī and the grandson of the Prophet. The observances differ greatly from country to country and from time to time, but the central point appears to be the continuity and identification which the rituals give the community. The material considered here will deal particularly with the sacred Shīʻa cities of Nejev and Karbala, which are sites historically connected to the martyrdom of Ḥusain and the development of Shīʻa consciousness.

The Historical Background

The seeds for the religious movement of the Shīʻa derived from both the political and religious aspects of early Islam; when ʻUmar, the second caliph, died in 644 C.E. the splits within the Muslim community became more pronounced. Medinese leaders formed a panel to decide who should succeed him, and bitterness and jealousy among them led them to nominate ʻUthmān b. ʻAffān, one of the earliest converts from the Umayyads (one of the main tribes that had opposed Muhammad to the last), who was very religious but who was not a strong leader. He standardized the Qur'ān, thus gaining the enmity of some Qur'ān-reciters who had variations of their own, and he made some minor regulations of the cult. His gravest difficulty was his insistence on giving the Umayyad family the choicest posts, and, although some of his relatives were capable, strong complaints were made about his nepotism. He did nothing to alleviate the problems of finance; ʻUmar's policy of having all funds transferred to Medina was continued, but now the sensibleness of that law was clouded by the nepotism of those in charge in Medina.[1] Contrary to accepted custom, lands taken in conquest were now claimed by the soldiers who took them as part of their booty; ʻAlī, the prophet's son-in-law appears to have sided with them. In fact, ʻAlī may have opposed the policies of ʻUmar from the beginning.[2] Since he was a good soldier, he became representative for all those who disagreed with the Medinese policies concerning land. When ʻUthmān was assassinated by a group of malcontents from Egypt, the Muslim community split over his successor. Most of the Medinese and the dissidents backed ʻAlī, who accepted the nomination; but another group, lead by ʻA'īsha, the Prophet's favorite wife, demanded that

'Alī punish those who had killed the chosen leader of Islam. 'Alī repaired to Kūfa, where his strongest support was found, and then a civil war erupted which has become known in Muslim history as the first *fitnah*.[3] Arabs from Syria, led by Mu'āwiyah, the governor of Syria, insisted that the Umayyad family be restored because of the implication of 'Alī in the assassination.

After inconclusive fighting the two sides agreed to arbitration, whereupon 'Alī's partisans split, the Khāriji party repudiated both men, Mu'āwiyah for his lack of legitimacy, and 'Alī because he had agreed that such an important issue as who should be caliph could be arbitrated. Those who supported 'Alī became known as Shī'ah 'Alī or the "party of 'Alī." Mu'āwiyah was proclaimed caliph in 660 by his followers, and when 'Alī was murdered by a Khāriji, Mu'āwiyah's leadership was accepted as a *fait accompli* by most Muslims. 'Alī's son Ḥasan sold his rights to the caliphate to Mu'āwiyah and retired to Medina on a generous pension.[4]

The immediate result of the altercation was ill feeling between the Arabs of Syria and those of more eastern sections (mainly Iraq), but this soon developed into permanent distrust and antagonism. 'Alī became the symbol of local opposition to the established political order, since no one from 'Alī's time on saw the political leader as in the caliphal tradition. Rather, the majority of the Muslims accepted that the community as a whole was rightly guided, that is, God had called out one community, the *jamā'ah*,[5] which would be the repository of the rightly guided community. This special quality was separate from the leadership but tied up with it by the will of God.

It was with Ḥusain, 'Alī's other son, that strong religious issues came to the fore. The Medinese people never forgave Mu'āwiyah for his method of coming to power, and for his moving the head of the government from Mecca and Medina to Damascus. They looked back on the days of Muhammad and the early caliphs as the ideal government, since then it had been ordered around the ancient models suggested by Muhammad, and carried out by strong personal ties.[6] Mu'āwiyah was the break with this tradition; he did not express the continuity of line which those who had been companions or associates[7] of the Prophet represented.

This tradition came to mean more than just a political candidate whose religious background was impeccable. Rather, by this time (circa 650), notions of authority became involved; the best candidates were those in a position to have experienced the *'ilm* or the way of Muhammad, since it was through Muhammad that the way had first been expressed. It was becoming increasingly believed that the proper authority was handed down through the Prophet's family, or someone closely associated with that family. Hence, ideas that the community should be loyal to 'Alī expressed how the true Islam was to be handed on. To this loyalty to 'Alī was added the religious piety concerning the Prophet, for those who regarded this as the legitimate method of transfer of authority linked the whole together into the "Ahl al-Bayt" or the people of the House, referring to the House of Muhammad.

To this must be added the independence, both political and religious, of the Kūfans. Kūfa represented the edge of the Arab stronghold; immigrants and converts from other ethnic stocks flooded its gates, making it rich in intellectual, social, and religious variety. These people were known as Mawāli, non-Arab converts, who had not known Muhammad and had come to Islam under the early expansion of the faith. They were not included in the groups who claimed the foremost positions in the community, since they could have no relationship with the primitive Meccan or Medinan community. Yet they were creative Muslims, and they resented the second-class fare which their late conversion imposed upon them. They implicitly rejected those who claimed their political position in Islam from their early conversion date or their Arabism. These Kūfans argued that it was the quality that meant the most in Islam, and they were the first to criticize the governors sent by the ruling clique in Damascus. Out of this rejection grew new ideas about succession; in most cases the old tribal form of appointment by agreement was rejected for appointment by religious capability. This movement found much in common with the Ahl al-Bayt people in opposing the Mu'āwiyah government. Many of its partisans argued for succession by family heir, and they were consequently open to Ḥusain, 'Alī's second son by Fāṭimah, when he came to them attempting to raise a revolt against the Umayyads.

The occasion for this rebellion was the succession of Yazīd, upon Mu'āwiyah's death. Mu'āwiyah had insisted that the community recognize Yazīd, his son, as his successor before his death, a device hitherto unknown in Islam. Yazīd did not have the skill his father had, and, in any case, problems were beginning to mount toward the end of Mu'āwiyah's career.[8] Meccans, Medinans, Kūfans, and many other people were eager to listen to Ḥusain's claim to the leadership of the Muslim community, especially since 'Alī's claims were now being recognized by many more than had orginally considered them when first proposed. Added to the situation was the growing awareness of loyalty to the family of Muhammad, and the material for the second *fitnah* was prepared.

Ḥusain set out for Kūfah, but before he arrived, the Syrian governor succeeded in putting down Kūfan interest in revolt. Ḥusain was left with only a small band;[9] 'Umar, the commander of the Yazīd's forces sent to intercept him, was told to seal Ḥusain and his family from the river so that they had no water. The denial of water has gone down in Muslim history as gross inhumanity since even sacrificial animals are not prevented from having water. Ḥusain refused to surrender, and his small force was isolated in the desert near Karbala, Iraq, and slaughtered. His death on the tenth day of the month of Muḥarram, 680 C.E., is the basis for the ta'ziya[10] and the rites which we are describing here.

But the death of Ḥusain did not immediately usher in the rituals or generate the religious meaning necessary for influencing the sustained interest of the Shī'a. Shī'ism was not yet an identifiable group in opposition to the majority; rather it was a collection of tendencies at the heart of which was protest. As the Umayyad dynasty became more and more associated with the life of ease denoted by dancing girls and drinking, the pious-minded people turned away from its support. While Umayyad leadership still appealed to the majority of Muslims as the guarantor of Muslim unity, more and more religious leaders were questioning whether Muslim intentions were being destroyed by a decadent caliphate tolerated as the price for unity. Even the more religiously sensitive among the Umayyad leaders, such as 'Umar II, encouraged a bureaucracy which put further distance between the caliph and the people.[11] Revolts and tension in the name of a return to more religious leadership became increasingly prevalent, until descendants of Muhammad's cousin 'Abd-Allah b. 'Abbās began insisting on their legitimacy through Shī'a arguments. Abū-Muslim went to Khurāsān, which became the focal point for Mawāli agitation, and began encouraging vengeance for the death of Ḥusain and other members of the Prophet's family. Religiously their deaths meant martyrdom, and loyalty to Muhammad's house became tantamount to preserving true Islam from the usurping Umayyads. By 748 all other rebellions had been put down except Abū-Muslim's, and he defeated the forces of Marwān in 750. Claiming 'Abu-l-'Abbās, a member of the Hāshimite family of Muhammad as caliph, Abū-Muslim seized control of Muslim territory from Khurāsān to Egypt.[12] The Abbāsids built their capital at Baghdad, attempting to break down the old power of the Arabs by assigning important roles to Mawāli. But they rejected the more rigorous Shī'a doctrines and made little of their supposed role as imāms with the true 'ilm.[13] The Shī'a were disappointed, and soon the Abbāsids put to death the more vocal Shī'ī leaders.[14] It was at this time that the distinctions between groups in Islam became noticeable. Those who accepted the Abbāsids as legitimate (if not as good as had been hoped) adopted their black gowns and black flags; those who did not, broke into opposition sects which have continued to today. The former group became known as the Sunnīs (indicating the broad community-based acceptance of the Abbāsid compromise). Those who did not became Shī'īs, members of the party of 'Alī. Each developed separate life styles which they tried to work out in the political and social order. As time passed, the majority of the Muslims accepted the style of life advocated by the Sunnīs; but the Shī'a remained a viable alternative, as it proposed its own interpretation of what it meant to be a Muslim.

Religious meaning thus developed from several areas in the Muslim community to provide the impetus for the Muḥarram rites: loyalty to the house of Muhammad, especially through the deaths of outstanding members such as 'Alī and Ḥusain;[15] the association of death with martyrdom in the sacred family; the belief that true knowledge passed through the imām, of which 'Alī was the chief, and that the community was only adhering to true Islam by maintaining allegiance to the imām's leadership;[16] the preservation of protest as a religious category designed to offset the evil of the ruling powers; the remembrance of a sacred history as a means for defining heritage and uniqueness in the face of tremendous odds; and the religious value of suffering according to the model set by the sacred heroes of the past.

The public celebrations could not have been enacted until Shī'a partisans controlled the sacred areas in Iraq. Under the Buwayhid leadership of the tenth century, the public rites were first authorized: "One of the greatest innovations introduced by the Mu'izz ad-Dawla was the custom of public mourning during the first 10 days of Muḥarram. This order was given in A.D. 963, that there might be an annual commemoration of the tragic death of the Imām Ḥusain."[17]

The Buwayhids did not claim to be caliphs; indeed they deposed the Abbāsid caliphs at will. They had come from the southern shore of the Caspian Sea originally, and had gradually moved into Shīraz, where they established their capital. They were convinced Shī'ites and they actively promoted Shī'a concerns; 'Abud al-Dawlah, for example, built the shrine over the site of 'Alī's tomb. It is from their time, then, that the major dimensions of Shī'a cult must be dated.[18]

Community Participation in the Rites

The observances involve the total concentration of the community at several levels; during the ten days of Muḥarram the cities of Nejev and Karbala are draped in black, with black cloth framing doorways and black flags everywhere in evidence.[19] Work is supposed to continue as usual, but in general there is a solemn air, heightened by the constant influx of pilgrims who come to share in the sacred hour or who have brought the bodies of the relatives for burial near the sacred precincts. Normalcy is curbed in the city by the required closing of all cafes, bars, moviehouses, and ice cream parlors, and by the cessation of activity denoting mirth or easy life style. Television's programming for the entire ten days is changed, with news items regarding the rites and religious discussions or live coverage of processions dominating. Radio features Qur'ān recitation, news items, and religious programs. No music or light-hearted fare is permitted.

Each enclave of the city organizes its own religious contributions to the rites; for example, the community of Hindiyya or Mahmoudiyya near Karbala organizes its own group of marchers so that, in addition to the overall sense of participation, each community within the larger whole forms a solid unity in ritual activity. Anyone within that community who wishes to be involved in the formal marches may do so; the procession itself is organized by the most respected religious member of each area. This individual need not be politically the most powerful; in fact, participation in the rites has been resisted at various times by the government. Since the Shī'īs have often been ruled by Sunnīs or at least rulers who did not share their views, the performance of the rites often implicitly assumes persecution. Even today, certain activities of the rites are prohibited by law, but they take place surreptitiously or in open violation of the government's official position. At any rate, the promotion and arrangement of the ritual activities brings a religious order into play, which grows out of community acceptance rather than political designation.

Probably nowhere is social participation more evident than in the remembrance ceremonies of the ta'ziya, the sacred drama that reenacts Ḥusain's death. The stories told during this ceremony do not simply retell his tragic history; they often go back to Adam and creation to trace the courage, bravery, and atrocity that accompanies God's children.[20] Ritual history refers to Muhammad, Fāṭimah, Ḥasan, 'Alī, and a host of other personages, angels, and jinn to depict this *heilsgeschichte*. In it Ḥusain is represented as a product of superior spiritual insight and needs; he undertook a trust at the beginning of time involving martyrdom for mankind. For example, in one scene Ḥusain cries out to God:

> O Lord! For the merit of Ḥusain's father, mother, and grandfather i.e. 'Alī, Fāṭimah, and the Prophet, deliver Ḥusain's pearl-producing eyes from the trouble of long expectation. Thou hast promised to invest me with the robe of martyrdom, to exalt my crown of glory on the high with this cutting dagger of the inhabitants of Kūfah. How glad I am to become a sacrifice for mankind! I do not know when Ḥusain's full moon will rise from her eastern horizon.[21]

Or in this conversation with Kulthūm, his sister:

> Trials, affiication, and pains, the thicker they fall on man, the better, dear sister, do they prepare him for his journey heavenward. We rejoice in tribulations, seeing they are but temporary, and yet they work out an eternal and blissful end. Though it is predestined that I should suffer martyrdom in this shameful manner, yet the treasury of everlasting happiness shall be at my disposal as a consequent reward. Thou must think of that, and be no longer sorry. The dust raised in the field of such battles is as highly esteemed by me, O sister, as the philosopher's stone was, in former times, by the alchemists; and the soil of Karbala is the sure remedy of my inward pains.[22]

Hence the reenactment of the drama becomes the occasion for celebrating the crucial meaning of religious death, setting humanity's ultimate value within a transcendent framework, and amplifying the positive aspects in the community's death conceptions. Death, even tortured death, is full of the highest forms of spiritual favor.

Ritual Observances

Personal identity in this story is worked out by participation in the retelling and reenactment in groups based on sexual distinction. The "public" expression is left to the men; "private" forms are for the women. The following description is by a young Iraqi woman, Nīdah al-Jassānī, who was born in Nejev:

> My grandmother's house was square-shaped, with a large courtyard in the center. Balconies looked down on the courtyard around which huge bolts of black cloth were hung. The women and children began filing in about dusk, and sat in circles around the mulla, the female story-teller. Sometimes she had an assistant who would take over when she was tired, or on some occasions, a member of the listening group could go into the center and tell part of the story. Everyone in the neighborhood was invited, and several qirā'a i.e., gatherings for the purpose of telling the story of Ḥusain could be held in the area. The women in the center were professional story-tellers usually, and they dressed in heavy black full-length dresses. They wore long veils called 'ubbiyyah. These story-tellers are not necessarily religious people. They are, however, known for their prowess at telling the stories, and the more call they get for their

services, the more money they can demand. Since my grandmother was giving one this year, she was responsible for paying the lady; sometimes the qirā'a is traditional in a family, and it will be carried on from mother to daughter, year after year. Moreover, if a qadi's (judge's) wife had it one night, it would be traditional that the next night it would move to another important family, like the mayor's wife, etc., so that one would know from year to year where to go for the story-telling. We knew too, that there was simultaneous qirā'a all over the city.

The story-telling began with the slow murmuring of the mulla in a sing-song way as she told the story. As she continued, the women gently smote their breasts, or patted their heads, and called out, "Yaa Ḥusain, Yaa Ḥusain." As the telling wore on, the women began to cry, in high, shrill-like voices, "Boooooo, Boooooo" in a kind of ritual crying. Rhythmic swaying and gentle pounding of the fist on the chest accompanied the rites.

Since the stories have a certain cadence, the mullas were considered to be very good if they could tell the story in such a way as to maintain the tempo. The telling had a kind of rhyme, which was told with fervor and love. My friends and neighbors sat around or in the balcony, most of them participating at some moment in the proceedings by rhythmic tapping of the breast, or crying in the ritual way. At the end of every episode, there would be a brief rest. The mulla would look through her little book where she had the stories written down, or her assistant would take her place in the center, and begin the recitation of another segment. Some of the ladies sat back and smoked, with the boys and girls hovering around, and required to sit quietly during the recitation. Of course, no older boys or men were allowed. Everybody in the room seemed united in mourning the tragic death of Ḥusain and tears trickled down the cheeks of some of the older and more religious ladies.[23]

Men too may join a qirā'a that is held in the street by the community; tents may be set up, a dais raised, and a mulla employed to tell the stories.[24] Crowds gather with much the same ritualized mourning as was evident in the preceding passage. In addition, reenactment of various events in the last days of Ḥusain's life can take place, especially the attack on Ḥusain's forces:

The forces of good i.e., Ḥusain, on green-caparisoned horses, and wearing cardboard helmets, fought with the forces of evil i.e., Mu'āwiyah in turbans and on yellow-caparisoned horses. Neutral elements, represented by the flag-bearers, tried to make peace and failed. By this time fifty or sixty horsemen filled the square, and the two groups of warriors galloped toward each other, met briefly in the center in a clash of wooden swords, then regrouped at each end in preparation for another assault. In between rounds, several small boys would run into the arena and rescue from the dust objects which Bob later told me were paper-mache arms and legs carried by the horsemen and thrown into the air after each assault to give an air of reality to the proceedings. With shouts and cries the women and men urged on the forces of Ḥusain and hissed the forces of Mu'āwiyah.

The legs of the horses ran with sweat, the cardboard helmets were wilting, and the silken tunics stuck to the backs of the horsemen. But the riders, at full gallop, continued to fire their rifles, and the smell of gunpowder was added to the odors of sweat and manure that drifted toward us from the arena.[25]

The climax of the public ceremonies is, of course, the rites for the return of Ḥusain's head.[26] Shī'a villages from all Iraq send groups to perform the ta'ziya procession in the sacred city of Karbala. The procession is headed by flag-bearers, who carry long poles at the top of which are fixed flags with verses in praise of Ḥusain or tin ornaments,[27] followed by horsemen with flags of black dressed in black with shields, swords, and helmets.[28] Behind this comes a white horse covered with a black blanket:[29] the blanket is sewn to represent arrow cuts, or, on some occasions, may have the arrows sewn into it to represent the many arrows that pierced Ḥusain. Next come older men or boys, who may carry flags, who are dressed in black, and who may have their faces blackened to represent their mourning.[30] They ritually beat their breasts as a sign of their sorrow. In some processions a cenotaph purporting to carry the head of Ḥusain follows.[31] Next come the various groups who practice the rite of flagellation. Some of these bear chains,[32] and all wear garments, either black or white, which they tie at the waist, leaving the upper part of their bodies bare. Elizabeth Fernea describes the scene this way:

> "Ohhhh-Hussein, most great most honored, we grieve for thee," called the leader, walking backward, step after measured step down the cleared aisle of the street. At this signal the chains were swung like incence burners across the body, out to the side; a silent half beat, marked by the thump of bare feet marching in unison, passed before the score of chains swung back to thud on the bared shoulders.
>
> "Yaaa Hussein," responded the young men.
>
> "Ohhhh-Hussein, most betrayed, we mourn for thee," cried the leader, shaking the sweat out of his eyes. Click went the chains across the body, out, and then the unbearable silent half beat. The crowd held its breath, letting it out in a concerted sigh as the chains struck the bare shoulders.
>
> "Yaaa-Hussein," answered the young men. Their shoulders were bruised blue from the ritual beatings, the kerchiefs around their heads blotched from perspiration. Still they kept up the sustained note, the measured beat, and the chains swung again like censers. The chains thudded and the chant swelled higher from a score of throats, from a hundred, as the taaziyas awaiting their turn inside the mosque were heard in the distance, in the silent half beat of the continuing ritual.
>
> Tears streamed down the faces of sobbing men standing near me, and the piercing wailing cries of the women spoke of loss and pain and grief and lamentation.[33]

A second group of ritual sufferers may likewise take part in the ceremony; these follow the same cadence, but with swords. In recent days, participants in this flagellation shave their heads, and medical attendants march with the group to care for those badly wounded. They may be dressed in white, or like the group before, stripped to the waist.

> The group, perhaps of a hundred, march in time through the streets. Their leader periodically brings them together into a circle where he retells some part of the story in ritual form. Then the group marches out again to the cries of "Yaaaa-Ḥusain." Those who brandish the sword swing it out and then bring it down with a thud on their forehead or scalp. Time and again the flat of the sword thuds against the skin,

> until it is red and puffed and stands out as if ready to burst. Then at some moment of the ritual, when sufficient ardor and religious feeling is attained, the sharp of the sword is brought down. The blood shoots out and down, running through eyes and beard and down over the gleaming white gown, or the sweating body. All the while the cadence of the procession continues with "Yaaaa-Ḥusain."[34]

The fervor of these rituals has, in the past, caused the death of several participants. For example, during the reenactment of the passion play in Iran, the headless bodies of the participants were played with exacting realism: some buried themselves to the head; others buried only their heads to give the appearance of decapitation.[35] During the hot summer, these burials were too exacting and some of the actors died. Sometimes individuals lose too much blood, or the heat is too much for their constitutions. Moreover, others take part in secret knifing rituals. Knives are thrust into stomachs and pulled out again; it is the mark of superior spirituality for these people if they do not bleed. Those who have witnessed this activity suggest the continued running of the knife into the body at the same place so that in time the blade may pass in without severing the flesh.[36] However, such practices are forbidden by the government; no one knows how many have died in ritually enacting these death scenes.[37]

Activities Common with Death Rituals

Many of the activities undertaken during Muḥarram are similar to those accompanying death at other times; when a close relative dies, a woman may throw dirt in the air or daub clay on her face. She dresses in black and does not participate in festive occasions or engage in pleasurable social events. During the heat of her sorrow, she will beat her breast with her closed fist and agonize with a high shrill ritual cry. If the deceased is a husband or father, qirā'a will be held, during which his good traits will be rehearsed. Like Ḥusain, the values of courage, determination, strength, steadfastness, and piety will be recalled, in much the same form as during the Muḥarram rites.

Men, during mourning, wear dark clothes, perhaps a black western tie (if they commonly wear western clothes), and probably will go unwashed and unshaven until the period of mourning is past. In some cases, a limited special food, or at least simple fare, is all the luxury allowed. Muḥarram calls for the same type of mourning.

The ritual black is, of course, common to all death watches; a house is draped with black upon a death. and some families may fly black flags. A Qur'ān reciter may be hired to sit at the head of the grave and silently read from the sacred word, but unlike Egyptian death watches, a reciter is not hired to chant in the presence of the mourning family. During Muḥarram personal piety may include hiring a Qur'ān reciter at the mosque. For those who can afford it, food may be given away as alms at the end of the rites; if the giver's family cannot prepare it, they must pay a restaurant or another family to prepare and distribute it to the poor.[38]

Multivalent Death

I have already noted the complex religious meanings in the development of the Muḥarram rituals; I will now turn to death as one facet of that meaning as it bears on Shīʿa self-understanding.

Western writers on the Muḥarram rites have given a wide variety of interpretations to the activities associated with Muḥarram; some have seen them as pagan survivals,[39] some, such as Erdmans, in his article "Der Ersprung der Ceremonien Hosein-Festes," regard them as revalorizations of ancient Tammuz rituals,[40] while others regard them as latently Christian.[41] For instance, Canon Sell saw the Shīʿa rites as indicative of the need for self-denial and self-sacrifice which, he felt, was offered in Christianity. His crowning statement is: "It has been well said that the death of Ḥusain as idealized in after ages, fills up this void in Islam; it is the womanly as against the masculine, the Christian as opposed to the Jewish element, that this story supplies to the work of Muhammad."[42]

But Muslim material has its own value system; even phrases such as "passion play," "martyrdom for the truth," and "dying for the people" must be used without presupposing Christian structures. This, I think, will be borne out by a careful consideration of death's meaning in the Shīʿa tradition.

Shīʿa doctrine holds that Ḥusain's steadfastness and courage in the face of death allow him to grant any who would ask him the freedom to enter paradise. Thus, Ḥusain's death is sacrificial only in its renunciation of a life of comfort, wealth, and safe anonymity for an identifiable role in salvation history. From the perspective of Shīʿa belief, Ḥusain's death was crucial for community fulfillment and salvation.

That qirāʾa are held for the mourning rites of every important personage indicates common grounds between Ḥusain and all other individuals. The commonness appears to focus on that which survives. It is not just that every man has a qirāʾa at death because rituals similar to Ḥusain's must be applied; rather what is abiding about each individual's life is how he worked out that spiritual model during his own existence and, structured by his family, environment, and natural abilities, fulfilled that model in his life. In addition, just as the drama of Ḥusain's death showed how the religious values permeated the details of his life, and in the end gave it its meaning, so the ordinary Shīʿa follower can rely on those same undergirding values.

The Muḥarram rites, from that perspective, show that even the values upheld in death are not of private derivation. Rather they are the accepted standards of meaning rising from the religious norms of the community to which all owe allegiance, and which derive originally from the God-directed history of that community. The reenactment and rehearsing of that sacred history during the Muḥarram rituals provide that opportunity to affirm and reinforce those values yearly.

The rituals of death often inspire terror, regardless of the culture; Shīʿa Islam is no different. Young children are usually prevented from seeing the marchers, and most will suggest that their first confrontation with the activities was fraught with shock and fear. The crying, the half-dazed participants, the tense mood that pervades, the packed streets, the black agony of the chains and knives lift everyone into a vivid experiential frame; personal death becomes dramatic and real. Little wonder that governments, mindful of human emotion and destructibility, have sometimes required communities to post a bond before the ceremonies will be permitted.[43]

Personal death is dramatically real, but the rites provide it with a religious context that modifies its terror. This is accomplished by the many recitations of the stories, both in the homes by the women and in the public squares by the men. Ḥusain's life is tragic; much of everyone's life is so, too. Death is often violent and uncalled-for, just like Husain's. But all this is mitigated by his archetypal existence: a plan set down at the beginning of creation, creatively working among the myriad aspects of personality and conflict, establishes for each and every person a sacred history. In this manner, religious value and personal value are merged into one scenario in which violent death figures only as the moment before supreme achievement. It is easy to see, then, how dying while participating in the rites is considered the height of religious blessedness, and death at such an auspicious moment would guarantee fantastic rewards in the other world.

The motivation behind the rites is merit more than sacrifice. This merit derives from several sources. For some, the model of Ḥusain is sufficient, and the value of the activities will have eternal significance. Others participate in the rites because of a prior commitment to God: a vow that if God does this for them, they will perform the ta'ziya, or if God prospers them in this manner, they will repay this goodness with a public demonstration of God's meaning to them. Sometimes the whole shape of life can be drawn from the meritorious qualities of the rites, as in Elizabeth Fernea's account of the woman who vowed that if God gave her a son, she would dedicate him to participating in the Muḥarram ceremonies. The son came, and when he grew, he participated in the ta'ziya as an expression of devotion to God for his personal existence.[44]

It is evident also that this merit has historical dimensions, for a lifetime of participation in the rites is considered an extremely important religious commitment. Ritual participation allows personal relations with God to be worked out in a public manner, adding new meaning to what it is to be religious during one's lifetime.

Moreover, the rites provide the vehicle for affirming the sacred history of the community in a concrete manner; while Ḥusain's martyrdom founded the mythological history of the Shī'a, it is the rites themselves that open the way for participation in that reality. By ritually recovering the archetypal Ḥusain, the devotee experiences the ongoing commitment of the whole community, and, as it were, begins again that reality in a hostile world. Hence, every stroke of the chain, every act of agony pushes aside the individual's personal meaning and puts him in touch with the reality of Ḥusain's death, thus introducing him to the ground of the community's existence.

There are other positive affirmations of death. Pilgrims travel great distances to be present at the sacred shrines of Kaẓimayn or Nejev or Karbala. The rites, when held abroad (i.e., in Iran, India, or Pakistan), utilize replicas of the shrine at Karbala. Those who are ill make a last heroic effort to reach the holy cities, particularly Nejev,[45] in order that they may die and be buried in the sacred precincts; relatives transport bodies many hot, dusty, weary miles just to bury them near the beloved shrines. Religious power and efficacy are closely connected, then, to the physical expressions of the imāms, whether in the reenactment of their deaths or in the presence of the shrines.

It would appear that the rites operate within the same "concrete" continuum: truth is embodied in every individual existence. But this brings with it an ambiguity. For the Shī'a, the 'ilm of Islam resides in the special guidance afforded the Prophet's family; community resilience and continuity depend on loyalty to that tradition. Persecution, treason, and death are part of that tradition, for the operation of truth in the world eventually leads to the impossible situation of making an ideal order operative in a hostile and opposing world. Why fight then? Because truth has been borne out in the historical life of the people, and anything less would repudiate all that gives both the person and the community meaning. Taken to its extreme, some form of death results from either alternative. Hence, the flagellations give expression to the quandary of a righteous group committed to the involvement of the transcendent in the moral, social, and political world; they are a cipher of a profound contradiction deeply felt by Shī'a Islam. The community must suffer in order that God's will be made evident. In this manner, the community dies continually, yet lives between the commitment to that death and the sure knowledge that anything else is a more profound death, a death unthinkable in its ramifications.

Notes

1. For example, he appointed his foster brother 'Abdullah, whom Muhammad had proscribed when he had taken Mecca, and who had been charged with altering the words of revelation (see Qur'ān 6:93), as head of Egypt; many other important offices, such as governor of Kūfah, were given to his family.

2. See Laura Veccia-Vaglieri, "Sulla origine della denominazione 'Sunniti'," *Studi Orientalistici in onore di Giorgio Leui della Vida*, vol. 2 (Rome, 1956), pp. 573–85.

3. Fitnah means "discomfiture," which shows that religious beliefs about the divine mission of the Muslim community would not allow the use of the term "civil war" to describe internal dissension.

4. Tabari, *Ta'rīkh al-Rusul*, ed. M.J. de Goeje, vol. 3 (Leiden, 1881–82), p. 3.

5. *Jamā'ah* means "whole"; hence the tendency from this point on to view the total community as a unit, despite local differences. Unity became a religious value to be preserved and institutionalized. It became a group called Ahl al-Sunnah wa-l-Jamā'ah, the People of the Custom and the Community, in distinction to the Shī'a 'Alī or party of 'Alī. From this comes the popular term "Sunnīs."

6. Mu'āwiya's power was based purely on the military support he received from the Syrians, who idolized him; see Tabari, *Ta'rīkh al-Rusul*, vol. 1, pp. 3409–10.

7. The Arabic word is *ṣaḥābah*; it probably should be used in the sense of "comrade," implying working together for a cause rather than the close association of companion.

8. Religiously, those of the Hijaz rebelled against his kingly role; he is called a *mulk* (king), and he utilized a royal throne, something offensive to all who remembered the grace and ordinariness of the Prophet and the *rāshidūn*; see Ya'qūbi, *Kitāb al-Buldān*, ed. M. Th. Houtsma, vol. 2 (Leiden, 1883), p. 257.

9. Ḥusain had about 200 in his party, some 60 of which were family. The band he faced numbered around 4000; hence the magnitude of his courage bordered on insanity.

10. Ta'ziya has a variety of meanings; see *Encyclopedia of Islam*, ed. M. Th. Houtsma et al. (Leiden, 1913–38): *Ta'ziya*. (Encyclopedia hereafter E.I.)

11. 'Umar II's policy of treating Mawālī and Arab alike meant that the caliphate could control official status in Islam, thereby increasing the centralization of government. It was by Hishām's time (724–743) that the real burden of this policy was felt.

12. See Tabari, vol. 2, pp. 1952 ff.

13. They were not above using religious ideas to further entrench their reign; for example, the notion was floated by the Abbāsids that authority would remain in their hands until Jesus the Messiah returned (see Tabari, vol. 3, p. 33), but their actions in putting down even those who were loyal 'Alids yet powerful (such as abu-Muslim, who was treacherously killed while having an audience with the caliph) soon showed their true colors.

14. E.g. Abū-Salamah, head of the Shī'īs in Iraq, had wanted someone of the Ahl al-Bayt elected caliph; he was killed. On the early Shī'a development see Marshal G.S. Hodgson, "How did the early Shī'a become sectarian," *Journal of the American Oriental Society* 75 (1955), 1–13.

15. For example, Ḥasan was said to have been poisoned by the Umayyads, according to legend, by the hand of his wife, Ja'dah, in 670; see Sir Lewis Pelly, *The Miracle Play of Ḥasan and Ḥusain*, vol. 1, (London, 1879), p. 154 ff.

16. See E.I.: *Imām*.

17. Dwight M. Donaldson, *The Shī'ite Religion* (London, 1933), p. 11. See also Mas'ūdi, *al-Tanbīh w-al-Ishrāf*, ed. M.J. de Goeje (Leiden, 1893–4), pp. 255–56.

18. That is, the public mourning for Ḥusain, and the special feast day marking the date when Muhammad appointed 'Alī his successor. The Sunnīs of course, did not accept as sound the ḥadīth indicating the latter.

19. Black was originally the color of Muhammad's flag; the Umayyads had white flags, while Husain's colors were green. The Abbasids adopted black as their color, as another indication of their legitimacy, and to it has now been added the traditional meaning of mourning. The following description is based on several written sources including: Denis de Rivoyre, *Les Vrais Arabes et leur Pays* (Paris, 1884), pp. 146–51; A.F. Badsha Husain, "Shiah Islam," *Muslim World* 31 (1941), 185–92; A.S. Tritton, "Popular Shī'ism," *British Society of Oriental and African Studies* 13 (1951), 829–839; T.M. Unvala, "The Moharram Festival in Persia," *Studi e materiali di Storia delle religioni* 3 (1927), 82–96; J. Robson, "The Muharram Ceremonies," *The Hibbert Journal* 54–55 (Oct. 1955-July 1957), 265–74; E.S. Stevens, *By Tigris and Euphrates* (London, 1923). Contemporary Shī'īs include: Muḥammad Maḥdi al-Jawāhirī (born in Nejev), Kadhim al-Jassānī (born in Nejev), his wife Mājida al-Nakīb al-Jassānī (born in Nejev), Nīdah al-Jassānī (born in Baghdad), and 'Abbas al-Wahad (born in Karbala).

20. The stories have certain themes, the essence of which is to be found in Pelly, *The Miracle Plays of Ḥasan and Ḥusain, passim*. I was unable to get a copy of the stories from Iraq, although all my sources said that the mullas could tell the story their own way, so long as the main notions of courage, steadfastness, holiness, treachery, etc. were maintained.

21. Pelly, op. cit., vol. 1, p. 52.

22. Ibid., vol. 2, p. 86.

23. Interview, Feb. 1973, Nīdah al-Jassānī. Women also ritually pat their forehead in mourning, per Mājida al-Jassānī, interview, June, 1973.

24. Kadhim al-Jassānī, interview, June 1973; Adam Olearius, *The Voyages and Travels of the Ambassadors from the Duke of Holstein to the Great Duke of Muscovy and the King of Persia*, tr. John Davies (London, 1662), pp. 235–36; James Morier, *A Second Journey Through Persia* (London, 1818), pp. 178–81.

25. Elizabeth Warnock Fernea, *Guests of the Sheik* (New York, 1965), pp. 208–9.

26. The fortieth day after the death of Husain.

27. See B.D. Erdmans, "Der Ursprung der Ceremonien des Hosein-Festes," *Zeitschrift für Assyriologie* (1894), 285, and Morier, *A Second Journey*, p. 180. In Morier's description, a dervish "chanted praises to the king," while being carried by a stout man bearing a long pole, *ibid.*; note pictures in Thomas Hughes. *A Dictionary of Islam* (London, 1896), p. 410.

28. Morier, *A Second Journey*, p. 181; Kadhim al-Jassānī.

29. Morier, *A Second Journey*, p. 182: all witnesses.

30. Kadhim al-Jassānī.

31. Morier, *A Second Journey*, p. 181. Kadhim al-Jassānī recalls a replica of the head of Ḥusain used in high school, when the play was presented, but not in the public rites.

32. I was unable to determine when chains became part of the ceremonies; they are not mentioned in the older accounts, knives and swords being utilized in every description. In the 17th century description of Olearius, the smaller youth used stones to hit each other (see *The Voyages and Travels of the Ambassadors*, p. 236) but no record is made of chains. Knives were still used in Nejev in 1921, according to Frederick Simpich, "Mystic Nedjef, The Shia Mecca," *National Geographic*, 1921, p. 597.

33. *Guests of the Sheik*, pp. 242–43.

34. Kadhim al-Jassānī, Nidah al-Jassānī.

35. Olearius, *Voyage and Travels*, p. 237. None of the witnesses had seen this enacted.

36. 'Abbas al-Wahab, interview, 1970. The efficacy of dying during celebration of the rites must encourage daring, for death then is regarded as tantamount to martyrdom (Olearius, *Voyage and Travels*, p. 237; Kadhim al-Jassānī).

37. Denis de Rivoyre said there were 20 to 30 left after the rites were performed in Istanbul; see *Les Vrais Arabes*, p. 151. It is also significant that in the Persian enactment of the rites special power is held to reside in the tears of those participating; Morier, *A Second Journey*, p. 179, records that the tears are collected, and, if given to a dying man, will restore him.

38. Mājida al-Nakīb al-Jassanī and Nabhā al-Jawāhirī.

39. ". . . these extravagances, I conjecture must resemble the practice of the priests of Baal who cried aloud and cut themselves after this manner with knives and lancets, till the blood gushed out upon them." Thomas Hughes, *A Dictionary of Islam* article: *Muḥarram*.

40. "Der Ursprung der Ceremonien," pp. 291 ff.

41. Morier, *The Second Journey*, takes a delight in quoting some verse from the Bible to explain an action, e.g. Luke, 18:13 is quoted as proof that smiting the breast has universal use (p. 179).

42. Rev. Canon Sell, *The Cult of 'Alī* (London, 1910), p. 3.

43. See for an example Fernea, *Guests of the Sheik*, p. 198.

44. Ibid., p. 202.

45. The legend behind the founding of Nejev is found in Stevens, *By Tigris and Euphrates*, pp. 28–29.

North American and Christian Traditions

And so I pass from incarnation to incarnation, and in every incarnation I struggle against him. I tear myself from him, and cannot tear myself away. I cannot be with him, and I cannot be without him.

Sholem Asch, *The Nazarene*

In Search of Paradigms: Death and Destiny in Seventeenth-Century North America

GLEN W. DAVIDSON

Mankind has yet to find an appropriate definition for "death," but all seem to agree that death and destiny are inextricably related. Sidney E. Mead has said that "a sense of destiny is . . . an element common to the mind of every Western nation that helps to define for its people their corporate sense of direction through the vast and misty labyrinth of history."[1] And a sense of mortality is an element common to the experience of every person, an element which helps to define the paradigms by which to gain access to the destiny of one's people.

For the Hurons, French, and English in seventeenth-century North America, destiny was uncertain in the New World. Although all three peoples had identities rooted in a specific geographic area, each group was in the midst of a period of radical transition in which older paradigms were losing their meaning. In a different historical period, Abraham Lincoln spoke for all "new" peoples when he observed that "if we could first know where we are, and whither we are tending, we could then better judge what to do, and how to do it."[2] There must be paradigms in order to judge what to do and paradigmatic rituals in order to know how to do it. For different reasons, each of these peoples struggled to determine where they were and whither they were tending. They were searching for paradigms.

It is the thesis of this essay that the "Fathers" of each of the people examined, as soon as they died, became the paradigms for their sons. But in finding the paradigms for destiny in their Fathers, the sons found themselves practicing paradigmatic rituals different from those practiced by the Fathers. As the community became established, it provided the paradigms to which the individual related for his sense of destiny; and in each individual's death an occasion was provided for the community to review its destiny.

All three peoples—of Huronia, New France, and New England—saw their destiny as being in Right Order, but in their search for paradigms the Hurons gave ritual priority to Right Act; the French gave ritual priority to Right Belief; and the Puritans gave ritual priority to Right Relationship. The Hurons were an established people when the French and English arrived. But they were not to survive as a people. Their paradigms were inadequate in helping them to adapt, not so much to the impact of the white man and his different paradigms, but rather to the onslaught of their own brothers. The peoples of New France and New England thought they were transplanting paradigms, only to find that the New World dictated a new destiny for each people, and new paradigms.

I will use the term destiny in two ways: as end in the Greek sense (*telos*), meaning fulfillment of purpose or design; and as end in the Latin sense (*finis*), meaning termination or cessation.

Right Act

Who were the Hurons? Our information comes only from sixteenth- and seventeenth-century European missionaries and explorers and from recent archaeological studies. "Huron" (French for peasant with unkempt head) was a nickname the French gave them because the hair style of the males looked like the headtuft of a wild boar.[3] In speaking to the first French inquisitors, the Hurons called themselves "Ouendat"—People-of-One-Land-Apart. In order to bring their furs to the French traders on the St. Lawrence River, they had to cross the lands of the Algonquins. The Hurons, although racially distinct from the Algonquins, usually were at peace with them. Their own racial and language affinities were with their traditional enemies the Iroquois, with whom they warred in competition for furs.

To other Indians, the Hurons referred to themselves by nations—the Bears, to the north; the Cord, to the east and south; and the Rock, in the central and southern areas along the peninsula that juts into Lake Huron and separates it from Georgian Bay. Huronia was small, about forty miles at its widest part from east to west, and little more from north to south. French traders estimated their population to be about 30,000 in the 1630s. They were located in a perfect spot for trapping fur-bearing animals, and the surrounding waters provided fish for sustenance through the harsh winters. Small as the territory was, it still took three or four days to traverse. It was large enough to give them a firm sense of cultural identity so that they came to believe their paradigmatic rituals were unchangeable. Their rituals, if the rites were to be efficacious, had to replicate exactly in act, time, and place the acts of their Fathers.

The Hurons were sedentary. Of all the *indigenes* (natives), the French thought they were the most compatible. They lived in permanent houses, and they cultivated crops. For three seasons of the year, they ate corn or maize and dried fish but had to rely on finding fish, bear, beaver, and moose to supplement their diet. Huron men governed the nations, hunted, fished, traded, built cabins, made war, and appeased demons and otherwise played games or lounged in long periods of intended ease. The women performed all duties about the houses, cultivated the fields, prepared the furs and skins, and carried baggage during journeys.

When the Jesuit missionary Jean de Brébeuf wrote to his Superior in 1635, he described the Hurons' myth of Order as personified by a "certain woman named *Eataensic*," who made earth and man. She had an assistant named *Jouskeha* with whom she governed the world. Jouskeha had care of the living and of the things that concern life, and consequently was said to be good. Eataensic had care of souls; and, because the Hurons believed that she made men die, they thought of her as wicked. The Hurons saw these creation deities as living like themselves "but without famine; [making] feasts as they do, [being] lustful as they are; in short, they imagine them exactly like themselves."[4]

To the French, the Huron's life was chaotic and subject to demonic forces. But the Hurons' world view coincided with their experience of nature, where each object of creation has its own way, its own spirit or soul—the more dangerous the object the more powerful its spirit. Their world view, they believed, imitated Order itself.

According to de Brébeuf, the Hurons conceived of their main soul being material and divisible.[5] After death, the soul separated from the body but did not abandon it. As with spirits in nature, "the souls of those who died in war formed a band apart, as do the souls of those who kill themselves. According to them, the village of souls is in no way unlike the village of the living. They go hunting, fishing, and into the woods, in a word, everything there is the same, but with a difference, that they do nothing day and night but groan and complain."[6]

The paradigmatic ritual for preparing a Huron's soul to be powerful in the afterlife was described in *Jesuit Relations* by François Le Merçier, one of de Brébeuf's companions. An Iroquois captive was brought to a Huron village and alternately tormented and treated kindly. He feasted lustily on sagamité, squashes, and fruits, which the Huron men and women provided him. But he sang defiant songs to show his courage and daring. He knew that this act of warrior courage would determine his place in the afterlife. As the captive Iroquois prepared for his testing, de Brébeuf approached him and offered an alternative: "He would in truth be miserable during the little life that remained to him, but . . . if he would listen to him, and would believe what he had to tell him, he would assure him of an eternal happiness in Heaven after his death."[7] De Brébeuf was offering him not only a different paradigm—based on belief—but a different quality of existence in the afterlife. The captive Iroquois accepted Holy Baptism, but instruction in such mysteries was neither uncommon nor unusual for a member of his people. Anything that would permit him to act out appropriately his status as a warrior in the face of death was legitimate preparation.

When the time for torture was at hand, the "Captain" of the Huron warriors reminded his men "to do their duty, representing to them the importance of this act, which was viewed, he said, by the Sun and by the God of War."[8] The horrifying torture, including jabbing at the most tender parts of the body, cutting away of flesh, and finally charring his body by fire—the most painful of deaths but the mode chosen by the victim—proved the Iroquois a worthy warrior. He had not sought death but he had learned the acts which would enable him to die properly and to pass into the land of the strongest spirits. No doubt, some of his best teachers had been Hurons. Now he was the paradigm.

After the Iroquois' death, his blood was drunk and his body was eaten by the Hurons in order that they could ingest his courage and, like him, be strong in the presence of other souls. They also effectively neutralized the power of an enemy's spirit. The Jesuits, however, were scandalized by this ritual, and they returned to their cabin to ingest the elements of the Mass.

De Brébeuf was to die in a similar way on 16 March 1649 when the Iroquois devastated Huronia. He had prayed to die a martyr's death, and he did. But before he died, the Iroquois vented their rage on him and his companion by cruel torture, including having whole sections of flesh cut away, scalding water poured over them, and a collar of red-hot hatchets placed around their necks. This latter torture created much agony. As described by Christophe Regnaut: "if [the victim] leaned forward, those [hatchets] about his shoulder would weigh the more on him; if he leaned back, those on his stomach made him suffer the same torment; if he would keep erect without leaning to one side or the other, the burning hatchet, applied equally on both sides, give him a double torture." Unlike the warriors' assumption that when they died their courageous act would put them in the abode of the powerful, de Brébeuf had preached that tenacious belief would give him access to a heaven of peace and happiness. Throughout his torture, he kept reminding the listeners, particularly his Christian converts, to be steadfast despite their suffering so that "they might die well, in order to go in company with him to Paradise."[9] The Iroquois derided him, saying, "Thou seest plainly that we treat thee as a friend, since we shall be the cause of thy eternal happiness; thank us, then, for these good offices which we render thee,—for the more thou shalt suffer, the more will thy God reward thee."[10] The Jesuit died courageously, crying "*Jesus taiteur*! Jesus, have mercy on us!"[11] One of the warriors tore open the upper part of his chest, ripped out his heart, and roasted and ate it. Others came to drink his blood, still warm, "which they drank with both hands—saying that Father de Brébeuf had been very courageous to endure such pain as they had given him, and that by drinking his blood, they would become courageous like him."[12]

The Feast of Courage was efficacious for the Hurons so long as there was an equilibrium of power between them and their enemies; but when they were overwhelmed as a people, the possibilities of an afterlife as anything other than subservient spirits to the Iroquois became all too evident. From the Jesuits, many Huron warriors saw that the Frenchman's paradigms permitted them not only to escape subservience, but to go to Heaven where, if the missionaries were to be believed, they would live in glory.

The Feast of Courage prepared the soul and the Feast of the Dead united it with both the living and the dead. The Feast of the Dead was a ritual of second burial. It bound the whole people together. The ceremony attending their final burial was so hallowed that if any traditional detail were omitted the entire nation would be doomed. Sons would be cut off from the Fathers. When referring to it, the Hurons used euphonisms and metaphors. To refer to the dead as dead would either be insulting or be cause for new mourning. As de Brébeuf explained: "They hardly ever speak of the Feast of the Dead, even in most solemn councils, except under the name of The Kettle. They appropriate to it all the terms of cookery. In speaking of hastening or postponing the 'Feast of the Dead,' they will speak of stirring up or scattering the embers beneath the Kettle. He who would say, 'the Kettle is overturned,' would mean, 'there will be no Feast of the Dead.'"

The Feast of the Dead, or of the souls, occurred every ten to twelve years. In order to perform the Kettle, rifts and schisms among the Hurons had to be healed or the souls could not be properly reunited. The bones of the forefathers were sacred and called *Atisken*, meaning the soul. Each family was responsible for performing the ritual for its own dead and each village or nation was obliged to choose a chief, called *Aiheonde*, who was responsible for directing the rites. Master of the Festival was called the *Anenkhiondic*.

The Feast began when the Aiheonde from each village led his people in silent procession to the cemetery where bodies of their dead had been stored on scaffolding awaiting second burial. After the men had lowered the bodies to the ground, the squaws and girls cried out, again and again, the names of their dead. De Brébeuf observed: "The flesh of some was quite gone, and there was only a parchment over their bones. Some bodies looked as if they had been dried and smoked, and showed scarcely any signs of putrefaction. Others were all swarming over with worms."[13]

After contemplating the remains, the women cleaned the bones from what remained of skin and flesh and wrapped the bones in furs. These were then carried back to their houses and hung on posts or propped up on the ground. Recently stored bodies were carried on litters. A feast was then prepared and consumed in the presence of the Atisken.

On the appointed day, the Aiheonde led his people to the Kettle. The men walked in procession wearing their most valuable robes and beads, their naked bodies smeared with paint. The squaws followed in file carrying the pouches of Atisken and the bodies.

The burial pit described by de Brébeuf was about twenty-five feet in diameter and ten feet deep. A circular scaffolding about ten feet high and twelve feet wide surrounded the excavation. Poles extended from the top of the scaffolding out toward the center of the pit. The bags of souls were suspended on the poles. Surrounding the scaffolding were posts which were erected in a circle about three thousand feet in circumference on which each family displayed presents it would distribute in honor of their ancestors.

The Hurons took up to a week for the final burial. While waiting, during daytime, young people engaged in sports and older people gambled. In the evening, everyone feasted and danced, and orators recalled the prowess of their ancestors.

When the Master of the Feast proclaimed that the ritual of burial would begin, the women took down the pouches of bones, opened them, and paid their last farewell with shrill lamentations. After a procession around the burial pit, the Master of the Feast ordered the bones to be placed back on the suspended poles and the bodies to be moved to the edge of the pit. At the next command, he announced what gifts were being made and who was donating such wealth to which recipient. In the pit, beaver robes were spread out along the bottom and sides. De Brébeuf calculated that about forty-eight robes, each of ten or more of the best grade of beaver skins, were used during the ceremony of 1636. Ten to twelve men worked in the pit arranging the bodies next to one another around the sides. In the middle of the pit, they placed three large kettles. That evening each group of families held its vigil near where the corpses of their relatives rested on beaver skins in the pit and their pouches of souls hung above on the poles.

About dawn, naked men on the scaffolding hurled the bones out of the pouches toward the center of the pit. Pit workers spread out and leveled the skulls and other bones which came hurling down on top of them. In the particular ceremony that de Brébeuf described, final burial was hastened because one of the bags holding the bones had fallen from the pole and dropped the twenty feet to the bottom of the pit with such a crash that it wakened those sleeping nearby. It was then necessary for all the people to bury their bones because their people "would be doomed forever if the bones were not buried altogether at the same time." Following placement of bones in the burial pit, the Anenkhiondic began a chant. The mourners joined him while the bones were leveled out about two feet from the top of the pit. Those in charge covered the bones with robes, mats, and large pieces of bark, and filled the pit with sandy soil over which they threw logs and poles.[14]

The Jesuits had buried fifteen or twenty Christians nearby and as the Chant of the Souls went on, the Jesuits said a *de Profundis*. De Brébeuf had participated in the Feast of the Dead on condition that those who had been baptized would be buried in a separate sacred spot. As on earlier occasions, a number of Hurons were so impressed with the French mode of burial that "several desired us to honor their burial in the same way."[15]

It must be noted, however, that it was the Huron manner of preserving bones that permitted the Jesuits to return de Brébeuf's remains to Quebec following his death. On that occasion, all flesh was removed from his bones, the bones were hardened in a low fire and placed in a pouch not of beaver fur but of silk. Unlike the Hurons, who believed that the soul of the departed continued to reside in the bones, the Catholics revered the bones only as relics by which to focus their paradigmatic rituals of Right Belief. The soul had passed on at death.

The Jesuits' paradigm also permitted them to maintain their sense of destiny even though they no longer dwelled on the same land as their fathers. While the Hurons thought of the abode of the souls as the specific burial mounds of Huronia, the French were able to shift their focus with their relics. Further, like their language, the Hurons' rituals were specific and concrete, whereas the French, like their language, could transfer paradigms by abstract and spiritual ideas. Many Hurons had become impressed with the French paradigms, because French paradigms were more flexible; they could be adjusted to varying contexts while the Hurons' were undeviating. Right Belief would allow Order to be carried in one's memory while Right Action was limited to a specific geographic area.

After the Iroquois destruction, the people of Huronia were either taken as captives or scattered. Those who had adopted the French paradigms accompanied the Jesuits to Quebec and resided there. Other Hurons settled in the region of Ohio and Indiana until the white man forced them to move. By the nineteenth century, remnants of a once proud people were confined to reservations in Oklahoma. In the move west, they had to leave behind their dead—the paradigmatic souls who gave them their sense of destiny. Not only were the paradigms lost, but their identity as a people was destroyed.

Right Belief

De Brébeuf's martyrdom became a paradigmatic event for the people of New France. "New France" referred to all territory which had been claimed by French explorers in the New World. But the early explorers had not thought of this primitive land, filled with mystery and savagery, as part of France's destiny. When Jacques Cartier explored the St. Lawrence River in 1534, his one obsession was to find a passageway to Cathay in order that the kingdom of Francis I could compete materially with Spain. By 1535, stopped by rapids near present-day Montreal, Cartier knew this was not the passageway to France's salvation. Tradition holds that, with mocking bitterness, Cartier named the rapids "La Chine"—China.[16] And he looked for other ways to Cathay.

Neither crown nor court showed much interest in the discovery of the St. Lawrence. But by 1603, a Breton sea captain and a Huguenot shipowner had obtained the fur trade monopoly in the St. Lawrence drainage and set about establishing trading posts for bartering with the Indians. Beaver pelts were soon to become the rage of European society. The amazed Indians were only too willing to part with their bounty for a metal utensil or weapons; but it was the Huguenot traders who prospered.

Moved in part by the explorers' touching reports about the savages' harsh living conditions and in part by the missionary zeal of religious orders like the Society of Jesus, some Frenchmen were eager to convert the natives of the New World to Catholicism. Both for religious and political reasons, the Calvinist traders worked to keep missionaries out, particularly the Jesuits. When court pressures forced passage for priests to care for winter inhabitants of the trading posts, a compromise was made and ecclesiastical responsibility was reserved to the gentle Franciscan priests, named Recollects. Since the traders desired neither permanent colonies nor to disrupt the Indians' life style, aspirations of men like Samuel de Champlain for a permanent colony at Quebec were thwarted. Even though the trading companies had promised the court that they would invest in permanent settlements, it was not until de Champlain and the Recollects obtained the help of the Jesuits that both the religious and political zeal of the French Catholic Revival could be sustained in America. The Huguenots' suspicions were soon confirmed: After the Jesuits were admitted to New France, the Calvinists lost influence and were expelled, only to find their revenge in the destiny of New England.

Even though de Champlain had founded Quebec in 1608, it was not until 1663, during the reign of Louis XIV, that the destiny of New France became clear. Jean-Baptiste Colbert, the King's administrative genius, established the colonists' mission:

To transplant in the New World that Right Order which was established in France —an Order in which all would know both their rightful places and their appropriate roles. Old France was exhausted from years of religious wars and political conflict. In New France, Order would be reestablished. New France now had its destiny. Colbert intended the colony to have two paradigms: the rule of the King and the faith of the Church. King Louis' struggles with Rome were reflected in the priorities!

Colbert tried to restrict immigration to faithful Catholics who had been raised in the Old World topographies similar to that of the St. Lawrence River valleys. If the mission of New France were to succeed, there had to be a stable population which could survive the rigors and isolation of this land. By 1669, the entire male population around Quebec had been organized into *Troupes de Terre* under Royal officers, which meant that the colony was prepared both to defend and to administer itself down to the last man. Land and *habitants* were divided into parishes.[17] Parish lines were symmetrically laid out and presided over by a *curé* (pastor). The family of the habitant,[18] encouraged by the King's men and the curés, had numerous children and was organized as a Holy Family. The husband's first name was usually Joseph and he passed it on to each of his sons. The wife's first name was usually Marie, and each daughter was called the same. Each individual not only knew his roles within the state but also knew his cosmic role as acted out according to the paradigm of the Holy Family.

Roles were clearly defined at every level of society from King to subject. Governors and bishops did have their difficulties determining limits of responsibility, which reflected the feuds that went on between King and Pope. But those controversies were based on the attempt by both sides to clarify lines of order. Most historians persist in calling French-Canadian society authoritarian, but that is hardly an adequate word to account for the fierce and individualistic spirit of the habitant, who was forced to show considerable innovativeness and independence simply to survive. The habitant's intention was to act "in order."

"In order" not only meant knowing one's status but also meant that one's place was predictable. Each parish was laid out in geometric precision along the river, and the church was built at the center. Establishment of the center did lead to controversy and tabernacles were moved to accommodate the opinions of the parishioners. They were moved only until the cemetery was established. Then the church was understood to be on its permanent site and the parish had its sacred spot around which the rituals of life were organized.

The rhythm of French-Canadian culture took its form within the cycles of nature, with the liturgical calendar being a counterpart of the seasons. But unlike the Hurons, the habitants did not understand themselves to be the children of nature; rather, nature was to serve the children of God. Time was understood as a unity of order. Many were the saint's days, festivals, and holidays, but two stand out for the purpose of my thesis: The Day of the Dead and Easter. The first day of November was, and is, the Day of the Dead when the holy souls not only were remembered but were addressed by prayers invoking their assistance for the benefit of the parish. It was, and is, the occasion when the mission of the living is united with the destiny of the Fathers. The stirrings of spring heralded the Easter event and on

Easter morning free-flowing water, released from the winter's snows, was collected and brought to the church to be blessed and given to the faithful to be ingested. Just as waters had come alive and had become united, so too would all of the holy souls in the Last Judgment. In particular, it would be the time when all of the holy souls of their people would be united.

But who were their holy souls? It is evident that the first generation of habitants faced uncertainty about the company of holy souls. The living order of King and Church was now being established in the New World as it was in the Old. There were the Church saints. But for many, emotional ties were with the holy souls of their relatives, and they were buried in France.

Theologians of the day may have been able to conceptualize disembodied souls and abstractions of unity and to envision the intervention of the host of faithful on their behalf, but the immigrant peasant could not. Isolation from their people was often translated into fear of dying away from the homeland. It was a major constraint on immigration and a prime motive for returning to the Old World. Just as when the great de Champlain died in 1635, and the Jesuit Superior who gave the funeral oration had assured the small body of faithful in Quebec that even though the Governor had "died far away from France, his name will not be any less glorious to posterity,"[19] nor will his mission be diminished; so now, the first generation of settlers was urged to focus on the mission. That was their destiny.

Paradigmatic rituals of Right Belief could be transferred to the New World, but it was in men like Jean de Brébeuf that the habitants found their holy souls. Relics of the New World martyrs were used to help first generation habitants adapt to their mission. De Brébeuf's skull was encased in a silver reliquary in Quebec in order that the habitant could see how the sacredness of martyrdom for the faith was one with the sacredness of the mission for the crown.

The habitants' myth of destiny, like that of other Roman Catholics in the seventeenth century, understood men to be assessed in two eschatological judgments: at death when the immortal soul is separated from the body and enters into its reward or torment, and the Last Judgment when the success or failure in reaching one's destiny is confirmed permanently. Although the Last Judgment is the end (*telos*) of history, the concern of the living focused on the first Judgment. It is there that their mission to establish the Order of New France would be tested. For those faithful to the mission, death would not cut them off from either their mission or their opportunity to be further purged from sin. In the interim between the two judgments, they would continue to help act out the cosmological drama of the faithful.

Confidence in being able to relate to the whole order of God's universe through holy souls had to await the second generation when they would have their own cherished dead nearby and at the center of their life. Then their mission would be to remember the mission of their fathers—the first generation.

Rituals of the Day of the Dead took on new meaning for the second generation in New France. Like their European counterparts, they burned memorial candles and arranged for the saying of the Mass for the benefit of the holy souls. But in remembrance of their holy souls was the liturgical union with the mission of New France. Right Belief gave way to Right Remembrance. Focus of mission shifted from the first generation's establishment of the paradigmatic settlement in the New World to remembering the fathers who had transplanted the paradigms of destiny. And the second generation adopted an oath of Right Remembrance as their creed. Often translated as "I remember," *Je me souviens* is more properly translated in its emphatic form—"I *do* remember."

Just as Father de Brébeuf had discovered that the Hurons were most concerned about the fact of death and the assumptions of a future life of either happiness in heaven or of eternal torment, so too did the habitant order his life around the fact of his mortality and his hopes for eternal happiness. While morality (Right Acts) was his code of behavior and political and ecclesiastical authority (Right Relationship) was his security, remembrance (Right Belief) became his prime ritual, which allowed his holy souls, rather than the holy souls of Europe, to become his paradigms for destiny. Like the Hurons but unlike the Calvinists, the site of burial for the habitant became *the* sacred spot where the Church would remain and around which new settlements were organized.

The cemeteries of New France were, and are, the symbols of destiny. In Quebec, and on the Island of St. Pierre, where the climate does not cause rapid physical deterioration of the corpse, crypts were designed with doors or portholes. There, beside the coffins, families could meditate. In each habitant's death and in visitation to the grave, there was occasion for measuring obedience to the mission to which each person—because he was French and Roman Catholic—had been called.

Je me souviens now refers to more than the mission of New France, however. It refers to more than the history of a people who have saved a vital culture even though they lost a war to the British. It also refers to the mission of each person to perpetuate the True Order and Identity established by their Fathers. Only in the persistence of a French culture is there testimony of a destiny which transcends an individual's death. To question this has long been taboo. Calls for assimilation of French Canadians into English Canadian culture challenge the taboo and may lead to political separatism in Canada.

Louis Hémon captured the sentiment of remembrance in his novel *Maria Chapdelaine*, when he has "the voice of Quebec" tell Maria: "We have held fast, so that it may be, many centuries hence, the world will look upon us and say: 'These people are of a race that knows not how to perish. . . . We are a testimony.'"[20]

At graveside, the creed is said: "I do remember"; and in that ritual, with its particular focus on an obedient and paradigmatic forebearer, the faithful living relate to a cosmological order which knows no end (*finis*) even though the France of the seventeenth century, and its order, no longer exists.

Right Relationship

The Puritans immigrated to the wilds of Massachusetts Bay not to transplant Old World culture in the New, but to establish a divinely ordered society which Europe had never had. The Puritan's mission was to create God's exemplary "city on a hill," which could be viewed by all mankind. Their mission had become clear to them while struggling in Europe to purify the Church of England. They thought of God, as William Stoughton preached in 1668, as "having sifted a whole Nation"—meaning England—"that he might send Choice Grain over into this wilderness" for reestablishing what had become lost when "in Adam's fall, we sinned all." Man's destiny depended on the success of their mission to show mankind how to be in right relationship with God.

William Hubbard spoke for all Puritans when he wrote, "order is the soul of the Universe."[21] The Catholics of New France did not disagree. For both peoples, the order of the universe was synonymous with God's will. But for the Catholic, some events in nature and in human history are of ungodly and demonic origin. For the Calvinist, no event occurs either in nature or in human history that is not an act of God.

Neither Catholic nor Calvinist assumed that sovereignty rested anywhere but with God. But the Catholics of New France thought that only King and Pope could adequately discern and therefore represent the meaning of Right Order. The Calvinists of New England thought that King and Pope never had the authority to discern divine will and therefore could not represent it. The paradigmatic model of authority for New France was an omnipotent, omniscient, omnipresent Father who was to be emulated at every level of social existence. The paradigmatic model of authority for New England was the covenant of the Old Testament people of Israel with a capricious God.

Puritan purity was based not on ethnic traditions (though they seemed unaware of assumptions peculiarly English), but on "owning" the paradigm of the covenant. Owning was impossible without proof of being in right relationship with God. The conversion experience was the proof needed, at least for the Fathers. All those receiving that sign of Grace were among the chosen people and constituted the "one Catholick church"—those saints who had died as well as those still waging earthly battle. Those who had received the sign of Grace comprised the visible church when they entered into congregational discipline.

Of equal importance to the corporate coming together of Puritan saints in building that city on a hill was the assumption that only the community of saints could discern the will of God in the present moment. The Covenant of Grace had set man back in right relation with God. But even the saints still bore the effects of Adam's fall in pridefully seeking knowledge independently of God. Therefore, no man could trust his own powers to discover God's will. Instead, each man's discerning of the signs of the time had to be tested by the community of gathered saints. The only way to salvation was through the destiny of the covenanted people.

In covenantal theology the Puritan found both assurance and anxiety. His assurance rested on the notion that a saint's obedience could be tested by discerning the state of the saint's prosperity. This led, in later generations, to a shift from emphasis on discerning the proper form of the covenant to discerning the proper maintenance of the covenant. Those who were in God's favor, the sons believed, showed it in their moral discipline and their prosperity. Those who transgressed the covenant failed in both assurance and assets. As old Ezra Stiles noted in various entries of his diary: "This day Ethan Allen died and went to Hell." "This day died Joseph Bellamy and went to Heaven, where he can dictate and domineer no longer."[22]

Covenantal theology was also the basis for the Puritan's anxiety. He was always fearful of falling or being led into disobedience of God's will. Like the Huron who feared offending some god if he failed to perform paradigmatic acts exactly, and the Catholic's fear of forgetting, the Calvinist obsessively monitored the position before God of himself and his neighbors. Had John Bunyan not been correct to portray the Pilgrim's progress fraught with danger right up to the gate of Heaven? Even at the threshold, at death, there is that trap door to Hell for those who become overconfident and arrogate to themselves divine affect.

In order not to misstep, many Puritans kept diaries, the better to review their mission. And they analyzed the diaries and autobiographies of saints in the "Church Triumphant" to see how they had transacted relationships. Diary keeping and reading became a paradigmatic ritual. The Puritan kept a diary not because he was infatuated with himself, though some were, but to keep a strict ledger of God's dealings with life, so that at any moment, and particularly at the point of death, he could review the long list of his transactions with God.

It was thought that the appropriate time to die was after an illness in which the adult saint was given a period of torment and testing and an opportunity to repent. Sudden death was an omen of unfaithfulness. When the antinomian heretic Anne Hutchinson met her death in New York, the Puritan faithful interpreted the Indians' butchery as divine confirmation of the sentence of exile the community had placed on her.

Clergymen kept careful tabs on the manner and rate of deaths in their parishes. Increase Mather wrote in *An Essay For the Recording of Illustrious Providences*: "There have been many sudden deaths in this country which should not pass without some remark; for when such strokes are multiplied there is undoubtedly a speaking voice of Providence therein; and so it hath been with us in New England this last year, and most of all the last summer. To my observation in August last, within the space of three or four weeks, there were twelve sudden deaths (and it may be others have observed more than I did), some of them being in respect of sundry circumstances exceeding awful."[23]

Mather was forced to note that "sudden death is not always a judgment unto those who are taken out of an evil world; it may be a mercy to them, and a warning unto others, as the prophet Ezekiel's wife was. Many of whom the world was not worthy, have been so removed out of it."[24] But if a Puritan saint were to have his choice, death would not come upon him suddenly, in order that he could be prepared and "exhibit the virtue of dying well." The diaries, history books, and theological treatises all record the Puritan's deep-seated belief that life's mission culminates in the event of peaceful death. For the saint, death is the time when he could truly be made free in the glory of God. All of life had been a period of preparation. Death closed the probationary period and was that arbitrary point beyond which evil is barred. For good or ill, the time of testing was over.

The Puritan ideal for the funeral was simplicity. The Westminster Assembly of the Church of Scotland, in 1645, published a "Directory for the Publick Worship of God," in which the Puritan divines declared: "When any person departeth this life, let the dead body, upon the day of burial, be decently attended from the house to the place appointed for public burial, and there immediately interred without any ceremony."[25] In New England, the ban on ceremony was interpreted specifically as an injunction to avoid the "popish" error of saying prayers for the dead, and no prayers were said at graveside. At times, with death striking the faithful faster than they could be buried, the corpse was placed in bare soil, with little more than a winding sheet around it. As the economy became more affluent, wooden boxes and then simple wooden coffins were used. Usually, the body would be wrapped in a shroud.

The occasion of death was used to instruct the living. A special sermon would be preached the Sunday following death when the pastor could call for the saints to renew their vigilance and prepare to meet the same fate as their departed brother. Cemeteries, too, were used for instructional purposes. Contrary to popular assumptions, the Puritans used art forms on gravestones "For the Civil use of . . . representation & remembrance of a person absent," as Samuel Mather wrote in 1672.[26] As early as 1650, the Puritans began to embellish headstones with skull and crossbones and epitaphs. Some warned the viewer that "Fugit Hora"—Time flees—and that he too, would be joining the dust. Others held forth promises like the one written as an elegy for John Foster by the Reverend Joseph Capen in 1681:

> Yes, though with dust thy body soiled be
> Yet at the Resurrection we shall see
> A fair Edition and of matchless worth,
> Free from Errata, new in Heaven set forth:
> 'Tis but a word from God the great Creatour,
> It shall be Done when He saith *Imprimatur*.[27]

The Puritan funeral expressed the hopes of eternal reward for the deceased and further served to sustain the surviving faithful in their own relationships of collective destiny.

The Puritan was not clear just when fulfillment of New England's mission would be. Like Calvin, the Puritans were less concerned about how long it would be until the Last Judgment than they were in putting down the "popish deception" that further testing went on for the individual's soul in the interim between death and the Last Judgment.

The Puritan did suspect, however, that even though the date of the Last Judgment was known only to God, that day was not far off, and he pictured the saints soon in Heaven. Of this much the Puritan was certain: When the Day of Judgment came, "a strict and straight account of all things done under the sun . . . all filthy facts and secret acts, however closely done and long concealed, are there revealed before the mid-day sun." Then the Just God will order the unregenerate to "depart . . . forever to endless misery, and then a man's soul becomes his own, cut off from its Maker, to live in a hell where they must lie and never die, though dying every day," for "God's direful wrath their bodies hath forever immortal made."[28]

The Puritan Fathers had answered their concerns for destiny by focusing on the nature of covenantal theology, assuming that in Right Relationship man had the paradigm for salvation. Their sons came to focus their concern on the maintenance of the covenant, assuming that Right Morality was its proper manifestation. The Fathers understood their mission to be the establishment of the covenanted society, and their sons understood their own mission to be the perpetuation of that society. This shift in mission did not cut the sons off, however, from either the paradigms or the destiny of the Fathers. Or so they hoped. On the contrary, the rituals of living well, of which learning to die well was a part, prepared the sons to meet that judgment which would determine success or failure of the mission to be in Right Order. But whatever the sons thought, their paradigmatic rituals for Right Order shifted from Right Relationship to Right Morality.

I find the roots of the dominating culture in North America to lie in the soil of the Puritan's city, not so much because the Puritans succeeded in making Right Relationship the paradigmatic ritual, but because their notion of peaceful death as the proof of fulfilled destiny (*telos*) prevails. For several hundred years this culture has focused on the peaceful death as the reward for the elect. Where the courageous death for the Huron and the martyred death for the French was proof of a paradigm's validity, the literature of New England culture can be summarized in a promise: The moral man can die in peace, his conscience clear and his body undefiled, prepared to meet his Lord and to dwell in that sleep which knows no evil, no conflict, no disappointment. His end (*telos*) is in Order.

In later generations, among sons who no longer call themselves Puritans but who continue to understand their own mission as the practice of right relationships through good manners and morals, there lies, unconscious, an origin of identity and a quest for destiny similar to the Puritan's. But unlike the Puritans, their shift from the paradigmatic ritual of Right Relationship to the paradigmatic ritual of Right Morality brings their focus back to the deceased. By the nineteenth century, in the Civil War, we witnessed the triumph of that ritual. An industry arose to preserve not just relics but whole bodies so that they could be returned to *their* people and be honored as models for selfless dying.

Although all three peoples had a three-directional sense of time, Right Act as a paradigmatic ritual focused on how to have access to destiny in the present, Right Belief focused on how to have access to destiny through the past, and Right Relationship focused on how to gain access in the future. For the Hurons, paradigmatic rituals of Right Act permitted them to have access to destiny only so long as they had direct access to their Fathers. But when the rituals could not be changed to accommodate the sons' forced moves, the sons lost contact with their origins. For the people of New France, paradigmatic rituals of Right Belief not only permitted them to have access to an Old World destiny but has permitted, in the ritual's altered form, the perpetuation of a destiny lost to Old France. For the people of New England, paradigmatic rituals of Right Relationship not only permitted them to establish a new sense of destiny but permitted, in the ritual's altered form, the reorganization of life in the face of new orders, philosophies, and theologies.

Whether the paradigmatic rituals from the Fathers of New France or New England can sustain late-twentieth-century sons, who find themselves in accelerating transitions, will largely depend on whether the paradigms for death point to a *telos* or a *finis*. Only with a *telos* can a community provide a paradigm to which an individual can relate for a sense of identity, and a community renew its sense of mission in the individual's death.

Notes

1. *The Lively Experiment* (New York: Harper & Row, 1963), p. 75.

2. "A House Divided," speech at Springield, Ill., 16 June 1858 in *The Collected Works of Abraham Lincoln*, ed. Roy P. Basler, 9 vols. (New Brunswick: Rutgers University Press, 1953), 2:461.

3. Samuel Eliot Morison notes that the French never called natives of North America "Indians." That was a term probably first used by Columbus and the Spaniards. Cartier consistently used the term *sauvages*; later French explorers used *peaux-rouges* (redskins), or, if they chose to be polite, *indigènes* (natives). *The European Discovery of America: The Northern Voyages A.D. 500–1600* (New York: Oxford University Press, 1974), p. 428.

4. *The Jesuit Relations and Allied Documents: Travels and Explorations of the Jesuit Missionaries in North America (1610–1791)*. Abridged version, ed. Edna Kenton (New York: Albert & Charles Boni, 1925), p. 112.

5. De Brébeuf describes illness as "living death" for the Hurons. For rituals used to restore the strength of the soul against the demons of illness, see Francis X. Talbot, *Saint Among the Hurons; The Life of Jean de Brébeuf* (New York: Doubleday, 1956), p. 72.

6. Ibid., p. 79.

7. Kenton, p. 128.

8. Ibid., p. 129.

9. Ibid., p. 221.

10. Ibid., p. 222.

11. Talbot, p. 299.

12. Kenton, p. 222.

13. Talbot, p. 148. The complete text of Père de Brébeuf's writings on the Hurons is found in vol. 10 of *The Jesuit Relations and Allied Documents*, ed. Reuben Gold Thwaites, 71 vol. (Cleveland: The Burrows Company, 1896–1901).

14. Ibid., p. 152.

15. Ibid., p. 132.

16. But as Morison notes, the sarcasm is LaSalle's, who followed Cartier in the next century, p. 415.

17. See Mason Wade, *The French Canadians*, rev. ed., 2 vol. (Toronto: Macmillan, 1968).

18. The significance of the word which the settlers took for themselves, *habitants*, is seen in an observation of Mircea Eliade. It means the people of "the universe that man constructs for himself by imitating the paradigmatic creation of the gods, the cosmogony." *The Sacred and The Profane* (New York: Harcourt, Brace & World, 1959), pp. 56–57.

19. Talbot, p. 157.

20. Louis Hémon, *Maria Chapdelaine: Récit du Canada Français* (Paris: Bernard Grasset, 1954), p. 241.

21. "The Happiness of a People . . . 1676," in Perry Miller and Thomas H. Johnson, eds., *The Puritans*, 2 vols. (New York: American Book Company, 1938), 1:247.

22. Alice Morse Earle, *Customs and Fashions in Old New England* (New York: Scribner's, 1906), p. 275.

23. Quoted in Perry Miller, *The American Puritans* (New York: Doubleday, 1956), p. 260.

24. Ibid.

25. Massachusetts Historical Society, *Proceedings*, vol. 17, pp. 168–69. Cited in Robert W. Habenstein and William M. Lamers, *The History of American Funeral Directing* (Milwaukee: Bulfin Printers, 1955), p. 197.

26. "A Testimony from the Scripture against Idolatry & Superstition," quoted in Dickran Tashjian and Ann Tashjian, *Memorials for Children of Change* (Middletown, Conn.: Wesleyan University Press, 1974), p. 8.

27. "Funeral Elegy," quoted in ibid., p. 196.

28. Michael Wigglesworth, "The Day of Doom," reprinted in Miller, *American Puritans*, pp. 282–94.

The Death of Father Abraham: The Assassination of Lincoln and Its Effect on Frontier Mythology

DONALD CAPPS

The recent interest of sociologists and historians in American civil religion has drawn particular attention to the religious dimensions of the American Presidency. Robert N. Bellah's catalytic article on civil religion in America, published in 1967, addressed the religious themes in Presidential inaugural addresses.[1] My paper deals not with the inauguration of a person's incumbency in the office but with its termination through untimely death. This aspect of American civil religion came to the fore in an extremely dramatic way with the assassination of President John F. Kennedy in 1963. From our vantage point in the 1970s, it can be said that President Kennedy's assassination and the funeral rites that followed it have proven at least as important as his inaugural address (which Bellah uses to introduce his pioneer study) in providing the existential impetus for scholarly interest in American civil religion.

The death of an incumbent President is of profound religious import. Death by assassination is especially so, since it thwarts the President in the accomplishment of his divinely appointed tasks. A President's death from natural causes may be understood to be consistent with divine will and thus does not necessarily thwart the nation's divinely appointed destiny. But to view assassination as consistent with divine will would violate one of the deepest convictions of civil religion in America, that is, that divinely appointed ends cannot be achieved through means inimical to the inalienable rights of individual citizens. Assassination, an act of murder, clearly violates those rights. Thus, the assassination of a President arbitrarily terminates his accomplishment of the divinely appointed acts he promised to carry out to the best of his ability at the time of his inauguration. And, although his successor may immediately don his predecessor's mantle and promise to carry on these appointed tasks, thus insuring continuity in the governance of the country, the nation itself is profoundly aware that God's purposes for his people may have been seriously threatened by this single, senseless act of personal violence. The assassination has quite literally changed the course of the nation's religious history and has placed in serious jeopardy the accomplishment of certain divinely appointed tasks once considered within the nation's reach. However, if one effect of the assassination of a President is to threaten the accomplishment of God's purposes for the nation, we should expect that an actual assassination would prompt the nation to reflect even more seriously on its spiritual destiny. An event of this magnitude might result in a significant revision, even transformation of American civil religion.

This study asks about the influence of an assassination of a President on the nation's religious consciousness. Does an assassination prompt greater reflection on the spiritual destiny of the American people? Does it significantly alter the nation's religious self-understanding? Although popular comparisons of the assassinations of Presidents Kennedy and Lincoln invite the historian of religion to deal with both assassinations in addressing these questions, this study is best served by focusing exclusively on the death of Abraham Lincoln. What were the effects of Lincoln's untimely death on the religious consciousness of the American people? Did his death significantly transform the religious temper of America and, if so, in what sense? The answer is that Lincoln's death contributed to the rise of a tragic religious perspective in America, and it was particularly responsible for the introduction of a tragic dimension into frontier mythology.

The Civil War and the Failure of the Myth-Dream

The suggestion of a tragic view of American religious history is not new. A useful point of departure for an analysis of Lincoln's assassination is Sidney E. Mead's suggestion that the Civil War was the turning point in American history in that it forced the nation for the first time to take an essentially tragic view of itself. In Mead's view, "Americans can most profoundly understand their collective and dynamic experience on this continent as a tragic drama and themselves as actors in that kind of play."[2] Mead acknowledges that other conceptions of the American experience are plausible, but he proposes that the tragic view recommends itself to those historians concerned with the mythical view of history. This tragic view is especially congruent with anthropologist Kenelm O.L. Burridge's emphasis on the "myth-dream" by which a people understands its origins, its present situation, and its ultimate destiny.[3]

Such a historian would then see that the American experience grew out of a myth-dream based on the conviction that man has the potential to be free. The dream of human freedom, the freedom of the people to govern themselves, was the myth on which America was founded and which infused its people with creative energy. This historian, in tracing the evolution of the myth of human freedom, would observe that "for a time at least these people exhibited such creative activity as to justify wise men in hoping that they might successfully incarnate their creative idea—their dream—in actuality." But if the angle of vision is changed from past to present, the myth-dream lacks power; "it does not produce in the beholder any clear impression of purpose and meaning." In Mead's judgment, this obvious discrepancy between the dream's original power and its present lack of purpose and meaning requires the historian to take a tragic view of the American experience. However, this tragic view would stand or fall, "not on the adequacy of my understanding and/or the persuasiveness of my presentation of the creative idea of America, but on the plausibility that there was a creative idea . . . which appeared so soundly based that wise men hoped that it could be incarnated in actuality, and that the result would have 'power.'"[4] The fact that it could not be so incarnated would then be the crux of the American tragedy.

The student of the American myth-dream, as historian, must explain the failure of the myth-dream. In Mead's judgment, the Civil War represents that critical historical juncture in the tragic drama when the dream lost its persuasive hold on the imaginations of wiser persons. The dream itself may survive the ravages of war, but the power behind the dream, confidence in its efficacy, suffers irreparable damage. Doubt colors the actions of even the boldest of dreamers, and the nation talks less about the dream becoming an actuality and more about the people having embarked on a great experiment that was as likely to fail as to succeed.

To Mead, Abraham Lincoln was foremost among those who recognized the deeper implications of the Civil War for the survival of the myth-dream. Lincoln understood that the dream had come to a severe time of testing, the outcome of which would have fateful implications for the nation's subsequent history. Lincoln's understanding of the implications of the Civil War for the dream's survival is revealed in his Gettysburg Address: "Our fathers brought forth on this continent a new nation, conceived in liberty, and dedicated to the proposition that all men are created equal. Now we are engaged in a great civil war, testing whether that nation, or any nation so conceived and so dedicated, can long endure." Lincoln made no effort to gloss over the tragic implications of this great experiment. At Gettysburg, "he could not and did not assert with finality that the dead had not died in vain. All that he could ask was that 'we here highly resolve that these dead shall not have died in vain; that this nation, under God, shall have a new birth of freedom.'"[5]

Mead concludes that the Civil War was the great turning point in the evolution of the dream. However the political results of the war are assessed, its effect on the myth-dream of the American people was truly devastating:

> For despite the clarity and power of Lincoln's articulation of the creative idea, the tremendous energy that was drawn out of the people in its defense, and the activity and technical skill they exhibited in its conduct, the shape of the "work" after the war either lacked power, or showed a demonic dimension by having a power contrary to the dream. . . .[6]

Thus, the Civil War marks that critical point in the history of America when the creative dream of the people lost its power:

> Here is the nub of the tragedy. It lies, not in the great technological and material development as such, and not even in the simple fact that the actuality of America

> appeared more and more ugly and less and less the progressive incarnation of the ideal. Rather it lay in the fading from the mind of the artist-people of the creative idea—the evaporation of their dream.[7]

With the Civil War, the dream of human freedom, as exemplified in its emphasis on the ability of a people to govern itself by reflection and choice, no longer had a persuasive hold on the nation's wiser inhabitants.

Mead's admittedly imaginative reconstruction of the American experience as the tragic evaporation of the myth-dream provides the backdrop for my discussion of Lincoln's assassination. Although the Civil War had already forced the nation to come to terms with the tragic character of the American experience, the assassination of Lincoln effectively destroyed all hope of the immediate recovery of the dream. There were differences of opinion as to the political consequences of the assassination, but, from the perspective of the myth-dream, the assassination removed the one individual potentially capable of reviving confidence in the dream. Thus, the nation saw the American tragedy personalized in its leader's untimely death.

The assassination personalized the tragic drama; it cast an aura of myth over Lincoln's previous life and career. As Lincoln scholar Richard N. Current observes:

> If Booth *had* missed, our knowledge of Lincoln undoubtedly would be much clearer than it is, much less clouded by mystery and myth. The awful fact of the assassination falls between us and the man. . . . Lincoln's whole life tends to become obscured by the circumstances of his death.[8]

Historians acknowledge that, given his role as President in a time of civil war, some mythicization was inevitable. Yet they also point out that the nation's spontaneous grief-reaction to Lincoln's death was so overwhelming and so universal that the mythic imagination generated by this emotional outpouring could be neither denied nor manipulated. David Donald, Civil War historian, captures the emotional tenor of these troubled times:

> The times and events of the Civil War had made a great popular leader necessary. There had been the emotional strain of war, the taut peril of defeat, the thrill of battles won, the release of peace. Then had come the calamitous, disastrous assassination. The people's grief was immediate and it was immense. . . . Mourning intensified grief. The trappings of death—the black-draped catafalque, the silent train that moved by a circuitous route over the land, the white-robed choirs that wailed a dirge, the crepe-veiled women, the stone-faced men—made Lincoln's passing seem even more calamitous. Over a million persons took a last sad look at the face in the casket and went away treasuring an unforgettable memory.[9]

To be sure, there was more to the nation's tragedy than the assassination of Lincoln. But this event was unique in directing the nation's attention to the finality of their tragedy. The myth-dream and hopes for its recovery were being laid to rest in the casket of their great popular leader.

The Assassination and Frontier Mythology

It is not enough to note that Lincoln's assassination contributed to the transformation of the American myth-dream in the direction of the tragic. It remains to ask how it did so, and what were the historical consequences of this transformation? Here we come to the constructive part of this essay, for, in my judgment, the role of Lincoln's death in transforming the American experience toward the deeper tragic sense is best demonstrated by its alteration of the nation's perception of Lincoln as a frontier hero.[10] Lincoln appealed to the public at the time of his candidacy because he represented the homely frontier virtues considered particularly valuable to a nation threatened with civil conflict. However, what the image of the frontiersman signified to the general public prior to his assassination—an essentially comic presence—was drastically altered after his assassination. Following his death, the frontier hero became a tragic figure consistent with the nation's realization of the tragic character of the American experience. By tracing the transformation of this major form of American heroism, therefore, it is possible to see how the American drama was assuming new tragic dimensions as a direct consequence of the assassination.

The popular view of Lincoln as frontier hero was no less an imposition of an imaginative schema on his life than the view of the American experience as a tragic drama. Why, then, should it be accorded particular attention here? Of all attempts to impose on Lincoln's life some imaginative schema, some interpretive structure, the view of Lincoln as frontier hero takes particular note of the tragic character of American life. Other imaginative schemas, such as those employed in Lincoln biography, are particularly concerned to account for the apparent discontinuity between his early years in frontier America and his later years as a wartime President. Although partly concerned with this apparent discontinuity between the "early" or "Western" and "late" or "Eastern" Lincoln, the frontier hero model pays considerably greater attention to the discontinuity between the living President and the dead hero. It does not primarily concern itself with the apparent discrepancies between Lincoln the rude frontiersman and Lincoln the polished political statesman, but with the radical disjunction between the man who guided the nation through its greatest internal crisis and the hero whose death symbolizes the diminishing of the American dream. Expressed in more prosaic terms, Lincoln's death directed the nation's self-understanding toward a deeper sense of its inherent tragic character; it called for a myth capable of establishing a meaningful connection between the effective political statesman and the dead hero. Among the various imaginative reconstructions of Lincoln's life, only the frontier hero myth has proven capable of establishing this connection, and this because only a tragic perspective can begin to account for the irrevocable link between Lincoln the political statesman and Lincoln the dead hero.

To substantiate this claim about the frontier hero myth, some of the imaginative schemas employed by Lincoln biographers must be considered. These schemas represent not simply the work of skilled writers but also the various popular conceptions of Lincoln that surfaced after his death, and so they provide valuable insights into the nation's efforts to understand the meaning of the man Lincoln.[11] However, these models are concerned primarily with the living Lincoln, not with the relation between Lincoln the political statesman and Lincoln the dead hero. They focus on the problem of how his early years on the frontier can be reconciled with his later years in the White House. They ask whether there is not some serious discrepancy between the rough frontier and the high purposes of the White House.

Thus biographers John G. Nicolay and John Hay attempt to bring Lincoln's past into conformity with his later years by idealizing the early frontier years. To these authors the gap between the frontier and the White House is largely imaginary, based on an altogether too negative view of frontier life. John T. Morse shifts away from such environmental explanations to psychological ones, pointing to some unspecified inner quality "which made Lincoln, as a young man, not much superior to his coarse surroundings" but which, "ripening and expanding rapidly and grandly with maturing years and a greater circle of humanity, made him what he was in later life."[12] The seeds of greatness were always there, they simply required nurturance. Hapgood offers the theory that conflicting tendencies could reside in the same individual, such that Lincoln "might reach as high as the saints in one direction and as high as Rabelais in another." He might be "the prairie male as well as the sage and martyr, the deft politician as well as the generous statesman." This position, suggesting that frontier and statesman Lincoln were two essential if conflicting dimensions of the total character structure, has generally led those who hold it to remark on Lincoln's mysterious or enigmatic quality.[13]

Some years later, Godfrey Charnwood attacked the problem by attempting to reduce the gap between the "commonness" and "greatness" of Lincoln. Lincoln, he suggests, was neither a spiritual genius nor a low clown of tricky mind, but a consistently quiet man who bent his powers to the vindication of certain principles. The contemporary Civil War historian David Donald appears to subscribe to this view when he notices that, after all, the common elements in the various interpretive schemas employed by biographers portray Lincoln as having all the decent qualities of a civilized person: patience, tolerance, humor, sympathy, kindliness, and sagacity. Hence, in this view, Lincoln is neither the great genius nor the Rabelaisian clown but a man of enduring civilized decency. However, Carl Sandburg would not achieve continuity between the early and late Lincoln at the price of denying him uncommon capacities for greatness and simplicity. Rather, he suggests that the weakness of previous interpretive schemas is their effort to derive Lincoln's greatness from his supposedly simple beginnings. He proposes, instead, that Lincoln's simplicity and greatness were cut from the same cloth. The frontier environment that made Lincoln a simple man also made him the great man. This view requires Sandburg to depict a frontier environment of unique complexity, one capable of producing a man of similar complexity. Hence, the prairie assumes "epic" proportions consistent with the epic of Lincoln himself. The frontier environment is itself the basis of continuity between the early and late, Western and Eastern Lincoln. There simplicity and greatness are mingled.

The psychobiographer L. Pierce Clark attempts to account for the continuity between the early and late Lincoln. He takes the position that the continuity in Lincoln's life is best understood as a series of major turning points, which have in common the death of a family member or estrangement in the area of romance. Clark traces Lincoln's psychological depressions to these personal losses and estrangements. On the other hand, he recognizes that these mental depressions are only half the story, because he contends that Lincoln had a remarkable capacity to recover from these emotional crises. Each crisis results in a "temporary setback" accompanied by mental depression, but each leads eventually to greater strength of character. In Clark's view, Lincoln's early experience of turning temporary setbacks into occasions for character building proved to be the source of his remarkable strength as the nation's leader.[14]

However, and here we begin to address the frontier hero myth more directly, Clark's schema contrasts significantly with the view expressed by William Herndon, Lincoln's law partner in Illinois. Instead of talking about turning points and temporary setbacks, Herndon characterized Lincoln's career as a steady rise from his origins in "stagnant, putrid pools" to the "topmost rung of the ladder." What interests Herndon is not an alleged alternation of forward and backward steps, but the enormous distance traversed from the bottommost rung in frontier Illinois to the topmost rung in the American Presidency. Herndon's structure undoubtedly fits with the Horatio Alger myth of the late nineteenth century, and it is worth noting in this regard that Alger himself wrote a story of Lincoln's life meant to inspire young boys to similar heights.[15] In contrast, Clark's schema reflects the fact that he wrote during the Great Depression of the 1930s. Not only does he center his attention on Lincoln's "depressions," but he also views "setbacks" as occasions for character building.

In short, efforts to establish the continuity between the early and later Lincoln have included creating an idealized picture of the frontier; pointing to some unique but unspecified quality in Lincoln which blossomed when he assumed the Presidency; suggesting that there were conflicting tendencies in the Lincoln personality which were there from the very beginning; attempting to show that he was a man of moderation and consistency, given neither to great achievements nor low chicanery; showing that the frontier environment was itself of such complexity that both Lincoln's greatness and his simplicity can be attributed to his frontier upbringing; emphasizing the turning points in Lincoln's career, each of which was marked by a pattern of temporary setback followed by intensified forward progress; accounting for continuity through a model based on steady but painstaking upward progress.

What can be concluded from this brief survey of the nation's efforts, as represented in Lincoln biography, to identify the basis of continuity in his life and career? Some of these efforts take better account of known facts about Lincoln than others. However, not one account comes to terms with the assassination. Although each theory addresses the apparent discontinuities between Lincoln's early frontier years and his later Presidential years, none addresses the apparent disjunction between the man who guided the nation through its greatest internal crisis and the hero whose death symbolizes the diminishment of the American dream. In this sense, none comes to terms with the profound tragedy of Lincoln, or, in dramatic terms, the tragic inevitability of his violent death.

None, that is, except the frontier hero myth which served as the basis for Herndon's imaginative schema. Unfortunately, although quite anxious to draw out the tragic implications of Lincoln's alleged romance with Ann Rutledge, Herndon fails to carry the frontier hero myth to its inevitably tragic conclusion in Lincoln's case, being content to show how Lincoln rose from his ignominious frontier origins to the Presidency. But this frontier hero model also enables us to establish the continuities between the living leader and the dead hero. Fundamental to this model was an essentially fatalistic attitude on the part of the frontiersman. Frontiersmen sensed that even the greatest persons could not enjoy the heights indefinitely, that eventually the acquisition of money, fame, or political prominence must be paid for. He was faced at the pinnacle of success with a cataclysmic fall; after the long hard struggle up, the ladder could be overturned in a moment. Evidence of such fatalism in Lincoln's later years is reflected in his premonitions of his untimely death.[16] And, after his death, reports of these premonitions were circulated as evidence that Lincoln viewed his life in essentially tragic terms.

Unfortunately, however, the tragic frontier hero myth has been seriously neglected in recent discussions of Lincoln as frontier hero. In his essay "The Folklore Lincoln," David Donald describes Lincoln as frontier hero in essentially comic terms. According to Donald, the major characteristics of the frontier hero are the storyteller, the shrewd bargainer, the chaste wooer, the henpecked husband, the man of great physical prowess, and the anticleric. Thus, Lincoln was portrayed as a great spinner of yarns; as the country lawyer who eschewed fine legal reasoning in favor of shrewd common sense; as the chaste and honorable wooer of Ann Rutledge, forbearing to plead his own case until it seemed certain her fiancé would not return to claim her; as the wrestling champion of New Salem and the indefatigable splitter of rails; and as the deeply religious man who preferred to avoid the formalities of church-going. In Donald's view Lincoln stood in the comic tradition of Davy Crockett, Mike Fink, and Paul Bunyan:

> The grotesque hero—the Gargantua or the Till Eulenspiegel—is one of the oldest and most familiar patterns in folk literature. In America the type had been already exemplified by such favorites as Davy Crockett, Mike Fink and Paul Bunyan. Of a like cut was the myth of Lincoln as frontier hero. . . . He was Old Abe, a Westerner, and his long flapping arms were not the wings of an angel.[17]

Other students of the Lincoln myth agree that Lincoln the frontier hero was essentially comic. Roy P. Basler describes him as "The drinking, cock-fighting, rough-and-tumble hero, 'the big buck of the lick' who dared anyone to 'come on and whet his horns,' the lover of broad humor."[18]

Basler points out, however, that in the years following Lincoln's death, there was a tendency to smooth the rough edges of Lincoln as frontier hero, to present a spiritualized Lincoln more congruent with the nation's desire to dignify this great American hero. But if spiritualization were the only way Lincoln's death influenced the frontier hero myth, it would make little sense to say that through his death the frontier hero came to represent the tragic dimension of the American experience. Spiritualization, although it certainly occurred, is not the same thing as the transformation of a hero myth. The real influence of Lincoln's death on the frontier hero myth was not spiritualization through the omission of rough frontierisms. Rather, its effect was to transform the myth through the introduction of a historically rooted tragic dimension into an otherwise comic folk myth.

How did Lincoln's death transform the frontier hero myth? The answer is simple, but its implications are profound. Consider the characteristics of the frontier hero as Donald enumerates them. Each characteristic represents a social role. Concerning sociality at the community level, the frontier hero is a spinner of yarns, the shrewd bargainer, the combatant, the eschewer of institutional religion; at the domestic level, he is the chaste wooer and henpecked husband. Among adult domestic roles, the father image is notoriously absent. And yet, as Basler points out, Lincoln's image as "Father Abraham" was a great source of consolation to the nation as it mourned his death:

> Lincoln as he walks at midnight is the symbol of all ideals of democratic humanity, but he is also the tender memory in apparition of the beloved personal saint, the folk Father Abraham. . . . The conventional picture given by the builders of the gentle legend is that of Father Abraham, a kindly, pleasant old man with a humorous smile which often fades into a look of sadness. He is forever enshrined in popular memory dressed in black, with tall hat and black shawl. The touch of earthiness is never in the picture drawn with loving fancy. He is never thought of as having any personal interest or ambition. It is only as the guardian angel of his children that he overlooks the vast arena of war and sadly smiles as the blood sinks into the thirsty sand. He bears his own burden uncomplainingly and gladly seeks to lighten the burden of others. His sad, plain features are simply glorious in their reflection of benignity, devotion, and a wisdom passing that of earth.[19]

Here, in the image of Father Abraham, is the sense of tragedy lacking in Donald's description of the frontier hero. Perhaps under normal conditions it was possible for Lincoln's contemporaries to identify as frontier heroes those who symbolized resentment of the domestic roles of husband and father. But the tragic implications of this omission of the father ideal were probably always just below the surface. In times of severe social stress, the need became great for a hero capable of embodying a father ideal. In spiritualized accounts of the life of Lincoln, therefore, concerted efforts were made to play down Lincoln's own resentment of the domestic roles of husband and father and to emphasize his role as the faithful, long-suffering father of a tragically divided national household.

Of course, this tragic transformation of the frontier hero model through recognition of Lincoln's father role did not introduce an entirely new element into frontier mythology. Basler notes that intimations of the Father Abraham image were evident in Lincoln's earlier frontier experiences, including his alleged gentleness toward animals as a child and his kindness toward widows and orphans as a circuit-riding lawyer. Yet, as John William Ward points out in his study of Andrew Jackson, these attributes were earlier accorded Jackson, also noted for his protection of children and women.[20] Thus, elements of the Father Abraham image predated Lincoln. Nonetheless, not until the event of Lincoln's assassination did the image of Father Abraham irrevocably transform the comic model of the frontier hero into an essentially tragic one. And, if a tendency toward fatalism was already part of the frontier hero model, Lincoln's sudden and violent death gave the model a previously inconceivable tragic depth.

It should also be acknowledged that efforts were made by Lincoln's contemporaries to view the tragedy in Christological terms. Parallels between the life and death of Jesus and of Lincoln were at hand: both were of humble birth, the one in a log cabin, the other in a manger. Their fathers were carpenters by trade. Both spoke in parables and homely sayings. And, of particular importance here, both went to their deaths on Good Friday, Lincoln having chosen Ford's Theatre because the play being presented there satirized the Northerner. Was this not itself a final act of suffering servanthood? Without discounting the mythic importance of these Christological parallels, it should be noted that they play largely on the element of coincidence and generally fail to penetrate the deeper levels of the tragedy of Lincoln's death.[21] As the Lincoln funeral train circled its way westward after the assassination, the grieving populace saw less the godforsaken son of man and more the immobile face of their dead Father Abraham. And, when poets like Vachel Lindsay proclaim, "He cannot sleep upon his hillside now. He is among us—as in times before," their words conjure up in our own minds less the image of the resurrected savior and more the presence of Father Abraham standing watch over his lost children of Israel.[22]

Father Abraham and American Civil Religion

In short, the effect of Lincoln's assassination was to transform the model frontiersman from comic to tragic hero. This transformation establishes a meaningful connection between the President, who guided the nation through civil war, and the sad-visaged Father who continues to walk the nation's streets at midnight. There is tragedy in this transformation, but at the same time wiser men have found power in the image of Father Abraham to partially replace their confidence in the original myth-dream. As R.W.B. Lewis points out, the dream of human freedom has been traditionally symbolized by the myth of Adam. However, the myth of Adam has supported the "resistance in America to the painful process of growing up . . . expressing itself in repeated efforts to revert to a lost childhood and a vanished Eden, and issuing repeatedly in a series of outcries at the freshly discovered capacity of the world to injure."[23] The Civil War, however, shifted the nation's attention from the youthful Adam to the aging Father Abraham. This shift, although certainly not a total replacement of the one image with the other, is nonetheless dramatic evidence of a significant change in the religious consciousness of the American populace.

From the standpoint of American civil religion, it can be noted that this change was already prefigured in Lincoln's second inaugural address. Discouraged by the fact that the termination of the war was not yet in sight, Lincoln sought an explanation for God's allowing it to continue. In this address, therefore, he pointed out that God's guarantee of the success of any humanly conceived project can no longer be assumed. All that can be done is to trust the Almighty who "has His own purposes" in history. Not the vigorous optimism of a nation in Adamic innocence, persuaded that it is embarked on divinely appointed tasks, but the wisdom accruing from the tragic awareness that, after all, human enterprises may bear little relation to God's purposes. Later, when explaining the views expressed in his second inaugural address, Lincoln acknowledged: "Men are not flattered by being shown that there has been a difference of purpose between the Almighty and them. To deny it, however, in this case, is to deny that there is a God governing the world."[24] In like fashion, the assassination of a President who had believed himself the instrument of God's purposes dramatizes this fundamental discontinuity between divine purpose and human enterprise. And because it does this, we sense that the sad benignity enveloping the face of Father Abraham has its basis in the tragic awareness that, whether the President lives or dies, the hand of God moves on.

Notes

1. "Civil Religion in America," *Daedalus* 96 (1967): 1–9.
2. "American History as a Tragic Drama," *The Journal of Religion* 52 (1972): 336.
3. *Mambu: A Melanesia Millennium* (London: MacMillan, 1960).
4. Mead, p. 342.
5. Ibid., p. 345.
6. Ibid., p. 359.
7. Ibid.
8. *The Lincoln Nobody Knows* (New York: Hill and Wang, 1958), pp. 272–73. The major book-length treatment of Lincoln's death and its mythic aftermath is Lloyd Lewis, *Myths After Lincoln* (New York: Harcourt, Brace, 1929).
9. "The Folklore Lincoln," in *Lincoln Reconsidered: Essays on the Civil War Era* (New York: Vintage Books, 1961), pp. 154, 145–46.
10. For brief but important discussions of the mythic transformations of the lives of historical personages after their deaths, see Mircea Eliade, *Myths, Dreams, and Mysteries*, trans. Philip Mairet (New York: Harper Torchbooks, 1960), pp. 32–33; *Cosmos and History*, trans. Willard R. Trask (New York: Harper Torchbooks, 1959), p. 42. For another important discussion of the relation of individual lives to mythic models, see Moses Hadas and Morton Smith, *Heroes and Gods: Spiritual Biography in Antiquity* (New York: Harper & Row, 1965).
11. A useful summary of the major Lincoln biographies written before 1935 is Roy P. Basler's *The Lincoln Legend: A Study in Changing Conceptions* (New York: Octagon Books, 1969), pp. 8–34. Another useful summary of Lincoln biography is Andrew Rolle, "A Biographical Lincoln," *Lincoln: A Contemporary Portrait*, ed. Allan Nevin and Irving Stone (Garden City N.Y.: Doubleday, 1962), pp. 193–207.

However, Rolle tends to dismiss the earlier biographies as historically weak, but I am giving them particular attention because they are mythologically significant. Whether biographies can be both historically reliable and mythologically significant is a question requiring more attention than it has been accorded to date. It may become an increasingly practical question in light of the fact that, as Erik H. Erikson points out, the contemporary historian "finds himself involved in ongoing history by an accelerated interplay of communication between the interpreters, as echoed by the mass media and the makers of history." *Life History and the Historical Moment* (New York: Norton, 1975), p. 114.

12. Quoted in Basler, p. 15.

13. Ibid., p. 18. Basler points out, for example, that Gamaliel Bradford, "who splendidly interpreted in his 'psychographies' so many American heroes, never attempted a portrait of Lincoln. I have checked his numerous comments on Lincoln scattered through several volumes. Together . . . they indicate an interest that is profound, and at the same time, an amount of uncertainty that is not common to Bradford's work as a whole. It is interesting to speculate that for the great 'psychographer' as for so many Lincoln biographers, Lincoln was too complex a soul. To quote Bradford's own phrase, 'He still smiles and remains impenetrable.'" P. 51.

14. *Lincoln: A Psychobiography* (New York: Scribner, 1933. See also his earlier article, "Unconscious Motives Underlying the Personalities of Great Statesmen and Their Relation to Epoch-Making Events (1.A Psychologic Study of Abraham Lincoln)," *The Psychoanalytic Review* 8 (1921):1–21.

15. David Donald contends that "the biographies of the Herndon school are stylized presentations of Western folklore. Herndon's own book recounts the epic of the frontier hero, transmogrified into the pattern of the sentimental novel." P. 162.

16. Accounts of Lincoln's premonitions of death by assassination abound. See, for example, Carl Sandburg's *Abraham Lincoln: The War Years* (New York: Dell, 1954), pp. 823–27.

17. Donald, p. 154.

18. Basler, p. 147.

19. Ibid., pp. 200, 125–26. The power of this image of Father Abraham to unify as well as console the nation is also attested by the fact that the Lincoln myth appealed to southerners' obligations to their own fathers. As Michael Davis points out: "The Lincoln legend . . . acted as a kind of force attracting Southerners back into the Union of their fathers. . . . The conscious conciliators of the New South found in Lincoln a most usable symbol of reunion; in praising Lincoln they announced to the North their willingness to share in those very national virtues for which the North had canonized Lincoln as its martyr-hero." *The Image of Lincoln in the South* (Knoxville: University of Tennessee Press, 1971), p. 170.

20. *Andrew Jackson: Symbol for an Age* (New York: Oxford University Press, 1953), pp. 197–98.

21. This is not to deny another significant link between Lincoln and Christ, i.e., the fact that scholars recognize similar historiographical problems in reconstructing the lives of Jesus and Lincoln. Van Harvey's observation is typical: "If historians are unable to decipher the mystery of Abraham Lincoln, even though they possess volumes of authentic sayings, intimate letters, and the accounts of eyewitnesses, are we to believe that we can encounter the real Jesus of Nazareth on the basis of a handful of sayings preserved in no chronological order by a community that was especially anxious to prove that he was the Messiah?" *The Historian and the Believer* (New York: Macmillan, 1966), p. 193.

22. It can be argued that the application of Christological motifs to Lincoln was an "elitest" phenomenon, especially common in the Eastern states, while the myth of Father Abraham was the product of "popular" religion on the Western frontier. Arthur F. Wright addresses the problem of the fusion of elite and popular mythic images in "Sui Yang-ti: Personality and Stereotype," *Confucianism and Chinese Civilization*, ed. Arthur F. Wright (New York: Atheneum, 1965). Wright points out: "It would be too much to say that the elite and popular images of Yang-ti fused into a single myth, but it is certain that the two images, influencing each other, have drawn closer together during the thirteen centuries since the death of Yang-ti" (p. 186).

23. R.W.B. Lewis, *The American Adam: Innocence, Tragedy, and Tradition in the Nineteenth Century* (Chicago: University of Chicago Press, 1955), p. 129.

24. From a letter addressed to Thurlow Weed quoted in *Current*, pp. 74–75.

Index